John Grant has been a freelance writer and
editor for the last five yea
He lives in the West C
graphic designer, and dau
*tory of Possibilities* and
Colin Wilson) and an ant
*Aries 1*. He is the auth
*Ideas* and *A Book of*
*About the Flaming Ghoulies* is also published by Panther
Books. He is an experienced lecturer and broadcaster.

By the same author

*The Truth About the Flaming Ghoulies*
*A Book of Numbers*
*A Directory of Discarded Ideas*
*The Directory of Possibilities*
(editor, with Colin Wilson)
*The Book of Time* (editor, with Colin Wilson)
*Aries 1* (editor)

JOHN GRANT

# Dreamers:

## A Geography of Dreamland

Since the young vigour that urges
Inwards to the heart
Is frail as age, no warcraft yet perfect,
While beyond age, leaf-withered,
Man goes three-footed,
No stronger than a child is,
A dream that falters in daylight.

– Aeschylus,
*Agamemnon*

**GRAFTON BOOKS**
A Division of the Collins Publishing Group

LONDON GLASGOW
TORONTO SYDNEY AUCKLAND

Grafton Books
A Division of the Collins Publishing Group
8 Grafton Street, London W1X 3LA

Published by Grafton Books 1986

First published in Great Britain by
Ashgrove Press Limited 1984



ISBN 0-586-06500-8

Printed and bound in Great Britain by
Collins, Glasgow

Set in Times

FOR JANE

whose dreams,
if there were any justice in this world,
would fill about ninety per cent of this book;
and whose bedroom door bears a sign saying:
NO BAD DREAMS
FRIENDLY MONSTERS ONLY
BY ORDER
Signed: Jane's Daddy

# Contents

# Acknowledgements

Many people have given me their help in the writing of this book. I have done my best to keep track of them all, but it's quite possible that in my usual chaotic fashion I've managed to miss out a crucial name or two. To those people, I apologize profusely.

David Bolt, my agent, and Robin Campbell, of Ashgrove Press, have given me every encouragement throughout the writing of *Dreamers*, as have Muriel Barnett and Donald and Margaret Stewart. Howard Harrison gave me help on composers' dreams (including his own); Jenny Randles not only told me about several fascinating dreams of her own but also put me on to a few good leads; J. B. Priestley kindly confirmed a suspicion of mine; Magis Books went out of their way to rush me a vital reference; V. I. Maund of the National Westminster Bank got off my back at the appropriate moments so that I could get on with research; Jonathon Davies of Radio Wales provided a spur of encouragement at just the right time; Sandra Shulman let me quote her dreams and touched me with her infectious enthusiasm; Peter Evans told me that my heresy wasn't; Shelley Rhode and Mark Gorton of Granada TV allowed me to work out a few ideas in public; Christopher Priest made a pithy comment; Signatures, of Gandy Street, Exeter, helped me with the Kenneth Grahame dreams; and Jane was herself.

Pauline Wakeham very kindly allowed me to quote her poem 'The Dream', as did Peter Cadle his poem 'Conflagration' (from *Afterthoughts*, available for a £1 postal order from Quiet Publications, 41 Ainger Road, London NW3).

Gerry Jutsum and John Pierce of Devonair gave sterling assistance in the collection of unpublished dreams. Through them I was put in contact with W. Palmer, S. Paskell, Susan Richardson, Ivor White, Pat Simpson, Phyllis Godbeer, Pamela Corby, Dorothy Furse and J. F. Raymond, all of whom kindly told me of their interesting dream-experiences, as well as Audrey Atkinson, Violet Casley and Ann White, with whom I corresponded at greater length and whose dreams are discussed in some detail in the text. To all of the 'Devonair Dreamers' my profound thanks.

I must thank, too, the people at the Westcountry Studies Library and the Exeter Central Reference Library. Unfortunately, as a result of government cutbacks on such needless expenses as public education, the Exeter Central Library has been of far less assistance to me than in the case of previous works; however, several individual members of staff have done their best in difficult circumstances to assist me, and so to them my gratitude (especially to Mrs Rakestrow).

It is with great sadness that I have to record that Donald Stewart is no longer around to disagree with my few humble psychological 'insights' (for none of which he was responsible!). I had looked forward to a thoroughly good argument with him – which I would inevitably have lost – when this book was published.

Catherine Barnett encouraged me to write this book when I didn't think I would, and throughout its writing has egged me on whenever I've shown signs of flagging; in addition, she took some of the burden of research off my back. In a very real sense, had it not been for her this book would never have been written. $4\pi + 0$.

JOHN GRANT

# Introduction

It's astonishing how little we understand dreaming – and astonishing, too, how many books and papers have been written on the subject without any consensus as to what dreaming actually *is*. Similarly, systems of dream-analysis are to be found vying with each other for recognition throughout the psychological and psychoanalytical literature. Each of these systems has something to commend it, yet in general they are all mutually contradictory and seem to have little relation to real life. This is a fact recognized by most students of the dream who have no axe to grind, who are not Jungians or Freudians or Adlerians or even Caycians; but to those who are convinced adherents to one of these faiths the notion is a heretical one.

The trouble is that it's a false heresy – of stature similar to the idea that we should nuke the Reds in the name of Christianity and freedom. In the same way that Christ advocated the turning of the other cheek, so one of the messiahs of dream-analysis, C. G. Jung, on occasion was moved to express caution:

> We must never forget in dream-analysis, even for a moment, that we move on treacherous ground where nothing is certain but uncertainty. A suitable warning to the dream-interpreter – if only it were not so paradoxical – would be: 'Do anything you like, only don't try to understand!' [*Modern Man in Search of a Soul*, trans. 1933.]

In other words, the rules are different in dreamland, and

our waking selves have no more understanding of those rules than Newton had of Einstein's Relativity.

But, as I've said, this doesn't stop humanity from *trying* to understand the rules. Trying is one thing – and obviously laudable – but what is dangerous is the frequently encountered dogmatism of those who are convinced that they *have* worked out the rules – or that someone else has worked out the rules for them.

In fact, we can go one further than that and ignore everyone's opinions. There are studies galore which attempt to explain both dreams and the act of dreaming; there are mountains of works polemicizing in favour of one system of dream-analysis or another. It would be a waste of time for me to try to add to them – not only because I am not qualified to do so, not only because I think that with the art in its present state such essays are foolhardy, but most importantly because I am simply not interested in the debate. With the true cowardice of the born scholar I prefer to flee from such contentious issues and concentrate instead on a comparatively neglected matter: the effects that dreams have had on the dreamers themselves.

This book, then, can be regarded as less of a geology of dreamland, more of a human geography; less of a cosmology, more of an astronomy. Inevitably, we shall find ourselves stumbling into the pitfalls of explanation or analysis from time to time, but for the most part I shall keep an alert lookout so that these can be deftly sidestepped. It is my own personal suspicion – 'opinion' would be too strong a word – that all attempts to analyze or explain dreams may be doomed for the simple reason that dreams actually *have* no meaning; but this is a notion regarded as heretical not just by the various psychoanalytic and parapsychological sects but also by the public at large, and so I shall keep quiet about it.

Dreams infest the creative output of Western civilization: a cliché. They are ubiquitously found in *all* terrestrial cultures, so far as I can establish, right down to the most 'primitive', where they have a position in society far more significant than in ours. Among some cultures, for example, if you dream of making love with your next-door-neighbour's spouse then either this means that you have really done so, in which case there can be complications, or it means that you ought to, in which case you can go ahead and commit adultery with the full approval of all concerned.

This central role of dreams in 'primitive' societies is not, however, reflected in our own. True, there are uncounted billions of poems about dreams; hardly a novel goes by without some reference to dreaming, and in many novels dreams play an important part; paintings and pieces of music with dream-allusions in their titles are not uncommon. But, outside the field of the paranormal, dreams are rarely regarded as having any importance beyond, perhaps, the psychological insights they provide into the individual. We accept that dreamland is a place we all frequently explore, but we regard it as if each of us had a *personal* dreamland. The notion that our nocturnal adventures take place on the same continent as everyone else's is – *pace* the Jungians – not a popular one.

That this should be the case is curious. It is probably ridiculous to suggest that everyone's dreams are enacted in the same country, but it is surprising how often, in comparing our own dreams with those of other people, we find that the topography of the dreamland we know ourselves is identical with that of the one 'they' explore. This is not an original observation; we shall come across it being made several times by different people from different ages. However, it seems odd that so few students of the dream have been moved to take the matter further.

Perhaps, like myself, they have noticed the curious fact but, because they have no notion of how even to start exploring the issue, have determined to ignore it. Certainly, the people who *have* toyed with the matter don't seem to have got very far with it.

Can it be, one wonders, that when we dream we 'travel to an astral plane', 'attain a higher level of consciousness', or whatever piece of jargon is in vogue at the moment? If so, then there is no worry about everybody's dreamland being the same place: the 'fifth dimension' is the 'fifth dimension' is the 'fifth dimension'. Here is William James on the subject:

> One conclusion was forced upon my mind . . . and my impression of its truth has ever since remained unshaken. It is that our normal waking consciousness, rational consciousness as we call it, is but one special type of consciousness, whilst all about it, parted from it by the filmiest of screens, there lie potential forms of consciousness entirely different. We may go through life without suspecting their existence; but apply the requisite stimulus, and at a touch they are there in all their completeness, definite types of mentality which probably somewhere have their field of application and adaptation. No account of the universe in its totality can be final which leaves these other forms of consciousness quite disregarded. How to regard them is the question – for they are discontinuous with ordinary consciousness. Yet they may determine attitudes though they cannot furnish formulas, and open a region though they fail to give a map. At any rate, they forbid a premature closing of our account with reality.

It is a fool who would disagree with much of what James says here; but unfortunately it is only too tempting to read between the lines and thereby find out what he is implying (or, to be charitable, what people think he's implying): that these other forms of consciousness involve flitting between 'astral planes', and that this is what we do when dreaming. That there are other forms of consciousness is only too evident – the dolphins don't seem to think the same way we do, and if we ever bump into extraterrestrial intelligences we are likely to find this difference magnified a thousandfold – but it seems to be merely confusing the issue to bring into the discussion of those differences such notions as other 'dimensions' and 'astral planes'. And to say that we visit these 'planes' in our dreams is to build illogical speculation upon illogical speculation.

This doesn't take us very far towards explaining why most if not all of us seem to visit the same dreamland. Is it possible that we are looking to the skies for enlightenment when we should be looking to the ground beneath our feet? Possibly so. While everyone except the racialist bigot accepts that human beings are morphologically and intellectually much the same – a state of affairs which has existed for at least millennia* – we seem reluctant to extend the comparison to the more arcane workings of the mind. If genetics can ordain that I, a Scot, am in appearance very much like an Australian Aborigine, then why cannot genetics similarly ordain that my dreams are very much like this? If he and I trace our family trees back far enough, after all, we discover that we're related and that our common ancestors were men and women much like ourselves. Of course, there will be culturally

* It is a perfectly tenable suggestion that, were we to use a time machine to fish one of our caveman ancestors out of the past, we would find that he (or she) was just as intelligent as ourselves. All that would be required would be an intensive educational course; our caveman, if young enough, would probably find this rigorous but not impossible. Culture shock would be something else, of course.

derived differences in the details of our dreams, but overall our dreams will be much the same: we will be visiting different parts of the same dreamland, and doing different things there, in exactly the same way that some people go to the West Indies to sunbathe, some to overthrow governments, some to study wildlife, and some to play cricket.

This is a depressing and unpopular view of what is generally regarded as a romantic and exciting phenomenon – or, at least, that's what you're probably thinking. I'm not so sure that I agree with you. To explain why, let me play upon the word 'romantic' for a moment.

In our culture romance is a subject relegated to the pages of hack novels or, failing that, to other people's lives. Princes and princesses are allowed to have great romances, either in real life or in fiction, and so are actresses and actors and other members of glamour professions. You and I, on the other hand, are allowed to experience great romance and be genuinely romantic only furtively, as it were. I can tell my wife how much I love her and everything she means to me at great length in private; but I get funny looks if I discuss the subject with someone else in public, unless I have the forethought to couch my romantic feelings in poetry or song. I am quite sure, to stress the example, that at least half of you winced embarrassedly at the fact that in the previous sentence I confessed to loving my wife.

In the same way that we banish romance from everyday life, discount it from our reckoning of the forces which determine our daily actions and devisions, so we do the same with dreams. We set them up on a pedestal, we regard them with something akin to mysticism, we even say that in many ways they are 'truer' than our waking conscious thoughts – and then we ignore them. The thrust of my argument is that this paradoxical behaviour has the effect of castrating our dreams and deliberately nullifying their importance, of fencing ourselves off from those other workings of our own minds. In many ways, then, my 'mechanistic' explanation of the fact that we all seem to travel to the same dreamland strikes me as more romantic than the 'gosh, wow' approach, in that it brings dreams into the embrace of our everyday lives rather than setting them apart in some unattainable distant province of the mind. To draw for a final time upon my analogy, it is surely much more romantic to be in love in real life than to read about doctors and nurses exchanging sweet nothings all over the badly printed pages of a pulp novel.

I don't propose to produce an extended justification for my premise that we are committing a grave error in relegating our dreams to the ranks of mere fancies, things which have nothing to do with mundane activities such as catching the 'bus and dealing with the Inland Revenue (although, in the latter case, there are certain Kafkaesque similarities). Mere fancies dreams quite possibly are, but nevertheless they can have a considerable effect on what we do in our waking lives. They may or may not reveal to us any great psychological truths about ourselves, but they are a fundamental part of our experience of life and in that sense are no less important than the sensations we have during our waking hours. At the very least, they allow us a richness of emotion and sensual experience which we can only too rarely experience in 'real life'.

Before proceeding, I think it is worthwhile to glance swiftly at what might be thought of as an intersection between dream-reality and waking-reality. I'm referring, of course, to the phenomenon known as lucid dreaming.

Lucid dreamers are lucky people. When they are dreaming they know that they are doing so, and often can go one step further to start directing their dreams.

They are thus able consciously to guide their own explorations of dreamland – and they have my envy! To give a fairly lightweight example, I recently had an infuriating dream in which I was manfully resisting seduction by some beautiful dream-figment woman, on the grounds that I was married. After I had resisted for some while I woke up, realized that she was only a dream and therefore fair game – and then I couldn't blasted well get back to sleep again. Had I been a lucid dreamer, on the other hand . . .

But lucid dreamers don't have it all their own way. In his book *The Romeo Error* (1974) Lyall Watson quotes a superb example of a lucid anxiety-dream from a paper by Charles McCreery published in *Proceedings of the Institute of Psychophysical Research 4* (1973):

> I now found myself with X (a minister friend) in a room at the other end of the corridor. I was telling him about the lucid dreams I had just had, and said suddenly as it occurred to me, 'And of course this is a dream now.'
>
> X said with an unhelpful smile, 'Well, it might be. How do you know?'
>
> 'Of course it is,' I said and crossed to the window. 'I am going to fly,' I said.
>
> 'Be awkward if it is not a dream, won't it?' said X . . .

Here we have an extreme example of the way in which, in lucid dreaming, the two logics of dreamland and the waking world combine. Each has a different set of rules, but that is not to say that the two sets are mutually incompatible – one is reminded, by way of analogy, of the current fashion for pointing up the similarities between the 'rules' of oriental metaphysics and those of occidental physics.

In a way, then, dreams are more important than we generally give them credit for because, as James said, they give us glimpses of different workings of the human consciousness. Their logic differs from 'common sense', but that does not mean that they are illogical, only that our definition of logic is too narrow a one: dreams are as logical and useful as lateral thinking, and in a similar way are important tools because they allow our minds fresh perspectives on the nature and meaning of existence.

They are important, too, because of the effects they have on us. They help some of us to create great works of literature or art. They convince some of us that we can foretell the future or that our souls are immortal and are incarnated in (mortal) life after life. They are the hidden stimuli for all manner of human activities, at both the individual and the global levels. At the most fundamental, they are a part of each and every one of us, and of crucial importance for this reason alone.

The concern of this book, then, is as already stated the interplay between people and their dreams. For practical reasons which are obvious, the 'dreamers' I discuss are those who have been influenced enough by a single dream or by the whole panoply of their dream-lives to be moved to write about their experiences; this they have done in books, articles or, in many cases, in letters. While unavoidable, this selection process is artificial – or, at least, it may be seen as conjuring up an artificial barrier between 'dreamers', on the one side, and the rest of us, on the other.

In reality, of course, we can forget the quotation marks around the word 'dreamers'. There is no such barrier between 'them' and 'us'. All o' God's children are dreamers.

# PART ONE

# Children of the Mind

My house is unveiled
            I cut the ribbon
            Look around
Anxiously repairs are complete
My bed is chosen
            I enter the room
            Caress the walls
            Taste, smell
Joyfully the windows, open, wide
A shaft of sunlight reveals
            A wizen hag with child
Approaching
            I greet her
            My arms are open
Tenderly the baby, delivered
            I receive

– Pauline Wakeham, 'A Dream'

# 1
# *Inner Spacemen*

It is our will
That thus enchains us to permitted ill –
We might be otherwise – we might be all
We dream of: happy, high, majestical.

– P. B. Shelley,
'Julian and Maddalo'

As dogs, cats, horses, and probably all the higher animals, even birds, have vivid dreams, and this is shewn by their movements and the sounds uttered, we must admit that they possess some power of imagination. There must be something special, which causes dogs to howl in the night, and especially during moonlight, in that remarkable and melancholy manner called baying.

– Charles Darwin,
*The Descent of Man*

like any man I've been a dreamer in my time:
I've walked the boards, I've conquered hordes,
I've made the ballrooms mine.
as captain under Genghis Khan I've kept the men in line . . .
funny how dreams never come true;
but my lady let me build a dream with you . . .

– Paul Barnett,
'Dreams'

I have a sneaking suspicion that more nonsense is written on the subject of dreams than on any other. Since each of us has, from time to time, one of those 'different' dreams

– one which shocks us, haunts us, imprints itself particularly strongly on our minds – it is only natural that we make the 'obvious' assumption that dreams *mean* something. Freud founded a whole school of psychological thought on the hypothesis that dreams could be analyzed and that the analysis revealed deep truths about the dreamer. Several people have made professions out of their own and other people's belief in paranormal dreaming. When in 1983 I made a radio broadcast on dreaming, virtually every person who wrote to me asked me to 'explain' their dreams, to 'say what they meant'.

Since we know very little about the how and why of dreaming, we're really on uncertain ground when we make the 'obvious' assumption. Humanity is going to look pretty silly if it turns out that dreams don't mean anything at all.

If that proves to be the case, will it mean that the study of dreams is a waste of time? I don't think so. In the first place, dreams are interesting, and anything that's interesting is worth studying, since the act of study itself advances our knowledge. In the second place, and probably more importantly, it is almost certain that our dreams allow us to view the workings of the unconscious (or right brain) at first hand. Whether the right brain has anything interesting to tell us is another matter altogether, and one to which we shall return from time to time throughout this book. And one must add the *caveat* that the usefulness of dreams in this respect is sharply reduced by the fact that we can use them to spy on the workings of only our own, individual unconscious; machines for projecting other people's dreams onto television screens, or whatever, still belong firmly in the realms of science fiction.

However, as I say, dreams are interesting, and they're important, too, if only in that they affect our waking actions. A couple of paragraphs ago the 'phone went, and Ivor White, when hearing what I was doing, mentioned an interesting wartime dream of his: it involved a German aircraft strafing the railway line nearby. The following morning he clocked on as usual for work on the railway, and sure enough the German 'plane turned up and did its strafing. Whether or not this was a precognitive dream is hard to say; but certainly it must have made White duck for cover just that little bit faster than otherwise he might have. (He himself thinks that the dream was 'a warning', and in a way it was.)

One possibility is that dreams may do their psychological stuff not because of any deep meaning necessarily locked up in them but rather because, like the *I Ching*, they focus the conscious mind's attention on something, or allow it to look at something in a new light. Let's continue with the analogy of the *I Ching* for a moment. This oriental 'divinatory' apparatus does not claim to predict the future, but to act as a guide to the user's future actions. Most readers will know the ritual, but for those who don't the idea is that, by dividing bundles of yarrow stalks or tossing coins, you create a 'hexagram', a little diagram consisting of six lines, some of which are solid and some broken. (If you're tossing three coins, a majority of heads gives you a solid line, a majority of tails a broken one.) There are 64 ($2^6$) possible hexagrams, each of which leads you to a different advising paragraph. For example, I've just been led to hexagram 51, which tells me:

> When great thunderclouds meet and clash like two mighty dragons fighting in the sky, people tremble fearfully at each succeeding shock; thus presence of mind is lost when it is most essential. Better, then, to be stout-hearted, letting fate and heaven decide the

issue, as you plan what course to follow when the storm has died down.

This is good if fairly vague advice for many situations; but had it come to me at a time of personal 'tempest' I might have been led to think it was a message from the gods.

It may very well be that dreams operate in rather the same way, that it's not so much that they give you direct insights into your problems but more that they lead you to think in a different way about them. Take for example the dream of Alexander the Great noted in Freud's *The Interpretation of Dreams* (and cited by Ullman *et al.* in *Dream Telepathy* as a telepathic dream!). Alexander was besieging Tyre when he had a dream about a satyr dancing on his shield – or so says Artemidorus. Aristander, the dream-interpreter, was told of this dream and, following the principle that dreams are often infested with visual and/or verbal puns, broke the word *satyros* down into *sa Tyre* ('Tyre is yours'). Sure enough, Alexander went on to take Tyre.

The important point here is that the dream didn't necessarily *predict* anything, nor did it reveal any deep psychological truth about the dreamer: all it did was confirm in Aiexander's mind something which he was already pretty certain about. We can take this one stage further: it's likely that it was not the dream but only *Aristander's interpretation of it* which confirmed Alexander in his views. Either way, the dream did not say: 'You will conquer Tyre.' At best, its sole effect was to focus Alexander's conscious mind on the subject, so that he realized consciously what he already knew unconsciously. That is, if he ever had the dream in the first place.

I don't want to get embroiled in the various theoretical arguments about the meanings and *raison d'être* of dreams

– this is, after all, a book about dreamers, not dream-analysis – but a few ideas on the subject appeal to me. I like Herbert Spencer's suggestion that all belief in the afterlife, spiritualism, reincarnation, etc., sprang from the primitive belief that in dreams the soul travels afar from the body. I think this is probably a 'psychological truth' – that is, something which isn't actually true but looks as if it ought to be.

Pliny the Elder believed that there are two quite different types of dreams corresponding to two different causes. One type of dream is born as a result of overeating or drinking too much (in other words, from indigestion), while dreams of the other type are sent by the gods. Obviously he was making the distinction we've already noted between 'only' dreams and 'different' dreams. Most of the dreams we'll be considering are, for obvious reasons, of the latter type – in that usually no one's driven to write down 'only' dreams.

It may be just a trick of the mind that we think there are 'different' dreams. For example, if dreams are quite random and meaningless then, just by chance, every now and then we're going to have one which is particularly vivid to us, individually, simply because it's touched some chord in our conscious minds. If this is unclear, think of the analogy of a wineglass shattering as an opera singer hits a high note. The wineglass resonates (to the point of destruction) because of *itself* and its relation with the high note, not because of the opera singer. She is, in a way, incidental: the destruction is the wineglass's 'fault'. Similarly, a dream may in itself be of no importance at all, but elements in it may make our conscious minds 'resonate'. Of course, the dream then *does* become important because we start thinking profoundly about it, and such introspection may effect changes in our overall personal philosophies, our lifestyles, and so on.

But of course Pliny is far from alone in ascribing importance to the 'different' dream. The *Epic of Gilgamesh*, the Bible, the *Iliad*, the *Odyssey* – most of the major works of the ancient past are packed with dreams, their effects and their interpretations. (We'll look at Joseph's dream-interpretation in some detail in Chapter Five.) Even in the *Book of Mormon* one is on only the seventh verse of the very first book (*1 Nephi*) when one comes across

> 7. . . and he cast himself upon his bed, being overcome with the Spirit and the things which he had seen.
> 8. And being thus overcome with the Spirit, he was carried away in a vision, even that he saw the heavens open, and he thought he saw God sitting upon his throne, surrounded with numberless concourses of angels in the attitude of singing and praising their God.

The ensuing pages are liberally littered with dream-references. If you believe that the Mormon prophet Joseph Smith was merely a charlatan, and that the *Book of Mormon* is nothing more than a clever pastiche, then clearly you must regard the prominence given to dreams in the book as being just a reflection of the prominence given to them in the Bible. Otherwise, the *Book of Mormon* must be recognized as carrying on a grand tradition.

The trouble is that even 'different' dreams can be hard to remember: there's nothing worse than wandering around all day haunted by the dream you had the night before and yet totally unable to remember what it was about. Carl Sagan, in his *The Dragons of Eden* (1977), has a proposed explanation for this 'forgettability' of dreams. He points out that, even if he has the most powerful of dreams, if he simply sits up in bed and thinks 'I'll never forget that!' then the chances are strong that he will. If, on the other hand, he tells his wife about it immediately, or writes it down, he later remembers the dream with ease. This, he suggests, may be a throwback to a time when our ancestors didn't have very many thoughts, and hence needed no mechanism to help remember them. In other words, we can remember things we've said or written because we can remember the act of saying or writing, or even remember the sounds and the written symbols; but we cannot remember the pure thoughts (in this case, dreams) themselves.

This is an elegant and entertaining suggestion, but as far as I can see it simply isn't true. Certainly, though, it's *easier* to remember dreams if you write them down first thing in the morning – as anyone who's ever kept a dream-diary will tell you. And there's another curious thing about keeping a dream-diary: doing so seems to generate far more dreams than you normally have. Now it would be easy enough to say that all that's happening is that you're remembering more of your dreams simply because you're making the effort to write them down. But I'm not sure that this is the case. While writing this book, I've woken up on far more mornings than usual *knowing* that I've been dreaming – even if, half an hour later, I can't remember anything about the dream. I'm not at all sure why this should be: possibly there's a higher than usual chance that my first thoughts of the morning will be concerned with the subject of dreaming, and this reminds me that I've been doing just that. But, if this is the case, it certainly hasn't happened consciously: most mornings my first thoughts are on a rather lower plane: dashing to the lavatory or wanting a cup of tea.

Another important consideration is the dividing line between dreamland and reality. In the *Chuang-tzu* (or *Nan-hua chen Ching*, literally *The Pure Classic of Nan-hua*), believed to be by the important Taoist philosopher

Chuang-tzu (or Juang-zu, Chwang-tse, etc.; *c.* 369-*c.* 286 B.C.), we come across the famous passage:

> Once I, Chuang-tzu, dreamt that I was a butterfly and that I was happy as a butterfly. I knew that I was quite pleased with myself, but I was not aware that I was Chuang-tzu. Suddenly I awoke, and there I was, quite obviously Chuang-tzu. I do not know whether I was a man dreaming I was a butterfly or a butterfly dreaming that I was a man. Between Chuang-tzu and the butterfly there must be some distinction. This is called the transformation of things.

The same sort of point – that dreams might be the reality and life only a dream – has been made by other people: Mark Twain's *The Prince and the Pauper* is based on this idea (see page 79). The notion has been picked up or reinvented by later thinkers: Descartes, Pascal, Schopenhauer and, as you might expect, the mystic G. I. Gurdjieff. The lynchpin of Gurdjieff's theories was, indeed, the idea that almost all of us live permanently in a dream; only by rigorous application of Gurdjieff's own techniques can any of us hope to become fully awake. Jack Kerouac seems confusedly to have tried to make Chuang-tzu's point:

> . . . the fact that everybody in the world dreams every night ties all mankind together shall we say in one unspoken Union and also proves that the world is really transcendental which the Communists do not believe because they think their dreams are 'unrealities' instead of visions of what they saw in their sleep.

On the other hand, he may have been trying to make a different point altogether: it's always hard to tell with Kerouac. D. H. Lawrence said, on a related topic,

> I can never decide whether my dreams are the result of my thoughts, or my thoughts the result of my dreams. It is very queer. But my dreams make conclusions for me. They decide things finally . . . Sleep seems to hammer out for me the logical conclusions of my vague days, and offer me them as dreams. It is a horrid feeling, not to be able to escape from one's own – what? – self-daemon – fate . . .

The dividing line between dreamland and reality lies, I think, where we choose to draw it.

## *Ordinary People*

It's a truism that ordinary people like you and me often have not-so-ordinary dreams. Ann White, for example, once had a fascinating dream in which everyone in the world except herself had turned into telephones:

> The telephones were all black and were all the dialling type (not press-button). They had wires attached to them but there were no switchboards or telephone boxes. The majority of telephones were on the floor but, just occasionally, one or two appeared on the type of large table used in offices. I was not a telephone and, although I felt no sense of power, throughout the whole dream I felt totally at ease – almost as if I were in control of all about me. Although I spoke on various telephones, at no time during the dream did a telephone ring. In fact, apart from talking (I cannot remember any actual conversations), it was a silent peaceful world. There were buildings, large open spaces (with telephones dotted about), but there was no movement of any kind. No cars, planes and, presumably, no wind because of the stillness. There were no plants, trees or animals (this is strange because these are important to

me). When I spoke on a telephone it was because *I* wanted to speak to that person. Otherwise all was silent.

This dream was in no way a nightmare . . . [1]

White's particular dreamland sounds like quite a fun place to be.

Recurring dreams, of varying degrees of interest, happen to many of us. Susan Richardson has had not one but three notable recurring dreams:

. . . Incidentally, I have been able to realize whilst actually in the middle of these dreams that I have dreamt them before.

1) This dream occurred frequently as a child but it is years now since it recurred. I was trying to escape from German soldiers who were chasing me. I picture clearly my parents' home which was four doors up from the corner of the road. My legs are like treacle with ball and chain attached to each and I always manage to get past two houses before waking up either crying or sweating.

2) I am on top of a very tall, narrow tower. There is a lift but this is always broken and I have therefore no alternative, if I want to get down, but to descent via an open spiral staircase on the outside of the building. Needless to say, I can't do it . . . I always wake up in an extreme state of panic.

3) I dream that I am ice skating, always with a long dress on, just gliding over the ice and always to music. It really is the most beautiful sensation. I adore skating and music and presumably this influences my subconscious . . . This dream I occasionally still have; when I do, I try to extend it as long as possible.

I have had other recurring dreams, mainly nightmarish, but these are not so clear. They do, however, frequently involve my little dog getting killed, and water and knives seem to loom large. As she [the dog] means everything to me, I wake up very distressed and soaking wet from crying. I have also had creative dreams and have solved problems whilst dreaming but I can't remember any specific instances, unfortunately.[2]

It sounds from this last sentence as if Richardson has encountered the phenomenon known as 'reading back' (see page 190).

These recurring dreams are of especial interest to dream-analysts because, of course, they reveal all sorts of naughty things about the dreamer's innermost self. Here's a recurring childhood dream which is packed with more sexual symbolism than the average copy of *Playboy*; alternatively, it might just as well mean that the dreamer, Catherine Stewart, was frightened of being chased by vicious animals.

I used to dream about horribly huge animals – a panther or a lion chasing me. When it caught up with me I would pretend I hadn't been running away at all, and be very nice to it. The setting for these dreams was never the jungle or anything like that, but our house, a friend's house and the local street. Sometimes I would try to 'control' the dream – you know, when you partly wake up and decide to make a happy ending. Then I'd fall properly to sleep again, part way through the process, and the happy ending would go all wrong. Like people would come with nets to capture the lion but it would break out and never go for the zookeepers or bystanders but follow me again.

I distinctly remember, too, entertaining a panther to afternoon tea . . .[3]

Phyllis Godbeer reports:

> I have had two recurring dreams all my adult life (I am now 65 years old) . . .
>
> One is I am heading towards the sea from the shore, delighted at the thought of a swim – when I get there the water is never deep enough to swim in, or else it is much too rough. Also at times it is a swimming pool, and on entering I find there is no water in it – a further disappointment.
>
> My next dream is I am looking for a lavatory, usually in a hotel or big establishment. When I finally find one after a great panic there are always people looking at me – no privacy, no doors.[4]

It's interesting to note that Godbeer's recurring dreams have persisted throughout her life, rather than vanished with puberty, as is so often the case. Mrs J. F. Raymond's dreams are rather more complicated.

> Occasionally I have dreamt of events before they have happened; e.g., whilst living in London I dreamt about an airliner crashing near Heathrow airport. The event, I am afraid, took place the following day. Another example of this was when the Menai Bridge went up in flames. I was standing beside a man and a woman who, seeing the fire, raised the alarm. I told my mother about it, and it was only when she pointed out the similarities between my story and the press column that I realized that I had been watching the disaster hundreds of miles away whilst fast asleep.

As we shall see in Chapters Four and Five, we shouldn't get too excited about dreams like these. There are perhaps half a million nightmares dreamt in Britain each night; it would be odd if some of them did not correspond reasonably well with real-life disasters of the following days. This is not to say that these dreams of Mrs Raymond's were definitely not paranormal: in this case we just don't know.

But on to her recurring dream:

One dream I have had since I was a child and turns up virtually every week, is one that I cannot comprehend at all.

I am standing in a big old house, made of dark stone (brown), and with high arc-shaped windows. It has long corridors, rather barren-looking, with a few rugs scattered about. I am not alone, but the people about me are all nameless faces.

The house is situated on the side of a hill overlooking a bay and is surrounded by trees. Below are many small houses, a number of them made of wood but with slate roofs. There is no beach to speak of, but there are boats moored to an old harbour wall.

The sky at first is very blue and the sun shines through the windows where I am standing at the hallway. Gradually the sky becomes overcast even whilst I am looking down at the sea; and with the darkness the waves begin to lash in the bay opening, causing spray to fly over the rocks and the harbour wall.

At the sound of a tinkling bell, the people about me all move to the windows. The ringing seems to come from inside somewhere, but while I am trying to see who is causing the sound it stops as quickly as it started.

Looking back out of the window, the sea has become a dark grey-green topped with rolling crests of white.

As I watch, the waves get bigger and bigger. I feel terrified and begin asking what's wrong, what is happening; but they shake off my hands and tell me to be quiet. They carry on drinking from glasses and laughing as they look out at the night.

To my horror, a massive wave about a hundred feet high (or perhaps more) sweeps in.

I scream, as I see the wooden houses and others below become engulfed, smashing like toy bricks. People are flung around everywhere, and I try to pull some of the men present away from the windows, begging them to do something.

They get angry and say that we are all right, the house is safe. Again I point out that people outside are drowning, but all they do is laugh and walk away.

Outside a big door that I hadn't noticed before, I hear people screaming and banging, pleading to come in.

I start running to the door, but it never gets any nearer. Then the voices stop and a great crashing sound echoes around me, and everything shakes and vibrates.

Crouched up against the wall, I look back to where the people in their evening attire are still standing. They still face the windows, but no one moves or speaks. The windows are almost completely covered by the sea-water, and the room is given a strange green tinge. Outside, men, women, and children – now dead – can be seen floating about.

A voice starts shouting above the roar 'Why? Why? Why?', over and over again. Then I realize it is myself asking the question.

Everyone alive in the hallway turns to look at me, but their faces are just white blanks. No eyes, mouths or any features at all except their hair and the rest of their bodies which are normal.

They begin to walk towards me and I begin to back away and then run from them. The only escape apart from the door is a very wide staircase. I begin to run up it; but suddenly it seems I am neither running up or down it, but rather straight ahead. In front is total blackness, and when I look back there is only blackness there as well. Suddenly I seem to trip and fall; and that is when I wake up, usually amid a heap of blankets and sheets.

It's the same every time without any deviation . . . [5]

This is one of those dreams which psychoanalysts itch to get their hands on: a couple of years' work on it and a professorship would be in the bag. That it's a dream of extraordinary vividness is obvious from the richness of Raymond's description of it (although we must remember that it's a dream she's had perhaps 1000 or 1500 times). To a psychoanalyst it's packed with rich symbolism, and reveals all there is to know about Raymond. Alternatively, it could easily be just a collection of several of her pet phobias, uuniting in a single nightmare.

## *Not-So-Ordinary People*

If perfectly ordinary people like Ann White and Mrs Raymond can have such curious, complicated dreams, one naturally wonders what the dreams of the not-so-ordinary can be like.

At the age of 19 months Helen Keller suffered an illness that left her deaf, dumb and almost completely blind. Even today, these disabilities would probably render the luckless individual totally handicapped, totally dependent on other people; in the 1880s the situation was, obviously, even worse. However, Keller was lucky enough to be 'discovered' in 1887 by Anne Sullivan (*née* Macy), who was herself partially blind. Sullivan became Keller's teacher and lifelong companion, teaching her the arts of speech and of understanding others' speech *via* the touch of the neck muscles. Keller adapted sufficiently to graduate from Radcliffe College, Cambridge (Mass.), in 1904, and to write several bestselling books.

Keller's dreams have an obvious fascination in that her records of them are almost unique. Blind, deaf and dumb, she nevertheless lived a full dream-life, seeing in her dreams things which she could not see during her waking hours. It is a pity that no answer survives (if indeed any was written) to G. Stanley Hall's 1901 letter to Sullivan, which reads in part:

> It would be specially interesting to know, what I have never seen, whether there has been anything that suggests spontaneous dreams of sex or any other indication of the awakening of this new consciousness.

The interest is not a prurient one: Keller must have experienced the physical changes of ageing, just like anyone else, and her reactions to them in dreams would have been fascinating. But otherwise the fullness of her dream-life, its sensual richness, can be gathered from this famous description:

> Once in my dreams I held in my hand a pearl. I have no memory-vision of a real pearl. The one I saw in my dream must, therefore, have been a creation of my imagination. It was a smooth, exquisitely molded crystal . . . My pearl was dew and fire, the velvety green of moss, the soft whiteness of lilies.

The interesting point here is that Keller was operating in reverse the process whereby many of us associate qualities with colours. Clearly she was taking qualities – e.g., the 'velvetiness' of moss – and deriving her ideas of colours from the tactile information. It's a pity we can't know what the colours were that she saw in her dreams.

She seems to have had at least one apparently clairvoyant or precognitive dream: she dreamt that her friend Bishop Phillips Brooks was dying, and found out some while later that this had indeed been the case.

Fortunately for us, Keller recorded a good many of her dreams. For example:

> I would often dream that I ran into a still, dark room, and that, while I stood there, I felt something fall heavily without any noise, causing the floor to shake up and down violently; and each time I woke up with a jump.

She noted, too, that when in dreamland she behaved and thought much as she did during her waking hours, except in the case of her relations with Sullivan, her teacher. In her dreams they quarrelled violently, or Sullivan would drag her towards disaster.

> One night we stood at the foot of a stairway that seemed to rise to the very stars, and she commanded me to climb it. I refused stubbornly, declaring that my feet would stumble, and I should be hurled from the dizzying heights. At last, unable to make me yield, she struck a match and flashing it in my face tried to make me swallow it. Still I resisted and remonstrated, and at last I tore myself away from her firm grasp. I rushed blindly in an opposite direction, pursued by my teacher and was just letting myself down into a cellar by a trapdoor when I awoke.

Occasionally she would see Sullivan like a distant figure, smiling in friendly fashion but for all that coldly. Once she saw Sullivan dressed in white like an angel falling into the turbulent waters beside the Niagara Falls. Keller jumped in to save her, but the best she could do was stop Sullivan from sinking. Finally she got her to the shore; but then Sullivan just strolled off, seemingly unconscious of the fact that she'd been in any danger or that Keller had endangered herself in the rescue.

It hardly takes a great imaginative leap to conclude

that in dreams such as these Keller was acting out her feelings of rebelliousness towards the good Annie Sullivan. Of the Niagara Falls dream she remarked: 'I was at a loss how to account for her ignoring me – that was worse than all our [dream-] quarrels put together.' Clearly, without Sullivan Keller might have become as nothing – regarded by all and sundry as a vegetable. But, in her way, Sullivan was a harsh dictator: Keller recorded how Sullivan refused to be satisfied with anything less than perfection on Keller's part. (It may well be that this perfectionism was responsible for Sullivan's success.) Although Keller was extremely intelligent, she was probably by no means a genius: she did well, but not outstandingly so, at college. Her guilt about 'failing' Sullivan was intensified by the fact that, by now, Sullivan was wrecking her own already poor eyesight by reading to Keller for four or five hours a day. (To save Sullivan's eyes, Keller began to claim that she had a phenomenal memory, and could recall precisely passages which she had, in fact, totally forgotten.)

Sullivan's attendance had also the effect of making Keller dream more.

> . . . before Miss Sullivan came to me, my dreams were few and far between, devoid of thought or coherency, except those of a purely physical nature . . . After Miss Sullivan came to me, the more I learned, the oftener I dreamed; but with the making of my mind there came many dreary fancies and vague terrors which troubled my sleep for a long time.

Here is one of the 'vague terrors':

> One cold winter night I was alone in my room. Miss Sullivan had put out the light and gone away, thinking I was sound asleep. Suddenly I felt my bed shake, and

> a wolf seemed to spring on me and snarl in my face. It was only a dream, but I thought it real, and my heart sank within me. I dared not scream, and I dared not stay in bed. Perhaps this was a confused recollection of the story I had heard not long before about Red Riding Hood. At all events I slipped down from the bed and nestled close to the fire which had not flickered out . . .

Helen Keller died on 1st June, 1968. Martin Luther King, whose campaigning she had supported, was assassinated on 4th April in that same year. It is fortunate that by that time Keller had little knowledge of the world around her: having conquered so triumphantly her disabilities, thanks largely to Sullivan's patience, it would have been ironic had she died in the knowledge that King had been murdered in his attempt to conquer disabilities which existed only in the eyes and minds of bigots.

Described in Flora Rheta Schreiber's book *Sybil* (1973), 'Sybil Dorsett' is of interest as one of the most extreme cases of multiple personality on record (we'll look at 'Eve', Chris Sizemore, in Chapter Five – see pages 275–9): there were no less than sixteen of her, fused, in the end, into a seventeenth – stable – personality, the 'real Sybil'.

In Schreiber's book we find various accounts of 'Sybil's' dreams, some of them apparently betraying her sexual attraction towards her father, who seems little to have deserved it. Here is a very typical example from the notes of Dr Cornelia Wilbur who, in the end successfully, treated 'Sybil':

> Men were pursuing her sexually. Her father was not there to rescue her. The pursuit continued and, too, the lack of rescue.

In other dreams 'Sybil' identified with the Jews in the Nazi concentration camps: according to Schreiber, 'Sybil' identified Hitler with her mother (sometimes her guard in the dream-camp was a white-haired lady whom Schreiber again identifies with 'Sybil's' mother): it seems likely that the identification was as a result of the belief that Hitler and her mother were both reincarnations of the Great Beast 666.

One dream is recounted at length by Schreiber. 'Sybil' is travelling on an inter-city train when suddenly it comes to a halt: she looks out and sees that a new, and huge, platform is being built by her father. All of a sudden she is outside the train, in a warehouse: she comes across a starving kitten moving sluggishly near the decapitated body of its mother. Then she sees that nearby are three further kittens of the dead mother-cat; she throws the dismembered remains of the cat into the river, but is anxious that she has not thrown them far enough, that they might float in to the shore. She turns to the three kittens, and finds that they are hiding three *more* kittens. She is beginning to look after them all when she wakes.

Wilbur and Schreiber between them produced an interpretation of this dream which is quite astonishingly boring. The kittens, you see, symbolized 'Sybil' herself; the train was life,

> moving towards a destination but stopped by new work (analysis), which meant reversing its route . . . to become one. The various degrees of starvation among the kittens symbolized the years during which Sybil had tried to live and work normally only to discover that she had come to the end of the line (the train again) in maintaining the ruse of normality.

And so on. Let's swiftly turn from this to an interesting recurring dream which she had:

> She was walking through a tremendous house, looking for her father, or in the same house he was looking for

> her, or they were searching for each other. She would go through room after room in a frustrated quest, knowing that her father was there some place, but knowing, too, that she couldn't find him.

An incestuous desire for her father, Wilbur believed. Well, yes, maybe – but alternatively it could just have been a typical insecurity dream. Only 'Sybil' really knows – and if it was the wrong personality who had the dream then even 'Sybil' cannot tell us.

## *The Quasi-Professionals*

As we shall soon see, a good number of people have not only had interesting dreams but have been driven to do serious research into dreams. There is, however, a rather smaller band of people who have been driven to do *unorthodox* research into dreaming, and most of whom have made a partial if not a good living out of the subject. Since most are concerned with paranormal dreaming, we shall discuss them in Part Two; but it's worth noting a few of their comments here.

An interesting piece of dream-imagery is reported by Joan Grant and Denys Kelsey in *Many Lifetimes* (1967). A close friend was dying of cancer, and had recurring dreams of being on the bank of a river, from the other side of which a hand was beckoning. Grant says that the river represented the border between life and death (remember the Styx): the friend's time was coming.

Sure enough, as the days and weeks passed, the river became gradually narrower – although sometimes it widened temporarily, so that the friend knew that she was for the moment further from death than usual. But she knew, too, that with the beckoning hand and the charming surrounds there was nothing to fear from death. At length the river narrowed until it was no more than a tumbling spring, and she knew that she could step across it easily. As you might expect, a few days later she died.

Grant and Kelsey interpret this in terms of life after death, and Grant talks about this river-symbol elsewhere. It seems much more interesting to speculate that the woman's unconscious (right brain) recognized that death was approaching, and used the medium of the dream, and suitable symbols, in order to communicate this to her – and to comfort her about the fact. She may, like many another sick person, have, unconsciously, positively welcomed death as a release from suffering.

Grant's own dreams are fascinating; we shall encounter them frequently later on.

The German philosopher Count Hermann Alexander Graf Keyserling (1880–1947) was widely regarded in his own time, and to an extent still, as a crackpot of the very first water. According to James Webb's *The Occult Establishment* (1976) Keyserling was 'the most influential guru of Central Europe between 1918 and 1933'; this is a tactful way of putting it. Webb tells too of Keyserling's meeting with an Irishwoman with whom he fell madly in love; apparently the two of them travelled together to Scotland, where Keyserling sat up the whole of one night by a lochside waiting for a kelpie to appear!

In the context of dreamers, Keyserling is important because of his extended correspondence with Jung. In June 1927 we find Jung interpreting one of Keyserling's dreams – in which he was repeatedly hanged – in terms of 'hanging' being a pun for 'suspense'. Keyserling agreed with this interpretation, although it does seem a little desperate – especially since Keyserling apparently dreamt quite frequently about being executed.

On 4th April, 1928, Keyserling claimed in a letter to Jung that he'd dreamt he was the last man alive on Earth, and that in this situation he'd laughed 'like a Homeric hero' (rather than a jackass) in his joy at the sense of 'cosmic stillness' surrounding him. On 20th August in the same year, Keyserling was writing to Jung about an interesting recurring dream: he dreamt that his father hadn't really died years before but was now living in 'reduced circumstances' and in secret. Keyserling, in the dream, was keen to meet up with his father, but his father wanted to 'vanish' and so the meeting never came about. This dream is particularly interesting to me because I had a similar one about my own dead father when I was a child. Keyserling's version of 'my' dream seems to have clung to him for a good while: a letter of Jung's dated 10th May, 1932, refers to the same dream, as recounted yet again by Keyserling a little while before. (Jack Kerouac had similar dreams – see page 88.)

The most important of all the unorthodox-theorist dreamers, if you'll forgive the ugliness of that expression, was undoubtedly Edgar Cayce.

Cayce was born in Hopkinsville, Kentucky, on 18th March, 1877. At the age of about seven or eight he had a vision of an angelic figure (it is claimed) which asked him what was his heart's desire. Cayce's heart's desire was to help other people; and so he was granted access to the Universal Consciousness, or Universal Mind. While sleeping, he would respond to questions put to him by those around him, and, it is said, he was soon able to diagnose the ailments of the attendants (including himself), and to prescribe efficacious, if bizarre, remedies.

Cayce found that any attempt to make a personal profit through his 'readings' soon incurred severe headaches and loss of voice. Although some people claimed to make vast amounts of money by following his guidance (some later lost the money by ignoring him), matters came to a head when a stockbroker ruthlessly picked his sleeping brain, profiting $20,000 thereby – no mean sum in the early 1900s – but bringing on the same dire symptoms in Cayce as if the psychic had been working for his own profit. Thereafter he insisted that someone he trusted – almost always his wife Gertrude – be there while he spoke in his sleep.

In the standard biography of him, *Edgar Cayce: The Sleeping Prophet*, Jess Stearn describes the procedure:

> He observed a regular ritual. Avoiding strictures of circulation, he would remove his jacket and tie, open his collar and loosen his cuffs, unlace his shoes. Then he would lie back on the couch in his study, placing his hands on his forehead. Often as not, he would smile pleasantly, before responding to the suggestion that he put himself to sleep. As a signal, Gertrude would lean over and touch his cheek. He would close his eyes, fold his hands over his chest, and begin to breathe deeply. Mrs Cayce, and Cayce's secretary and trusted aide, Gladys Davis, would close their own eyes in prayer. As Cayce sighed, breathing evenly, as anyone would in a nap, Gertrude would speak softly, making the suggestion that induced the reading.

Questions would then be put to him, and to these he would reply either succinctly or in terms of ambiguous orotundity: religious references were dotted around liberally.

To describe this process as 'dreaming' may seem to be stretching things a little. However, it does seem to parallel closely the process at work among G. M. Glaskin and his friends in the 'Christos Experiment' – the chief difference being that they described their visual and sensual experiences while Cayce seems to have described words or meanings that hopped into his unconscious (see pages 387–97).

While in this state Cayce performed at least 600 or so dream-interpretations, many of them of his own dreams. This is not the place to go into the symbol-system he used in such interpretations – especially since the system is not outrageous. A rabbit, for example, referred to sex or to timidity; a house was the body or family; dead leaves were faeces; a boat was 'life's great adventure'; fire was rage, destruction, or a cleansing force (depending upon context); a bumpy road ahead meant that difficulties were in store; and so on. Thus if you dreamt you were driving along a bumpy road when you saw your house was on fire you knew you were really in the dead leaves.

One man came to him with a nightmare. He had been standing in his back yard, and found there was something inside the cloth of the cuff of his left sleeve. It proved to be a cocoon, which broke open to release a little black spider and lots of eggs, which stuck to the dreamer's sleeve. As he struggled to get these off the spider ran away, speaking about its mother and growing all the time. A little later – by which time the beast was several inches across and had a red spot to alleviate the blackness – it had built a web all over the inside of the back of his house. He forced it outside, and it started to build its web over the outside of the back of his house. Using his straw hat *à l'*Oddjob, he felled it, and then hacked it to bits with a knife.

Cayce's interpretation was that the spider was Another Woman who was causing the (married) dreamer strains in both financial and emotional senses. Unless the dreamer changed his ways, he would lose his wife (who, despite his efforts, knew about the liaison) and his children. The house seems to have represented both his body and his family life, while the stickiness of the spider's eggs seems to have represented all the little complications – so hard to get out of – which his duplicity entailed.[6]

Many of Cayce's interpretations were briefer and more lucid. One poor fellow sent him the terse dream-description: 'Dreamed I died.' Most people who believe in the paranormal believe that such dreams are Not Good News, but Cayce's interpretation was more optimistic. The dream signified a rebirth of the spirit through the death of purely materialistic influences on the dreamer. Even more to the point were the instructions given to a dreamer in response to a more elaborate dream: he was to stop staying up late, improve his eating habits, and change his milkman because the milk he was getting had not been properly sterilized.

Cayce was fairly direct, too, about one of his own dreams, in which he saw himself going to some heavenly church to pray. An angel-figure showed him a room filled with gift-wrapped packages, and explained that these were waiting here in Limbo because people had lost their faith before the gifts could be delivered. Cayce took this to mean that he should get a move on with his work in healing and prediction.

Between 1925 and 1926 Cayce was interested in the apparently precognitive dreams of a young woman. In one she was chatting up an old flame; and sure enough she later divorced her husband to marry the old flame, who promptly left her. She dreamt that one of her children was feeble-minded (she had yet to bear a child in real life); 25 years later one of her (adult) children lost his sanity – a rather tenuous connection! She dreamt that her husband stopped coming home; and five years later he did, because they were divorced. She dreamt that her mother was going to die; and sure enough, in the fullness of time, the mother *did* die. She dreamt that her cousin was getting married; and some months later the cousin married.

Set out as baldly as this, the supposed predictions are

hardly startling. But there are further reasons for creeping doubts. The dreams were so clear, so straightforward, that in virtually every instance all that Cayce had to do by way of interpretation was to say: 'Yes, that's what's going to happen.' As we shall see in Chapters Four and Five, paranormal dreams – if such things exist at all – simply don't work that way. Loaded with symbolism, they give partial, fragmented visions of the reality; yet only one of this woman's 'prophetic' dreams seems to have been like this (it's not mentioned in the list above, and need not concern us here). *All* of her dreams can be explained in terms of orthodox psychology and require no invocation of the paranormal.

My hunch is that the explanation is embarrassingly simple. I think she was pulling Cayce's leg.

## *The Professionals*

Psychologists, surprisingly enough, are people too – and as people they dream like everyone else. Where the psychologists are, more correctly, psychoanalysts, thousands upon thousands of their dreams have been passed down to us. For obvious reasons, if you're interested in studying dreams, the ones you're most likely to consider in detail are your own: after all, they're the only ones you've experienced first-hand.

The French physician Alfred Maury (1817–1892) is generally regarded as the first person to have made a proper scientific study of dreams – although Artemidorus had an occasionally hilarious stab at it in the 2nd century. Maury gathered and studied over 3000 dream-reports; the results of his researches were first published in 1861.

He it was who first proposed that there is a huge discrepancy between dream-time and real-time. His breakthrough came as a result of a very famous dream. It was set in the time of the French Revolution, and Maury walked around talking to people, witnessing the atrocities and the achievements; in due course he was himself condemned to death. The detail of the dream was rich, and its subjective timescale long. The dream ended in the instant that he felt the guillotine on the back of his neck . . . and in the instant that he was awoken by a bedstaff dropping onto the back of his neck.

Refusing to believe that his dream could in any way involve short-term precognition (i.e., that his mind had known the bedstaff was going to fall soon, and so had hurriedly created the whole dream just so that the real blow could coincide with that of the dream-blade), Maury proposed that this entire, rich, extensive dream had happened in the instant between the pain of the impact and his awakening.

Maury performed some experiments on the production of dreams by external stimuli. Some of his successes are noted by Freud in *The Interpretation of Dreams* (1900). As Maury slept, helpers tickled his nose with a feather: he dreamt that he was being tortured by the use of a mask the inside of which was covered in pitch, so that as the mask was taken away his facial skin was removed. In another experiment scissors were grated against pliers: the sound made him dream of bells pealing, and then of the ringing of alarm bells. Another stimulus used was to bring a hot iron close to his face: he dreamt that thieves had burst into the house and were forcing its occupants to surrender their money by sticking their feet into hot braziers (a charming practice which had not, in fact, been uncommon a century or so earlier, during the Revolution). A burning match was held under his nose: he dreamt he was at sea and his ship's powder magazine had just exploded. Light was shone through red paper onto his face: he dreamt of hot weather, and of being once more in a storm in the English Channel which he'd experienced in real life a while before. And, as a final example, a drop of water was splashed onto his forehead: he dreamt he was in Italy, drinking white wine and sweating profusely.

As a result of all these experiments, Maury concluded that external stimuli could indeed generate dreams. However, the connections seem to be pretty tenuous in some cases. As Freud notes, only some of the stimuli supplied corresponded with the sleeper's dreams; so at best all that could be claimed is that stimuli may or may not generate dreams. Moreover, the connection between stimulus and dream is not strong even in the 'successful' experiments described above. In the mask-filled-with-pitch dream the only connection was the fact that the face was involved; red light is not really much like hot weather; and so on.

Freud quotes a few examples of dreams apparently prompted by external stimuli which other people have had. Napoleon was once asleep in a carriage when a bomb went off nearby; he awoke shouting, 'We are undermined!' (In French the pun works even better: *miner* is to undermine and *mine* is mine.) A man once dreamt he was teaching a class of boys; when he had explained his point he asked one of the pupils if he'd understood. 'Oh, ja!' shrieked the boy maniacally. As the dreamer began to rebuke the lad, the rest of the class took up the cry: 'Orja!', then 'Eurjo!', and then a final distortion from these nonsense-words to '*Feuerjo*!' (Fire!). Sure enough, the sleeper woke up to cries of '*Feuerjo*!' from the street below.

F. W. Hildebrandt used to be awoken by his alarm-clock each morning; after a good number of mornings, he noticed that quite often a complicated dream would lead up to some denouement that seemed to be a product of the sound of the clock. Freud tells us of three.

In one, Hildebrandt was strolling through the fields when he spotted a village church. He made his way towards it and, before going in, browsed among the tombstones for a while. A bellringer climbed the tower and, some time later, the churchbell began to peal . . . and the alarm-clock went off.

In another Hildebrandt dreamt that he was going on a sleigh-ride. There was a long delay before the sleigh arrived and he and his friends climbed into it. The sleigh-bells jangled as the sleigh moved off . . . the alarm-clock went off.

In a third he saw a maid carrying a pile of crockery. He warned her she might drop it, and an argument ensued: she knew her own job, thank you very much. Sure enough, a while later she dropped the lot . . . the alarm-clock went off.

Carl Sagan has commented that he often has 'plot' dreams in which the final denouement hinges on various little clues, which had seemed irrelevant at the time, scattered through the earlier parts of the dream. It seems that the same sort of phenomenon as with Hildebrandt's alarm-clock is at work.

I wonder if what's happening might be that the dreaming self is creating false memories. Most of our conception of the world about us is based on memories: to take an obvious example, if we laugh at a joke we (generally) start laughing after the punchline – in other words, we laugh at the *memory* of the joke as a whole rather than at the joke as it is being told. Now, if we dream that something's happening – a ringing bell or a startling denouement – it's perfectly possible that our dreaming self may, in seeking for an explanation of the event, create a complete set of false memories. Then, when we wake up, we remember the false memories as if we'd dreamt the whole episode.[7]

I should add that this is only a personal speculation. However, it does seem to allow an explanation of such dreams as Maury's guillotining and Hildebrandt's alarm-clock while still admitting today's accepted truth that dream-time passes at a rate not significantly different from real-time.

James Burnett, Lord Monboddo (1714–1799), was in many ways a sort of latterday Renaissance man; to put it conversely, he was a man of such curious beliefs and eccentricities that it is hard not to sympathize with the suggestion of some of his contemporaries that he was a crank. For example, he maintained that all human children are born with tails, but that these are adroitly clipped off by the midwife before the father is allowed to look at his newborn. Again, he was a staunch advocate of the hypothesis that orangutans are a species of humanity rather than apes.[8] Because he has become something of a figure of fun among the comparatively few who remember him today (and something of a figure of fun to his contemporaries, too, including Boswell and Peacock; the latter immortalized him as Sir Oran Haut-ton in *Melincourt*), one tends to forget that he was the author of *Antient Metaphysics* (1779–99). This is a vast work on philosophy and natural philosophy, a large part of whose second volume is concerned with dreams.

But let us retrace our steps a little. In early 1778 Monboddo was so seriously ill that he was expected to die. In a dream he met a beautiful woman, a philosopher, who lectured to him for hours in French. Her words were words of great wisdom – for did she not confirm to him so many of his own ideas? He awoke in the morning determined to write down as full an account as possible of what she had said – but all he could manage was a page of notes on Man's cradle-land. But in physical terms, when he awoke that morning, he found that he was cured.

Although he could recall so little of the dream's contents, it had a profound effect on him, one which was to last for the rest of his life. Soon after the dream, he talked with Boswell about it; and added that during his illness he'd realized the great fallacy of being frightened of death, that a man accustomed to mental pursuits would be truly happy in the hereafter. Boswell was originally rather impressed, but within days the rather unpleasant little gossip was spreading the story everywhere as a juicy example of Monboddo's peculiarity. He 'entertained' Lord Kames, who was over 80 and in poor health, with the tale of 'Monboddo, who told me that during his late fever he had been some hours in Elysium'. Kames did not deign to reply when Boswell added that Monboddo had said 'a Man who is afraid of death must be very miserable'. Boswell laughed fit to bust; Kames, in his circumstances, was less amused.

But, if the dream supplied Boswell with nothing more than a good tale to tell over the port, it altered and exaggerated Monboddo's philosophy quite drastically. Since his ideas had been confirmed by the dream-philosopher, they must be more than mere speculations: he was *right*, dammit, *right*. And his mystical leanings, always pronounced, gradually became dominant. While these changes in one sense made his philosophy more valuable, in that it attempted to marry the (then) modern stark mechanism with the older, more humanistic approach to matters cosmogonic, in another sense they destroyed all of its potential value: there is no one easier to ignore than the bigot convinced that every word he says is true.

Naturally the dream affected his ideas on dreams in general. In *Antient Metaphysics* he tells us that dreams are important because it is during them that the mind functions in a totally pure state, and at its best. Where the mind, during the waking hours, relies for its raw materials on the evidences of the senses, at night it uses those images which are presented to it by the 'phantasia'. The phantasia have reached a rudimentary stage of development in some of the higher animals, who dream (see Darwin's remarks at the head of this chapter); but they have yet to develop in young children, who perforce cannot dream.[9]

Monboddo elegantly proves that the mind is not tied in any way to the body. The mind is of course immaterial; in order to occupy or be tied to any particular part of the body, it would have to have a spatial dimension, and therefore would be material – which, as noted, it most certainly isn't. Being immaterial, the mind can roam wherever it wants, in time or in space, in this Universe or any other. The obvious – in fact, the *necessary* – conclusion is that in dreams, when the mind is working in its pure form, we can see the past or the future; that when we dream we are somewhere else we really *are* somewhere else. In short, Monboddo's ideas imply an acceptance of precognitive, telepathic and all the other sorts of paranormal dreams.

Henry Havelock Ellis (1859–1939), who did more than virtually anyone else to allow sexuality to start to be treated as part of the full spectrum of humanity's activities and interests, and therefore as a respectable object of discussion, study and scientific research, had an interesting relationship with Freud. In fact, some of his earlier ideas fit in very well with Freud's; later, however, he was to be one of the many who rejected the Freudian notion that *every* dream springs from the desire for wish-fulfilment, and thereafter the thinking of the two men diverged somewhat radically.

Leaving their arguments aside, Ellis is of interest also in that he carried out a study on the correlations between dreaming and stomach upsets. That there might be such a connection is probable: although I've never noticed that late-night cheese binges have given me nightmares, the popular belief that they do is a very strong one, and there is no evidence that it should be rejected as a mere baseless superstition.

Vincent Brome, in his biography of Ellis, quotes him as follows:

> Sleeping consciousness, blindfolded and blundering, a prey to these massive waves from below, and fumbling about desperately for some explanation, jumps at the idea that only the attempt to escape some terrible danger or the guilty consciousness of some awful crime can account for this immense emotional uproar.

I'm not certain but that this idea doesn't have a lot going for it. As Freud himself noticed, there are 'different' dreams and 'only' dreams; we all know that there is a profound emotional difference between the former (which can affect us for hours, days or even years after waking) and the latter. Freud chose to explain the former as being dreams which referred to real-life memories, however obscured by symbolism. My instincts hint that Ellis may have been closer to the truth – especially since even some nightmares fall into the 'only' dreams category, forgotten soon after awakening or remembered only as a subject for a good story to tell one's friends.

Hmmm. 'Different' dreams as the product of indigestion. Freud must be spinning in his grave.

Herbert Silberer was a devotee of Freud's who did some important work on the interpretation of dreams. One of his techniques of investigation was, at the onset of drowsiness, to think about some problem that he had not solved, then to record the subsequent dream to see how it reflected the problem. A single example of this should be enough.

The problem under contemplation was

> . . . the purpose of the metaphysical studies I am about to undertake. The purpose is, I reflect, to work my way through ever higher forms of consciousness, that is, levels of existence, in my quest after the basis of existence.

The succeeding dream was of him sliding a long knife under a layer-cake, preparatory to lifting out a slice.

No connection at all, you might think (and so might I). But, as Silberer explains, the dream is a restatement of the problem. In real life he sometimes had to perform this mundane chore, and it involved carefully working the knife under the cake ('work my way through'). The layers of the cake are of course the 'levels of existence', and the underside of the cake is likewise the 'basis of existence'.

Freud could be cruel to his devotees. He seems to have respected much of Silberer's work, but nevertheless rejected him on a personal basis – a matter which depressed Silberer considerably. Here is the complete text of a letter Freud sent him in April 1922:

> Dear Sir,
> I request that you do not make the intended visit with me. As the result of the observations and impressions of recent years, I no longer desire personal contact with you.
> Very truly yours,
> Freud.

Silberer committed suicide in January 1923.

In *Modern Man in Search of a Soul* (trans., 1933) C.

G. Jung tells an interesting tale which is of some note in any discussion of the question of dream-analysis as a route to the diagnosis and cure of a neurosis. A young woman had been to three analysts, and at the beginning of each treatment she had had a distinct new dream – distinct, although all three dreams were obviously related.

In the first, she knew that she must cross a frontier into another country, but she did not know where the frontier was and no one could help her find it; the treatment was unsuccessful. In the second she had to cross the frontier, but it was night and she couldn't find the customs post. After searching for a while, she saw a light in the distance, and assumed it must be the post; but to get there she had to cross a valley and go through a dark wood. She got lost in the wood and then, to her horror, realized that there was somebody travelling furtively alongside her. At this point, her fellow-traveller leapt upon her, clinging to her like a madman, and she awoke in terror. (A rather similar dream collected by Wesley resulted in a man being hanged – see page 204.) The treatment was unsuccessful, and was discontinued.

The third analyst was Jung himself. In this case, the woman dreamt that she had already crossed the frontier, and was now in a Swiss customs post. All she had with her was her handbag, and so she believed that she had nothing to declare; however, the customs officer delved deep into the bag and came out with 'two full-sized mattresses'.

Now – to follow Jung for a moment – the interesting thing in this dream-sequence is not purely the matter of the progression from one dream to the next. Nor has it anything to do with the root cause of her neurosis: as Jung points out, when he did eventually track down her neurosis it had nothing whatsoever to do with her dreams.

But the dreams were not meaningless. What they represented were her *anticipation of the difficulties she was going to have with each of her three analysts*. In other words, there was a sad case of 'positive feedback', whereby the very fact that she was going to submit to analysis – including analysis of her dreams – *generated* dreams.

I find all this rather difficult to follow; but then I find Jung's ideas pretty opaque at the best of times. You'll excuse me if I take the easy option and skip athletically away from much of the theoretical aspect of Jung's work. This may or may not be cowardly: I've yet to find a psychologist who can explain the theory to me without the need for strong drinks. Let's stick to the dreams.

In 1944 Jung had a dream reminiscent of Chuang-tzu's (see page 10). He was on a hiking holiday when he came to a wayside church: inside there were none of the usual church accoutrements, only a 'wonderful flower arrangement' and a meditating yogi. The dreaming Jung knew that it was not a question of himself dreaming the yogi but of the yogi dreaming him: when the yogi awoke, Jung would cease to exist.

Jung states that the yogi represents his 'unconscious prenatal wholeness', the very essence of himself which projects itself in three-dimensional human form in the real world. That it should represent itself as a yogi involves the idea of the Orient and hence a philosophical/psychic structure alien to the Occident. The religious setting indicates that Jung's inmost self had 'renounced existence in the hereafter' (the dream occurred after a serious illness).

He relates this dream to one which has a similar 'feel' to it, but which involved UFOs ('flying saucers' – see page 260); this dream occurred in 1958. He saw from his house two lens-shaped UFOs; then a third stopped within a few hundred yards of him. It was like the objective lens of a telescope. It moved off, immediately to be replaced by another lens: this time the lens was connected to a magic lantern and pointed straight at him. Still half-asleep, he thought to himself that, whereas we think that UFOs are projections of the human mind, perhaps it's the other way around: perhaps we are the projections of the UFOs. Who, he wondered, operated the 'magic lantern' which controls the projections that are ourselves?

In January 1943, in a letter to a correspondent whose name is lost to us but whom Jung considered to be an amateur in the art of dream-interpretation, we find the following:

> The question of dream psychology is a very difficult topic which can be discussed with some prospect of success only if one has the necessary rudiments of knowledge together with thorough practical experience. The fact of having dreams is not nearly enough. You also have a digestive system but this is not nearly enough to make you a physiological chemist.

Such considerations don't seem to have stopped Jung from regarding himself as a dream-interpreter *par excellence* – and, to be fair, within his own conceptual framework he was. Even he had to admit, however, that sometimes he was beat. Take the case of a certain 'Mr O', to whom Jung wrote on 30th April, 1947:

> The fact is that you have an uncannily extensive [dream] material one can hardly hope to cope with, at least I couldn't muster the amount of energy that would be required to deal with your dreams properly. In order to keep up with them one would need at least three hours a week . . . You are not only informed enough but also intelligent enough to go on for a long stretch

> on the assumption that I'm buried and that there is no analyst for you under the changing moon except the one that is in your own heart. As you will understand, this does not mean at all that you analyse and interpret your dreams according to rules of thumb, but that you do what we call [coming to terms with the unconscious], which is a dialectical procedure you carry through with yourself with the aid of active imagination . . .

The method known as 'active imagination' is, to the nearest order of magnitude, incomprehensible to the layman. In *The Directory of Possibilities* (1981) Colin Wilson summed it up thus:

> [Jung] asserted that it was possible to 'descend into the unconscious' while wide awake, to conjure up a scene with a sense of its total reality, and to explore it consciously.

This is a far clearer explanation than any Jung gave. In fact, Jung's next letter to 'Mr O', dated 2nd May, 1947 (the posts were obviously faster then), begins: 'I'm somewhat astonished that you haven't learned yet to apply what I call "active imagination" . . .' Jung's several letters to 'Mr O' from that month then proceed to interpret 'Mr O's' dreams in alchemical terms of the utmost opacity.

A long-time correspondent with Jung was a certain 'Dr S'. In 1947 he wrote to Jung about a dream he had had in which he had been standing alongside a bank of terminal moraine; on the far side of the moraine he had seen a single star shining brightly from the depths of a dark forest. 'Dr S' had been studying Indian philosophy and Sanskrit: he was currently going through various psychological crises.

'Dr S's' dream is not of thundering interest in itself; what *is* interesting is the terseness with which Jung was able to provide a 'complete analysis' of the dream.

> I gather from your description that you are indeed climbing too high. Sanskrit and India really are a bit much. You must turn back to the simple things, just as your dream says, to the forest. There you will find the star. You must set off in search of yourself; you will find yourself again only in the simple and forgotten things. Why not, literally, go into the forest for a time? Sometimes a tree tells you more than can be read in books.

This is all very well, but the *I Ching* would probably have produced similarly vague advice at much less cost.

'Dr S' was favoured in 1935 with a curious utterance from Jung concerning the dreamer's *attitude* to his/her own dreams:

> Your question about dreams relates to the little explored problem of the attitude of the dreamer to what is dreamt. There are various levels of realization, different degrees of intensity and enfeeblement of the dream experience . . . when I am on the point of waking from a dream, this expresses itself in a kind of pushing away of the dream experience, so that it looks as if someone else were experiencing the dream and I were getting only a report of it. Conversely, it very often happens that, at the beginning of a dream, one merely experiences something like the beginning of a cinema show, or that one knows something has been said earlier, or that one has maintained an opinion, and that only with deeper sleep does one enter into the real action as an active protagonist. Then, suddenly, one is in the dream. I would be very chary of the assumption of 'make-believe'. I would have good reason for doubting whether there is such a thing in dreams at all.

On the one hand we can get excited about one of history's greatest dreamers describing his own sensations during dreaming. On the other, we can notice that he's saying, time after time, that dream-analysis is a load of rubbish. Yet, again and again, he analyzes his own dreams and those of other people.

But what of Jung's own dreams?

More than once after her death in 1955 Jung dreamt of his wife, Emma. In one dream he saw her as she had been in her thirties, dressed in the most beautiful dress she had ever worn. She was motionless, and he knew that it was not the real she that he was looking at, somehow, but a sort of portrait containing all of the experiences of their marriage, from their youthful love onwards, and including even her death.

Again, he woke one day knowing that he had spent an entire day with his wife in the south of France, where she was continuing her lifelong (and unfinished, until 1958, by Marie-Louise von Franz) study of the Holy Grail. Jung dismissed the idea that his dream might be telling him to finish her work for her; yet he found the notion that she was continuing with it even after death 'held a measure of reassurance' for him.

He wrote extensively to Father Victor White, then Professor of Dogmatic Theology at Blackfriars, Oxford, about his dreams. On 19th December, 1947, and 30th January, 1948, he wrote of a dream he had had on the night of 18th/19th December, 1947. He had recently found himself inexorably driven to write an essay, against his will (he had been suffering from insomnia and didn't feel up to intellectual hard work), which developed – in some part thanks to the encouragement he received *via* dreams – into a major discussion of Christ, the anti-Christ, and the developing power of the latter over the centuries from A.D.1000 until its near success during 1939–45.

His dream of 18th/19th December, 1947, concerned his

meeting up with three friendly Catholic priests, one of whom, he adds, 'had a remarkable library'. Jung, as some kind of soldier, had to sleep in a barracks which was so crowded that the men were two to a bed. By the time Jung went to bed the other occupant, a venerable old man with white hair and a long white beard, was already there. '. . . I thought and felt: *Indignus sum Domine* [Lord, I am unworthy]. I know Him very well: He was my "guru" more than 30 years ago . . .' (Here Jung refers to a much earlier fantasy about superior insight being incarnate in the figure of Philemon.) As Jung slipped into bed beside the 'guru' the dream ended and he awoke.

In a letter from 30th January, 1948, he tells of a further, linked dream. It started with the figure of the priest who had the 'remarkable library' and the question: 'How is it possible that my mother celebrates her 70th birthday in this year 1948 while I am reaching my 74th year?' (In fact, his mother had died in 1923, at the age of 74.) Because the figure of the priest is strongly reminiscent of Jung's father (who died in 1896), Jung finds himself in his father's house. Before answering the question, his father leads him up onto the first floor, where there is a peculiar room which Jung realizes is his father's: it is more like a gallery than a room, with a bridge leading from the gallery to a central 'cuplike' platform.

According to Jung, this room was very much like those of the Moghul Emperor Akbar the Great's (1542–1605) *diwan-i-khas*, or audience rooms, where 'he used to discuss philosophy and religion with the representatives of all philosophies and all creeds'. To Jung the dream's meaning was reasonably obvious, since he had indeed been discussing matters religious and philosophical with White and others: he knew that his own 'creed' had been 'prescribed to me by a hand far above my reach', and for that reason alone felt that he had no right to meddle with the 'creeds' of other people. (White was a Dominican.)

In 1915 Jung wrote in a letter to the Swiss psychotherapist Hans Schmid (1881–1932) of a dream in which he had been digging a hole in his garden. From the hole gushed forth water from a spring, and so the dreaming Jung had to dig another hole down which he could channel the waters back into the ground. His interpretation of this dream is expressed with his usual charming opacity, but as far as I can understand he relates it to the role of the analytical psychologist: while it is important that he 'cracks' a particular symbol of the individual's unconscious to find the 'seed' within, he must remember that the symbol is there to *protect* the 'seed', and that this protection should not be removed. The dream, then – which took place some years before the letter and before Jung's break with Freud – signified his latent dissatisfaction with psychoanalysis, which he felt left the individual's 'seeds' exposed and vulnerable.

In a letter dated 23rd July, 1949, Jung recalls the Clark Conference of 1909. He mentions travelling on the same boat as Freud, and says that the two of them spent much of their time analyzing each other's dreams both on the boat and while they were in the USA. In February 1936, though, Jung explained in a letter to the US neurologist Smith Jelliffe that one of the principal reasons for his split from Freud was the matter of Freud's dream-interpretations. And in a letter written in 1950 he explains this in layman's terms:

> I also couldn't agree with his theory of dreams as wish-fulfilments. Freud, I'm afraid, misunderstood theoretical doubt or criticism as a personal resistance and I couldn't agree with him that his view was right.

This criticism of Freud – which is indeed a personal one – seems to have been totally justified. We've already noticed Silberer's suicide after his callous rejection by Freud; another dissenter in the Freudian camp was Victor Tausk, whose suicide was definitely in direct response to Freud's behaviour. Freud seems to have been a benevolent daddy just so long as his 'children' didn't disagree with him, think too much for themselves, or grow too big for their boots.

In *Man and His Symbols* and *Memories, Dreams, Reflections* Jung describes the critical incident in the series of dream-interpretations he engaged in with Freud. Jung requested personal details from Freud's private life as associations to assist in the interpretation of one of Freud's dreams. These Freud refused to supply because 'I cannot risk my authority'. As Jung remarked, 'At that moment he lost it altogether' – without the details it was impossible, in terms of psychoanalysis, for Jung to make a decent stab at analyzing the dream, something which Freud knew better than anyone else.

The final straw for Jung came with Freud's attempts to analyze what Jung regarded as one of his (Jung's) most important dreams – the one which in due course was to prompt him to put forward his idea of the 'collective unconscious'.

Jung dreamt he was in a house that, while unknown to him, was nevertheless his own house; i.e., he was conscious of the fact that it was the place where he lived. He was in the upper of the house's two storeys, in a salon furnished in the rococo style and hung with fine pictures. He went down to the ground floor to see what it looked like, and found that it was much older: 15th- or 16th-century, he guessed, with a red brick floor and mediaeval furnishings. In due course he came to a stout door, which he opened to find a flight of stairs leading down to the cellar, a 'beautifully vaulted room which looked exceedingly ancient' – in fact, he soon inferred that the walls were Roman. He raised a slab in the floor and descended a narrow flight of stairs to find himself in a cave, on whose floor were bits of broken pottery and some scattered bones, including two human skulls.

To us the imagery might be obvious: the dream portrayed in symbolic form the whole pageant of Man's past history, the process which had led to the genesis of the dreamer himself. To Jung, the same sort of a thing was true, except that the descent from storey to storey represented his peeling-away of progressively deeper layers of his unconscious, until he reached the primitive human being locked up inside himself.

To Freud, though, the dream was – had to be – an expression of some deep personal emotion. What concerned him most were the two skulls. 'He returned to them repeatedly,' wrote Jung,

> and urged me to find a *wish* in connection with them . . . I knew perfectly well, of course, what he was driving at: that secret death-wishes were concealed in the dream. 'But what does he really expect of me?' I thought to myself. Towards whom would I have death-wishes?

Jung had partly made up his own mind about what the dream meant; but he wasn't too keen to force his own ideas into the limelight – he was at the time uncertain of himself, and wanted to learn from Freud.

But Freud kept pressing the question until eventually, in exasperation, Jung lied to him: he said the skulls were those of his wife and his sister-in-law. He chose those two because, since he had not long been married, they were the two people towards whom he was least likely to feel any death-wish whatsoever. Freud was delighted by Jung's 'confession', and interpreted the dream much as you may imagine.

Jung had already been questioning, if silently, the foundations of Freudian analysis (or so he says), and the dream seemed to him to be the climax of – indeed, the answer to – the questioning. If the dream was, in essence, a diagram of the human mind, then that diagram was different from any which Freud might draw. Take into account that Freud made such a mess of the analysis, imposing his own preconceptions upon it, and it is hardly surprising that his disciple broke out of the fold.

Freud was, in general, not very good at obeying his own rules. In *The Interpretation of Dreams* he describes over a hundred of his own dreams; but throughout his analysis of them he fails to produce any personal details which might assist the analysis. Moreover, one gets the impression that he has censored not only the private details but also the dreams themselves. In some cases one wonders if he's invented the dreams to fit his theories, because the fit is almost too good. Of course, one can't tell: since the theories were born from his dream-studies, and since the dreams he knew best were for obvious reasons his own, it's only to be expected that they fitted his theories snugly. Still, one wonders.

## *The Subjects*

As a result of a nightmare, Bertha Pappenheim was to achieve fame in the annals of psychiatry under the pseudonym 'Anna O'.

She had been sitting by her father's deathbed when she fell asleep; in a slightly different sense of the term, her arm too fell asleep. She dreamt that a great black serpent was wriggling towards her father, and that she was unable to fight it off because of her paralyzed arm. Even prayer was useless, because all she could recall were some stanzas in English. She was woken by a noise outside.

This would be of no more interest than any other nightmare were it not for the fact that, the following day, she saw a crooked branch of a tree, rather like a wriggling serpent, and at once contracted a paralysis of the arm. All sorts of other hysterical symptoms followed: she developed a squint, found herself unable to eat or drink, went deaf and was struck dumb, and began to exhibit the curious characteristic of living over again, while displaying a quite different personality, events which had happened *exactly* one year before. Her new, alternate personality spoke only English, seemed only semi-conscious, and hallucinated.

Pappenheim was cured by Josef Breuer (1842–1925) in the early 1880s; he was using a form of hypnotherapy, although he didn't know it. When Pappenheim was her 'other' self she was in something very close to a hypnotic trance, and Breuer discovered that, if in this state she could be induced to talk about what had originated her various symptoms, they disappeared. And the progenitors of the symptoms could be so everyday that they'd never otherwise have been discovered, let alone cured. For example, her inability to drink was born from having seen a puppy drink from a glass. As soon as she talked about this event she demanded a drink; after she had downed it both the 'other' Pappenheim and the 'real' one no longer suffered from the symptom.

This case was to gain even greater significance when Breuer's acquaintance Sigmund Freud made the connection between (a) Pappenheim's hysteric condition, (b) hypnotism, and (c) the notion of the unconscious. So Pappenheim's nightmare was to be a major factor in the moulding of psychoanalysis.

There is extant only one of the case-histories of Freud's

'great cases', and it is one of the three which Freud himself conducted – that of the Wolf-Man. I should state instantly that, while the patient's 'code-name' might make you think of lycanthropy, Freud invented it because of the man's passionate and unreasonable fear of wolves, as manifested in his dreams. I'll look shortly at the Wolf-Man's 'core dream'; but first I want to skip through a few details of his life, for reasons which will soon be evident.

He was born on Christmas Eve, 1886, according to the Julian calendar (6th January, 1887, according to the Gregorian calendar used outside Russia), near Kherson in the Ukraine to a wealthy family. At one point during his early childhood a certain English governess called Miss Oven was employed to look after him and his elder sister, Anna. She stayed for only a few months, but during this time seems to have taken sadistic pleasure in torturing Serge (the Wolf-Man) at every opportunity; after a little, Anna, who was two and a half years his senior, joined in as deputy tormentor. His parents were absent at the time, and so he was defenceless.

One day Anna teased him with the promise of showing him a picture of a pretty girl. She led him on for as long as possible, finally and abruptly confronting him with an illustration of a rampant wolf about to swallow Little Red Riding-Hood. Since it terrified him, she repeated the trick many times thereafter. She also, when he was a few months from his fourth birthday, 'seduced' him – that is, made him expose his genitalia so that she could play with them. This, too, was repeated a number of times, until his revulsion for the act forced him, he claimed in later life, to put a stop to it.

Suicide was to surround the Wolf-Man's life. Anna was to poison herself in the summer of 1906. His father died at the age of 49, probably from an overdose of a sleeping-draught and possibly deliberately. His wife was to kill herself in 1938, as the Nazis' power grew towards apparent omnipotence. These and other tragedies in his life, combined with the traumas of his infancy, make it unsurprising that he was a suitable case for treatment: he underwent analysis with Freud from 1910 until 1914 (it stopped the day after the Archduke's assassination) and again in 1919–20.

The Wolf-Man's 'core dream' was a recurring one. It first made its appearance on the night before his fourth birthday; in Russia, his birthday coincided with Christmas. He dreamt that it was night and that he was lying in bed. Outside the window at the foot of his bed were (in both reality and the dream) some walnut trees. It was winter.

Suddenly the window crashed open. To his horror, he saw that six or seven big white wolves were sitting in the walnut tree directly outside his window. The wolves had big bushy tails, like foxes', while they were dog-like in that their ears pricked up when something attracted their attention. He awoke screaming: the wolves might eat him. Even awake, such had been the realism of the dream that it was some time before his nurse could persuade him that there were no wolves out there.

Naturally enough, for years afterwards he was terrified of having nightmares.

The analysis by both Freud and the Wolf-Man himself of this dream is of more than passing interest, and we shall look into it in some detail. In the early stages it seemed clear that the wolf-connection arose from Anna's sadistic trick; the whiteness of the wolves reminded Serge of his father's flocks of sheep (many of whom he had seen die in an epidemic; his father, incidentally, conducted wolf-hunts and attendant festivities on the estate). That the wolves were in the tree seemed to refer to a tale his grandfather had sometimes told him. In this story, a tailor was sitting at work when an old wolf leapt into the room, ready to devour him. The tailor responded – with superhuman courage! – by pulling the beast's tail off, so that it ran away in terror and pain. But a while later the tailor was in a forest when a pack of wolves made for him; one of the pack was the wolf whose tail he'd pulled off. He fled up a tree. But his enemy, being both unnaturally intelligent for a wolf and filled with an understandable desire for vengeance, suggested that the pack form a vulpine pyramid, with himself at the bottom. The tailor waited until they were in place and then yelled: 'Catch the grey one by his tail!' This terrified his old adversary afresh: he ran off and the pyramid collapsed in chaos.

Children's stories seem to have improved a bit since then.

Freud noted in passing the dream-wolves' bushy tails. These were as a compensation for the loss of the tail of the wolf in the story. Moreover, the removal of the tail seemed to represent castration: since the wolf was specified as an old one, there seemed to be a hint that the desired castratee was Serge's father.

But Freud was puzzled by the fact that there were *several* wolves. In 'Little Red Riding-Hood', of course, there's only the one. Could Serge have been mistaken about the book whose illustration Anna had used to frighten him? Yes, it seemed: there was a story called 'The Wolf and the Seven Little Goats', in which both the numbers six and seven turned up, six of the goats being consumed by the wolf while the seventh hid inside a long-case clock. A tree appears in the story: the wolf snoozes under it after having downed the goats. And there are strong parallels with 'Little Red Riding-Hood': the wolf is cut open to release its meal. Even whiteness makes its appearance: because the goats recognize the wolf by its grey paw, it goes and dips it, by way of disguise, in some flour.

So, in these preliminary stages of interpretation, it seemed that one could make a case for the rampant wolf representing Serge's father, whom he feared and whom he wished to castrate. The symbolism derived from the two – if not three – nursery stories as well as, possibly, childhood threats during play such as 'I'll gobble you right up'. Of course, it could all simply have been a kid's nightmare, but this consideration was rejected out of hand.

Freud went very much further than this. His in-depth analysis can be looked on, in one way, as a fantastic piece of deduction; in another, as an extraordinary example of the power of the human mind to delude itself in order to make facts fit preconceived theories, however difficult this might prove to be.

Two things had struck Serge most forcibly about the dream. First, that it had such a quality of reality that it intruded itself when he was awake (in other words, it was a 'different' dream); second, that all the while in the dream the wolves were quite motionless but with their attention focussed on him.

Freud claimed that the 'quality of reality' indicated that the dream referred to a real-life event, rather than being a mere fantasy. If Serge was four when he first had the dream, then the real-life scene must have occurred very early in his childhood. Moreover, in the scene there must have been some element of stillness and fixed attention.

Serge himself provided a new link in the chain. Right at the start of the dream, the window had crashed open of its own accord: might this not represent his eyes popping open as he suddenly awoke? If so, then it must have been the infant himself who had remained still and attentive on awakening. But, if this sort of transposition from the wolves to himself had taken place in the dream, so too, it was logical to assume, there had been a transposition in terms of the scene witnessed: in other words, he had woken not to a scene of tranquillity but to a violent one.

Serge now said that the tree was a Christmas tree (this helped Freud date the first appearance of the dream). But, instead of being the bearer of goodies and gifts, this Christmas tree bore wolves. He was terrified of being eaten by the wolves . . . which represented his father. Yet at the same time he wanted sex with his father.[10] A violent scene; a sense of horror; sex with his father – what else could the infant have seen but 'what sexual satisfaction from his father was like'?

To be fair, to the naïve it can look as if, when a couple are making love, the man were assaulting the woman. Or, come to think of it, as if the woman were assaulting the man.

At this stage in the analysis, Serge began to dream a number of variants of the 'core dream'. Freud does not describe all these variants in detail (even had he done so, there would have been no space to discuss them here); however, from his earlier analysis of the 'core dream' and from the additional or different details in the new versions, Freud was able to construct a really quite astonishingly precise scenario.

When he had been eighteen months old Serge had suffered a bout of malaria which would become particularly severe during the afternoons, reaching a climax at about 5.00 P.M. (For decades afterwards his depressions followed the same diurnal cycle.) One day, set to sleep in his cot in his parents' bedroom, he had awoken to find them making love – not just once, but three times in a row, so the adult Serge's brain suddenly told him (although this could have been a false memory). He'd been able to see clearly the actions of both parents' genitalia: this was because, at least part of the time, his father had been making love to his mother from behind, thereby giving rise to the symbol of the terrifying rampant wolf, with the woman submissive and crouching like an animal.[11]

This could be taken slightly further. The rampant posture of the wolf was important. Not only was this the posture in the illustration with which Anna had frightened him (and which he eventually, as an adult, tracked down), it was also the only posture in which he found pictured wolves frightening. Indeed, this posture was almost more important than the animal: in his childhood he had had a nightmare about a rampant lion the night before a new tutor had been about to arrive, the lion substituting for the wolf much as, in reality, the tutor was to substitute for the father. And the submissive posture of his mother affected him, too: as an adult, he was able to gain pleasure from sex only when it was performed in this way, and the most strikingly sexual attribute of any woman was, for him, her bottom – especially if it was big and fleshy.

How was this memory of something he'd seen at eighteen months transformed into the four-year-old's dream? Easy. Take the story of the wolves and the tailor, and remember that the de-tailed ('castrated') wolf was at the bottom of the pile. Take the number six or seven from the tale of the wolf and the goats. Take the fact that Serge wanted sex with his father, and that this would of necessity imply that he, Serge, be castrated – because wasn't it obvious that his mother had been? Take the 'real' circumstance: the sudden awakening, and the stillness, and the attention. Mix all these ingredients up well together, give them a good stir, and you have a dream of a window throwing itself open and wolves sitting in a tree . . . watching.[12]

Vast numbers of the Wolf-Man's later dreams are on record, but they need hardly concern us here. Many of them feature wolves, many of them suggest his father's or his own castration, many have homosexual elements. They make, *en masse* or even singly, pretty tedious reading. But I thought it worth looking at this one – one of the most famous in the history of psychology – in detail, since it seems to me to exemplify perfectly two points.

Firstly, even the simplest dream can have an extremely complicated genesis, each of its components being drawn from a plurality of sources, and each of them having a specific and by no means always obvious meaning to the dreamer.

Secondly, there is great peril in dream-interpretation. The entire 'primal scene' of the parents making love is evidenced *solely* by the dream and Freud's interpretation of it. It may very well never have happened, in which case the entire interpretation is a farrago.[11]

## *Two Suitable Cases for Analysis*

A friend of mine, whom I shall call Miranda because that isn't her name, has a recurring nightmare. She comes home unexpectedly and as she closes the door she hears a noise upstairs in the bedroom. Thinking that the dog is up there, possibly making a mess of the clothes, she runs up the stairs shouting at it. But when she gets to the bedroom she finds that the noise was caused by her husband making violent love to the lodger. When they notice Miranda in the doorway, they stop; and then the other woman giggles. 'Why don't you come and join in?' she says.

At this point Miranda wakes and is violently sick.

This is clearly a dream that cries out for Freudian analysis. Running up the stairs – a sure symbol for sexual intercourse. The mention of the dog – yes, there's something sexual there. Maybe Miranda has unconscious lesbian tendencies, and would really *like* to go to bed with another woman? Maybe she'd just prefer a *ménage à trois*? Perhaps the whole thing means that she wants to castrate the lodger's grandfather?

In fact, Miranda has this dream because the incident described actually happened. All the dream does is replay it to her – time after time after time.

Perhaps a psychoanalyst would nevertheless be able to make an interesting interpretation of this dream; perhaps some of the details are different in the dream from the way they were in real life, and these are significant. Nevertheless, there are so many dreams one comes across which do not seem to require – or even be susceptible to – any kind of analysis or interpretation at all that one begins to wonder if the whole business of analyzing *any* dream is simply a waste of time.

Graham Greene recalls in his *A Sort of Life* (1971) being under psychoanalysis and being required to narrate his dreams each morning; if he couldn't remember the dream he had to invent one, and his psychoanalyst, Kenneth Richmond, would analyze the invention instead. (Greene remarks that, curiously, all of these invented dreams 'began with a pig'.)

One morning the young Greene was in terror. The only dream he could remember from the night was an erotic one – and it was about Zoe, Richmond's wife. What should he do – lie? However, he had respect enough for psychoanalysis (and presumably Richmond) not to dodge the issue.

'And now,' Richmond said, after a little talk on general theory, 'we'll get down to last night's dream.'

I cleared my dry throat. 'I can only remember one.'

'Let's have it.'

'I was in bed,' I said.

'Where?'

'Here.'

He made a note on his pad. I took a breath and plunged.

'There was a knock on the door and Zoe came in. She was naked. She leaned over me. One of her breasts nearly touched my mouth. I woke up.'

'What's your association to breasts?' Richmond asked, setting his stop-watch.

'Tube train,' I said after a long pause.

'Five seconds,' Richmond said.

# 2
## *The Creative Dreamers*

Very old are we men;
Our dreams are tales
Told in dim Eden
By Eve's nightingales;
We wake and whisper awhile,
But, the day gone by,
Silence and sleep like fields
Of amaranth lie.

– Walter de la Mare,
'All That's Past'

'ring ring'
    'knock knock'
'yes,
what is it?'

'I thought I should
    tell you
that your house
    is on fire.'

'oh not now please
we're having dinner'

– Peter Cadle,
'Conflagration'

It is a popular truism that creative artists – painters, writers, composers – derive much of their inspiration from their dream lives. Like so many other popular truisms, this one is only partly correct. True, some famous creations have had their origins in dreams – Stevenson's *Dr Jekyll and Mr Hyde* is the classic example – but most pieces of imaginative writing based closely on one of the author's dreams are fairly substandard. The laws of the dream-world are different from those of waking reality: what we accept as logical in a dream, circumstances which may have been profoundly emotive when we were dream-experiencing them, somehow fail to make the transition to the printed page. It's very much the same sort of phenomenon as the one that can have us waking in terror from a nightmare and then, over breakfast the next morning, laughing about the truly preposterous antics of that nightmare. Where dreams have been transformed into powerful works of art, it is because the creator's waking self took his or her original idea from a dream and then quite consciously adapted it and modified it for consumption by the waking minds of the audience. We shall see this time and again as we look at the great army of 'creative dreamers'.

Composers seem to have a different problem from the other artists. Mozart claimed that he wrote the most stunning pieces of music in his sleep, but then couldn't remember them when he woke up. The modern composer Howard Harrison echoes this: he says that he has often woken up knowing nothing about the piece of music he's been listening to except that it was 'absolutely fantastic'.

He recalls, however, one exception to this general rule. It occurred while he was still a student at Dartington College, in the southwest of England.[1] In common with contemporaries, he was preparing for recitals, during which the students would be marked for their performance of their own pieces of music. One night Harrison dreamt that he went to see the recital of a friend of his, and when he awoke he could remember the tune that the friend had been playing. At lunchtime he told several of his fellow-students about his curious dream, and hummed the tune to them. 'What was strange,' he says, 'is that

that afternoon you could hear all the people in the rehearsal rooms trying out variations on *my* tune.'

Karlheinz Stockhausen, too, has claimed to receive all sorts of musical inspiration in dreams. In some cases the inspiration has come about in the same sort of way as the problem-solving dreams which many of us have: he has been working away until late at night on a particularly tricky piece of music, has given up in desperation, and then has dream-solved the difficulty that had been holding him up. In other cases, though, he has dream-composed complete pieces of music – right down to the clothing and positioning of the players.

His composition *Telemusik* seems to have come to him in a series of waking dreams:

> TELEMUSIK was composed between January and April, 1966, in the studio for electronic music of the Japanese Radio Nippon Hoso Kyokai, Tokyo. During my first 8 or 9 days in Tokyo I could not sleep: one vision came again and again, a vision of sounds, new technical processes, formal relationships, pictures of notation, human relationships – all at once and in a network too tangled up to be unravelled in *one* logical process. In all this I wanted to come closer to the realization of an old dream: to take a step further in the direction of composing not 'my' music, but a music of the whole world, of all countries and all races. I am certain you will hear them in TELEMUSIK . . .

He then proceeds to tell us what an excellent composition *Telemusik* is.

More dramatic was his dream composition of the lesser known work *Trans*, which is scored for a visible string section bathed in red-violet light and an offstage collection of other players. An important element is a stereo tape-recording of a weaving chair, which is played first from one side then the other of the stage through a pair of loudspeakers. He is not certain where the idea for the weaving chair came from, but says that it might have been a partial memory of an experience in Bali, when he visited a roomful of weaving girls.

Other composers have said that they, too, have received musical inspirations in their dreams: they include Stravinsky, Saint-Saëns, Tartini (the 'Devil's Trill' sonata) and the contemporary Argentinian composer Mauricio Kagel.

## *The Crossword Connection*

While it is in the field of literature that the vast majority of dream creations can be found, the other arts are well represented. In fact, dream creativity can extend right outside the arts, sometimes to trivial and sometimes to important effect: a number of important scientific or technological discoveries have been made as a result of problem-solving dreams, as we shall see. At the trivial end of the scale, Violet Casley, a self-styled crossword fanatic, frequently invents crosswords in her dreams; the really galling thing is that not always can she solve the crosswords. This might be because the clues are simply gibberish – but, in that case, it's surprising that others of the clues are not, and prove to be perfectly solvable. It seems possible that her subconscious really is inventing clues which are too difficult for her.

Casley has been kind enough to supply me with an example of her dream-failure to solve part of a crossword. Before being stumped, she had filled in the word 'jet' in response to the clue 'he echoes far and wide'; 'jovial' for 'miners' monarch's disposition'; 'solaced' for 'placated'. Her grid then looked like this:

J E T<br>
O<br>
V<br>
I<br>
A<br>
S O L A C E D

The next clue was 'equine', and the solution had to fill the gap running downwards from 'T' to 'C'. Even when awake, she could see no solution.

My initial reaction was that the clues she had solved were slightly skew-logical. 'Solaced', for example, doesn't really mean 'placated', although in certain circumstances the two words can have very similar thought-meanings. Similarly, Pluto rather than Jove would seem to be the 'miners' monarch'. So my first guess for the unsolved clue was 'Trojic', a little known variant of 'Trojan', as in the famous horse. Unfortunately, my guess was so little known that even the full edition of the OED failed to list it. This doesn't exactly mean that the word doesn't exist, but the discovery rather took the wind out of my sails.

I then began to think in terms of skew-logic. 'Equine' is close enough to 'equinox', in pun-language. Could it be that there was a thing called the 'equine' related to the equinox? I scoured dictionaries, encyclopaedias and astronomical reference books without success – until I noticed that 'tropic' fits into Casley's grid. The tropics are, of course, very much related to the equinoxes, in that the tropics mark the position of the Sun at the solstices. Moreover, and this seemed to me the clincher, not far from the tropics on the terrestrial globe are the . . . Horse Latitudes!

I 'phoned Casley excitedly. She pointed out to me that this sort of pun was reasonable, since she'd worked out why the clue 'miners' monarch's disposition' yielded 'jovial'. Just think of Old King Cole . . .

Obviously, with so many strained puns involved, I can't really claim to have definitively cracked the problem; but there is enough of a concentration of ideas into a single nexus for me to feel justified in claiming that I'm at least quite probably right. The combination of skew-logic and pun is so typical of the dream that it can be considered almost symptomatic.

## *A Saintly Digression*

While it is one thing to dream up a poem, crossword, novel, short story or whatever, perhaps the most exciting effort of creative dreaming on record was the creation of a brand-new saint. This is what happened in the case of Saint Cordula, the evidence for whose existence is based solely on dreams, those dreams themselves being based on a legend of extremely doubtful provenance.

The legend is that of Ursula and her eleven thousand virgins. This has it that the British Ursula, in order to avoid marriage to a pagan, fled from the court of her royal father to Rome, taking 10,999 virginal chums with her. On the way back from Rome, this army of unsullied femininity was massacred by the Huns at Cologne.

The origins of the legend are obscure – although it seems certain that a group of young women were indeed martyred at Cologne. However, we can trace the tale as far back as the 9th century, when it was generally accepted that eleven – rather than eleven thousand – virgins, under the leadership of a virgin called either Pinnosa or Ursula, had been put to death as a result both of their Christianity and of their determined retention of their maidenhoods. Our ancestors, who had a notoriously cavalier way with numbers, promptly multiplied the figure a thousand-fold – just to make the story better. When, in the 12th century, an ancient cemetery was unearthed at Cologne, its contents were immediately claimed to be the remains of Ursula's army.

In about the middle of that century a nun called Helentrudis (according to Baring-Gould's *Lives of the Saints*) dreamt that she met a young woman who had been one of Ursula's virgins. She had hidden herself away while the Huns were massacring the others; but, the following day, her conscience had forced her to come out of hiding and be killed like all her cronies. She held out her hand to show Helentrudis her name, which was inscribed on her palm 'in fiery characters'. This name was Cordula.

Thanks to Helentrudis's dream, and to nothing else, Cordula was promptly canonized. But this was not to be her only dream-appearance. In 1238 one Ingebrand von Rurke, a Knight Hospitaller of St John of Jerusalem, from Cologne, dreamt of encountering a beautiful maiden who asked him to dig up her remains. The following morning he told his prior about this dream, and was advised to do nothing, but just wait and see what happened.

The next night she appeared again, and somewhat tartly asked him why she had not been dug up.

> 'Because,' said Sir Ingebrand, 'you did not tell me where to dig.'
>
> 'You will find me,' said the apparition, 'in the orchard of the priory, under the filbert tree.'
>
> When the prior heard this, he was greatly delighted. 'But,' said he, 'you must first ascertain her name.'
>
> Next night the maiden appeared with cloudy brow, and rated the knight soundly for his laziness and want of gallantry in not attending to a lady's request, though proffered twice. Sir Ingebrand apologized, and said

that he only waited to be told her name. Thereupon the virgin bade him look her in the face. He did so, and read on her brow in gold letters, 'Cordulo Virgo Regina'. The knight thereupon jumped out of bed, and ran to the prior, and told him, 'Her name is Cordula. And a very appropriate name too; for Cordula means a little heart, and a sweet little heart she is!'[2]

In the morning, they dug in the relevant spot and found some bones which, as sacred relics, have since been claimed to have miraculous powers. As have the bones of another body of St Cordula, discovered in Cologne two years earlier. Curiously enough, the bones of a third body of St Cordula have similar powers . . .

Before leaping to the conclusion that St Cordula's greatest miracle was to have three corpses, we should remember the revelations received by a certain Herman Joseph, which throw a considerable deal of light on the matter. There were, you see, not one but *two* virgins called Cordula in Ursula's army. One of them was the sister of Saint Columba and the other a daughter of Count Quirinus. That still leaves an extra Saint Cordula to be accounted for, but at least it's progress.

## *Nightmare Depictions*

One of the most famous – or, if you prefer, notorious – paintings of the 18th century is generally regarded as having been, at least in part, born from dreams. The painting is *The Nightmare*, by John Henry Fuseli (christened Johann Heinrich Füssli), which was first exhibited at the Royal Academy in 1782.

The picture is semierotic, with a slight but quite distinct overlay of sadism. It shows a sleeping woman draped aesthetically across a couch, with a horrific dwarfish figure seated firmly and heavily on her chest. A fire-eyed horse – the 'mare' of the nightmare – stares hellishly at the scene. Despite these ghoulish ingredients, it's difficult to work out exactly what it is that makes the picture such an affecting and disturbing one. But it most certainly is a powerful work – as witnessed by the fact that countless imitations derived from it were produced, as well as by the storm of controversy it raised when first exhibited.[3]

Whether the picture's nastiness derives from the fact that it was genuinely inspired by Fuseli's nightmares, or whether – as seems more likely – it's a result merely of a deliberate attempt on his part to produce a picture as nasty as possible, is anyone's guess. But the feeling of an oppressive weight on the chest is certainly a typical feature of many nightmares.

An interesting creative dreamer in the field of the visual arts was Austin Osman Spare (1886–1956), a painter and draughtsman whose early promise – he was still a teenager when he first exhibited at the Royal Academy – was never quite realized. In addition to his artistic activities, he was what we would call in everyday language a sexual magician; more correctly, according to his executor and biographer Kenneth Grant (in *Images and Oracles of Austin Osman Spare*, 1975), Spare was a sorcerer, in that he sought to ensnare (ensorcel) spirits rather than to cast spells, as would a magician proper. His two vocations – art and sorcery – rapidly became inseparably intermingled, and he spent the latter part of his life as a recluse, trying to capture on paper the bizarre images brought up either from his subconscious or from 'spaces beyond space' where lurked occult entities – choose for yourself which of the two sources you prefer to believe in.

The role of the dream in his occult theory is rather hard to access. It seems that he regarded dreams not as products of the mind but as the mind making excursions into those 'spaces beyond space'. To quote Grant:

> The dream is the cosmos which appears as the great outside; the past, 'all otherness', the self explicit and remote, replete with the images of desire. The dreamer is the self within, implicit, elusive, generating glamours [spells] for desire-fulfilment, controlling *ids* and incarnating beliefs in flesh for further pleasuring in self-love.

If that isn't 100% comprehensible to you, don't worry about it.

Spare reported a very curious thing about his own dreams. This was that in some of them he found himself gazing at perspectives so far from our everyday ones that he was quite incapable of drawing them. This was all the more peculiar in that normally he could translate his dreams onto paper without any difficulty. His theory was that these strange dreams were precognitive: he was peeking into a future incarnation of his in which he would be able to 'reify' (occultly bring into existence) the geometries of an age far distant in either the past or the future.

Spare claimed that much of his work was produced automatically through him by an occult entity called 'Black Eagle'. On occasions, he said, he would wake up to discover that he – Spare – was asleep. Some of these automatic drawings have about them such a genuine feeling of evil that George Bernard Shaw was once driven to remark: 'Spare's medicine is too strong for the average man.'

Before we leave him, there is one tale about Spare which, while totally irrelevant in this context, certainly bears repeating. Determined to prove to a visitor that all his talk about possessing occult powers was not just so much piffle, Spare proposed to cause rose-petals to fall magically like snow from the ceiling of his room. Suitable preparations were made, suitable incantations uttered, and then . . . through the rotten ceiling fell the lavatory from the floor above.

## *'Poor Col.'*

> . . . closed my eyes and instantly there appeared a [spectre] of a pheasant's tail, that altered through various degradations into round wrinkly shapes, as of horse excrement, or . . . round baked apples, with exactly the same colour, the same circular intra-circular wrinkles. I started out of bed, lit my candles, and noted it down . . . I went to the window to empty my urine-pot, and wondered at the simple grandeur of the view.

So Samuel Taylor Coleridge, writing in late 1803.[4] And it would not be too outrageous an overstatement to say that Coleridge's entire life, and certainly his poetic writings, were shaped by his dream-life. However, the correspondence between his dreams and his writings is not as direct as might be thought – as we shall see.

In his childhood his dreams were profoundly affected by his having read the *1001 Nights*, especially by the tale he found there of a man compelled to quest until he found a totally pure virgin. The impact of this tale may help to explain why, throughout his life, the poet was to seek to mould all the women he met and fell for into the form of chaste, pure, essentially sexless maidens. Like Ruskin, his image of the ideal woman was incompatible with the messy process of actual physical love. This incompatibility was to wreck his marriage: how could his wife, with whom he knew he had had sex, ever hope to compete in his esteem with those other fair unattainables?

The adult Coleridge was to be unable to adopt as pragmatic an approach to problems as did his father. The vicar of Ottery St Mary, on hearing that the book was giving his boy nightmares, simply burnt it.

Nevertheless, nightmares continued to haunt Samuel from childhood right through to the end of his days – he once estimated that three nights out of four he awoke screaming from sleep – and these nightmares found their way, willy-nilly, into his poetry, whether or not he consciously willed them to be expressed there. That said, he was certainly interested in the subject: we know that in 1795 he was actively and busily engaged in a study of dreams, using as his main reference *An Enquiry Into the Nature of the Human Soul* (1733) by Andrew Baxter (1686/7–1750).

His notebooks contain countless accounts of nightmares and anxiety dreams; and in his 'The Pains of Sleep' (written in 1803 and revised some time before 1816) he made an open statement of the terrors which sleep and its dreams caused him:

> But yester-night I prayed aloud
> In anguish and in agony,
> Up-starting from the fiendish crowd
> Of shapes and thoughts that tortured me:
> Desire with loathing strangely mixt,
> On wild or hateful objects fixt.
> Sense of revenge, the powerless will,
> Still baffled and consuming still;
> Sense of intolerable wrong,
> And men whom I despis'd made strong!
> Vain-glorious threats, unmanly vaunting,
> Bad men my boasts and fury taunting:
> Rage, sensual passion, mad'ning Brawl,
> And shame and terror over all!

Deeds to be hid which were not hid,
Which all confused I could not know
Whether I suffered, or I did:
For all was Guilt, and Shame, and Woe,
My own or others still the same
Life-stifling fear, soul-stifling shame.

And so on and so forth for quite a long time.[5] The key words in the poem are obviously those such as 'guilt', 'shame' and 'woe'; later we have

Such punishments, I said, were due
To natures deepliest stained with sin, –
Still to be stirring up anew
The self-created Hell within, . . .

and studies of Coleridge's accounts of his nightmares, as well as of his less lucid references to them in his poetry, show that they were rooted in a sort of ubiquitous sense of guilt which Coleridge felt about virtually everything he did or thought.

He had had a fairly hellish childhood (although one can't help feeling that it was to a certain extent a 'self-created Hell'): his father died when he was a boy, and four brothers and a sister were to die before he reached the age of twenty. Teasing and taunting drove him to attack his elder brother with a kitchen knife, after which he was sent to be brought up as an orphan at Christ's Hospital. Not surprisingly, he felt he was an outcast, and had a deep sense of guilt about the way his family seemed to be paying with their lives for his sins – a preoccupation which was to emerge in 'The Rime of the Ancient Mariner', where the protagonist's shipmates all lose their lives as a result of his crime, yet he himself suffers a worse fate, survival. Coleridge had been, so he thought, rejected by his mother; there are parallels here with

Christabel's mother, who died in childbirth – the ultimate rejection of one's child. Yet Coleridge believed in the sanctity of motherhood: his emotional conclusion was therefore necessarily that *he* must have been the one at fault.

We shall return to Coleridge's deep guilt feelings – especially that of sexual guilt – in Chapter Three, when we look more generally at his dreams. Here our prime concern is the effect his dreams had on his creative output. First, though, we must swiftly brush off a popular misapprehension.

It is generally assumed that the dreams which overflowed into Coleridge's writings were opium dreams, rather than normal sleeping ones. (De Quincey's opium dreams are described in *Confessions of an English Opium Eater* (1822, 1856) and in his various dream-works.) However, the converse seems to be the case, for the dreams he recorded seem to show little or no change in character as he became addicted to the drug: if anything, he took to opium in order to counter the misery of his nightmares – that is, to assure himself a decent night's sleep. Of course, as therapy turned into dependence, the worst happened: here was Coleridge, the committed anti-sensualist, gaining sensual pleasure from a drug which he could no longer go without. One more guilt – of course – to add to the list.

Moreover, his three major 'visionary' poems date from 1797 (debate that 'Kubla Khan' was written in 1798 is quite probably misleading), a time before his addiction reached its height – as well as a time when he was severely emotionally disturbed: in a series of autobiographical letters written around this period he was recalling the agonies of his childhood. And so we have the sinister, daemonic mother-figure of Geraldine in 'Christabel'; the guilt-ridden perpetual outcast at the heart of

'The Rime of the Ancient Mariner'; and the ripe and graphic sexual/sensual images of 'Khubla Khan':

> But oh! that deep romantic chasm which slanted
> Down the green hill athwart a cedarn cover! . . .
> And from this chasm, with ceaseless turmoil seething,
> As if this earth in fast thick pants were breathing,
> A mighty fountain momently was forced:
> Amid whose swift half-intermitted burst . . .

Mention of 'Kubla Khan' brings us, of course, to Coleridge's most celebrated dream of all. The story is well known. Under the influence of opium (which, while it may not have generated dreams, most certainly facilitated their conscious or unconscious transposition from his mind onto the page), Coleridge is supposed to have composed not 'less than two to three hundred lines' of a poem sparked off by the fact that, before succumbing to trance or sleep, he had been reading the following lines in *Purchas his Pilgrimage*:

> In Xamdu did Cublai Can build a stately Palace, encompassing sixteen miles of plaine ground with a wall, wherein are fertile Meddowes, pleasant Springs, delightfull Streames, and all sorts of beasts of chase and game, and in the middest thereof a sumptuous house of pleasure.

According to Coleridge's own account, he awoke and began feverishly to scribble down this major poem which he had been 'given'. Alas, he had written only some fifty lines when

> . . . he was unfortunately called out by a person on business from Porlock, and detained by him above an hour, and on his return to his room, found, to his no small surprise and mortification, that though he still

retained some vague and dim recollection of the general purport of the vision, yet, with the exception of some eight or ten scattered lines and images, all the rest had passed away like the images on the surface of a stream into which a stone has been cast, but, alas! without the after restoration of the latter![6]

Well, it's a good tale, but there seem to be some discrepancies. For example, Coleridge was living some miles from Porlock, so it is unlikely that the mysterious 'person on business from Porlock' would have popped out merely on the off-chance of finding him at home. So he presumably had an appointment . . . but, if so, surely Coleridge wouldn't have been so foolish as to dose himself up with opium just before it? – especially since Coleridge at this time was reluctant to admit his dependence on the drug, and so would have done his best to conceal the fact that he made use of it, especially in front of a stranger.

It seems sad to bid farewell to 'the seminal Man from Porlock', as Stephen Pile so gleefully hails him in *The Book of Heroic Failures* (1979), but certainly Coleridge's story is, at best, not the whole one. It would not be the first time he lied about the creation of one of his works.

Perhaps the most striking reason for doubting Coleridge's account is the fact that 'Kubla Khan' is, as it stands, too complete a work. Its first 36 lines tell of a vision, while the succeeding (and concluding) 18 lines ruefully lament the loss of that vision, while acknowledging that even a taste of 'the milk of Paradise' is a great privilege. Surely, then, the 'soul' of the poem lies in these final 18 lines, the yearning to return to the magic land which provides the setting for so many fantasy tales from the last century or more. It is conceivable, therefore, that one of two things happened: firstly, Coleridge may have had an entrancing dream, apparently pointless like most dreams, and in cold sobriety recorded his sense of loss at being unable to reenter the dream; or, secondly, he may have had the dream, tried to record it, lost track or inspiration, and then or later used the 36-line fragment as the basis of the full poem describing his sense of loss, as above.

Either way, it seems likely that it was Coleridge the conscious poet who composed 'Kubla Khan', not Coleridge the dreamer.

All is not quite as it may seem with the dream origin of 'The Rime of the Ancient Mariner', too. The initial inspiration for this work did indeed come from a dream . . . but not one of Coleridge's own. A neighbour, John Cruikshank, recounted to the poet a powerful dream which he had had and which included the vision of a 'skeleton ship, with figures in it'. Around this image Coleridge built the poem, although it seems certain that much of what he added came from his own dreams (and think of the 'Night-mare LIFE-IN-DEATH').

About the whole poem, in fact, there is a curious dream-like inconsequentiality: if one attempted to write a synopsis of the story-line one would end up with a very weak tale indeed. It gains its power from the fact that, like so many dreams, it contains in addition to the apparently pointless plot some deep, underlying truths about the nature of human existence. And, of course, there is the nightmarish quality of the unrelenting feeling of impending doom.

We are lucky that the waking poet was a creative genius: nowhere else can we find such graphic descriptions of the nightmare world as in his diaries (see Chapter Three) – even though they are often infuriatingly slipshod and/or affectedly poetic. How far his creativity was born from his nightmares, how far his drug use enabled him to transfer the wild rompings of his imagination, on occasion, to paper – these are things which we shall never know, of course. All that we can say is that, had it not been for him, the fortunate majority of us could have had no real conception of the sheer Hell endured by the soul who suffers perpetually from the assaults of nightmare.

## *Less Famous Creative Dreams*

The dreaming Coleridge, on the other hand, was rather less of a creative genius. While the waking Coleridge took dreams, spun them together, and wove 'Kubla Khan' and 'The Rime of the Ancient Mariner', his sleeping counterpart produced this:

> Here sleeps at length poor Col. and without screaming
> Who died, as he had always lived, a-dreaming:
> Shot dead, while sleeping, by the gout within
> Alone, and all unknown, at Ed'nboro' in an inn.

I've dwelt at some length on Coleridge's dream-creativity, because it seems to me to be typical. Dreams can be responsible for rare inspiration, and the end-result be a masterpiece, but taken by themselves dreams produce unsatisfying stories or short bursts of doggerel – although Swinburne claimed that the first three stanzas of 'Spring in Winter' came to him in a dream. More typical is the verse which Tennyson dreamt at the age of ten:

> May a cock sparrow
> Write to a barrow?
> I hope you'll excuse
> My infantile muse.

According to Lewis Carroll, Tennyson's other dream composition was 'an enormously long poem about fairies, which began with very long lines that gradually got shorter, and ended with fifty or sixty lines of two syllables each'. Sir John Squire dream-composed what seemed to him a masterpiece until the critical fingers of cold dawn touched it:

> There was a boy grew twenty inch, yes,
> Twenty inch a year,
> It might have made his mother flinch, but
> She was quite a dear;
> Yes, she was excellent,
> And she was well content
> To watch her offspring forge ahead in his
> Peculiar sphere.

More successful in popular if not always in critical terms was the horror-story writer H. P. Lovecraft, who probably produced most of his stories – about the Cthulhu Mythos and the Old Ones – as a result of the dreadful nightmares he experienced from childhood onwards, but the dreams seem to have contributed only to the *mood* of the stories. Perhaps they'd have been better written had the dreams done the whole job: 'indescribable, unimaginably horrifying, stinking of all that is dark and dank and dirty and repulsive, incomprehensibly disgusting . . .' represents the first 10% or so of a typical Lovecraftian adjectival clause.

At a slightly higher level, the Gothic novelist Ann Radcliffe used to eat indigestible foods at bedtime to give herself inspiring nightmares. In an unpublished parody, Ray Thompson has combined both genres to give a three-page Lovecraftian description of the plateful of food he found sitting in front of him at a fast-food establishment.

It may seem presumptuous to quote my own experiences of creative dreams – in fact, it is – but I'll do so because they've allowed me, perhaps, some first-hand insight into the reasons why stories written as direct transcripts of dreams tend to be unsatisfying.[7] I find that there are two problems which between them 'account for' most of my creative dreams.

In the first place, on most mornings when I wake up thinking 'Wow! That dream would make a good story!', I continued thinking so for the first half-hour or so of the day. Of course, I'm only too aware that dream-plots need extensive revision, but nevertheless, during the time that the whole ambient feeling of the dream is still fresh and recallable in my mind, I feel confident that – especially because of the new plot-angles my conscious mind is thinking up – I'm onto a good thing. At the end of the half-hour, I suddenly realize that my great Booker Prize-winning story is in reality the worst bathetic drivel.

But this isn't always what happens. On occasion I find the combination of the dream itself and my later, conscious, plot manipulations still seems as if it could be put together to make a pretty good tale. And so I head for the typewriter. About a page and a half later I pick up what I've written, tear it into many little shreds, and jump up and down on the pile. At least for me, there is a barrier between the story I've dreamt and the story I might write; perhaps because of my insufficient skill as a writer, there is no way I can cross this barrier. It's rather like having a 'writer's block' even though one's raring to write.

The most curious part of it all, perhaps, is that all this doesn't mean that I mentally ditch the stories. They're still there, locked up inside my head, but I know I'll probably never write them.

As I say, then, these two effects taken together may account for the fact that the dream directly transformed into story or poem is often so unsatisfactory: either the author should never have tried to do anything with the dream in the first place, or he or she was well justified in trying but the attempt was a failure for the sort of reason I've described.

Why should a writer lose his or her critical faculties and fail to censor the worst outpourings – or, at least, to burn the results rather than publish them? I think this is possibly because of the very profound effects our dreams have on us. We seem to experience things in our dreams in some way much more vividly than we do in real life. Emotions are magnified, scenes are more beautiful, and so forth.

That this might be the case is suggested by the fact that very often writers produce their worst dream-inspired work when they are emotionally upset. At such times, of course, there's a good chance that one will dream more (unless one's using drink to blot out reality's misery); but in addition one's more vulnerable to the emotive, affecting power of one's dreams.

Mark Twain is a case in point. Late in his life he was in a state of abject misery: his daughter had died and he was in deep debt. Like Edward VI in Twain's *The Prince and the Pauper* (1882), who dreamt of being a pauper so vividly that – reminiscently of Chuang-tzu (see page 10) – he began to wonder whether he was a prince dreaming he was a pauper or a pauper dreaming he was a prince, Twain began to have difficulty in telling one world – the 'Twain world' – from another – the 'Clemens world'. His real life began to seem to him to be nothing more than a dream: after all, boat-boys from the Mississippi just *didn't* – really didn't – turn into internationally acclaimed writers. As one might expect in somebody suffering from this sort of mental confusion, his nightmares began to oppress him. Moreover, his waking self was shocked and horrified by some of the things his dreaming self quite happily got up to.

As Kaplan has pointed out (in his excellent *Mr Clemens*

*and Mark Twain*), the late 1890s were the right time to be worrying about such things, for Freud's notion of the unconscious was all the rage. The idea was that, in essence, each of us is two different creatures, quite different and rarely in communication. This did not really satisfy Twain, though: he refused to believe that the conscious and the unconscious could operate simultaneously, and so required a rather more sophisticated model of the situation.

Now Twain's recorded dreams often had a sexual content – although Twain himself was too naïve to realize that sex was embroiled in all those crazy dream-symbols. One night in late 1896 or early 1897, however, he had a dream about which even he could have had little doubt:

> I was suddenly in the presence of a negro wench who was sitting in grassy open country . . . She was very vivid to me – round black face, shiny black eyes, thick lips, very white regular teeth showing through her smile. She was about 22, and plump . . . and good-natured and not at all bad-looking. She had but one garment on – a coarse tow-linen shirt that reached from her neck to her ankles without a break. She sold me a pie . . . She was eating one herself with a tin teaspoon. She made a disgusting proposition to me. Although it was disgusting it did not surprise me – for I was young (I was never old in a dream yet) and it seemed quite natural that it should come from her . . . I merely made a chaffing remark, brushing aside the matter – a little jeeringly – and this embarrassed her and she made an awkward pretence that I had misunderstood her. I . . . asked for a spoon to eat my pie with. She had but the one, and she took it out of her mouth, in a quite matter-of-course way, and offered it to me. My stomach rose – there everything vanished

> . . . My, how vivid it all was! Even to the texture of her shirt, its dull white colour, and the pale brown tint of a stain on the shoulder of it.[8]

All seemed to become clear to the waking Twain: the Mark Twain of his dreams was actually a different person from himself. This other fellow could do things and see things and think things which were anathema to the waking Twain. The most famous of all such antics of his dream-self was his appearance on a platform dressed only in his nightshirt. When he said to the assembled audience that he was Mark Twain, no one would believe him!

Twain exploited his dreams for creative purposes over the next couple of years – and also the curious 'role reversal' whereby reality became dream and dream became reality – to produce a whole series of dream-tales. Significantly, in context of my argument, none of these dream-tales are great fictions – although the posthumously published *The Mysterious Stranger* has a certain sombre appeal – but they served one important purpose. They kept him sane when his mind was slipping – thanks to his miserable circumstances – inexorably towards the borderlands of madness. In a sense, then, his dreams were therapeutic, rather than truly creative.

Not, of course, that one has anything against psychotherapy. But I suggest that Twain's experience shows that the combination of the mind being in upheaval, and therefore quite uncritical, and the gullibility of the dream-persona makes for bad artistry.

## *Not Quite Great Art*

Some writers, of course, are honest enough to admit that, while their dream-creations may in a way be fascinating, they are not Great Art. One such was John Keats. In fact, it would be difficult to find a better and more direct example than the one recounted in a letter of his to George and Georgiana Keats. The letter is dated 12th February to 3rd May, 1819: if this should seem a long time to work on a letter, bear in mind that it's nearly 20,000 words long.

> The fifth canto of Dante pleases me more and more – it is that one in which he meets with Paulo and Francesca – I had passed many days in rather a low state of mind and in the midst of them I dreamt of being in that region of Hell. The dream was one of the most delightful enjoyments I ever had in my life – I floated about the whirling atmosphere as it is described with a beautiful figure to whose lips mine were joined as it seem'd for an age – and in the midst of all this cold and darkness I was warm – even flowery tree tops sprung up and we rested on them sometimes with the lightness of a cloud till the wind blew us away again – I tried a Sonnnet upon it – there are fourteen lines but nothing of what I felt in it – o that I could dream it every night –
>
> As Hermes once took to his feathers light
> When lulled Argus, baffled, swoon'd and slept
> So on a delphic reed my idle spright
> So play'd, so charm'd so conquer'd, so bereft
> The dragon world of all its hundred eyes
> And seeing it asleep so fled away: –
> Not to pure Ida with its snow-cold skies
> Nor unto Tempe where Jove grieved that day,
> But to that second circle of sad hell,
> Where in the gust, the whirlwind and the flaw
> Of Rain and hailstones lovers need not tell
> Their sorrows – Pale were the sweet lips I saw

Pale were the lips I kiss'd and fair the form
I floated with about that melancholy storm –

The key words here are of course Keats's own: the sonnet had 'nothing of what I felt in it'. Here it would seem he is referring to the difficulty I described earlier, that of somehow hauling the content of a dream over the barrier of cold daylight to set it down on paper.

There are of course exceptions – or claimed exceptions – to the rule. In his *The Paranormal* (1978) the British wirter Stan Gooch discusses his dreams at some length. He says that he has often dreamt complete short stories, and frequently also jokes so funny that he has woken up because he has been laughing so much at them. Interestingly enough, he says that, while the stories still seem pretty good in the grim light of morning, the jokes are . . . well, I suppose it all depends on the way you dream them.

Probably all of us have shared the experience of dreaming a joke which was either incomprehensible or just plain unfunny when recalled in the morning. In a radio-broadcast appeal which I made for dreams during the summer of 1983, I stressed that I would be particularly interested to hear from people who had dreamt jokes which they still found funny (as opposed to dreams which were funny in recollection, but not necessarily at the time): there was not a single response to my plea, although I was sent plenty of examples of all the other types of dreams I asked for.[9]

Gooch mentions, too, having had 'adventure dreams' which are such rollickingly good fun that on occasion he has deliberately made himself go back to sleep again after the alarm-clock has woken him, in order that the fun may carry on. These he correlates with periods of tedium or idleness in real life; but the most interesting thing about them is that they are, he claims, self-consistent – '. . . in the dream anyone who is killed remains killed, for example. I remember one dream where I myself was shot dead – and that was the end of the dream.' But not, thankfully, the end of Gooch.

He refers, however, to the 'barrier problem'. He is a developing lucid dreamer – that is, a person who is conscious of the fact that he or she is dreaming, and can in some cases direct the dream. '. . . I can only say that the dream world which I enter for extended periods as, nevertheless, a fully conscious individual is of a beauty and a wonder that I have no words to convey.' In other words, the barrier still exists even if you have consciously directed the dream.

## *Hypnagogic Lucidity*

However, if the creative artist can not only solve the 'barrier problem' but also direct the dreams, the resulting mixture is likely to be very heady stuff indeed.

One such dreamer was Edgar Allan Poe. Often enough it's been said that if you just sit down and read a few stories by Poe you know that here is a man who dreamt vividly, who lived by his dreams in more ways than one: after all, if you can't stop yourself having nightmares, you could do a whole lot worse than turn a few bucks by writing them down.[10] However, the trouble is that insights like this can be misleading. Ask the horror writers of your choice if they have nightmares and they'll say: 'Yes. Of course. Everyone has nightmares.' But is this where the ideas for their horror stories come from? Quite probably the answer will be no. As we shall see, Stevenson's Jekyll and Hyde may have started their bizarre double act in a nightmare, but the story which he finally wrote was a product more of his conscious mind than of the nightmare.

So one's intuition on reading the works of Poe could be a false one – and, in fact, it more or less is. He did indeed get a lot of material out of his dreams, but not the dreams he had while he was asleep. He was lucky enough to be a lucid hypnagogic dreamer, which means both that he could have vivid dreams while he was only half-asleep, and that he was quite conscious that they were only dreams and in some cases could direct them.[11] 'These "fancies" have in them a pleasurable ecstasy as far beyond the most pleasurable of the world of wakefulness, or of [sleeping] dreams, as the Heaven of the Northman mythology is beyond its Hell,' he wrote, echoing Gooch's words of a couple of paragraphs ago.

Again, he wrote in the guise of the narrator of 'Eleanora' (1842): 'They who dream by day are cognizant of many things that escape those who dream only by night . . . In their grey vision they obtain glimpses of eternity, and thrill, on awaking, to find that they have been upon the verge of the great secret.'

In his column, 'Marginalia', he tells us that these hypnagogic dreams weren't just hit-and-miss affairs. In the first place, he was able to 'control . . . the existence of the condition'. In the second place, he adds,

> I have proceeded so far . . . as to prevent the lapse from *the point* of which I speak – the point of blending between wakefulness and sleep. Not that I can *continue* the condition – not that I can render the point more than a point – but that I can startle myself from the point into wakefulness – *and thus transfer the point itself into the realm of Memory* – convey its impressions, or more properly their recollections, to a situation where (although still for a very brief period) I can survey them with the eye of analysis.

Note that, once again, here is a creative artist stressing the important role of that 'eye of analysis'.

But how much did these waking dreams contribute to his literary output? A fair deal, we have to admit – especially to some of the poems. But, just as it was Coleridge the poet who wrote 'Kubla Khan', so it was Poe the poet who produced lines based on his visions. That is, the poems didn't spring straight from his visions, all neatly cooked up by his subconscious: he used the medium of poetry *to describe what he had seen.* As for the stories, it can probably never be proved one way or the other: one guesses that the 'eye of analysis' probably played as large – if not larger – a part as the original dreams themselves.

To digress a little just before leaving Poe: Walt Whitman had an interesting dream.

> . . . I saw a vessel on the sea, at midnight, in a storm. It was no great full-rigg'd ship, nor majestic steamer, steering firmly through the gale, but seem'd one of those superb little schooner yachts I had often seen lying anchor'd, rocking so jauntily, in the waters around New York, or up Long Island sound – now flying uncontroll'd with torn sails and broken spars through the wild sleet and the wind and waves of the night. On the deck was a slender, slight, beautiful figure, a dim man apparently enjoying the terror, the murk, and the dislocation of which he was the center and the victim. That picture of my lurid dream might stand for Edgar Poe, his spirit, his fortunes, and his poems – themselves all lurid dreams.

I'm rather uncertain about this vision of Whitman's. Somehow, it makes Poe out to be a sort of milkwater character wreaking his vengeance on the world with 'lurid dreams'; that would be a fair description of Lovecraft, but Poe was a rather more positive person than Whitman's sketch would suggest.

I have also a terrible, unjustified sneaking suspicion that Whitman simply invented his 'dream' in order to make a point.

## *Stream of Unconsciousness*

Jack Kerouac, on the other hand, I can quite believe transferred his dreams straight from his memories of them onto the paper. His reputation has had, to say the very least, its ups and downs. His confused tales, written in self-conscious stream-of-consciousness format, were in their day set reading for a whole generation; today it seems to be the fashion to dismiss them as derivative and pretentious pulp literature . . . to the extent that, astonishingly, Kerouac merits not even a mention in the index, let alone an entry in his own right, in the *Encyclopedia Americana* (1978 edition). That this most American of reference books should omit him altogether is rather rough justice.

However, let's not get embroiled in the literary argument: either you like Kerouac or you don't;[12] either you find his style revelatory or you find it infuriating. What is of interest in our context is the dreamlike quality of so many of his writings. The basic reason for it is fairly simple, I think: dreams, like Kerouac's tales, are stream-of-consciousness stories. But there is perhaps more to it than that.

In 1961 he published his *Book of Dreams*, a random collection spontaneously 'scribbled after I woke from my sleep . . . sometimes written before I was even wide awake'. It is immediately evident from it that his dream-life had a fundamental effect on his writing. The same characters appear in his dreams as in *On the Road, The*

*Subterraneans* and *The Dharma Bums* – albeit under different names: in fact, Kerouac prefaced his *Book of Dreams* with a key to who's who. Moreover, there's little by way of qualitative distinction between his spontaneously and no doubt sleepily written dream-accounts and his fictions: unless you actually look at *Book of Dreams* properly you can't tell it from any of his other books, which is presumably why it's classified as fiction in several reference works.

To do more than tap the surface of the collection is clearly impossible: he gives us nearly 250 dream-accounts and, while some are simple – perhaps only a sentence or two – many describe complex full-length sequences of dreams, while quite a few are just straightforwardly incomprehensible. However, three strands clearly emerge as predominant: dreams about his father, dreams about cats, and especially dreams about sex.

Some of the dreams about his dead father are much what you would expect from a bereaved son – in one Kerouac finds himself digging graves, one of which is his father's – but there's a curious preponderance of dreams about his father having, quite literally, returned from the dead. In one he came back as a 'drunkard and didn't answer or give a shit – Intractable as a bad child'; elsewhere Kerouac remarks: 'God how heavily he carries his carrion corpse around in these repetitious dreams, with what a hopeless, pale almost invisible face, so joyless.' In most if not all cases where Kerouac dreamt about his father, it seems that he woke up the following morning oppressed by guilt.

Similarly, there are many dreams concerning his cats and possible injury to them. For example, he finds himself on a cliff, a cat struggling and clawing in his arms. He thinks the cat would be better on its own, and throws it onto a beam. The cat slithers and slides off it, bounces off another beam, and falls to the sands a hundred feet beneath him, spinning 'like a rollercoaster at the beach'.

I have a sneaking suspicion that the cats in Kerouac's dreams fulfil a sexual function of some kind, and also that Kerouac guessed it. However, when it came to dreams of blatant, full-frontal sexuality, he suffered no dearth. In fact, if I'd had anything like some of his sexual dreams, I don't think I'd have written them down – even in a personal diary.

Few of them are to do with happy, normal sex. Even when he dreams of spending the night with Marlene Dietrich, the ecstasy is marred by the fact that she's taking photographs of him for a three-page spread in *Life* magazine. Most concern sexual humiliation of some kind or another – being spied on when in action; making love to a woman who won't stop talking about trivia; having a minute penis and children laughing at it; and so on. However, there's a fair admixture of paedophilia and other perversions, and an underlying strain of homosexuality.

Here are a couple of typical examples of his humiliation or frustration:

An old friend asks him to 'comfort' her. He is uncertain whether she means she wants him to make love to her (which he'd like) or not, and so resolves to be a gentleman and play things her way. She promptly has a frenzied sexual encounter against the wall with a burly passing sailor, and Kerouac naturally feels a little miffed.[13] He tries the same strong-arm tactics as the sailor did, but she wriggles away from him.

Again, he is having an affair with a coloured girl. They plan to make love, but by the time they get around to it it's too late – she has to go to work, leaving him more than a mite frustrated and uncertain.[14]

In the same sort of vein of humiliation and frustration,

there's a most curious Portnoy-style dream in which he's making love to a girl, Peaches, who refuses to let him make love in the normal way: instead, she holds a piece of steak between her legs, so that it acts as an artificial vagina. Then he meets a beautiful (probably rich) middle-aged woman who takes him back to her house, and they start to have an affair. She feeds him so well that he can no longer eat his packed lunches at college, and all the people in the class, with the exception of Peaches, realize that he's having an affair. As so often happens, the dream lingered on into wakefulness: he lay in bed thinking for a while that he must persuade Peaches to give up the steak, before he realized that it was all only a dream.

Slightly different in neurosis is

> Those awful Amazon women of Rome have got me as one of their slaves dancing in their torture chorus, a ritual, in the Circus – people watch laffing, clapping – the sexual dance – they'll stick you with a spear if you don't dance – the big brunette runs up, grabs me, pulls me, makes me do lewd suggestive stuff with her, all a formal written dance but I'm a reluctant slave, unhappy paramour – the crowd roars glad – it's also a kind of basketball floor, the St Louis parochial floor – . . .

And one asexual dream of his which appeals to me is set in a friend's living room. She is telling him about a great but forgotten Greek writer called Plipias or Snipias who, when his father absconded with the family fortunes, went to live with his young boyfriend on a remote island. Kerouac's friend stresses one of Plipias' (or Snipias') sayings: 'I never go on strike against man, because I love him.' Both the friend and Kerouac concur that this is a saying of great wisdom. Once again, the dream-self is much impressed by the banal – just as Coleridge's was by his 'Ed'nboro'' quatrain.

As I've said, Kerouac's dreams could be taken and used almost verbatim as straightforward pieces of Kerouac fiction, and this is almost certainly what to a great extent he did. In many ways, though, he doesn't seem to have realized quite how much about himself his dreams revealed: I suppose that when he introduced some of the riper scenes into his fiction they were accepted by his audience as being merely the kind of things that hoboes – professional hoboes, 'bound for glory' – got up to in their spare time.[15]

## *The Brownies*

But the great advantage of writing in a stream-of-consciousness style is that all sorts of dream snippets can be thrown into the general morass and no one will notice the difference. This can't, of course, be the case if the writer is working with orthodox prose, as did that most remarkable of the literary creative dreamers, Robert Louis Stevenson. One of his nightmares is almost as well known as Coleridge's probably spurious 'Kubla Khan' dream: it became the novel *Dr Jekyll and Mr Hyde* (1886). In *Across the Plains* (1892) Stevenson discusses the matter:

> I had long been trying to write a story on this subject, to find a body, a vehicle, for that strong sense of man's double being which must at times come in upon and overwhelm the mind of every thinking creature. I had even written one, *The Travelling Companion*, which was returned by an editor on the plea that it was a work of genius and indecent, and which I burned the other day on the ground that it was not a work of genius, and that *Jekyll* had supplanted it. Then came one of those financial fluctuations . . . For two days I

> went about racking my brains for a plot of any sort; and on the second night I dreamed the scene at the window, and a scene afterward split in two, in which Hyde, pursued for some crime, took the powder and underwent the change in the present of his pursuers. All the rest was made awake, and consciously . . . All that was given me was the matter of three scenes, and the central idea of a voluntary change becoming involuntary.

Stevenson himself doesn't tell quite the whole story. He was awoken in the middle of the night by his wife, who had been disturbed by his tossing and shouting: she thought he was having a nightmare – as indeed he was – and her purpose was merely to help. She was a little surprised when Stevenson was quite sharp with her: he had been halfway through dreaming up a rattling good thriller.

He worked quickly on the story, finishing the first draft within about three days. Unfortunately, when his wife read it she commented that he had written it as little more than his original description implied: it was a rattling good thriller. Did he not realize that there was a serious moral question that could be raised here? Stevenson took her point. He threw away the first draft and over the next three days wrote the second, which is the version we read today.[16]

This was by no means the first story that Stevenson had, quite literally, dreamt up. Indeed, to go by his own description, he seems to have been quite businesslike about the whole matter of creative dreaming. Writing of himself in the third person, he says:

> This honest fellow had long been in the custom of settling himself to sleep with tales, and so had his

> father before him; but these were irresponsible inventions, told for the teller's pleasure, with no eye to the crass public or the thwart reviewer: tales where a thread might be dropped, or one adventure quitted for another, on fancy's least suggestion. So that the little people who manage man's internal theatre had not yet received a very rigorous training; and played upon their stage like children who should have slipped into the house and found it empty, rather than like drilled actors performing a set piece to a huge hall of faces. But presently my dreamer began to turn his former amusement of story-telling to (what is called) account; by which I mean that he began to write and sell his tales. Here was he, and here were the little people who did that part of his business, in quite new conditions.

In other words the unrefined dreams had to be taken and shaped, turned from structureless fantasies into stories:

> . . . the pleasure, in one word, had become a business; and that not only for the dreamer, but for the little people of his theatre. These understood the change as well as he. When he lay down to prepare himself for sleep, he no longer sought amusement, but printable and profitable tales; and after he had dozed off in his box-seat, his little people continued their evolutions with the same mercantile designs . . . for the most part, whether awake or asleep, he is simply occupied – he or his little people – in consciously making stories for the market. This dreamer (like many other persons) has encountered some trifling vicissitudes of fortune. When the bank begins to send letters and the butcher to linger at the back gate . . .

(It's nice to know that I'm not the only one.)

> . . . he sets to belabouring his brains after a story, for that is his readiest money-winner; and, behold! at once

> the little people begin to bestir themselves in the same quest, and labour all night long . . . No fear of his being frightened now; applause, growing applause, growing interest, growing exultation in his own cleverness (for he takes all the credit), and at last a jubilant leap to wakefulness, with the cry, 'I have it, that'll do!' upon his lips . . .

Although he never says so in so many words, it does seem that Stevenson was a lucid dreamer – one who put his talent to good use. As we have seen, so many dream-creations have been of little value – Mark Twain's, for example, were the low-point of his literary career. Perhaps this is because the dreamers were, like most of us, unable to control their dreams. Perhaps, on the other hand, they simply failed to realize – as Stevenson so emphatically insists *he* realized – that dreams must be shaped and honed, plotted and structured, before they can become readable stories. Stevenson seems almost unique in having wedded the inventiveness of his 'little people', or 'Brownies', to his craft as a writer without, as it were, the join showing.

His Brownies 'do one-half my work for me while I am fast asleep, and in all human likelihood, do the rest for me as well, when I am wide awake and fondly suppose I do it for myself'. At a guess, he was being deliberately over-modest – and even more so when he added:

> . . . my conscious ego, the denizen of the pineal gland unless he has changed his residence since Descartes, the man with the conscience and the variable bank-account, the man with the hat and the boots, and the privilege of voting and not carrying his candidate at the general elections – I am sometimes tempted to suppose he is no story-teller at all, but a creature as matter of fact as any cheesemonger or any cheese . . .

He is being a little more honest and a little less self-effacing when he talks about the role of his Brownies in the creation of *Dr Jekyll and Mr Hyde*. You'll recall that 'All the rest was made awake, and consciously',

> although I think I can trace in it much of the manner of my Brownies. The meaning of the tale is therefore mine, and had long pre-existed in my garden of Adonis, and tried one body after another in vain; indeed, I do most of the morality, worse luck! and my Brownies have not a rudiment of what we call a conscience. Mine, too, is the setting, mine the characters . . . Will it be thought ungenerous, after I have been so liberally ladling out praise to my unseen collaborators, if I here toss them over, bound hand and foot, into the arena of the critics? For the business of the powders, which so many have censured, is, I am relieved to say, not mine at all but the Brownies'.

He'd doubtless have felt less guilty about blaming the Brownies for the foaming mugfuls of lurid liquid which so many Dr Jekylls have downed on the cinema screen – the ridiculous products of other people's Brownies, no doubt.

Leave that aside. While Stevenson might confess to having played the major role in the writing of *Jekyll and Hyde*, this was not always the case. The Brownies did almost all of the work in the production of the 'not very defensible story of *Olalla*':

> Here the court, the mother, the mother's niche, Olalla, Olalla's chamber, the meetings on the stair, the broken window, the ugly scene of the bite, were all given me in bulk and detail as I have tried to write them; to this I added only the external scenery (for in my dream I never was beyond the court), the portrait, the characters of Felipe and the priest, the moral, such as it is,

and the last pages, such as, alas! they are. And I may even say that in this case the moral itself was given me; for it arose immediately on comparison of the mother and the daughter, and from the hideous trick of atavism in the first . . .

In other words, as I was saying a little while ago, if writers don't apply their *craft* to their dreams, but simply write them down the way they were, the results can be far from good – as the writers themselves will later realize, to their profound embarrassment. But Stevenson took the matter further: in *Across the Plains* he summarizes a typical example of a story that came to him, fully formed, in a dream; he comments that 'it soon became plain that in this spirited tale there were unmarketable elements' (i.e., naughty bits).

The dream-self is the son of a rich man who has recently remarried. His young wife 'was supposed to suffer cruelly and to loathe her yoke'. Father and son meet in an isolated spot, far from home, and argue; in a fit of temper the son strikes the father dead. However, when the father's body is found it is assumed he died from natural causes, and the son inherits placidly enough.

The father's widow, however, is left nothing; and so she lives on in the family manor – as does the son, naturally. Friendship springs up between them, but then the son becomes suspicious that she has an inkling of his guilt in the little matter of patricide . . . yet still he is strangely drawn to her. Their life together becomes a curious one, 'full of broken dialogue, challenging glances, and suppressed passion'.

One day the dreamer spots the woman heading for the railway station, and he follows her. Sure enough, she goes – with him in tow – to the lonely cliffs where he killed his father, and there she finds a damning piece of evidence. Just as she does so, she trips and falls over the precipice, hanging on by some convenient undergrowth; the dream-self automatically rescues her.

She knows, and he knows that she knows, and so on, but they can't bring it out into the open. Life back home becomes purgatory for the young man – she is clearly holding the piece of evidence over him, as a blackmail tool – until one day he gives in and ransacks her room, searching for the vital object. She catches him in the act, and he puts the piece of evidence back where he found it; she says nothing to him, and tells her maid a lie about the reason why the room is in such chaos.

The next morning at breakfast, things rather naturally become too much for the dream-self. He leaps to his feet and begs her to put him out of his misery . . .

> Why did she torture him so? she knew all, she knew he was no enemy to her; why did she not denounce him at once? What signified her whole behaviour? why did she torture him? and yet again, why did she torture him? And when he had done, she fell upon her knees, and with outstretched hands: 'Do you not understand?' she cried. 'I love you!'
>
> Hereupon, with a pang of wonder and mercantile delight, the dreamer awoke.

Well, as Stevenson might have said to his Brownies, a good tale needs a good teller . . .

The story as a whole seems innocuous enough to us now, but presumably Stevenson felt that it was too strong – if the implications were thought about – for the Victorian stomach. Indeed,

> For the most part, it will be seen, my Brownies are somewhat fantastic, like their stories hot and hot, full of passion and the picturesque, alive with animating

incident; and they have no prejudice against the supernatural. But the other day they gave me a surprise, entertaining me with a love-story, a little April comedy, which I ought certainly to hand over to the author of *A Chance Acquaintance*,[17] for he could write it as it should be written, and I am sure (although I mean to try) that I cannot.

## Some Guides

Various of the 'reincarnatory' dreamers have had dreams which the uncharitable might describe as creative: Joan Grant, Taylor Caldwell, Edward Lucas White and G. M. Glaskin spring immediately to mind. However, for the purposes of argument we shall assume that the results of their dreams are not historical novels but genuine 'memories' of bygone lifetimes, and deal with them later (see Chapter Six).

However, it's worth noting that Glaskin, who – when not reliving his existence in prehistory – is a full-time novelist, has had some dreams which are set apart from his 'reincarnatory' ones, and which can genuinely be described as creative. Towards the end of his *Windows of the Mind: The Christos Experiment* (1974) he describes some of the results of these dreams. His long story 'The Road to Nowhere' was, he says, totally the product of dreaming, while his novels *O Loneliness* and *Flight to Landfall* either sprang 'in their entirety direct from a dream, or an image derived from a dream'. He dreamt his play *Turn on the Heat* scene for scene, if not word for word; when awake he felt that it was being dictated to him in some way by its deceased protagonist, Marilyn Monroe. Sections of his other novels were dream-inspired, especially *A Change of Mind*. At the time of writing, he was working on a novel provisionally entitled

*Alicia*, which was based on a frequently recurring dream: one section, which had come to him in a much earlier dream, had already appeared as the long story 'The Ice Yacht'.

Another vaguely creative dream of his was of a succession of windows, from little plain ones to colossal stained-glass ones, with people standing in or by them. He awoke happily, since he instantly realized that this succession of scenes would make an excellent opening for the television adaptation of his first book on the 'Christos Experience' (*Windows of the Mind*). He may or may not have been right about this: the proposed TV adaptation has yet to be made.[18]

Another modern writer known for her nonfiction is Sandra Shulman, whose twenty-odd books nevertheless include some novels – romances, published under a pseudonym. A couple of scenes in two of them – *The Degenerates* (1971) and *The Florentine* (1972) – come from dreams:

> They were better in the dreams, of course; when I fleshed them out for real they didn't make quite the same impression on me. Both are violent and nasty. I have a horrible unconscious, haven't I? Come to think of it, my conscious isn't much better . . .

Shulman is of particular interest in this context in that one of her books – *Nightmare* (1979) – is one of the classics on the geography of dreamland.

And a very curious example of creative dreaming came up in 1983 with the publication of the Booker-shortlisted novel *Flying to Nowhere*, by John Fuller. In a *Guardian* review of the book, Robert Nye noted strong similarities between it and the bestselling *The Name of the Rose*, by Umberto Eco, which had been published in Italian in 1980 and in English translation in July 1983, four months after

Fuller's book. Could it be, asked Nye, that Fuller had read an English review of Eco's book and then later had a dream which was to form the basis of his own novel?

The response to the suggestion from Fuller's publisher was immediate. *Flying to Nowhere* was indeed based on one of Fuller's dreams, but the dream had come to him as long ago as 1977 – as could be proved by Fuller's notes and synopsis dating from that time. Fuller had known nothing of *The Name of the Rose* until the publication of the English translation, by which time, of course, his own book was already in the shops.

The curious part of it all is that Fuller allowed six years to elapse between his original dream and the publication of his (very short) novel, and that when it did appear it did so almost simultaneously with the novel which it so strongly resembles. Moreover, both books achieved bestsellerdom around the same time. I don't want to make anything of the coincidence – I think it unlikely that telepathy or any other paranormal power was at work – but it does seem tempting to suggest that this tale is an example of the 'there is a tide in the affairs of men . . .' factor.

## *Dreamers in Disguise – With Diamonds*

But what of the dark fantasists? Lovecraft we've met, and Stevenson, too – not to mention Poe. Whenever one reads a work by a writer of horror-fantasy (as opposed to straightforward horror-sadism), one immediately begins to think that the author must be a dreamer. As I've noted, very often one may be wrong in so thinking; nonetheless, there's a definite correlation between profuse dreamers, on the one hand, and fantasy writers, on the other. If the dreams are nightmares, then the fantasies tend, quite naturally, to be dark. This correlation probably arises because in fantasy, as in dreams, there are no rules – which is precisely why fantasy is a genre of fiction which infuriates so many people. In its closest relative, science fiction, if the hero is falling into a vat of boiling oil, there's a good reason why he's able to get out of the scrape (that antigravity device he got free with his cigarettes back in Chapter Two, or whatever); but in fantasy – as in dreams – that discipline isn't there. He escapes because his nostrils, by sheer coincidence, twitch into exactly the right configuration to invoke the supernatural being who . . . do I have to go on?

I am being unkind to fantasy writers, some of whose works I enjoy.[19] Near the top of my list of fantasists comes Ambrose Bierce: although today he is remembered as, at his best, a dark fantasist *par excellence*, in his day he was notable as a journalist and literary critic of such acerbity and scurrilousness that he was blamed both for the suicide of the minor (very minor) poet David Lessor Lezinsky – the charge was probably well founded – and for the assassination of the 25th US President, William McKinley – in which instance Bierce was, probably to his profound regret, totally innocent.

Bierce's fantasies, published in collections such as *Can Such Things Be?* (1893), have a dreamlike quality, and many are almost certainly based on the nightmares that plagued him during his youth. Many have as their background thc carnage of the Civil War, in which, as a young man, he played a distinguished part (he was a confirmed anti-slaver). Frequently they express his life-long belief – probably also born from his war experiences – that humanity is merely a sick joke, and death the greatest joke of all. However, the dreamlike quality which helps to instil numb horror in the reader all too often renders his fantasies rather poor things, for improbable coincidences – just like the ones that characterize so many dreams and nightmares – abound. A typical Bierce story might have a soldier shooting what he thinks is his enemy, only to find he has killed his long-lost father or lover. The horrific description of stark death is wasted when the reader balks in incredulity at the plot.[20]

Bierce's great final card trick, which really oughtn't to concern us here, was inexplicably to disappear. The mystery is perhaps not quite so great as it might seem: he vanished while travelling as a 'tourist' to see the Madero Revolution in Mexico. In that part of the world, quite a lot of other people were disappearing without trace at the time. Still, it is charming to come across Charles Fort's explanation of the disappearance: since there vanished at about the same time an unfortunate called Ambrose Small, clearly some malevolent entity was in the business of 'collecting Ambroses'.

How much of Bierce's fiction derived from his dreams is a moot question: one has to say 'quite a lot', judging by all the evidence, but one's hard put to find specific examples. The same is true of Rudyard Kipling, as we shall see shortly: of *course* he made great use of his dreams in his writing, but . . . er . . . in which stories exactly? In some instances, though, one can be much more precise. The distinguished dramatic critic and minor playwright William Archer (1856–1924) is today probably remembered – if at all – only for his play *The Green Goddess*. Although it is impossible to be certain that he told the truth, it is generally agreed that, just as he described, this play came to him in its entirety in a dream. He was in fact an inveterate dreamer, and kept a dream-diary for long periods, although none of his other dreams were of any note.

However, if it's difficult to pin down which of Bierce's or Kipling's stories came directly from dreams, life becomes even more tricky when one comes to Charles

Kingsley. In a letter he wrote to John Buller on the 19th of March, 1857, he said:

> I feel deeply the change in one's imagination during the last twenty years. As a child I never could distinguish between dreams and imaginations, imaginations from waking impressions; and was often enough thought to be romancing when I was relating a real impression. In ill health from overwork aabout 16 to 18, I had spectral illusions often . . . accompanied with frightful nervous excitability, and inability to settle to any work, though always working at something in a fierce, desultory way. At twenty I found out tobacco. The spectres vanished; the power of dull application arose; and for the first time in my life, I began to be master of my own brain.
>
> Now, I am in general the most prosaic and matter-of-fact of persons. I cannot dream if I try. I go to my brain as to a storehouse or carpenter's shop, from which I take out coolly what I want, and put it into the best shape I can . . .

What's so remarkable about this letter? Quite simply, it is that Kingsley appears to be lying through his teeth: by all accounts, he was plagued by dreams and nightmares throughout his life. This is of a pattern with the rest of his behaviour, which was unconventional to the point of downright madness.

In a slightly different context, here is a relation of a dream taken from a letter he wrote to his wife Frances (Fanny) after the death in 1844 of his brother Gerald at sea:

> I saw him twice last night in two different dreams – strong and well – and so much grown – and I kissed him and wept over him – and woke to the everlasting No!

In her biography of him, *Charles Kingsley* (1975), Brenda Colloms directly contradicts his version of the role of the dream in his creative writing. Apparently he earned the criticism of many of his contemporaries for his habit of incorporating his own dreams wholesale into his novels. And there are, of course, strong dreamlike elements in *The Water Babies*, his most famous book.

## *Scientific Romancers*

Other writers are generally a little more honest, either with themselves or with others, about the contributions dreams have made to their creativity. In some cases, one suspects that they have actually overstated the importance of dreams. Clearly this is not the place to go into lengthy discussions of a hundred ghastly stories ending: 'I awoke. It had all been only a dream.' Nevertheless, one particular case is of especial interest: that of Johannes Kepler.

A towering figure in the history of astronomy, Kepler was also the author of a curious little work called *Somnium* ('The Dream'), which was published posthumously, in 1634. As early as 1593 he had written a dissertation in which he demonstrated what would be seen by an observer situated on the Moon, according to the then-new Copernican Theory (that the planets went around the Sun). In about 1609 Kepler recast his material in semi-fictional form, his narrator being transported to the Moon by a demon which his mother had conjured up. The manuscript of this version was stolen soon afterwards, and not much later Kepler's own mother was on trial for witchcraft; the two facts are possibly not unrelated.

The version which has come down to us was prepared in the 1620s, during which decade Kepler also added to it extremely extensive notes – taken together, the notes are substantially longer than the main text itself.

Kepler writes that, some time during 1608, he fell asleep and dreamt that he was reading a book he'd got at a fair. It is the narrator of *this* book whose mother conjured up the demon! – there, that foiled the witch-hunters. Most of the account thereafter makes it clear that Kepler was merely using the format of a dream-fiction in order to 'sweeten the pill' of the astronomy he was expounding.

Most of all, but not all. Before the mother conjured up the demon, we are told of some of the narrator's earlier adventures. He was sold into slavery by his mother; the ship's captain who purchased him then took him on a voyage. In due course the boat ended up in Denmark, where the narrator was stranded, with the instruction that he was to take a message to the great astronomer Tycho Brahe.[21] Leaving Tycho after a few years, our hero returned home to find his mother contrite – as well she should have been. After this, she conjured up the demon.

This opening section of *Somnium* is in stark contrast to the rest of the book, which sticks pretty closely to its astronomical subject matter. Even when Kepler talks of lunar inhabitants and their society, his speculations are strictly rational ones (for his day) rather than carefree fictions. Why should he have chosen to open his book with such a fantastic sequence of events? One has the sneaking suspicion that they did, perhaps, come from a genuine dream.

One interesting additional point: On her reunion with her son, the witch-mother says that 'now she was ready to die, since she was leaving behind a son who would inherit her knowledge, the only thing she possessed'. Tycho is reported to have died saying: 'Oh that it may not appear that I have lived in vain.' Kepler inherited Tycho's knowledge in the shape of the complete records of the most accurate and extensive series of observations that had ever been undertaken, and so Tycho did not live in vain. The parallel is a curious one.

Jules Verne, a science-fiction writer from a rather later age, used the dream framework in his *Hector Servadac* (1877), although it is not until the end of the book that the reader is told that all the preceding adventures have been merely a dream. The reader might, however, have already had a suspicion that this was the case: as Verne's biographer and grandson, Jean Jules-Verne, comments rather acidly, 'the basic hypothesis is so unlikely that the reader suspects from the outset that it will all turn out to be somebody's dream'. The hypothesis in question is that a comet has a grazing collision with the Earth and carries off into space a small stretch of land, complete with its occupants. They whiz around the cosmos in cheerful Vernean style.[22]

Others of his books may have been born from dreams – perhaps not specific dreams, but just a general climate of them: nightmares, on the one hand; happy dreams, on the other. Certainly we know that he had dreams about *Around the World in Eighty Days* (1873) while writing it, but it's impossible to tell if the dreams sparked off by the writing of the tale actually affected the future course of the tale. It has been claimed that *Child of the Cavern* (1877) contains deep-seated dream-elements relating to the unrequited passions of his youth, but I find this unconvincing. As you might expect from the title, the whole adventure is set in a great underground cavern – which 'obviously' symbolizes his unconscious, womb or whatever you care to choose (well, perhaps not his womb). In fact, Verne set the story in a cavern because he wanted to explore the idea of a whole community living underground, an idea that was vetoed by his literary agent. Verne therefore made do with a cavern.

Those unrequited passions of his youth which I mentioned did, by the way, affect his dream-life at the time. When he was infatuated with his cousin Caroline Tronson he noted that 'She has been in my dreams more than once'. She married someone else. Soon afterwards, so did Herminie Arnault-Grossetière, with whom he had also been infatuated.[23] This sparked off a dream which he described in a letter to his mother (dated 30th July, 1848). The bride and groom are in the bridal chamber, doing what people generally do in bridal chambers, and

> . . . all that dark night long, a man in rags and tatters had sharpened his teeth on the door knocker. Ah, my dear mother, this dreadful idea woke me up with a bound – and now your letter informs me that my dream was true! What misfortunes I foresee! Poor fellow! But I shall always say, 'Forgive him, father, for he knows not what he does.' Personally, I shall console myself by killing the first black cat I meet![24]

## *A Strong Infusion of Dreams*

Kingsley said that dreams played little part in his writing, but he was a liar. Kepler and Verne used the notion of dreams in their imaginative works, but it seems that real dreams had at best only a mild influence. (The same appears to be true of the British writer Christopher Priest, although one of his novels is called *A Dream of Wessex* – published in the USA under the hideous title *The Perfect Lover* – and he has written also the 'Dream Archipelago' series of stories.)

As we have seen, however, dreams play a major role in the creativity of many writers who are far from unwilling to admit it. One such is the British novelist Graham Greene – even if he did not confess the importance to him of his dreams one would suspect it. In his *The Ministry of Fear* (1943), for example, virtually an entire chapter – 'Between Sleeping and Waking' – early in the book is taken up with an extended description of a dream sequence, a description which rings true.

The protagonist, who years ago murdered his ill wife in a 'mercy killing', is fleeing through the London Blitz, believing that he is being sought by the police in connection with a quite different murder, one which he most certainly hasn't committed. He takes cover in an air-raid shelter, and when he sleeps he finds himself to be a boy again, in a childhood garden with his mother, trying desperately to tell her that he has killed his wife. Her sole response, however insistent he becomes, is: 'My little boy couldn't kill anyone.' He tries to tell her about the Blitz, about the shattering of the world she had known in her lifetime, but she cannot believe him.

And the scene shifts to a field, where he is putting a wounded rat out of its misery by clobbering it with a cricket bat: the nurse who catches him in the act thinks he is indulging in a fit of juvenile sadism.

And the scene shifts to find him in a lane, filled with all the gaucherie of young love, waiting for a girl who doesn't come.

And in the end he is urged by a policeman – who speaks in a woman's voice – to go to where a rat lies bleeding in a urinal, a place 'where even the ground whined when he pressed it, as if it had learnt the trick of suffering'. When he asks to be allowed to go home, the policeman tells him that this *is* home, that there is nowhere else. He cannot move: he cannot bear to hurt the ground any further.

This sequence – of anxiety dream transmuting into nightmare – while it bears the signs of Greene's conscious artistry, could have been written only by a dreamer. It is, of course, impossible to tell to what extent it is based on any particular dream or dreams of Greene himself . . . although there are traces in it of his own childhood experiences, as readers of his *A Sort of Life* (1971) will find. If more evidence of the importance of his dreams were required, the very fact that he should devote to this dream-sequence so much of what is otherwise a more conventional (and excellent) thriller should, in itself, be conclusive.

It's curious how, in the mind of a creative artist, real life can be percolated through the medium of the dream to produce something quite different; this 'something quite different' can, by reason of its dissemination in printed or other form, in turn affect real life. In Greene's early days as a writer, when he had had a few novels accepted but was still as often as not receiving rejection letters, and when financial disaster was rearing its ugly head yet again, he had a typical anxiety-dream. He had been sent to prison for five years; there was no escape. The dream carried over into consciousness: he awoke with the sad thought in his mind that he would not be living with his wife again until she had passed the age of thirty.[25]

This dream, he tells us, was the germ of his novel *It's a Battlefield*. The novel was accepted, and the very worries which had produced the dream in the first place were dissipated. I am constantly expecting, with excited apprehension, a creative dream which will have this powerful effect.

Hopping backwards in time some two and a half centuries, we come across another creative dreamer who is in many ways very like Greene – although their actual literary output could hardly be more different. The dreamer in question is the 'Immortal Dreamer' himself, John Bunyan. Before we look at his dreams, we must swiftly skip through some biographical data in order to make sense of what follows.

A tinker by trade, Bunyan entered the Bedford separatist church of John Gifford in about 1655; the sect was rather like the Baptist church, perhaps even more like the modern Congregationalist churches, in tone. Gifford's church, and Bunyan himself, were frequently at loggerheads with the Quakers, since both groups appealed to roughly the same section of the populace. In modern commercial terms, the squabbles were over the fair division of the market.

With the Restoration there came a crackdown on separatist churches; and on 12th November, 1660, Bunyan was brought before the local magistrates, charged with holding a service along lines not in accordance with those approved by the Church of England. Owing to his refusal to promise that he would not repeat his dastardly crime, Bunyan was sent to Bedford Jail, where he was left to rot from January, 1661, until March, 1672, and Charles II's Declaration of Indulgence to the Nonconformists. During this long period in prison, Bunyan probably began his *The Pilgrim's Progress from This World to That Which is to Come*.[26]

In his autobiography, *Grace Abounding to the Chief of Sinners* (1666), Bunyan tells us of his dissolute youth, and makes especial mention of the nightmares which plagued him during his early years. These must have made a tremendous impression on him, for there is a vividness about his recollections, nearly thirty years later, of not so much the *contents* of the dreams but the powerful feelings they engendered in him.

> Yea, so setled and rooted was I in these things [his youthful sins], that they became as a second Nature to me; the which, as I also have with soberness considered

since, did so offend the Lord, that even in my childhood he did scare and affright me with fearful dreams, and did terrifie me with dreadful visions. For often, after I had spent this and the other day in sin, I have in my bed been greatly afflicted, while asleep, with the apprehensions of Devils, and wicked spirits, who still, as I then thought, laboured to draw me away with them; of which I could never be rid.

Also I should at these years be greatly afflicted and troubled with the thoughts of the day of Judgment, and that both night and day, and should tremble at the thoughts of fearful torments of Hell-fire; still fearing that it would be my lot to be found at last amongst those Devils and Hellish Fiends, who are there bound down with the chains and bonds of eternal darkness.

These things, I say, when I was but a childe, about nine or ten years old, did so distress my Soul, that then in the midst of my many sports and childish vanities, amidst my vain companions, I was afflicted in my mind therewith, yet could I not let go my sins: yea, I was so overcome with despair of Life and Heaven, that then I should often wish, either that there had been no Hell, or that I had been a Devil; supposing they were onely tormentors; that if it must needs be, that I indeed went thither, I might be rather a tormentor, than tormented my self.

A while after, these terrible dreams did leave me . . .

Since Bunyan was only eight or nine years old at the time, and hence capable (one assumes) of only the most minor of sins, one can't help feeling that in this instance at least the Almighty was being a trifle harsh with the lad.

As far as the contents of the dreams are concerned, we

can guess something of them from a passage which appears quite early in *The Pilgrim's Progress*. (The work as a whole was, of course, ostensibly a dream.[27]) At the House of the Interpreter, Christian sees many wonderful things and meets, among others, the Man in the Iron Cage of Despair and a character dubbed by Bunyan (in Part II of the work) 'the Dreamer'. He tells Christian and the Interpreter about his dream, which is packed with the imagery referred to in the section I've quoted from *Grace Abounding*:

> This night as I was in my sleep, I Dreamed, and behold the Heavens grew exceeding black; also it thundered and lightned in most fearful wise, that it put me into an Agony. So I looked up in my Dream, and saw the Clouds rack at an unusual rate, upon which I heard a great sound of a Trumpet, and saw also a Man sit upon a Cloud, attended with the thousands of Heaven; they were all in flaming fire, also the Heavens was on a burning flame.
>
> I heard then a voice, saying, *Arise ye Dead, and come to Judgment*; and with that the Rocks rent, the Graves opened, and the Dead that were therein came forth; some of them were exceeding glad, and looked upward; and some sought to hide themselves under the Mountains: Then I saw the Man that sat upon the Cloud, open the Book; and bid the World draw near. Yet there was by reason of a Fiery flame that issued out and came from before him, a convenient distance betwixt him and them, as betwixt the Judge and the Prisoners at the Bar.
>
> I heard it also proclaimed to them that attended on the Man that sat on the Cloud, *Gather together the Tares, the Chaff, and Stubble, and cast them into the burning Lake*; and with that the Bottomless pit opened,

just whereabout I stood; out of the mouth of which there came in an abundant manner Smoak, and Coals of fire, with hideous noises.

It was also said to the same persons *Gather my wheat into my Garner*. And with that I saw many catch'd up and carried away into the Clouds, but I was left behind. I also sought to hide my self, but I could not; for the Man that sat upon the Cloud, still kept his eye upon me: my sins also came into mind, and my Conscience did accuse me on every side. Upon this I awaked from my sleep.

On the one hand, it would be all too easy to dismiss this description as a mere concoction of Biblical imagery produced in order to make a religious point – and, indeed, there is about it something more than slightly reminiscent of the more lurid pages of *Revelation*. On the other hand, such a dismissal would probably be a mistake: there is too much here of the genuine nightmare.

We can imagine the young Bunyan, in his waking hours bombarded from all sides by the more theatrical and less contemplative aspects of Christianity. There he is, tossing and turning on his bed as his unconscious tries to make what it can of the threats of hellfire, the grossly exaggerated juvenile naughtinesses, and the inability to understand a spiritual law beyond that of vengeance and retribution. Collect together a bundle of the resulting nightmares, and you're bound to end up with something very like the description Bunyan gives us through the lips of 'the Dreamer'. Add to that the exact description of the anxiety state which often immediately precedes the end of a nightmare – 'my Conscience did accuse me on every side' – and you have fairly convincing proof that Bunyan is describing his nightmares to us.

## *Monsters Made Flesh*

We must discuss a further couple of creative dreamers before we look at some of the 'inventive dreamers' who have made scientific breakthroughs or technological advances. At that point we will be able to look at the results of our survey and perhaps draw some conclusions about the nature of creative dreaming.

The first of these two dreamers is Rudyard Kipling.[28] He was an unusual, rather schizophrenic man, and so it is hardly surprising that his dream-life – more specifically, his nightmare-life – was a fairly active one. He frequently exhibited signs of being frightened of the opposite sex – an attitude which surfaces in such writings as 'The Man Who Would Be King' (in *The Phantom Rickshaw*, 1888), where a man achieves godhood among a remote tribe only to lose his life when he insists on taking a wife, who vengefully demonstrates his mortality.

The same adolescent fear of women is to be found in the recurrence in his work of fey 'dream-girls', feminine ideals who were infinitely appealing and yet untouchable. The original of these 'dream-girls' was possibly Flo Garrard, his childhood sweetheart, who throughout his life was a candle to his moth. In his letters to his female friends (and to some others who he wished to ensure remained close), it is interesting to note that his handwriting actually changed discernibly to become more like theirs. In the light of all this, his dream sex-life must have been odd; unfortunately we can't say any more than that.

As I've hinted, throughout his life he was tormented by those evil siblings, insomnia and the nightmare. One recurring nightmare – of a sightless face which pursued him silently – found its expression in his rather disturbing little horror story, 'At the End of the Passage' (in *Life's*

*Handicap*, 1891). Four men are playing cards, somewhere in colonial India. The host is clearly in a bad way: he confesses that he has been troubled by the nightmare of the sightless face, and that he is convinced that one day soon it will catch him and that then he will die.

However, his guests have imperative duties elsewhere, and so they can't hang around to look after him. When they return for another bout of cards the following week they find him (predictably) dead, his eyes staring in horror. One of the party photographs the dead man's eyes, and is shocked by what he finds imprinted on them – a reference to the old theory that the eyes of the dead retain the final image seen before death. While this additional bonus bucketful of horror is, of course, silly (and Kipling must have known it to be so), it is certainly true that people can quite literally be scared to death,[29] and there seems no reason to believe that nightmares cannot do the scaring. It is a very old joke that this matter is hard to prove.

Another nightmare-tale is 'In the Same Boat' (in *A Diversity of Creatures*, 1917). Here two people are able to conquer their recurring terror by telling each other about their experience of it, and by the sheer effort of their wills. Curiously, Kipling casts the nightmare almost as a character in the story, as something external which torments the two.

The paranormal infests much of Kipling's work, and so it comes as something of a surprise to learn that he was generally fairly sceptical about its reality – even though he is on record as having had at least one dream which he regarded as precognitive.

He dreamt that he was attending a ceremony, at the end of which a stranger accosted him, saying that he wanted a word with him. Six weeks later, Kipling was attending a war memorial service, and suddenly realized that he was reliving the circumstances of the dream. Sure enough, at the end of the service a stranger came up and accosted him, asking for a brief word.

This would be more interesting were it not for the overwhelming temptation to regard Kipling's account as his rationalization (if that's an appropriate word!) in later life of a particularly powerful experience of *déjà vu*, for which phenomenon there are, of course, non-psychic explanations. However, even if this is indeed the case, the important point is that Kipling *believed* that the dream had been precognitive – hence the oddness of his scepticism about matters paranormal.

There is a dreamlike quality about much of Kipling's work, notably in the books for which he is probably best remembered today – those books which, while ostensibly for children, are quite deliberately aimed at adults as well: *The Jungle Book* (1894), *The Second Jungle Book* (1895), *The Just-So Stories* (1902) and *Puck of Pook's Hill* (1906). It is less overt in the almost equally famous *Stalky & Co.* (1899) and *Kim* (1901), although you can discern in both of them a strong element of wish-fulfilment which, if it was not born from dreams proper, must have had its roots in fancies and daydreams. It is possible that the enigmatic nature of the 'voices' which Kipling used throughout his writing – for only rarely does Kipling himself play the part of narrator – is largely a result of the indefinite boundary in his life between the dream-world and reality.

We have talked about some of the most famous of creative dreams as well as about some of the more obscure. The two most famous dreams we have so far encountered have been Coleridge's non-dream of 'Kubla Khan' and Stevenson's nightmare which gave rise to *Dr Jekyll and Mr Hyde*. There is a third creative dream which is at least as well known as these two, and which has probably had more of an effect on Western popular culture than both of them put together. It is, of course, Mary Shelley's dream which gave rise to *Frankenstein*.

It all happened in 1816, when the Shelleys were staying near Byron and one of his mistresses, Claire (Jane) Clairmont. One night, at Byron's Villa Diodati, when the company – the Shelleys, Byron, Clairmont and Dr William Polidori (who was madly in love with Mary) – had been reading the French translations of some German horror stories, Byron leapt up and cried that all present should write a ghost story. He added, to Mary: 'You and I will publish ours together.'

Byron's, Polidori's and Percy Shelley's stories all came to nothing, although Shelley became demonstratively nervous about anything to do with the occult. On 18th June, 1816, Byron recited Coleridge's 'Christabel' to such effect that Shelley ran from the room screaming, later confessing to Mary that he had hallucinated that she was naked, with eyes in place of her nipples.

Despite – or perhaps even because of? – Byron's rather patronizing remark to her, it was of course Mary who produced the only horror story to come out of the exercise. We all know that it was born as a result of a nightmare; here is her own description of it.

> My imagination, unbidden, possessed and guided me, gifting the successive images that arose in my mind with a vividness far beyond the usual bounds of reveries. I saw with shut eyes, but acute mental vision – I saw the pale student of unhallowed arts kneeling beside the thing he had put together – I saw the hideous phantasm of a man stretched out, and then, on the working of some powerful engine, show signs of life, and stir with an uneasy, half-vital motion. Frightful must it be; for supremely frightful would be the effect of any human

endeavour to mock the stupendous mechanism of the Creator of the world. His success would terrify the artist; he would rush away from his odious handiwork, horror-stricken. He would hope that, left to itself, the slight spark of life which he had communicated would fade; that this thing which had received such imperfect animation would subside into dead matter, and he might sleep in the belief that the silence of the grave would quench forever the transient existence of the hideous corpse which he had looked upon as the cradle of life. He sleeps; but he is awakened; he opens his eyes; behold, the horrid thing stands at his bedside, opening his curtain and looking on him with yellow, watery, but speculative eyes.

I opened mine in horror. The idea so possessed my mind that a thrill of fear ran through me, and I wished to exchange the ghastly image of my fancy for the realities around. I see them still: the very room, the dark parquet, the closed shutters with the moonlight struggling through, and the sense I had that the glassy lake and the white high Alps were beyond. I could not so easily get rid of my hideous phantom; still it haunted me. I must try to think of something else. I recurred to my ghastly story – my tiresome, unlucky ghost story! Oh! If I could only contrive one which might frighten my reader as I myself had been frightened that night!

Swift as light and cheering was the idea that broke in upon me. 'I have found it! What terrified me will terrify others; and I need only describe the spectre which had haunted my midnight pillow.' On the morrow I announced that I had thought of a story . . .

And describe that spectre she did in her novel *Frankenstein: or, The Modern Prometheus*, which was published in 1818 and is to this day probably the most famous horror novel in the English language – with the possible exception of Bram Stoker's *Dracula* (1897) – and, indeed, one of the most famous novels in the English language. The story (or, more accurately, adaptations thereof) has been filmed countless times, with the monster, nameless in the novel, generally taking on the name of its creator. The extent to which the monster has entered popular mythology can be judged by the fact that in some movies, although the name 'Frankenstein' occurs in the title, neither the monster nor the scientist makes an appearance.[30]

All this from the nightmare of a young woman. Well, not quite: you have to remember that any of us could have had the nightmare; it was the genius of the young woman that turned the nightmare into a whole branch of modern mythology.

I know of only one example of dreaming producing a political speech. The dreamer was Senator Chauncey Depew.

In 1898 Depew was scheduled to give the nomination speech at the Republican Convention for Theodore Roosevelt's bid to become Governor of New York. A few days before the speech was due to be delivered, Depew was relaxing in his chair on his verandah when he dozed off and dreamt that he was at the convention. The chairman called him to give his speech in support of Roosevelt, and he rose to deliver one of his finest performances. The applause was ecstatic. On awakening, Depew rushed to his study and swiftly wrote down the speech he had just dream-delivered; and sure enough he gave it to an enthusiastic reception at the convention a few days later.

Some fans of the paranormal regard Depew's dream as precognitive, and claim that in it he saw all sorts of details of the convention (e.g., the chairman's face) which he could not possibly have known in advance. This is unverifiable. However, if it was indeed true, we have a lovely little example of a timeloop at work. (A timeloop is one of the hypothetical temporal paradoxes which are generally taken to indicate that time travel and its mental equivalent, precognition, cannot occur.) If you think about it, Depew's dream only came true because he had had the dream; had he not dreamt about the scene, he would have delivered a (presumably) quite different speech. If Depew didn't write the speech, and if the dream really was precognitive, then *who did*? Answer that question according to your own tastes.

## *Inventive Dreamers and Dream Discoveries*

Closely allied to creative dreaming, as I've already remarked, is 'inventive dreaming', in which the dreamer solves a problem in such a way that the result is a new invention or discovery.

Problem-solving in dreams is not uncommon. Almost always the problems are personal, of interest solely to the dreamer. Pat Simpson, for example, dreamt '. . . about helping people as I am a Christian worker and was worried about not being able to help *non* Christians. When I awoke a word was in my mind . . .' The word was 'surreptitiously' – but just before you dismiss this problem-solving as trivial, you ought to realize that Simpson *did not know the meaning of the word 'surreptitiously'*.[31]

In the field of dream discoveries and inventions, unlike other creative dreaming, the emotions don't seem to be playing a part, so it's rather difficult to explain glibly *why* so many dream inventions should prove, when subjected to a wakeful eye in the morning, to be so silly. I think it may well be because there *is* an emotion involved, the 'Amn't I a clever boy?' emotion (which is akin to, but not identical with, pride). In our dream we think to ourselves 'This great discovery was made by me!' This exultant thrill takes us over in an extremely exaggerated way, so we treat the discovery that apples fall as cosmic, and think not at all about any deductions that could be made from our observation. And some of the discoveries can be bizarre indeed, as a number of examples from drug-induced dreams show. One drugged experimenter discovered the ultimate secret of life, the Universe and everything, and wrote it down. When he came out from under the influence, he excitedly leapt to consult his piece of paper. He read: 'Please flush after using.'

William James had the same sort of experience using nitrous oxide, and made the cosmos-busting discovery that

> Higgamus, hoggamus,
> Woman's monogamous.
> Hoggamus, higgamus,
> Man is polygamous.

In a similar vein, Winston Churchill dreamt an important discovery and wrote it down. In the morning he discovered that the whole world was suffused with the smell of turpentine. Archbishop Benson dreamt that he had been made Poet Laureate and was reciting his latest creation to Queen Victoria. It was a fine poem, and as he awoke he was still reciting it. The surviving couplet is

> Your latest atmospheric device
> Is all composed of dust and lice.

William Morris could remember only the first line of his similar work of genius: 'The moonlight slept on a treacle sea.'

So much for that. But in his *Powers of Mind* (1975), which contains two of the examples quoted above (among others), Adam Smith cites an experience of his own which is rather more complicated. Under the influence of a drug, he realized at last how the Universe is constructed, and he carefully drew a molecule of DNA. Of course, when he 'awoke', it didn't take long to find out that what he'd drawn wasn't a DNA molecule – he was, after all, no chemist.

But there was something astonishing. What he had drawn *was* a molecule – of a plastic called Delrin (trade name). From what dim recess of his brain had he lugged the molecular structure of a chemical he'd barely, if at all, heard of? Moreover, had it not been for the accident of time that someone else had discovered the stuff first, his would have been a quite significant dream discovery.

Or would it? Probably not. Smith's own view – and he's almost certainly correct – is that a diagram of it appeared in some book or magazine he'd once read. Although he hadn't looked at the diagram, his unconscious had spotted it out of the corner of his eye and stored it away for later reference. Then, by coincidence or otherwise, his subconscious had spurted the diagram into his dream.

However, although the majority of dream creativity is fairly dire, on occasion a masterpiece is produced; and exactly the same is true of dream discovery. For example, the great biologist Louis Agassiz (1807–1873) had a problem with a fossil fish: only part of the fish's body was visible, and he was having some difficulty working out his reconstruction of the rest of it. The really maddening part was that the rest of the creature was probably present in the rock in fossil form, but he didn't want to risk destroying those parts by employing the 'Grant technique of fossil analysis'; *viz.*, hitting the thing with a hammer and seeing what happens.

Agassiz eventually put the problem from his mind and went on to other things. However, a little later he dreamt of the body of the fish in its entirety. Unfortunately, he was unable to remember the details of his dream on awakening. This time he was more convinced that the answer was lurking in his subconscious, and put paper and pen by his bedside. Sure enough, the dream came back to him the following night, and he was able to scribble down the reconstruction as seen in his dream. As you might expect – because I wouldn't be telling the story otherwise – the dream proved to be correct.

The tale is told in the biography of Agassiz written by his widow and, as far as I can establish, nowhere else. There's no reason to doubt her word, of course; but I have the suspicion that she elaborated the details a little – quite unconsciously. However, we can probably be fairly certain that Agassiz was much helped by his dream, which presumably drew together fragments of observation recorded by his brain just below the conscious level.

We can be more precise about four other famous dream discoveries: the dreamers were Kekulé, Loewi, Hilprecht and Howe.[32,33]

Friedrich August Kekulé von Stradonitz was a major figure in the history of chemistry. His first major contribution concerned the way in which atoms join onto each other, most notably the atoms of the element carbon, which element is the fundamental one for life as we know it.

Carbon, as Kekulé showed, has four bonds; more correctly, it has a valency of 4. It is, therefore, capable of bonding with 4 hydrogen atoms (hydrogen has a valency of 1 – $CH^4$ is methane), 2 oxygen atoms (oxygen's valency is 2 – $CO^2$ is of course carbon dioxide), and so forth.

More importantly, he pointed out that by *joining into each other*, using 1, 2 or 3 of their available bonds, carbon atoms could become the backbones of long chain molecules.

Additionally, isomers – pairs of compounds with the same chemical composition but quite different chemical properties – could now be explained quite simply. For example, both dimethyl ether and ethyl alcohol have the same apparent formula, $C^2H^5OH$, but their structural formulae reveal that they are in fact quite different substances: simplified, the two formulae are $CH^3$-O-$CH^3$ (dimethyl ether) and $CH^3$-$CH^2$-OH (ethyl alcohol).

All this was important enough, but Kekulé's most significant contribution to science, the discovery that carbon atoms could form not only chain but *ring* molecules, came to him in a dream. The structure of benzene (and other so-called 'unsaturated' molecules) had been causing chemists great difficulty. $C^6H^6$ was the formula – but it just didn't seem that you could make a workable chain molecule out of it. Kekulé was working hard on the problem when he had his dream – several versions of which are to be found in the popular scientific folklore. Many have him sitting on a 'bus, dozing off; but here, to settle all the arguments, is Kekulé's own version:

> . . . my mind was elsewhere. I turned the chair to the fireplace and fell half-asleep. Again the atoms gambolled in front of my eyes. Smaller groups this time kept modestly in the background. My mind's eye, trained by repeated visions of the same sort, now distinguished larger formations, of various shapes. Long chains . . . everything in the movement, twisting and turning like snakes. And look: what was that? One snake grabbed its own tail, and mockingly the shape

whirled before my eyes. I awoke as if struck by lightning; this time again I spent the rest of the night working out the consequences.

The snake swallowing its tail. What had been suddenly revealed to him was that the structure of the benzene molecule is

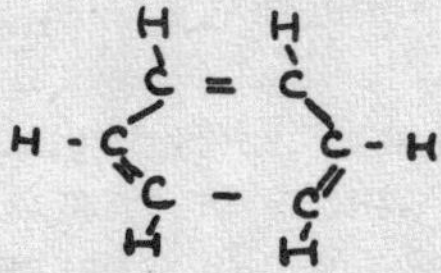


In other words, the carbon (C) atoms are capable of bonding together in such a way as to form a ring, with the hydrogen atoms clinging on around the edges. This was an astonishing conceptual leap, and its significance to organic chemistry cannot be exaggerated: there is a good chance that you, the reader, would not have survived to read this book had it not been for Kekulé's dream breakthrough.

Otto Loewi's breakthrough was a more modest one, in terms of its repercussions, but nevertheless it was significant. He shared with the British biologist Sir Henry Hallett Dale the 1936 Nobel Prize for Physiology or Medicine for their work in elucidating the chemical nature of the transmission of nerve impulses.

In 1771 the Italian anatomist Luigi Galvani had discovered serendipitously that the transmission of nerve impulses is electrical in nature: this he had discovered by applying electric currents to frogs' legs and watching them twitch. However, Loewi was convinced that chemical reactions were involved in the process, too: the problem was, how could he experimentally prove it? The answer came to him in 1921 in a dream – but there was a complication.

> . . . I awoke, turned on the light, and jotted down a few notes on a tiny slip of thin paper. Then I fell asleep again. It occurred to me at six o'clock in the morning that during the night I had written down something most important, but I was unable to decipher the scrawl.

This is the sort of thing that's constantly happening. We make these fantastic discoveries, but . . . In fact, of course, it's one of the clichés of dream-lore that, if you don't take care to write down or tape-record your dream as soon as you awake, you're very likely to forget it. That said, it's generally assumed to be the act of writing/recording that helps you remember the dream, not the being able to read or listen to what you've written or said. Still, in Loewi's case, all was fortunately not lost:

> The next night, at three o'clock, the idea returned. It was the design of an experiment to determine whether or not the hypothesis of chemical transmission that I had uttered seventeen years ago was correct. I got up immediately, went to the laboratory, and performed a single experiment on a frog heart according to the nocturnal design.[34]

By five o'clock that morning, the experiment was done and the point proved. He had taken two frog hearts and filled one with Ringer solution; he stimulated the vagus nerve of this heart (an action which causes the beating of the heart to slow down). He then transferred the Ringer solution to the other heart, which

> slowed and its beats diminished just as if its vagus had been stimulated. Similarly, when the accelerator nerve was stimulated and the Ringer from this period transferred, the second heart speeded up and its beats increased. These results unequivocally proved that the

> nerves do not influence the heart directly but liberate from their terminals specific chemical substances which, in their turn, cause the well known modifications of the function of the heart characteristic of the stimulation of its nerves.

Loewi called the chemical he had discovered 'vagus matter', *Vagusstoff*; Dale shared the Nobel Prize with him because he was able to show that *Vagusstoff* was in fact acetylcholine, a compound which he had isolated from the fungus ergot. It is depressing to note that Loewi, a Jew, was allowed to leave Austria (he was working at the University of Graz) to receive his Nobel Prize only on condition that he turn over the cash part of it to the Nazis. This was better than it could have been: for a while, because of his Jewishness, he'd been under sentence of death. After working for a few years in Britain he went to the United States, becoming a naturalized citizen in 1946. There he lived until his death in 1961.

Although the dream-revelation of Professor Herman Volrath Hilprecht (1859–1925) is at a somewhat lower level than the ones we've been considering, it has nevertheless acquired a certain fame because the story is such a fascinating one.

Hilprecht was an archaeologist. The team working at the temple of Bel at Nippur had asked him to decipher the inscriptions on two agate fragments which seemed to be from two separate finger-rings (the two fragments were of different colours). Hilprecht wrestled hard with the problem, but got approximately nowhere: the best he could do was to tentatively date one of them to the period 1700–1100 B.C. – not very accurate!

This was the situation right up until Hilprecht had corrected the final proofs of his book on the expedition's discoveries. That night he dreamt that a Nippur priest came to him and took him to the temple's treasure chamber. The priest then told him:

> The two fragments which you have published separately upon pages 22 and 26 belong together, are not finger-rings, and their history is as follows: King Kurigalzu once sent to the temple of Bel, among other articles of agate and lapis lazuli, an inscribed votive cylinder of agate. Then we priests suddenly received the command to make for the statue of the god Ninib a pair of ear-rings of agate; we were in great dismay, since there was no agate as raw material at hand. In order to carry out the command there was nothing for us to do but cut the votive cylinder into three parts, thus making three rings, each of which contained a portion of the original inscription. The first two rings served as ear-rings for the statue of the god; the two fragments which have given you so much trouble are portions from them. If you will put the two together you will find confirmation of my words. But the third ring you have not found in the course of your excavations, and you never will find it.

Immediately Hilprecht bounded out of bed and told his wife all about his dream 'that I might not forget it'. The following morning he looked at the drawings of the fragments from which he'd been working, and was astonished to find that the evidence there supported his dream. (It's a little surprising that he was astonished. You'd have thought the first thing to spring to his mind would have been that his unconscious had been doing some detective work based on precisely that evidence.) However, there was one major difficulty: although he had never seen the fragments themselves, it was quite certain that they were of different colours. How could this be, if both had been cut from the same votive cylinder?

A while later he was in Constantinople, in whose Imperial Museum the fragments were kept. The two were indeed of different colours – in fact, they'd been classified quite separately – but when he was allowed to handle them Hilprecht discovered that they did fit together: their different colours arose from veining in the original agate. His dream-priest had told him the truth; or, to put it another way, his unconscious mind had said to him, 'Elementary, my dear Watson', and proceeded to explain everything.

In strictly scientific terms, Elias Howe's dream invention is disappearingly trivial when placed alongside the discoveries of, say, Loewi and Kekulé. In practical terms, so far as the everyday consumer is concerned, his invention was, however, of colossally greater importance:[35] it was the first practicable sewing-machine, which he patented in 1846. Oddly enough, at first no one was much interested in the device in his homeland, the United States, and so he travelled to Britain, where he sold the patent rights for a modest sum. In direst poverty, he returned to the States in 1849 to find that other people were marketing sewing-machines based largely on his design; one such was Isaac Merrit Singer. After a tedious battle through the courts, Howe's claim was vindicated in 1854; royalties were paid to him for every sewing-machine manufactured. Naturally, in due course he became a very rich man.

He claimed that for years he had been trying without success to invent a sewing-machine; like everyone else, he had been thinking in terms of the conventional needle, which has its hole at the blunt(er) end. One night he dreamt that he had been captured by a savage tribe who told him that he would be speared to death unless, within twenty-four hours, he could produce a working sewing-machine.

As the deadline approached, the dreaming Howe grew more and more desperate in his search for inspiration, but still he could find no answer to his problem. Finally, the tribesmen raised their spears to kill him . . . and he noticed that near the tip of each spear was a hole.

He woke shivering from his nightmare, but this final impression of the dream was firmly imprinted on his brain. Inspired by it, he very shortly thereafter produced the first working lock-stitch[36] sewing-machine, an invention made possible solely because of his dream-insight that the hole should be at the needle's tip, not at the rear end.

I refuse to make any jokes about his unconscious having tipped him off.

## *The Art of Creative Dreaming*

I have dealt all the cards of my creative-dreamer pack – well, at least, all the ones that I haven't got hidden up my sleeve. Our survey of the field has been an extensive one. Can we begin to draw together the threads from all these tales of dreamers and their dreams and begin to weave together some kind of a tapestry portraying creative dreaming, the art of, as she really is?

First of all, let's look at one of the more trivial – or apparently so! – patterns that have emerged. A sizeable proportion of the creative dreamers we've looked at have been science-fiction writers. This might just be an indication that I'm interested in science fiction, but I don't think so. After all, there's no escaping the fact that Mary Shelley's *Frankenstein* is generally considered to be the first science-fiction novel proper; that Robert Louis Stevenson's *Dr Jekyll and Mr Hyde* was an important, seminal novel in the field; or that Jules Verne was probably the greatest science romancer of all time.[37] The other writers we've considered who've been involved in science fiction are: Ambrose Bierce, Gavin Glaskin, John Grant, Johannes Kepler, Rudyard Kipling, H. P. Lovecraft (I'm being charitable here), Edgar Allan Poe and Mark Twain. Somewhere around the fringes are Taylor Caldwell, Jack Kerouac and the artist Austin Osman Spare.

One could add in fantasists like Charles Kingsley – but there I think one would be clouding the issue. You see, it's easy enough to say that one can expect dreams to produce fantasies – for reasons which are obvious. But science fiction is quite distinct from fantasy. Science fiction has rules whereas fantasy doesn't and dreams don't. Science fiction obeys Sturgeon's 90% law (90% of *everything* is crud), but fantasy requires the related 99% law – *and so do creative dreams*. That this overwhelming preponderance of dreams obeys the 99% law is less than immediately obvious until one thinks about all the 'creative' dreams that have, fortunately, never made it into print.

So why should so many dreams have produced science fiction? To return to a point I've made several times, it's probably because *raw* dreams make lousy fiction. The dream-self and the dream-world simply don't follow the rules that the real self and the real world have to. I can think 'til I'm blue in the face that it would be nice to jump out of my window and float gently upwards, but it won't happen – in the real world. In the dream-world, however, it most certainly could (and, according to the Freudians, in so doing prove something about my sexuality). Similarly, in science fiction – as we've seen – I'd plummet like a stone if I tried the trick in Chapter Six, unless, in Chapter Two, I'd got hold of an antigravity device for some reason. In fantasy, I needn't have the antigravity device: I'd be saved by some *deus ex machina* or other.

If we can think, then, about science fiction as being a sort of fantasy onto which rules have been grafted, we get close to the picture I've painted of the successful creative dreamer. Without the rules – without the intervention of the conscious creative artist – the result is almost certain to be unsatisfying, slightly frustrating . . .

We can take this argument a little further by considering the different functions of the right and left brains.[38] I don't want to plunge into a detailed discussion of the subject here, but in essence we can think of their being two people inside each of us. Inside the left brain lives the conscious 'me', the one that's typing these words. Inside the right brain lives a strangely inarticulate fellow who can only rarely express him- or herself. The right-brain self is not a million miles removed from Freud's notion of the unconscious. Experiments over the last few years have shown that this model of the brain is more than just a model: it seems to be what the brain's actually like (although in some people the sides are reversed, and in a very few cases the sides are, as it were, mixed up together).

Dreaming is a right-brain activity. This primaeval person living inside our brain doesn't have much of a say during our waking hours, so makes the most of it while we're asleep. Since our right-brain selves aren't very good at little things like logic, our dreams likewise flout all known forms of logic; or, occasionally, as with the 'inventive dreamers', they take logical leaps which our left brains would look at with an expression of frank disgust. As examples, we have the mathematician Jacques Hadamard, who often found solutions to problems came to him in a flash as he was awoken, and Albert Einstein, who suddenly and for the first time *understood* the temporal aspect of Relativity while getting out of bed one morning. The right brain makes an important contribution to our fantasy world; it enables us to win money on the races or advance human progress through the logic-hopping medium of the hunch; and it is possibly capable of paranormal feats.[38]

The trouble is that the 'I' who reads the story is the left brain. Among children, who are much more right-brain than adults, fairy tales are extremely popular. Fairy tales are pretty unstructured things – try to discover the *point* of something like 'Cinderella' or, to move a fraction away from fairy tales, 'Goldilocks and the Three Bears' or 'Little Red Riding-Hood'. To left-brain adults the stories are primest piffle (unless filmed by Walt Disney): the popular children's stories among adults are intellectual fantasies like *Alice Through the Looking-Glass* and *The House at Pooh Corner*, or well structured fantasies like *The Lion, the Witch and the Wardrobe* and, just, *The Hobbit*; *The Wind in the Willows* is a related example of the latter category.

As I say, the average adult reader is a left-brain one: he or she finds dream-stories – if rendered plain – illogical, infuriating or just downright nonsensical. In order to be made acceptable to – or interesting to – the reader, the artist has to take his or her right-brain production, the dream, and apply the left brain to it. Over and over again we've seen how creative dreamers – the successful ones – have either done exactly this or have gone through the analogous process of building a story up from a couple of of 'revelatory' scenes which appeared in dreams (as in the examples of *Dr Jekyll and Mr Hyde*, page 91, and *Frankenstein*, page 117).

This is rather a pity. Clearly if we could fuse the ideas from our left and right brains together we'd have a much more *whole* way of looking at the Universe. In a curious kind of a way, this is very much what the modern physicist is asking us to try to do: we can understand something like the quantum theory either in terms of our right brains ('gut-understanding'), and thereby glimpse at the reality, or we can understand it purely in terms of the mathematics involved ('head-understanding'). There is no middle path available . . . *but* there is the possibility of understanding the theory in terms of both gut and head – in other words, in terms of both right brain and left. The same is true of something like Relativity: almost all physical scientists understand it in terms of the maths, but ask them if they *understand* it and most will either admit that they don't or show clear signs that, whatever they say, in fact they don't. A few, however, understand it with both gut and head: they have fused the ideas from their right and left brains.[39]

But this fusion is a rare thing, and it's only rarely realized in terms of the creative dreamer (probably more so in the field of music than elsewhere). The Stevensons, the Shelleys – they're the rare ones. Much more frequent are the Twains, whose dream works would never have got into print had it not been for the fact that he was a famous and *selling* author.

So, what exactly is the nature of creative dreaming? Well, it seems to be a matter of taking something coughed up by the right brain, attracting the attention of the left during one of the few opportunities it has to do so (the dream), and then using the left brain either to hone or to develop the idea passed across by the right brain. Some creative artists seem to have been content simply to take the hints from dreamland and incorporate them into what they were already doing. Others, like Stevenson, have relied very heavily on the productions of dreamland, but have nevertheless realized the crucial value of the left-brain intervention. Yet others, like Lovecraft, have let their unconscious hang out on the line for all to see: all that I can say is that, if you think Lovecraft's works are masterpieces of literature, you're entitled to your opinion.

And yet the mention of Lovecraft brings me to an important aspect of creative dreaming. I think his stories are junk, but nevertheless I recognize that, on occasion, they touch a primitive chord inside me. Just occasionally, while I'm coughing and spitting over the absurd drivel that is supposed to be a tale, I find myself oddly chilled, staring out of the window and thinking to myself, 'It's nonsense, but *what if* . . . ?'[40] In other words, the right brain is in contact with, and can express, some truths which are at the very core of the human experience – whether they be infinitely terrifying or infinitely pleasurable – and these can be made available *to* our left brains without the interpretative censor *of* our left brains. But these truths are isolated things: tell someone that they're going to be eaten alive and they'll be terrified (because the notion of being eaten alive is fundamentally a terrifying one), but tell them they're also going to be flayed, boiled, pickled, hung, strangled, shot, castrated (if relevant), pressed, burnt – and all the other things that human beings tell themselves they're justified in doing to other human beings – and your victim will inevitably giggle. You can only kill them once.

The situation is similar with the outpourings of the right brain. Sticking to very frightening images, the average audience of a horror film today is there only for the laughs: as horrific idea piles upon horrific idea, the whole thing becomes so implausible that the only reaction is laughter. But take movies like *Don't Look Now* and *The Possession of Joel Delaney*. The first took only one and the second only two[41] of the fundamental (right-brain) horrors, yet both scared the average audience silly. The creators involved had taken the nightmare and toned it down so that it was frightening to the waking self, more sceptical than the dream-self.

So the art of creative dreaming is not so much concerned with dreaming itself as with the art of *using* dreams. Tonight I may dream about a man who swallows a chemical and turns into a fiend; but tomorrow it's unlikely that I'll be able to write a seminal novel based on my dream. All successful creative dreamers must needs be artists in their own right; all artists are not necessarily creative dreamers; most creative dreamers are not artists, and therefore their creative dreams go for nothing.

Dreams do not provide a short-cut to genius.

# 3

# *Dreaming Creators*

If there were dreams to sell,
    What would you buy?
Some cost a passing bell;
    Some a light sigh,
That shakes from Life's fresh crown
Only a roseleaf down.
If there were dreams to sell,
Merry and sad to tell,
And the crier rung the bell,
    What would you buy?

– Thomas Lovell Beddoes,
'Dream-Pedlary'

Dreaming, in the literal and metaphorical sense, seems to be an essential part of psychic metabolism – as essential as its counterpart, the formation and automization of habits. Without this daily dip into the ancient sources of mental life we would probably all become desiccated automata. And without the more spectacular exploratory dives of the creative individual, there would be no science and no art.

– Arthur Koestler,
*The Act of Creation*

You will no doubt have noticed a certain vein of frustration running through parts of the preceding chapter. Everyone dreams – whether or not they realize and/or admit it – and creative artists are no exception, yet all too often we are unable to establish a firm relationship between an artist's dream-life and his or her creative output for the simple reason that the dreams were, deliberately or accidentally, allowed to go unrecorded or are otherwise lost to us. The frustration arises because, while we *know* that dreams must have played a part in the creativity of virtually every artist in history (we know this because otherwise artists would be strange beings indeed), we cannot point firmly at every single example of this having happened. We have to use some guesswork.

As a minor digression, it's interesting to note that creative artists are not unanimous in their admission that dreams play a part in the creative process, even if only an indirect one. In a letter dated 1st September, 1843, to his friend Professor Cornelius Conway Felton, no less a writer than Charles Dickens came out with a theory of creative dreaming – or, rather, of its nonexistence . . . a theory which is, quite simply, belied by the facts. Here, slightly repunctuated, is what he had to say on the subject, accompanied by his account of a rather delicious nightmare:

> I very often dream I am in America again; but, strange to say, I never dream of you. I am always endeavouring to get home in disguise, and have a dreary sense of the distance. Apropos of dreams, is it not a strange thing if writers of fiction never dream of their own creations: recollecting I suppose, even in their dreams, that they have no real existence? *I* never dreamed of any of my own characters and I feel it so impossible that I wager Scott never did of his, real as they are.[1]
>
> I had a good piece of absurdity in my head a night or two ago. I dreamed that somebody was dead. I don't know whom, but it's not to the purpose. It was a private gentleman and a particular friend; and I was greatly overcome when the news was broken to me (very delicately) by a gentleman in a cocked hat, top boots, and a sheet. Nothing else.
>
> 'Good God,' I said. 'Is he dead?'

> 'He is as dead, Sir,' rejoined the gentleman, 'as a door-nail. But we must all die, Mr Dickens – sooner or later, my dear Sir.'
>
> 'Ah!' I said. 'Yes. To be sure. Very true. But what did he die of?'
>
> The gentleman burst into a flood of tears, and said, in a voice broken by emotion, 'He christened his youngest child, Sir, with a toasting-fork.'
>
> I was never in my life so affected as at his having fallen a victim to this complaint. It carried a conviction to my mind that he never could have recovered. I knew that it was the most interesting and fatal malady in the world; and I wrung the gentleman's hand in a convulsion of respectful admiration – for I felt that this explanation did equal honour to his head and his heart!

Dickens' refusal to believe in creative dreaming is, however, fairly atypical. Numerous other creative artists have been less definite about the subject, merely ignoring it or, most annoyingly of all, recalling only minor dreams which have had little or no effect on their literary output. Some of these minor dreams can be fun, though; and I'm especially fond of an anxiety dream experienced by the great historian, Lord Macaulay.

> [My younger niece] came to me with a penitential face, and told me that she had a great sin to confess; that Pepys's Diary was all a forgery, and that she had forged it. I was in the greatest dismay. 'What! I have been quoting in reviews, and in my *History*, a forgery of yours as a book of the highest authority. How shall I ever hold up my head again?' I awoke with the fright, poor Alice's supplicating voice still in my ears.

I, too, sincerely hope that Macaulay's niece didn't forge Pepys' diary, because later in this chapter I plan to look at some of the dreams that Pepys recorded there.

A far more pompous gentleman than Macaulay was Samuel Johnson. He, too, had what must have been for him a profoundly nightmarish anxiety-dream. Bennet Langton's account of it is to be found quoted in Boswell's *Life of Samuel Johnson*.

> He related, that he had once in a dream a contest of wit with some other person, and that he was very much mortified by imagining that his opponent had the better of him. 'Now, (said he,) one may mark here the effect of sleep in weakening the power of reflection; for had not my judgement failed me, I should have seen, that the wit of this supposed antagonist, by whose superiority I felt myself depressed, was as much furnished by me, as that which I thought I had been uttering in my own character.'

In other words, the dream served only to reinforce Johnson's conviction that he was a whole lot cleverer than all the rest of us put together.

Skipping nimbly through the genres and the centuries alike, we come across other examples of writers recording their minor dreams but failing to note those which have had a more profound influence on their work. A rather different case is the dream recounted by Agatha Christie in her autobiography – 'rather different' in that this recurring nightmare obviously had a very profound effect on her as a youngster.

In fact, what terrified the child was not a recurring nightmare *per se* but a recurring nightmare-figure who intruded into all sorts of dreams, transforming a straightforward dream into a nightmare simply by making his appearance. She thought of him as 'the Gunman', because he was carrying a musket – although she quite specifically mentions that at no time was she frightened by the thought that he might use this musket on her. He looked like 'a Frenchman in grey-blue uniform, powdered hair in a queue and a kind of three-cornered hat'. A normal happy dream would, often enough, suddenly be disrupted by a deep feeling of unease and the knowledge that there 'was someone – someone *who ought not to be there*' (her italics). Then she'd see 'the Gunman', his eyes would meet hers, and she'd wake up screaming.

In later childhood, the dreams took on a far more sinister character:

> Sometimes, as we sat round a tea-table [in a dream], I would look across at a friend, or a member of the family, and I would suddenly realize that it was *not* Dorothy or Phyllis or Monty, or my mother or whoever it might be. The pale blue eyes in the familiar face met mine – under the familiar appearance. *It was really the Gunman.*

Terrifying enough for an adult: it's no wonder the child woke up screaming.

A nightmare of a rather different ilk befell the great tragic actress Sarah Siddons, who dreamt on one occasion that she was on stage, acting, when all of a sudden her teeth dropped out. The really nightmarish aspect of the whole experience occurred not when she was dreaming but afterwards, when she told a friend about the dream. Don't worry, said the friend: you'll still be a fine actress long after your teeth have *really* fallen out. Cold comfort there. (Many people believe that dreams of teeth falling out foretell imminent death.)

In more recent times, the popular actress and media-dubbed sex symbol Farrah Fawcett-Majors, of 'Charlie's Angels' fame, has talked of one of her nightmares. While appearing during 1983 in an off-Broadway play, as a rape victim bent on exacting violent revenge, she told the press:

> Since taking this part I've had the most amazing dreams. I was in an elevator and two men got in, pressed the 'Hold' button, and told me: 'Take off your clothes.' The main thought going through my head was: 'Don't kill me. I'll take my clothes off. I'll do anything. But please don't kill me.'

Threepence on it that the two men in the elevator were journalists.

Like Siddons and Fawcett-Majors, the writer Sandra Shulman has had nightmares born from her profession. I wonder how many other writers have suffered this particular anxiety-dream, or some version of it:

> I always experience the most uncomfortable dreams whenever a manuscript is due to be delivered to a publisher. The nightmare is set in an editorial office and around a table sit innumerable editors, some whom I know, others quite unfamiliar. They circulate copies of my book and make scathing comments about it and the writer. When eventually I catch a glimpse of what they're reading I understand their scorn: the pages are either quite blank or are covered with 'Jabberwocky' nonsense.

Certainly the poet Gavin Ewart has had something like it – two different versions of the same dream, in fact. In the first, the editor who is to handle his new book turns out to be a middle-aged woman who is President of the Poetry Readers' Association. Her members, she explains, will consider many of the poems in the new collection dangerously pornographic. She takes a foot-long blue pencil and scores through all the offending poems, until only one is left. Ewart describes this poem as being 'about feeding a horse with lumps of sugar'.

The other version of this recurring dream involves the

new editor being an American called Chuck. Chuck has decided that the book needs to be heavily copy-edited – in fact, rewritten. All the difficult words are expunged; references to 'nobodies' like Firbank and Telemann are removed; no line is left more than two words long; and, to add insult to all this injury, Chuck 'criticizes the poems for lack of positive thinking'.

Shulman too is quite accustomed to recurring dreams, it seems. In a letter to me on the subject she cites two others:

> (a) Travelling in a lift which shoots out of the top of the building. I had this dream even before I came to live on the top floor of this block, and every now and then I get the heeby-jeebies while I'm *awake* in the lift.
> (b) I'm in one of those high-ceilinged Regency drawing-rooms on the first or second floor of a house . . . long windows reach from floor to ceiling. I'm holding on to the floor by my fingernails because everything seems to be tipping towards windows which are suddenly unglazed and definitely hazardous.

And one more brief account before we start looking in a little more detail at some of the other dreaming creators. This time it's a very sad little tale. The poet Coventry Patmore (1823–1896), a friend of Tennyson and Ruskin, was the victim of a really vicious trick of his own mind. One night he dreamt that his wife had died; and naturally this filled him with very considerable grief. When he awoke from the nightmare, he lay for a while in the blissful glow of relief that we all experience on discovering that 'Thank God! – it was just a dream!' But a little while later Patmore remembered suddenly that, in reality, his wife *had* died a few weeks earlier . . .

A tragedy for the poet who produced, in *The Angel in the House*, this charming sleep-related stanza:

'I saw you take his kiss!' ''Tis true.'
'O, modesty!' ''Twas strictly kept:
He thought me asleep; at least, I knew
He thought I thought he thought I slept.'

Yes, well . . .

## *Dream-Fictions*

As far back in time as you care to go, literature betrays the fact that, not only did people dreams – as you might expect – but that their dreams were in almost every respect very much like ours are today, a fact which is slightly less obvious. Dreamers are to be found aplenty in the Bible, the most famous being Joseph, whose dream-interpretations we shall encounter in Chapter Five (see pages 288–90). Many writers have used the dream format as a 'frame' for their fantasies or, more often, religious polemics: we have already discussed Bunyan's *Pilgrim's Progress*, and in similar vein there is *The Vision Concerning Piers Plowman*, generally believed (probably wrongly) to have been written between 1360 and 1399 by William Langland. William Morris made extensive use of the 'dream-method' in his work, either overtly or by creating what Jack Lindsay has described as a 'sort of dream-blurring and transposition of time-relationships'. In perhaps his finest work, *Through the Looking -Glass* (1872), Lewis Carroll presents us with the surreal idea that all the characters and events of the books are . . . well, read it for yourself:

'It's only the Red King snoring,' said Tweedledee.

'Come and look at him!' the brothers cried, and they each took one of Alice's hands, and led her up to where the King was sleeping.

'Isn't he a *lovely* sight?' said Tweedledum.

Alice couldn't say honestly that he was. He had a tall red night-cap on, with a tassel, and he was lying crumpled up into a sort of untidy heap, and snoring loud – 'fit to snore his head off!' as Tweedledum remarked.

'I'm afraid he'll catch cold with lying on the damp grass,' said Alice, who was a very thoughtful little girl.

'He's dreaming now,' said Tweedledee: 'and what do you think he's dreaming about?'

Alice said, 'Nobody can guess that.'

'Why, about *you!*' Tweedledee exclaimed, clapping his hands triumphantly. 'And if he left off dreaming about you, where do you suppose you'd be?'

'Where I am now, of course,' said Alice.

'Not you!' Tweedledee retorted contemptuously. 'You'd be nowhere. Why, you're only a sort of thing in his dream!'

'If that there King was to wake,' added Tweedledum, 'you'd go out – bang! – just like a candle!'

'I shouldn't!' Alice exclaimed indignantly. 'Besides, if *I'm* only a sort of thing in his dream, what are *you*, I should like to know?'

'Ditto,' said Tweedledum.

'Ditto, ditto!' cried Tweedledee.

He shouted this so loud that Alice couldn't help saying, 'Hush! You'll be waking him, I'm afraid, if you make so much noise.'

'Well, it's no use *your* talking about waking him,' said Tweedledum, 'when you're only one of the things in his dream. You know very well you're not real.'

'I *am* real!' said Alice, and began to cry.

'You won't make yourself a bit realler by crying,' Tweedledee remarked: 'there's nothing to cry about.'

'If I wasn't real,' Alice said – half-laughing through

> her tears, it all seemed so ridiculous – 'I shouldn't be able to cry.'
>
> 'I hope you don't suppose those are real tears?' Tweedledum interrupted in a tone of great contempt . . .

James Thurber conjures up the spectre of the daydream with wicked ease in 'The Secret Life of Walter Mitty' (included in *My World – And Welcome to It*, 1942). Mitty, nagged by a shrewish wife, escapes into worlds where he is a heroic aircraft pilot, the world's finest surgeon about to save the life of a millionaire, a crack shot coping suavely with the DA while on trial for his life, the bravest fighter pilot of them all . . .

Probably the most remarkable of all dream-fictions is Nathanael West's *The Dream Life of Balso Snell* (1931), a surreal novel which, despite the fact that it is very short, is best not read lightly or when you've got one too many drinks inside you. Even if you're stone-cold sober, it can take quite some little while after reading *Balso Snell* before you can reliably differentiate between fact and fantasy. The same is true of John Franklin Bardin's *Devil Take the Blue-Tail Fly* (1948).

## *The Best That Ever Was Dreamed*

But these are all dream-fictions. They tell us that their creators were only too familiar with dreamland, but they tell us nothing about the dreams themselves. Some writers, however, have been good enough to leave detailed accounts for us in their diaries or letters – the latter, of course, being understandably less frank and more carefully censored than the former.

The very world 'diaries' makes one think almost inevitably of Samuel Pepys, and indeed the great diarist did describe a handful of his dreams for posterity – surprisingly few, in view of the extent to which he recorded the other minutiae of his daily life. Most, but not all, of the dreams he describes step just beyond the confines of good taste; bear with me, however, while I talk briefly about the exceptions first.

Two events in particular caused Pepys to have recurring dreams: the Great Fire of London, in 1666, and the death of his mother, in 1667. His nightmares about the fire were much as you might expect – rapacious conflagration, toppling houses, and the like – and indeed Pepys himself declined to be specific about them. His dreams about his mother are, however, of greater interest. Here is his diary entry, in part, for 29th June, 1667:[2]

> Up, having had many ugly dreams tonight – of my father and my sister and mother's coming to us and meeting my wife and me at the gate of the office going out – they all in laced suits, and come, they told me, to be with me this May-day. My mother told me she lacked a pair of gloves, and I remembered a pair of my wife's in my chamber and resolved she should have them. But then recollected how my mother came to be here and I was in mourning for her; and so thinking it to be a mistake in our thinking her all this while dead [*sic*], I did contrive that it should be said to any that enquired, that it was my mother-in-law, my wife's mother, that was dead and we in mourning for. This dream troubled me and I waked.

Curiously enough, I myself had a very similar sort of dream as a child some while after the death of my father, who died having just addressed a conference far from home. I dreamt that the reports of his death were based purely on a rumour put about by the chatterbox barber whose shop was just up the road from my home. I can vividly remember waking up and, for the first ten minutes or so, having great difficulty in working out whether my father was dead or alive. A sort of converse dream to Coventry Patmore's, in a way.

This was not Pepys' only dream that night. He fell asleep again and dreamt one of several which all have a certain something in common. He dreamt that

> I had great pain of the stone in making water, and that once I looked upon my yard in making water at the steps before my door, and there I took hold of the end of a thing and pulled it out, and it was a turd; and it came into my mind that I was in the same condition with my aunt Pepys, my uncle Robert's wife. And by and by, on the like occasion, I pulled out something and flung [it] on the ground – it looked like slime or snot, and presently it swelled and turned into a gray kind of Bird, and I would have taken it in my hand [had it not] run from me to the corner of the door, going into the garden . . . These dreams did trouble me mightily all night.

Scatological dreams are not uncommon, it seems: we shall encounter more of them when we are discussing other dreamers. Pepys himself seems to have had quite a few. From his entry for 28th May, 1660:

> This night I had a strange dream of bepissing myself, which I really did; and having kicked the clothes off, I got cold and found myself all muck-wet in the morning and had a great deal of pain in making water, which made me very melancholy.

No wonder! From 3rd December, 1661:

> . . . had a very bad night by dreams of my wife's riding with me, and her horse throwing her and breaking her

> leg. And then I dreamt that I had one of my testicles swelled, and in such pain that I waked with it; and had a great deal of pain there a very great while, till I fell asleep again, and such apprehensions I had of it that when I rose and trussed up myself, thinking that it had been no dream – till in the daytime I found myself very well at ease and remembered that I did dream so; and did dream that Mr Creed was with me and that I did complain to him of it, and he said he had the same pain in his left which I had in my right stone – which pleased me much to remember.

From 15th February, 1663:

> This morning my wife did wake me, being frightened with the noise I made in my sleep, being a dream that one our sea-maisters [*sic*] did desire to see the St John's Isle of my [no longer extant] drawing; which methought I showed him, but methought he did handle it so hard that it put me to very horrid pain; and what should this be but my cods, which after I woke were in very great pain for a good while – which what a strange extravagant dream it was.

But Pepys, fortunately for him, had other dreams involving his 'cods' which were of a rather pleasanter nature. Here he is writing about his famous dream of the night of 14th/15th August, 1665:

> . . . something put my last night's dream into my head, which I think is the best that ever was dreamed – which was, that I had my lady Castlemayne in my armes and was admitted to use all the dalliance I desired with her, and then dreamed that this could not be awake but that it was only a dream.[3] But that since it was a dream and that I took so much real pleasure in it, what a happy thing it would be, if when we are in our graves

> (as Shakespeare resembles it), we could dream, and dream but such dreams as this – that then we should not need to be so fearful of death as we are this plague-time.[4]

(The Shakespeare reference is of course to Hamlet's 'To die, to sleep;/To sleep: perchance to dream: ay, there's the rub;/For in that sleep of death what dreams may come/When we have shuffled off this mortal coil,/Must give us pause.')

Erotic dreams seem to have been reasonably frequent experiences for Pepys – but, pleasurable as they might be at the time, they could land him in hot water later. Here he writes on 5th December, 1668, a while after his wife Elizabeth had discovered that he had been having his celebrated affair with Deb Willmott, and had decreed that the dalliance must stop:

> Up, after a little talk with my wife which troubled me, she being ever since our late difference mighty watchful of sleep and dreams, and will not be persuaded but [that] I do dream of Deb, and doth tell me that I speak in my dreams and that this night I did cry 'Huzzy!' and it must be she – and now and then I start otherwise than I used to do, she says; which I know not, for I do not know that I dream of her more than usual, though I cannot deny that my thoughts waking do run now and then, against my will and judgement, upon her, for that only is wanting to undo me, being now in every other thing as to my mind most happy – and may still be so but for my own fault, if I be ketched loving anybody but my wife again.

Elizabeth was not beyond trying to discover hard evidence of his unconscious sins, as we find from his entry for 7th February, 1669:

My wife mighty peevish in the morning about my lying unquietly at nights, and she will have it that it is a late practice, from my evil thoughts in my dreams; and I do often find that in my dreams she doth lay her hand upon my cockerel to observe what she can. And mightily she is troubled about it, but all blew over; and I up and to church, and so home to dinner, where she [was] in a worse fit, which lasted all the afternoon, and shut herself up in her closet; and I mightily grieved and vexed, and could not get her to tell me what ayled her, or to let me into her closet; but at last she did, where I found her crying on the ground, and I could not please her; but I did at last find that she did plainly expound it to me: it was that she did believe me false to her with Jane, and did rip up three or four most silly circumstances, of her [Jane] not rising till I came out of my chamber and letting me thereby see her dressing herself, and that I must needs go into her chamber and was [impotent] with her; which was so silly, and so far from truth, that I could not be troubled at it, though I could not wonder at her being troubled, if she had these thoughts. And therefore she would lie from me, and caused sheets to be put in the blue room and would have Jane to lie with her, lest I should come to her. At last, I did give her such satisfaction, that we were mighty good friends and went to bed betimes, where yo did hazer very well con her, and did this night by chance the first night poner my digito en her thing, which did do her much pleasure; but I pray God that ella doth not think that yo did know before – or get a trick of liking it. So para sleep.[5]

It's interesting to note that Pepys was by this time in the unhappy position of getting hell from his wife whether or not he was guilty of having erotic interludes either in real life or in his dreams. The odd thing about the whole episode is Elizabeth's test of his dream-self's fidelity to her, by laying her hand 'upon my cockerel'. She must have been extremely unobservant of her husband's customary morning condition in all the years before his affair with Deb; and she must also have convinced herself that it was impossible for Pepys to have an erotic dream about her, Elizabeth. Either way, of course, poor old Pepys was on a hiding to nothing.

## *'Poor Col.' Revisited*

Pepys may have been upset about the aftermath of his nocturnal joys, but at least while he was asleep he was enjoying the joys themselves. Others have been less fortunate: St Hilary of Poitiers found to his horror that as soon as he closed his eyes in sleep he found himself surrounded by beautiful naked women; and St Margaret of Cortona had the disagreeable hallucination that she was being followed around her cell by a demon who sang scatological songs and tried to get her to join in with him in the choruses.

In a sense, it is all very well for saints to be tormented by any rampant sexuality in their dreams – it's their job to be able to cope with such things, after all – but sinners are not immune to feelings of guilt either during or after an erotic dream. We have already described Samuel Taylor Coleridge's creative dreams at some length (see pages 69–76); he must now return to the centre of our stage, for he was tormented throughout his life by dreams of such a startling obscenity that they were worlds away from any notion of the erotic. Of the many guilts which he experienced as a result of these and others of his dreams, sexual guilt was among the more severe.

In fact, incestuous urges are not far beneath the surface

in many of his works – there is something very close to lesbian incest in 'Christabel', for example. In some of his dreams there are symptoms of latent homosexual leanings, although one must avoid reading too much into this: it is all too easy to find evidence of homosexuality in virtually anything you care to name. Heterosexual physical love held its horrors, too; although he confessed to having sown wild oats as a youth, in his twenties he developed a fear of 'sensuality' in all its forms, especially sex between two people who did not have the deepest form of love for each other. Since he had contracted an extremely unhappy marriage with a woman whom he did not love, yet 'did his duty' and fathered her children, and since he was as physically passionate a man as any other, his subconscious was inevitably tortured by the contradictions in his emotions. When he did find love, it is almost certain that he was unable to bring himself to consummate it, because adultery and fornication were every whit as disgusting as unloving marital sex.

One can understand the hideous tangle his personal moral code had led him into: on the one hand it was all right to make love with his wife yet, because he didn't really love her, it wasn't all right at all, it was sinful; and, on the other hand, it was permissible to make love with the woman he did love yet, conversely, it was not permissible, it was again sinful because it would be adultery! To someone already neurotic about emotional rejection (see page 71), this conflict must have been absolutely hellish; at the purely physical level, Coleridge renounced even the safety-valve of masturbation. Like everyone else, he was at heart a sensualist; but, unlike most of us, he had made his conscious mind clamp down so hard upon his natural sensuality that even his unconscious only dimly perceived the truth. And when it did reveal the truth, it tended to do so suddenly, and very graphically.

We shall return to Coleridge's sexual nightmares in a moment; but first we should notice that guilts of other kinds emerged in his dreams as well. Long before his separation from his wife and children, he had been appalled to find out what most parents accept without thinking about it: that paternal (or maternal) love is tempered by occasional brief hatred for one's children, children being the frequently infuriating little people that they are.

In his notebook he records, for example, a dream about his son Hartley which he had in the early morning of 28th October, 1803:[6]

> Dozing, dreamt of Hartley as at his christening – how, as he was asked who redeemed him, and was to say 'God the Son', he went on, humming and hawing, in one hum and haw, like a boy who knows a thing and will not make the effort to recollect it – so as to irritate me greatly . . .

He had already awakened the household with screaming nightmares earlier that night; one must ruefully concede that things inside poor Coleridge's mind were pretty bad. His dream about Hartley might not at first seem particularly terrifying to you, until you realize that the dream contains the following elements: the child is apparently rejecting the Church's teachings; the child is being deliberately annoying to his father; the father is guilty about being annoyed. Guilty. (It has been suggested that, in addition, this dream provides further evidence of Coleridge's inner conflicts and divisions because it took place *before* Hartley's christening – i.e., that the boy in the dream represents Coleridge himself – but this seems to me to be stretching things too far.)

In another 1803 dream he and his wife Sara were both dead, and were trying to find the children. Coleridge did not in fact fear death – he was convinced that there was an afterlife waiting for him – and so he was troubled by this nightmare rather than seriously upset by it. But this was not generally the case: in a letter of 16th September, 1803, Coleridge wrote to Tom Wedgewood (like Coleridge a drug addict) that

> the Night is my Hell, sleeping my tormenting Angel. Three nights out of four I fall asleep, struggling to lie awake – my frequent Night-screams have almost made me a nuisance in my own house. Dreams with me are no Shadows, but the very Substances and foot-thick Calamities of my Life.

One suspects that he was much more than 'almost' a nuisance to the rest of the household. But this was hardly his fault, if his nightmare of 10th November, 1803, is anything to go by.

> Awoke after long struggles and wtih faint screaming from a persecuting dream. The tale of the dream began in two *images* – in two sons of a nobleman, desperately fond of shooting – brought out by the footman to resign their property, and to be made to believe that they had none. They were far too cunning for that, as they struggled and resisted their cruel wrongers . . . I became they; the duality vanished. Boyer and Christ's Hospital became concerned . . . and I was conjuring him . . . to have pity on a nobleman's orphan, when I was carried back to bed, and was struggling up against an unknown impediment. Some woman on the other side [was] about to relieve me, when a noise of one of the doors, strongly associated with Mrs Coleridge's coming in to awake me; the first thing I became

> conscious of was a faint double scream that I uttered . . .

The 'struggling up against an unknown impediment' is strongly reminiscent of the feeling of suffocation so often associated with nightmares – a matter we'll return to in a moment. And Christ's Hospital, where Coleridge was brought up as an orphan after a fit of fury during which he attacked his elder brother with a kitchen knife (see page 71), featured often in his nightmares. Here he is a few weeks later:

> I dreamt among other wild melancholy things . . . that I came up into one of our Christ's Hospital wards, and sitting by a bed was told that it was Davy in it, who in attempts to enlighten mankind had inflicted ghastly wounds on himself and must henceforth live bedridden. The image before my eyes, instead of Davy, was a wretched dwarf with only three fingers . . .

The 'wretched dwarf with only three fingers' was not, as you might anachronistically have suspected, Mickey Mouse: in fact 'Davy' was Sir Humphry Davy, the great chemist and lecturer. It's rather surprising, in a way, that this dream isn't cited in the paranormal literature as an example of a precognitive dream, because Davy was indeed to contribute to his own early death by his foolhardiness when experimenting. His most dangerous habit was to inhale quantities of the gases he was working with so that he could note the results! For example, he breathed four whole quarts (4.55 litres) of hydrogen, almost suffocating himself. (It's a good job he didn't try to calm his nerves with a cigarette.) This practice was almost certainly the reason why, from 1811 onwards, Davy was an invalid.

But the most direct reference which the dream appears

to make is to an incident in 1812 when Davy foolishly caused the explosion of some nitrogen trichloride, a highly dangerous chemical, and almost lost his eyesight – among other injuries – as a result. However, we should not try to make too much of this. As I say, Davy's foolhardiness was well known, especially to friends, of whom Coleridge was one, and so there is nothing strange in the poet dreaming that one day the chemist would cause himself a serious injury.

Coleridge's sexual nightmares betray a distortion of the normal sexual impulse so extreme as to be virtually perverted. Here are three examples from his notebooks, dating from 1800, 1802 and 1803:

> . . . a most frightful dream of a woman whose features were blended wth darkness catching hold of my right eye and attempting to pull it out. I caught hold of her arm fast – a horrid feel. Wordsworth cried out aloud to me, hearing my scream; heard his cry and thought it cruel he did not come, but did not wake till his cry was repeated a third time. The woman's name [was] Ebon Ebon Thalud. When I awoke, my right eyelid swelled.

Speculation abounds as to the meaning of 'Ebon Ebon Thalud': most explanations are tortuous, and it's perfectly possible that the name is simply meaningless. It is tempting, however, to note that the woman's features 'blended with darkness', that 'ebon' means 'black', and to remember the delightful 'Abyssinian maid' of 'Kubla Khan' (a poem which can be interpreted as packed with overt sexual imagery) whose sweet song alone could draw the poet back to Paradise: did Coleridge suffer yet a further guilt over what to him would have seemed still another moral crime, the finding of black women sexually attractive? Does the attempted plucking out of his eye (he suffered on and off from psychosomatic eye-pains) represent an essay at symbolic castration and thereby the assuagement of his guilt? The whole hypothesis has its attractions – principally the fact that it can't be proved one way or the other.

Here, in our second example, is a whole tempest of sexual imagery:

> . . . I dreamt that I was asleep in the cloister at Christ's Hospital and had awoken with a pain in my hand from some corrosion. Boys and nurses' daughters peeping at me . . . I dreamt of Dorothy, William and Mary [the Wordsworths], and that Dorothy was altered in every feature, a fat, thick-limbed and rather red-haired – in short, no resemblance to her at all – and I said, 'If I did not *know* you to be Dorothy, I never should suppose it.' 'Why,' says she, 'I have not a feature the same', and yet I was not surprised . . .
>
> I was followed up and down by a frightful pale woman who, I thought, wanted to kiss me, and had the property of giving a shameful disease by breathing in the face.
>
> And again I dreamt that a figure of a woman of gigantic height, dim and indefinite and smokelike, appeared, and that I was forced to run up towards it. And then it changed to a stool, and then appeared again in another place, and again I went up in great fright, and it changed to some other common thing . . .

The 'pain in my hand from some corrosion' seems likely, in the light of later dreams, to be a reference to the evils of masturbation. The transmutation of the 'gigantic' woman into what is generally regarded as a male symbol by analysts, a three-legged stool, is perhaps reminiscent of the way in which, in Coleridge's projected third part of 'Christabel', the tall mother-figure of Geraldine was to be transformed into a simulacrum of Christabel's betrothed. The 'frightful pale woman' can *surely* be none other than the 'Night-mare LIFE-IN-DEATH' whose 'skin was white as leprosy' and who 'thicks man's blood with cold'. (In an earlier version of 'The Rime of the Ancient Mariner' we find that 'she is far liker Death than he;/Her flesh makes the still air cold'.) So, at least, run the psychoanalytic interpretations of this series of nightmares, which provides fertile ground also for the literary detective. However, I think one can be forgiven for feeling a little sceptical – except, perhaps, in the case of 'pain in my hand from some corrosion' being an allusion to the poet's guilt over masturbation. It is perhaps difficult for us today to realize what a mortal sin masturbation was accepted to be at the time, thanks to the preaching of the Church – although nowhere in the Bible is the practice condemned, or even mentioned. (It comes as something of a surprise to discover that even St Paul missed it.)

Our third example contains one of those vague possible allusions to latent homosexuality. It's interesting to note, in passing, that a woman can be paid off with a mere shilling while a man costs a full three guineas!

> . . . Out rushes a university harlot, who insists on my going with her. Offer her a shilling – seem to get away a moment, when she overtakes me again. I am not to go to another while she is '*biting*' – these were her words. This will not satisfy her . . . The harlot in white with her open bosom certainly was the Cambridge Girl . . . One thing noticeable in an after-dream: a little weak contemptible wretch offering his services, and I (as before afraid to refuse them) literally and distinctly remembered a former dream, in which I had suffered most severely, this wretch leaping on me and grasping my scrotum. I therefore most politely assured him of

> the three guineas, but I meant only to get rid of him . . . and still affected by sleep, in an half-upright posture struggling, as I thought, against involuntarily sinking back into sleep, and consequent suffocation. 'Twas then I screamed . . .

There is probably no one who has not at one time or another suffered the suffocating feeling that Coleridge describes; indeed, it's this very sensation which has led the nightmare – both before and since Fuseli's time (see page 66) – to be depicted in the form of a hag or goblin squatting on the sleeper's chest. There are two further curious points here. Firstly, the suffocating feeling is linked by some psychologists to sexual frustration or repression. Secondly, the chest-squatting image of the nightmare is definitely linked with the old idea of incubi and succubi, respectively male and female demons who come along and have intercourse with you while you're asleep. The connection between nightmare and demon arises because the demon, like the nightmare, presses down heavily – suffocatingly – on you as it has its wicked way. It would seem, therefore, tenable that all three elements – nightmares, seductive demons, and sexual frustration – are inseparably intertwined. Perhaps our forefathers had a deeper understanding of psychology than we credit them with; more likely, they simply observed that nightmares, with which the suffocating feeling is often associated, frequently have a strong sexual content.

## *Miller's Tales*

It is therefore difficult to establish whether creative artists (a) have a greater number of erotic dreams than most of us (or are more likely to write down details of their sexual dreams, in their personal diaries if not for publication) or (b) simply have more nightmares than the rest of us. Whichever of the options is the correct one (most likely, it's a mixture), there certainly seems to be a strong relationship between sexual dreams and creativity.

But the relationship is certainly there. We've already looked at some of the more printable sexual dreams of Jack Kerouac, for example. It probably comes as no shock to discover that Henry Miller, too, suffered from erotic nightmares. In fact, simply to read a novel by him is to know that you are in the presence of a dreamer: this powerful suspicion is confirmed when you learn that, like Kerouac, Coleridge, and so on, for a long time he kept a dream-diary from which he drew material, occasionally, for his writings.

Miller's perceptive biographer, Jay Martin, in *Always Merry and Bright* (1978), tells us about whole sackfuls of the writer's dreams, which are almost always fascinating – in a chilling sort of a way. Many of them are, as hinted, not suitable reading material for the prudish or sensitive – and this leads me to wonder why, with comparatively few exceptions (e.g., Pepys, Coleridge), earlier writers seem not to have recorded any of their dreams which might have had the same horrific and/or sexual intensity as those which more modern writers such as Miller and Kerouac have written about. An obvious explanation would be that only in the last few decades has it become permissible for us to confess the *real* contents of our dreams; but there is a contrary explanation which is not ridiculous. It is possible that, as our society has become in many ways more brutal and certainly more permeated by the erotic, so our dreams have reacted to this progression. The dreams have drawn on the symbols present in the real world around us (something which J. G.

Ballard has done to produce his dreamlike horror fantasies such as *Crash* (1973), which mixes eroticism with brutal road accidents and 'motorway madness'). If this is the case, then our ancestors' dreams really may have been of tamer stuff than ours.

Let me develop this briefly, by use of analogy. We are currently seeing a continuing eruption of violence, erotica and sexual pornography in the cinema and, to a far greater extent, in the video film. It is the claim of antipornographers that such movies actually inspire imitative deeds by members of the audience, and there is a certain amount of (controversial) evidence to support the claim. In this view, then, the movies are the leaders and society tags along in their wake. In the case of purely erotic movies – although the average antipornographer fails to make the distinction – this doesn't really matter, and may actually be a good thing. But when sadism enters the scene the effect, if indeed it exists, obviously *is* crucially important.

Unfortunately for the argument, the evidence in its favour from surveys carried out to date is at best ambiguous, at worst dismissive.[7] Either violent movies actually defuse the latent sadism of the audience, who get their rather revolting kicks vicariously, or they are merely expressions of a sickness already present in society. In other words, if this thesis is correct, society is the leader and the movies the followers.

If so (and my own feeling is that the truth actually lies somewhere between the two propositions, though not necessarily in the centre), then it seems perfectly possible that modern dreams really are more violent and pornographic than those of our ancestors. Two factors would be at work. Not only would the dreams be directly reflecting our society, they would also be reacting to the fact that our *conscious* minds are today allowed to think thoughts and discuss ideas which would have been taboo or even totally unknown a few decades ago. To be sure, society in the past was crueller than it is today, in the main – a trend regretted by those of ultraconservative views. But, while we do not (are not allowed to?) flock to see public torture and execution, modern society has a brutalizing effect brought about thanks to such factors as overpopulation and technological advance, an effect which has been at best sporadically present in the past – at least among the literate classes. In the past, the only way this brutalizing effect could be created was by slavery – or by abject poverty, which was much the same thing and very much more widespread. Today, because of improvements in communications, and so forth, our masters can handle us with softer gloves; but most of us have little more control over our lives than did the poor of the Victorian slums, even though the quality of our lives has been improved a millionfold. The brutalizing effect is therefore, to an extent, enhanced today because there is no obvious 'enemy' responsible for the mind-rotting brutalities of daily life. In the real 1984, as opposed to the fictional one, there is no Big Brother to rebel against – and that makes the situation worse.

The brutalizing effect I've been talking about seems manifest in Miller's dreams, a few of which we'll discuss.

Miller had been reluctant about his second marriage, which seems to have been doomed from the start. In the autumn of 1926 he suffered from a recurring nightmare – a nightmare which, paradoxically, always left him with a strange feeling of satisfaction. He was hitch-hiking in the southern USA at night when suddenly he was seized and shoved into a pen. His assailant forced him up against an old fence and felt inside his anus, then took a rusty knife and cut his stomach and genitals to shreds. And then suddenly he was on a hearse-like streetcar; then being dumped back into the neighbourhood where he had endured all kinds of youthful miseries. As Jay Martin says, 'He felt a cruel joy in seeing the death of his hopes, even in dreams' – the same sort of satisfaction you see on the face of the long-term unemployed when, just as they expected, their most recent job-application comes to nothing.

A couple of years later found him convinced that his wife was deceiving him with a lesbian lover. Once again, his misery surfaced in the form of a recurring nightmare. He and his wife were (he dreamt) staying in some castle, when, one day, he saw that the lover was inside one of the rooms. At once he realized that she had been lurking there all along. He found his way to the darkened room, where he saw that she was dressed as a nun; and she was contorting her body in such a way that it had taken on the general shape of a skull. She was weeping and moaning, and he watched her, sympathizing, for a while. When he left her he found that the castle walls had turned bright red . . . and there was his first wife lying sensuously on a great bed.

The really curious aspect of this dream is that it was this last image, of his first wife on a bed, which *really* horrified him – for reasons he could not explain.

A third dream, and then we must leave Miller.[8]

In 1933 he was contemplating marriage to Anaïs Nin – although there was the odd undivorced spouse getting in the way of such plans. At the same time, it seems he was anxious to scour every last shred of romance out of the affair: he took a delight in describing to her, in detail, his liaisons with other women, including hordes of harlots. In particular, he became physically infatuated with one of these prostitutes; in one ghastly instance, Nin gave him some money to buy clothing after they had made joyful, passionate romantic love. He immediately spent the money on persuading the whore, Nys, to allow him to perform cunnilingus with her . . . and then he told Nin all about it. The reasons for this astonishing behaviour seem to be that, because she was married to her Hugo and he to his June, their liaison could only be an adulterous one. Adultery, Miller conceived, could not be romantic: marriage, on the other hand, would be. Since the existing relationship could not be romantic, there was no way in which he was going to act in a romantic fashion towards Nin.

His dreams reflected this immoral dilemma. In one he was seated across the table from Nin's mother, who was calling him most of the words omitted from the dictionary and telling him that he had ruined her daughter. Listening from an easy chair was Nin's brother – or was it her husband, Hugo? At last Miller was so infuriated that after each of the mother's remarks he yelled: 'What do you mean by that?' In the end, he vaulted the table and started to strangle the old woman . . . who promptly was transmogrified into the mother of a friend of his. Significantly, this 'new' woman was one whom Miller had always regarded as an ideal of motherhood.

It takes very little effort to interpret the message of this dream – yet it did not stop Miller from continuing simultaneously to woo Nin and recount to her his orgiastic exploits with Nys and the other women of the streets. As Jay Martin says, he 'should have listened to his dreams'.

## *A Critic's Comments*

The same sort of posthumous advice could be given to the art critic John Ruskin, who today has several claims to fame in the popular memory: his judgement of Whistler's painting 'Nocturne in Black and Gold' ('I have seen, and heard, much of cockney impudence before now; but never expected to hear a coxcomb ask two hundred guineas for flinging a pot of paint in the public's face'); his curious antipathy towards sex (he seems to have been revolted by his wife's body from the night when, after their marriage, he discovered for the first time that women have pubic hair); and his subsequent cuckolding by the more capillophile Millais.

However, Ruskin is well worth remembering for his nightmares, too, some of which seem certainly to have been rooted in his ambiguous attitude towards adult women.

For example, in August 1867, when he was much in love with one Rose La Touche, but also languishing in a nursing home in Norwood, he dreamt that he had obtained a private audience with Louis XV. He wanted to speak with the king, but found himself struck dumb. Louis, however, told him that he had 'just seen a lovely Irish girl, whose name was Rose' and who, on hearing the name 'Ruskin', 'had been terribly and brightly startled'. Ruskin was very much disturbed by this dream – probably, one suspects, because in it his dream-mind was being more honest about Rose's true feelings towards him than his conscious mind would have been.

By March of the following year, things were getting grim. Rose's parents were destroying her notes to him, and forcing her to return his letters unread. Moreover, her brother, who had been engaged to Ruskin's cousin, had broken off his own engagement, thereby destroying a potentially useful link between Ruskin and Rose. Ruskin was understandably very bitter about all this.[9] In March 1868 he dreamt of a snake which suddenly became very fat and leech-like, and clung to his hand until he awoke. Elsewhere he had compared Mrs La Touche's character with that of a serpent 'without the poison'.

In December 1872 he dreamt that he was looking after a little girl: much more, one suspects, to his taste than grown women like his wife, Effie, or Rose La Touche. The girl sat at a table eating with the spirits of Wisdom and Death. The spirits were beautiful, but icy cold (like Coleridge's 'LIFE-IN-DEATH' Mark I – see page 159): Ruskin was anxious that she should not hurt herself by touching them. In carefree fashion, the child asked the spirits why it was that they never smiled, in response to which Death *did* smile – an unpopular move, so far as Ruskin was concerned, because Death showed too many teeth. However, the little girl did not seem to notice this. Ruskin, on the other hand, awoke in the cold sweat of terror.

And in December 1875 he had what he himself described as the ghastliest nightmare ever to afflict him. In a room full of pictures he came across one showing a surgeon dissecting himself – 'It was worse than dissecting: *tearing*'. What the surgeon was doing to his own head was so revolting that Ruskin could not bring himself to write down the details!

## Not *for the Children*

Even writers of 'cosy' children's classics have been subject to agonizing nightmares, often of a sexual nature or with some sexual content. Books such as *Peter Pan* and *The Wind in the Willows* seem a long way from such considerations, but their authors were victims nevertheless.

Sir James Barrie, the author of *Peter Pan*, was a curious character, and there have been constant speculations about his sexuality for the best part of a century. One rumour has it that he was impotent; another that his wife, Mary, told friends that sexual relations had stopped after their marriage; a third, produced by John Middleton

Murry, had it that Barrie was a sexual deviant and demanded that Mary indulge in various perversions with him. No one knows – and it hardly matters! – but some light on his attitude towards women may be shed by the remark in his notebook: 'Greatest horror – dream I am married – wake up shrieking.' Nevertheless he had a well known penchant for pretty young actresses: a bizarre mixture.

He amplified his terse note in an article called 'My Ghastly Dream' published in the *Edinburgh Evening Dispatch* in 1887:

> When this horrid nightmare got hold of me, and how, I cannot say, but it has made me the most unfortunate of men.
>
> In my early boyhood it was a sheet that tried to choke me in the night. At school it was my awful bed-fellow with whom I wrestled nightly while all the other boys in the dormitory slept with their consciences at rest. It had assumed shape at that time: leering, but fatally fascinating; it was never the same yet always recognizable.

Rather like Agatha Christie's 'Gunman' (see page 140).

> One of the horrors of my dream was that I knew how it would come each time, and from where. I do not recall it in my childhood, but they tell me that, asleep in my cot, I would fling my arms about wildly as if fighting a ghost. It would thus seem that my nightmare was with me even then, though perhaps only as a shapeless mass that a too lively imagination was soon to resolve into a woman. My weird dream never varies now. Always I see myself being married . . .
>
> My ghastly nightmare always begins in the same way. I seem to know that I have gone to bed, and then I see

> myself slowly waking up in a misty world. As I realize where I am the mist dissolves; and the heavy shapeless mass that weighed upon me in the night time when I was a boy, assumes the form of a woman, beautiful and cruel, with a bridal veil over her face.[10]

The woman approaches him rapidly and, although reluctantly, he follows her when she beckons. They fly to the church he attended as a child, and find all the wedding guests waiting there for them. One night, he says, she came for him in a cart, into which he was thrown 'by invisible hands'. An aging Cupid – apparently another of Barrie's recurring dream-figures – taunts him all the way to the church by jabbing him with an arrow. His cries of pain serve merely to amuse his two escorts.

One can see why the conscious Barrie had mixed feelings about the prospect of marriage: if this was the 'marriage of his dreams', what the hell was the real thing going to be like? In fact, as it was to prove, the real thing was going to be shambolic.

But the greater debate about his sexuality concerns his relationship with the sons of Arthur Llewelyn Davies and his wife Sylvia (daughter of George du Maurier): George, Jack, Peter, Michael and Nicholas ('Nico'). When Peter Davies, who founded the well known publishing company Peter Davies Ltd., committed suicide in 1960 it was the claim of the press that it was the real Peter Pan who had died. But Barrie himself always used to maintain that no single one of the five boys had been the model for Peter Pan: instead, he had produced the character as an amalgamation of all five of them. One is tempted to suggest that even this isn't quite the truth: perhaps the *real* Peter Pan was Barrie himself.

At any rate, that Barrie loved the boys seems beyond question; that there was a trace of sexuality involved in that love has been a persistent rumour. It is worth noting that in his excellent *J. M. Barrie and the Lost Boys* (1979) Andrew Birkin cites Nico as saying he was utterly sure that Barrie had never had the least shade of homosexual interest in any of them.

On 19th May, 1921, Michael Davies died in a drowning accident: Barrie himself thought that it might have been suicide, and the idea was prevalent among family and friends. And Barrie was shattered by the event. In letters he referred to recurring dreams about going to the scene of the tragedy to look for Michael and give him some warning. From his notebook:[11]

> On 7th November, 1922, I dreamt that he came back to me, not knowing that he was drowned, and that I kept this knowledge from him, and we went on for another year in the old way till the fatal 19th approached again, and he became very sad not knowing why, and I feared what was to happen but never let on . . . When the day came I had devised schemes to make it impossible for him to leave me yet doubted they could help – and he rose in the night and put on the old clothes and came to look at me, as he thought, asleep . . . I went with him, holding his hand and he liked it and when we came to the place – that pool – he said goodbye to me and went into it and sank just as before . . .

Almost exactly a year earlier, on 7th May, 1920, the writer Kenneth Grahame suffered a very similar tragedy; that the suspected suicide was that of his son, Alastair, doesn't necessarily mean that his grief was any greater than Barrie's, because in both cases the bond between the writer and the dead youth was a close one. Yet, if Grahame suffered from nightmares in the wake of the event, I have been unable to find any record of them. I suspect this is because Grahame was aware of the importance of PR: he censored out of even his private writings anything that might damage his reputation amongst posterity.

During his lifetime Grahame was often described as the finest contemporary master of English prose, and yet today he is thought of – if at all – as a children's writer pure and simple, the author of *The Wind in the Willows* and some other books whose titles you can never quite remember. Paradoxically, when *The Wind in the Willows* was published in 1908 it was regarded by critics and public alike as being something of a disappointment, a book unworthy of the author of *The Golden Age* (1895) and *Dream Days* (1898). These two books of short stories had a tone which was regarded as revolutionary by the late-Victorian reading public. The stories were *about* children, yet they were not *for* children; and they attempted to describe the way in which children really feel about the adults around them rather than the way in which adults would fondly like to imagine they are seen by their loving offspring.

Both books are filled with childhood fantasies: often the only route whereby the children can escape the miseries imposed upon them by the adults, the 'Olympians', is the retreat into a dream-world of their own creation, where adults durst not intrude. It is a world where you can eat as many chocolates as you like – the hard ones *and* the soft ones – and still not be sick, where soldiers march about at your behest and fire their rifles in the air just to make you feel grand, where you can take to sea in a sailing-ship and fight off the Spanish fleet single-handed in the sure knowledge that you're going to be victorious.

If one has to choose a single story which best represents Grahame's imaginings in this respect then one is drawn unerringly to 'Mutabile Semper', which appears in *Dream Days*.

The plot is simple enough. A small boy (the narrator) is wandering along the road when he meets a little girl new to the area. They chat: he is attracted to her for reasons he does not understand. Eventually she weasels out of him that he has a dream-world – in fact, several – and asks to be allowed to share it with him. As he continues to describe it she eagerly suggests a few 'improvements'; for example, the soldiers shouldn't be allowed to fire their guns because she doesn't like loud noises. They agree to meet again.

> As I sped along to the tryst, again I accompanied my new comrade along the corridors of my pet palace into which I had so hastily introduced her; and on reflection I began to see that it wouldn't work properly. I had made a mistake, and those were not the surroundings in which she was most fitted to shine. However, it really did not matter much; I had other palaces to place at her disposal – plenty of 'em; and on a further acquaintance with and knowledge of her tastes, no doubt I could find something to suit her.
>
> There was a real Arabian one, for instance . . .

Now this is all very well: children do indeed have dream-worlds. But in Grahame's account of his narrator's dream-world there is something a little unconvincing. A child's dream-world exists only during the time it is being played in or actively thought about; often enough it endures for no longer than an hour, a new one being invented on the morrow. It doesn't have some kind of autonomous existence which can be tampered with as you might tamper with the objects of the real world, or the world you might have created in a piece of fiction. One feels that Grahame is making exactly the same mistake as all the other writers for and about children before him (and a good many who were to follow): he is idealizing his subjects. The difference – the 'revolutionary' difference – is of course that, whereas the other writers romanticized their young protagonists into cute, obedient, cuddlesome, fluffy little things, Grahame romanticized them into free-thinking individuals whose cerebral adventures into fantasy were as important as their everyday activities in the real world. And children are not really like that: they are dreamers, to be sure, but from an adult's point of view they are chillingly rational ones. They may go hunting tigers with apparently total conviction, but their dream-world vanishes at the veriest hint that a jam sandwich might be in the offing.

Both *The Golden Age* and *Dream Days* strike the modern reader as rather twee books, and as soon as you notice that there is more than a smack of falsehood, of conscious artifice, about one of their major components – the dream- and fantasy-lives of the children – you become merely impatient with them. And it is probably for this reason that Grahame's fame today rests almost exclusively on his 'disappointing' *The Wind in the Willows*.

However, accounts are extant of his real, as opposed to his fictional, dreams. In *Beyond the Wild Wood* (1982) Peter Green presents one such account, from a letter written by Grahame to Helen Dunham. This was a recurring dream:

> First, there would be a sense of smugness, of cushioned comfort, of home-coming. Next, a gradual awakening to consciousness in a certain little room, very dear and familiar, sequestered in some corner of the more populous and roaring part of London: solitary, the world walled out, but full of a brooding sense of peace and of possession. At times I would make my way there, unerringly, through the wet and windy streets,

climb the well known staircase, open the ever-welcoming door. More often I was there already, ensconced in the most comfortable chair in the world, the lamp lit, the fire glowing ruddily. But always the same feeling of a homecoming, of the world shut out, of the ideal encasement. On the shelves were a few books – a very few – but just the editions I had sighed for, the editions which refuse to turn up, or which poverty glowers at on alien shelves. On the walls were a print or two, a woodcut, an etching – not many. Old loves, all of them, apparitions that had flashed across the field of view in sales-rooms and vanished again in a blaze of three figures; but never possessed – until now. All was modest – O, so very modest! But all was my very own, and, what was more, everything in that room was exactly right.

In some ways it's hardly surprising that Grahame's recurring dream should have been of such commonplace, mundane security, for his childhood had been a hellish one. His mother died when he was very young, and the children were packed off by their father – who soon after relapsed into alcoholism – to live with relatives. As with anyone else's relatives, some of Grahame's were good with children and some weren't. Rejected (as it seemed) by their father, and at the mercy of adults whose whims were, at least initially, unpredictable because unfamiliar . . . it is quite surprising that the young Grahames didn't grow up to be psychopaths. Security, then, must have seemed to the boy Kenneth a state which might never be attained. Matters were hardly helped when his uncle, who held the purse-strings, decided it was all very well for Kenneth's older brother to go up to Oxford but that he was damned if he was going to pay for Kenneth to enjoy the same privilege: the young fellow should get himself a decent dead-end job – as a clerk in the Bank of England, for example. (In fact, Grahame eventually rose to be Secretary of the Bank.)

I suspect, then, that the 'room' Grahame describes with such affection was the *real* dream-world of his childhood – that all the stuff about chocolates and soldiers was just so much nonsense produced for an adoring readership. In his childhood, life itself must have seemed quite eventful enough without having to have action-packed dreams as well. It seems possible, then, that he dreamt of his cosy, placid secure room in the same way that blue-movie stars probably dream about being desert-island castaways.[12]

In parallel with his role as unimaginative dreamer, Grahame was – or so it has always struck me – a singularly unimaginative writer. Carroll and Milne – the two authors whose names are most often cited alongside Grahame's – produced books in which every page bounces and sparkles with imaginative invention. *The Wind in the Willows*, Grahame's comparable work, is pedestrian reading indeed if tackeld immediately after a healthy dose of *Through the Looking-Glass* or *The House at Pooh Corner*.

That said, it seems likely that many of Toad's adventures in *The Wind in the Willows* were born from Grahame's dreams – or, more specifically, his nightmares and anxiety-dreams. For he was in the position of being a rebel without the courage to go out and do any actual rebelling: in one way he wanted, like Toad, to create chaos and mayhem; in another, he was terrified of accidentally letting himself do just that.[13]

The presence of the anxiety-dreams is overt to the point of crashing obviousness. Take Toad's arrival at the station, disguised as a washerwoman, only to find that he has forgotten to bring any money with him; or any of the book's several chase scenes. The clearest example of this sort of thing occurs not in *The Wind in the Willows* but in another piece of writing which Grahame did for his son Alastair ('Mouse'), 'Bertie's Escapade'. This was a short story tossed off in about 1904 for the lad's nursery magazine, *The Merry Thought*, and concerned the nocturnal adventures of Bertie Pig in company with Alastair's two pet rabbits.

> Mr. Grahame's night was a very disturbed one, owing to agitating dreams. He dreamt that the house was broken into by burglars, and he wanted to get up and go down and catch them, but he could not move hand or foot. He heard them ransacking his pantry . . . plundering his wine-cellar, and still he could not move a muscle. Then he dreamt that he was at one of the great City Banquets that he used to go to, and he heard the Chairman propose the health of 'The King' and there was a great cheering. And he thought of a most excellent speech to make in reply – a really clever speech. And he tried to make it, but they held him down in his chair and wouldn't let him. And then he dreamt that the Chairman actually proposed . . . the health of Mr. Grahame! and he got up to reply, and he couldn't think of anything to say! And he stood there, for hours and hours it seemed, in a dead silence, the glittering eyes of the guests – there were hundreds and hundreds of guests – all fixed on him, and still he couldn't think of anything to say! Till at last the Chairman rose, 'He can't think of anything to say! *Turn him out*!' Then the waiters fell on him and dragged him from the room and threw him into the street, and flung his hat and coat after him . . . [14]

The person who hasn't had an anxiety-dream much like this one is a *rara avis* indeed. Most striking is the manifest fear of being shown publicly to be incompetent; also, there is the element of impotence, of the inability to respond in the correct (virile?) manner.

Somehow, and I'm not sure quite why it should be, I find it hard to be sympathetic towards Grahame. His childhood was a misery, true, and a large part of his adulthood was a drudgery and a frustration. Yet somehow one feels that he became a writer because it was the fashionable thing to do; that in most matters he chose to run with the hares and course with the hounds; and that, once he had retired from the Bank and the world had brought fame and wealth to his doorstep, the rampant eccentricity into which both he and his wife lapsed was calculated rather than sincere. In short, I can't help feeling he was something of a sham. His dreams – such of them as we have – have rather the same quality: not for Grahame the flamboyant pornography of a Coleridge or the apocalyptic baroque of a Bunyan. No, for Grahame any powerful urges and fears that might have been tussling in his unconscious could express themselves only in Walter-Mitty worries about looking like a fool in public. Rather like his writings, his dreams were slight – and, at base, rather insincere.

Unless, of course, he entered some Muslim Paradise every night, but simply dared not write about it . . .

## *Struggling With Dreams*

The British writer E. L. Grant Watson (1885–1970) was not so shy. In early 1954 he wrote to C. G. Jung about two interesting dreams which he had had. In the first, he had carried around for years the entrails of a magic horse which had been killed in a battle. One day, as he went downstairs, he met the resuscitated horse on the way up. The beast then ate its own entrails and was ready to be ridden once more.

The other dream is more complicated. It begins with Watson in a theatre. The cast are lying down on the stage, as if dead, but they are talking to each other, and in the end Watson joins them. Next he finds himself in a desert, being guided by two Hindu men; he sees that his feet are those of an old man. Things are made worse by an initiation ceremony he has to undergo in which his feet are cut about prior to his having to stand in boiling water. Then, in a big concave mirror, he sees an idealized image of himself; and is told by his erstwhile guides to travel on through the desert on his own. Naturally, he promptly meets two further Hindu guides, and these take him to a strange building packed with people, among whom are his father, mother and stepfather. Then he has to undertake a long climb, which finishes with him at the edge of a precipice listening to a 'mystery voice' which tells him to jump. He refuses several times before finally giving in. The dream ends with him swimming 'deliciously into the blue of eternity'.

Jung's interpretation of this dream was typically imperspicuous. Reassuringly, he told Watson that 'such dreams occur at the gateway of death . . . They don't predict it but they show you the right way to approach the end.' Very cheering.

As far as I can establish, Jung never had a chance to pronounce similarly on the dreams of Franz Kafka – rather a pity, because the results could hardly have failed to achieve new depths of incomprehensibility. In fact, it would be difficult to overestimate the importance of dreams in Kafka's life: his novels and stories themselves bear all the true hallmarks of the nightmare. At the end of 1911, his friend, biographer and 'agent', Max Brod, remarked in his diary: 'Nothing but Kafka's own dreams seems to interest him any more.' And at about the same time Kafka wrote in his own diary: '. . . the writing of my autobiography would be sheer pleasure, because it would go so easily, just like writing down one's dreams, and yet would have an entirely different result, a great result that would influence me forever, and that would at the same time be accessible to the understanding and feeling of everyone else.' Of course, Kafka never did quite get around to writing his autobiography, and so one has to be satisfied with Nahum N. Glatzer's stimulating compilation of Kafka's autobiographical writings and the writer's collections of love-letters, *Letters to Felice* and *Letters to Milena*. Of the latter, Brod commented: 'To my mind they belong among the most significant love-letters of all time and will ultimately take their place beside the ardently humble letters of Julie de l'Espinasse.'

On 2nd October, 1911, Kafka recorded:

> Sleepless night, the third in a row. I fall asleep soundly, but after an hour I wake up, as though I had laid my head in the wrong hole. I am completely awake, have the feeling that I have not slept at all or only under a thin skin, have before me anew the labour of falling asleep and feel myself rejected by sleep. And for the rest of the night, until about five, thus it remains, so that indeed I sleep but at the same time vivid dreams keep me awake. I sleep alongside myself, so to speak, while I myself must struggle with dreams. About five the last trace of sleep is exhausted, I just dream, which is more exhausting than wakefulness.

Disturbed nights like this are often regarded as a sign of the intellectual in a state of deep depression, and they seem to have dogged Kafka throughout his life. Other authors, not a million kilometres from this typewriter, periodically have the same problem – the description of sleeping 'alongside myself, so to speak' rings chillingly true – but it's a little hard to go along with Kafka's statement that 'I believe this sleeplessness comes only because I write'. It would seem more likely that it came about *despite* his writing – his expiation – or possibly that his writing was a product of the sleepless, dream-tormented nights.

As I say, the condition lasted all his life. Only a couple of years before his death in 1924 we find him writing: 'Almost impossible to sleep; plagued by dreams, as if they were being scratched on me, on a stubborn material.' And, returning to November 1911, we have:

> As a result of the last few nights spent in wild dreams but with scarcely a few snatches of sleep, I was so incoherent this morning, felt nothing but my forehead, saw a halfway bearable condition only far beyond my present one, and in sheer readiness to die would have been glad simply to have curled up in a ball on the cement floor of the corridor . . .

In the years 1920–21 Kafka had the second of his great unhappy love affairs. The target of his affections was a married woman, Milena Jesenská, whom he described as being 'a living fire, the like of which I have never seen before'. Details of the affair are obscure: from his diary are missing the pages for the period 9th January, 1920, to 15th October, 1921 (exclusive), and it is likely that he removed these pages before lending Jesenská his diaries. Another possibility is that it was she who removed these pages before, after Kafka's death, giving the diaries to Brod along with the manuscripts of *The Castle* and *America*. Whoever was responsible for the censorship – and it was probably Kafka himself – the missing pages seem certain to have been those which described his futile love.

She appeared in his dreams, though, as we know from one of Kafka's letters to Brod (late January, 1921):

> I have hardly slept, but I had two comforters. In the first place, severe headaches . . . And then I had this dream, the last of a whole welter: on my left sat a child dressed only in a vest (I was not quite sure, or rather I could not remember, whether it was my child, but that did not bother me) and on my right sat Milena; both of them snuggled up close to me, and I told them a story about my wallet, which I had lost and then found again, but which I had not yet opened and so did not know whether my money was still in it. But even if it was lost it did not matter, as long as I had the two of them by my side . . .
>
> That was the dream, but the reality is that three weeks ago (after many similar letters, albeit not as definitive as this one, which reflects the dire necessity that has now signalled, and will continue to signal, the end for me) I made just one request: that [Milena] should not write to me any more, and should take steps to ensure that we do not see one another again.

Perhaps Kafka 'should have listened to his dreams', as Jay Martin remarked of Henry Miller in a rather similar context.

Two living writers who listened to their dreams to such effect that many of their works are redolent of dreamland and its tangled functionings are J. B. Priestley and Graham Greene; the former we shall consider again in Chapters 4 and 5, while we have already discussed the latter in Chapters 1 and 2. Nonetheless, both are worth briefly considering here – especially Priestley, whose profound interest in dreams seems to have impelled him to describe more clearly than perhaps any other living creative artist the importance of dreams in every aspect of his life.

For example, in his anthology *Delight* he lists dreams

as one of his 114 'delights'. He expresses his wonderment that any of us – *all* of us – by the simple expedient of going to bed and falling asleep can wander 'into another kind of existence': 'As a child I could never understand why grown-ups took dreaming so calmly when they could make such a fuss about any holiday. This still puzzles me. I am mystified by people who say they never dream and appear to have no interest in the subject. It is much more astonishing than if they said they never went out for a walk.'

He expresses his astonishment, too, over the way in which we of the West seem to think of dreams as trivial things, not really part of real life. As I mentioned in the Introduction to this book (see page *xiv*), this is a point which has occurred to me as well: so far as I know, while many people have attempted to redress the balance by attempting to force dreams to the centre of the stage, as it were, no one has ever done the essential sociological research to find out *why* our culture so undervalues the importance of the dream. We use references to dreams liberally in our poetry, prose and public oratory – think of the power of Martin Luther King's repeated 'I have a dream'[15] – but in 'real life' we relegate them to the trivial. The *Shorter Oxford English Dictionary* (1965 edn.), for example, in its entries on dream-subjects defines the ancillary meanings of the words only in pejorative terms. A dream is – apart from the thing you have while asleep – 'a vision of the fancy indulged in when awake (*esp*. as being unreal or idle); reverie, castle-in-the-air', which is a long way from the sense in which King used the word. The word 'dreamer' gets a slightly better deal, but only slightly: '*1*. One who dreams; a visionary; an idle speculator. *2*. A puff-bird.' No, I don't know what a puff-bird is either.

Priestley sings enthusiastically the praises of dreaming

even despite the fact that he admits to having nightmares just as much as the rest of us.

> This dream life is often overshadowed by huge mysterious anxieties, with luggage that cannot be packed and trains that refuse to be caught; and both persons and scenes there are not as dependable and solid as they are in waking life, so that Brown and Smith merge into one person while Robinson splits into two . . . and there are moments of desolation or terror that are worse than anything we have known under the sun. Yet this other life has its interests, its gaieties, its . . .

And so on. Priestley must indeed be a courageous devotee of dreaming if he can honestly wake in the middle of the night from a nightmare and still think, *at that moment*, that it's all worth it for the privilege of dreaming! Especially since one's mind has a nasty tendency to remember the nightmares – to be haunted by them – for weeks, months or years afterwards, while the pleasurable dreams are only too inclined to slip off, wraith-like, into the mists of forgetfulness.

Graham Green can remember nightmares right back as far as his childhood, which is more than I can do but which, I gather from conversation with friends, is not especially uncommon. (*Recurring* childhood nightmares are, as you might expect, much more easily remembered than others.) Greene had frequent dreams of drowning – which were possibly inspired originally by an attack of hay-fever, during which he felt as if his lungs were filling with water. And he had a recurring nightmare of a witch jumping on him from behind, digging her nails into him: one time he dreamt that he turned and fought her, and after that he never had that nightmare again. Since his celebrated adventures as a youth playing Russian roulette he has had occasional dreams of trying to shoot at enemies only to find that 'the bullets are discharged without the force to penetrate' – an anxiety-dream which belongs aside all those missed trains.

In later life, long after the death of his father, whom he had respected but to whom he had not been close, Greene's submerged childhood love for the man would manifest itself in his dreams. In them, his father was confined to hospital, away from the family: sometimes he would return, but never for long, 'a silent solitary man, not really cured, who would have to go back again into exile'. These dreams, says Greene, he can remember so clearly that sometimes he has to remind himself that, in fact, his father lived with the family until the end of his days.

The final dream in the series, ten years after his father's death, saw Greene driving along with his mother. His father, by the side of the road, hitched a lift with them and told them excitedly that today he had been released from hospital. (Greene, a Catholic, points up the symbolic parallels with the notion of Purgatory.) At about the same time as this dream, Greene's mother also dreamt about her deceased husband. She had (in reality) broken her hip, and while in hospital had dreamt of her misery that her husband had failed to visit or even write to her; this misery carried over into real life when she awoke. Even awake, 'she felt unhappy because of his silence'.

## *A Certain Young Lady?*

Dreams such as these can be interpreted either as contacts with the spirit world (or whatever) or as the unconscious churning over the circumstances of the individual's mundane or emotional life for auto-psychotherapeutic or other purposes. It is more popular, in general, to opt for the former explanation; and one has to confess that it's difficult to explain *all* dreams of the arcane in strictly psychological terms. In the second part of this book we shall look in closer detail at such experiences, but in the meantime let's bid farewell to the world of creativity, the fringe-land where the intellect and the dream-mind combine forces, with a charming example of the dreamer as joker.

The dreamer in this case is the 'wrong' Sir Walter Raleigh, the British critic of, writer on and professor of English literature, who lived 1861–1922. In a letter from Ceylon to his sister Jessie, dated October 1886, he wrote:

> Do you know the poems of the Australian poet, Gordon?[16] I dreamt I asked you the question, stating it as my opinion that they completely superseded the Psalms of David – an obviously incorrect view. You replied that the Psalms of David were inspired, and a discussion ensued on the nature of inspiration. Driven from the position that everything was inspired, I maintained that nothing was verbally inspired, and that it was not worth while calling anything inspired, for in their stupidest moments the critics read more into Shakespeare than he ever meant. I was confuted by your producing a 'Synoptical Scheme of the Verbal Inspiration of the Psalms of David' printed in the form of a shilling novel and written by P.
>
> From this it appeared that the verbal inspiration was supplied to the Psalmist something in the form of *bouts rimés* [rhyme-endings], one word of each verse was given and David had to supply the rest as best he could from his own head. In spite of his striking success at this game, it was proposed to omit in future copies of the Bible all the 'human' part and print only the inspired words, which made absolute nonsense. This proposal was warmly supported by the Psalmist's namesake, Mr. David E., who had written a pamphlet and

formed an influential League which was about to return to Parliament.

I can't help but listen to the tiny voice at the back of my mind which suggests that somehow, somehow, Macaulay's mischievous niece had a hand in this dream. Not content with forging Pepys' diary, she was now intent on obliterating most of the psalms . . .

No, no, the whole idea's ridiculous. Or, again, perhaps you'd best read Part Two before you decide whether or not you want to agree with me.

## PART TWO
# The Country of the Strange

when Alice awoke she was all alone
    but past all hope of caring.
the train rattled through
a country station or two
    with empty houses staring.
she wanted to move
walk up and down for a while
but found that she could not stand;
her sight fastened for a sickened moment or two
    on the crablike claw of her hand.
        (and who could touch her
        and who could teach her
        that time is in confusion?
        conviction, knowledge and understanding
        are all parts of its illusion.)
and then she saw in her leathery palm
the reflection of an angel,
its hand upon her shoulder . . .

– Paul Barnett, 'History Book'

# 4
## *The Country of the Strange*

I saw their starv'd lips in the gloam
With horrid warning gapèd wide,
And I awoke, and found me here
On the cold hill side.

– John Keats,
'La Belle Dame Sans Merci'

*Caesar:* Nor heaven nor earth have been at peace to-night:
Thrice hath Calpurnia in her sleep cried out,
'Help, ho! They murder Caesar!'

– William Shakespeare,
*Julius Caesar*

After a television broadcast in October 1983 I was much berated by a couple of members of the studio audience for two of the points that I had made. The first was that I estimated that 95% or so of the dreams generally recognized as paranormal could in fact be reasonably simply explained in prosaic terms. The second was that I was unimpressed by 'precognitive' or 'clairvoyant' dreams of major catastrophe, because it is impossible to separate out any which might indeed have a parnormal genesis from the vast mass of *apparently* paranormal dreams which arise purely from the statistical fact that a lot of dreams are dreamt. For example, in the United Kingdom alone perhaps half a million or even a million nightmares are experienced each night. It would be rather startling if at least a handful of these didn't correspond in some way

– perhaps even quite closely – to any particular disaster which had happened that night or in the succeeding few days.

I should have known better and kept my heresy to myself. One person announced that she had had precognitive dreams about the Yorkshire Ripper.[1] The dreams involved a man slashing at her with knives, and each time she had the dream she knew that the Ripper would strike within a few days or, at worst, weeks. In fact, during the height of his career, such a prediction about the murderer was not especially dramatic; moreover, the nickname 'Ripper' misled the public, because the weapon was a hammer, not a knife. Another member of the audience described to me at great length an astonishing dream which she had had during one of the recent embassy sieges: the most significant element of the dream-prediction seemed to be that the siege would end with shots being fired, which indeed it did a few days later. Once again, I fail to be startled by this prediction.

The problem about any attempt to discuss matters paranormal is that there is so much dross; and this problem is intensified a millionfold when the narrower area of enquiry is into paranormal dreams. Some dream-stories are either fraudulent or apocryphal; some are born from misunderstandings; and many arise through the phenomenon described in the classic *Phantasms of the Living* (1886) as 'reading back'. 'Reading back' is the process which starts when a real-life event bears a chance resemblance to something dreamt; the more the dreamer thinks about it, the more coincidences he or she 'remembers' between the dream and the reality; until the dreamer is quite honestly convinced that the dream was precisely identical with the reality. Where one can detect fraud or misunderstanding by tracing the dream back to source, and recognize apocryphal tales for what they are, unprovable one way or the other, examples of 'reading back' are extremely hard to weed out. As a general rule, one can say that most dreams which correspond exactly to the reality involve some 'reading back', but one cannot therefore say definitely that there was not *some* element of telepathy, clairvoyance, precognition or whatever involved in the dream as dreamt. As an example of what I mean, let's look briefly at the case of Eileen J. Garrett.

Garrett (1893–1970) was one of the most famous of 20th-century mediums. Born in Ireland, she did her early work in the UK before becoming a US citizen; she had been originally invited to the States in 1931 by the American Society for Psychic Research. In 1951 she founded in New York the Parapsychology Foundation, of which she remained president until her death. It's interesting to note in passing that, while she was generally regarded by others as a spirit medium – i.e., one communicating with the dead – she herself preferred to think that her various experiences were of a psychological rather than a spiritualist origin.

In the book *Telepathy* (1941) she tells of a striking example of dream telepathy. One Sunday in London she had the nagging feeling that her daughter, who was away at boarding school, was in distress of some kind. However, she dismissed this as unimportant on remembering that, at about this time every Sunday, the girl would be in the process of writing her weekly letter to her parents: Garrett believed that 'I had "caught" her thoughts'.

That night Garrett dreamt that her daughter appeared to her and said: 'I have not written you, dear, as my chest hurt. Tonight I am coughing, and have a fever. When the [headmistress] found that I hadn't written, she was very cross, and called me neglectful and undutiful.

But now she has been in my room, and understands that I am not well.' One assumes the child actually said in the dream words to this effect, rather than employing this strange, stilted tone.

The following day, the weekly school letter didn't arrive, and so Garrett took to the telephone.[2] The headmistress told her that the daughter was indeed in bed with a bad chest cold, and said that the illness had been responsible for the girl's 'sullen behaviour' and refusal to buckle down to writing home.

Now this is, of course, an absolutely spot-on telepathic dream – if we are to believe Garrett's recollection of it. Much later, in 1960, she began to work with Montague Ullman and his colleagues on telepathic dreaming, and the researchers must have looked forward excitedly to repeating such dramatic results. Unfortunately, the results that they did come up with are of that peculiar suggestive type which committed believers in ESP regard as astonishingly significant, and which all the rest of us find less than entirely convincing. For example, in *Dream Telepathy* (1973; probably the most important modern book on the subject), Ullman, Krippner and Vaughan describe an experiment in which Ullman was thinking about Howard Fast's novel *Spartacus* while Garrett slept. She dreamt that she went to a cinema where the newly released movie version of *Spartacus* was showing, but didn't actually go in. One can't really rate this 'telepathic dream' much higher than the interesting-coincidence level, especially since the movie was the 'talk of the town' at the time. Further dreams which she had that same night did, to be fair, raise the odds against pure coincidence somewhat, but not to the level where simple coincidence seemed an *impossible* explanation.

This seems to be a characteristic of telepathic dreams:

lots of people can give fantastic examples of really pinpoint accurate telepathic dreams which they've experienced; but when the dreamers are brought into the laboratory all that can be produced are vague allusions and similarities (not always close ones) to the 'target' object or picture which the experimenter is concentrating on. We can't go into the details of the way in which Ullman and his colleagues evaluated the results they obtained when guinea pigs were encouraged to dream about pictures which were being studied by the experimenters, but the techniques of evaluation do seem to me to allow complexes of vague similarities between dream and 'target' picture to determine that the dream is counted as a bullseye. (See pages 236–8.)

For example, in *Dream Telepathy* we find a case where the picture[3] was of a scene in India. The main figure has a bow and arrows; another man looks vaguely as if he has a rifle over his shoulder (in fact, it's a stick), and has a bundle of cloth at his feet; a third figure is playing a stringed instrument. There's a shelter in the background, and almost lost in the picture is a stake with a rope tied around it. The three men all have something on their heads.

The dreamer involved was Robert Van de Castle, the team's star at the telepathic art. He got the three men, all right, but in a Wild West scene (a pun on 'Indians'?); the three were standing rather than, as in the picture, seated. They were wearing berets, and all held rifles with the butts resting on the ground beside them. A bedroll featured. One of the main elements of the dream-scene was a rope – but the only rope in the picture features merely as an obscure detail; to be fair, Van de Castle thought that a collection of strings (the stringed instrument?) was important, too.

But all this isn't desperately impressive. I think we're

justified in politely forgetting about the rope, even though Van de Castle was insistent that it dominated his dream. We're left with the three human figures, the roll of cloth, the strings on the instrument, and the stick that looks a bit like a rifle. Yet Van de Castle gave this dream a rating of 100%: it was a 'direct hit'!

Distortions of fact like this – whether deliberate or unconscious – do not help one to decide whether or not such phenomena as dream-telepathy actually exist.

Nevertheless, however sceptical one might be about the whole topic of the paranormal, I think it would be a dishonest person who claimed that he or she did not have a profound visceral belief that in our dreams we are able to foresee the future or communicate telepathically with our fellows. This deep belief is illogical, and is unshaken by any contrary evidence. For my own part, I am not convinced that paranormal phenomena actually occur, and I will do quite a lot of work to find mundane explanations for even the most improbable of events; and yet the part of me that believes in dream-miracles will not keep silent. So, while I happily explain away a good 95% of 'paranormal' dreams, as I've noted, I find myself, against my will, being prepared to concede that the paranormal may indeed be at work in the remaining 5% of dreams – or at least in some of them. Unlike most other people, who are heavily prejudiced either in favour of or against the paranormal, I find myself prejudiced in favour of the 'don't know' category. So, if you find me being apparently too harsh or too gullible about the paranormal in this second part of the book, please be assured that I agree wholeheartedly with you, whatever you say.

With exceptions which I will clearly label, the dreams which I'll discuss belong to the 5% which I find difficult to explain without invoking a 'something else' which may or may not be the paranormal. I know that in some cases I've been hoodwinked; I just don't know which those cases are. I think that some of the 'mysteries' probably arose because the dreamer's unconscious picked up and correlated all sorts of relevant scraps of data without the conscious knowing anything about it. Once again, I don't know which dreams originated this way. And so on and so forth.

One of the most exciting recent notions in parapsychology is that, by tape-recording in a deserted room, you can, if you're lucky, start picking up subtle noises which you can interpret as the voices of the dead. Without going into too much detail, it seems quite probable that what you're really doing is creating what sound engineers call 'white noise', on listening to which you can hear anything you choose to hear.[4] It's rather like being able to 'listen' to pop records when you're travelling at a steady speed down the motorway: your ears pick out the bits of the road-hum (a sort of frequency-restricted white noise) that they want to hear, and sure enough the sound of the pop record is perfectly re-created for you.

Lyall Watson has pointed out that there is a bizarre parallel between recording the dead and experiencing dreams. The voices are jumbled and say strange things – often surrealistic things. Watson suggests that, if we accept that it's possible that recording equipment can pick up people's thoughts (if for no other reason than that they are actually unconsciously subvocalizing these thoughts), it seems no great logical extension to propose that perhaps the recorders are picking up thoughts transmitted through the people present in the room by the souls of the departed.

He points out that the best results are obtained when people in some way emotionally involved with someone dead are in the room: sure enough, it is this 'someone dead' whose voice will be heard on the tape. But it does seem to me that, if we accept that recorders can pick up very subtle subvocalizations, and if the people in the room have just said to the thin air, 'Good evening, my friends in the Beyond' (to quote Watson), then it is hardly surprising that those people will think about their favourite dead acquaintance and unconsciously subvocalize accordingly. Even more probably, nothing like subvocalization is involved: having thought about Auntie Nora, the experimenters will, as sure as eggs are eggs, 'hear' Auntie Nora's voice mixed up in all that white noise.

I've tried it and . . .

However, there is as Watson points out a strong possibility that the phenomenon at work is directly related to the dreaming process. It is often possible to dream of someone dead; the more common thing is to dream of someone you haven't seen for years, whether they're dead or not. Naturally, your dream about them is jumbled – in the way that most other dreams are. Your unconscious, the source of your dreams, speaks with a forked tongue. Is it not likely that, when you're listening 'open-mindedly' to white noise, your unconscious is taking the opportunity of speaking to you – hence the jumble and the surrealism?

If this is the case, then the use of white-noise generators may well supply us with an invaluable tool for the study of dreams, most significantly in terms of the way it may give us direct access to them. And, if we are able to establish immediately the contents of a 'dream' obtained in this way, then all the arguments about the existence or nonexistence of paranormal dreams should be swiftly settled. Unfortunately, it's been quite some little while since I started looking forward eagerly to the results of such research: either it hasn't been done or the results have been prosaic.

Paranormal dreams – like the paranormal itself – can be classified in various ways. For the purposes of this book, I've decided to divide the subject up into the following classes: the mystic and revelationary; the telepathic; the clairvoyant; instances involving or associated with Unidentified Flying Objects and presumed aliens; dreams in whcih the dreamer 'entertains visitors' or 'travels afar'; and diagnostic or healing dreams. Obviously there's a fair overlap between any two of these categories; and all of them may be involved when it comes to precognitive (or predictive) dreams. Since precognitive dreaming is by far the most important type of paranormal dreaming – or, at least, it's the most popular – it is discussed in Chapter Five. Reincarnation dreams, in which the dreamer 'visits a previous life', are really rather outwith the field of the parnormal, in that either they're of purely psychological interest or they involve the survival of the soul after death (choose whichever explanation you prefer); a third possibility is that they are generated by 'timeslips' or telepathic communication across the centuries. Again they are discussed separately, in Chapter Seven.

A number of 'classic' dream-tales are told frequently and have established themselves as generally accepted 'true stories'. In most cases they are impossible to verify, and were probably born from the fertile fields of popular mythology. I think it's of interest to leaf rapidly through a few examples of the type of dream-story which I, personally, distrust. If nothing else, they're quite fun.

## *Stranger Than Fact*

In his life of Dante, Giovanni Boccaccio tells of a curious example of dream clairvoyance (or you may prefer to describe it as a spirit visitation). After Dante's death it was found that thirteen cantos of the *Divine Comedy* were missing, and it was suggested that Dante's two sons, Jacopo and Piero, both of whom were minor poets, should finish their father's work. One night Jacopo dreamt that his father came to him and showed him the thirteen cantos, hidden in a niche in the wall behind a picture. Jacopo rose from his bed, knocked up his father's friend Pier Giardino, and went with him to Dante's old house, where they awoke the new occupant. Sure enough, the cantos were found mouldering behind the picture, in a niche which had gone unnoticed during the earlier searches for them.

The tale is a good one, and enjoyed widespread currency at the time. Of course, from the vantage-point of the 20th century, it's impossible to decide whether the tale is truth or fiction, and Boccaccio was not particularly concerned to track down corroboration of it from other sources. If we accept that Jacopo did indeed have a dream, it's perfectly likely that the dream simply reminded him of the hidden niche which he had long since forgotten about. Who can say?

If the passage of the centuries makes us doubtful about the veracity of a written record, how much more sceptical must we be about an oral tradition. A famous dream-tale, which is almost certainly of apocryphal status and yet which is often cited in 'wow!' dream-books, concerns John Chapman, the tinker and peddler of Swaffham, whose sudden acquisition of great wealth is evidenced by the memorials to him which remain in the Church of St Peter and St Paul in that town. (Swaffham is in Norfolk, about one third of the way long the A47 from King's Lynn to Norwich.)

The legend has it that one day the impoverished Chapman dreamt that, if he went to London and hung around near London Bridge, he'd meet a man who'd put him in the way of great riches. When the tinker awoke the next morning he immediately packed some supplies and set off on foot, ignoring the scornful catcalls of his wife. After walking the hundred or so miles to London, he took up his position at one end of London Bridge – and there he waited for three whole days. At the end of this time the owner of one of the shops on the bridge, who'd seen him standing patiently there, came up and asked him what he was up to. Chapman told the tale of his dream.

The shopkeeper scoffed. He, too, had had a curious dream recently, but he wasn't such a fool as to traipse a hundred miles through bad weather on the strength of it. He'd dreamt about a tinker who lived in Swaffham, Norfolk, called John Chapman. In the dream the tinker had a tree in his garden, and under the tree was buried a pot of gold.

Chapman made good time on the way home, and attacked the ground beneath his tree like a terrier after a buried bone. Sure enough, he found the pot of coins. There was better to follow. The pot's lid had an inscription on it which Chapman, who could not read, had translated by someone else in the village: it said that there was an even bigger hoard buried deeper down. This proved to be true, and Chapman's fortune was made.

A little while after this, it was generally decided by the locals that the old church was falling to bits, and so the villagers levied a tax on everybody to pay for its rebuilding. Chapman had not publicized his new-found riches, and so was asked for only the usual pittance. However, he volunteered to give generously – paying for the construction of the whole of the northern aisle. That's why he's remembered in the church to this day.

This story dates from the middle of the 15th century and yet it is – astonishingly – as I say still quoted as a genuine example of the clairvoyant or precognitive dream at work! All right, say the credulous, perhaps some of the details are a little unreliable after all these years, thanks to distortions and embellishments introduced during oral repetition; but fundamentally it all happened just as the legend says it did. I simply do not believe this. Not only is the tale itself pretty incredible, it simply doesn't 'ring true': dreams don't work like that. Is it not far, far more likely that the humble tinker (if he ever existed) escaped from his grinding poverty in exactly the same way that many poor people have done both before and since, by turning to crime? The tale of the two pots of gold would seem to lend support to this hypothesis: Chapman pulls off a heist and resolves never to be tempted again (he does this far from home, perhaps going to London to do so). However, in due course the money runs out, and thus he ignores his virtuous resolution and perpetrates another crime. But his conscience troubles him and so, in order to appease a presumably wrathful God, he guiltily makes a large contribution to the church's reconstruction fund, swearing all those involved to secrecy. However, as in all small communities, the lifetime of a secret is measured in nanoseconds, and so the question as to the source of Chapman's wealth arises publicly. 'I had this dream, you see . . .' he explains to the gullible villagers.

I may be wrong. It may not have happened like that at all. Every word of the legend may be gospel. But I think my explanation – or something along those lines – is much more likely; and anyway the matter can now never be proved either one way or the other.

Wrong but sensational explanations for perfectly normal occurrences can pass into the public consciousness almost without delay. A few weeks before I wrote these words, the disc jockey and compere David Jacobs saw what he thought was a UFO, and the tale was splashed all over some of the gutter-press front pages. In fact, what he saw was an extremely bright meteor, which was witnessed as such by thousands of other people. Only those newspapers which had missed out on the first sensation bothered to report this – and of course it didn't make such good headlines. Yesterday I had lunch with a perfectly intelligent human being who assumed that the object Jacobs saw was a mysterious entity unknown to nature. My friend had simply missed the explanation because he reads the wrong newspaper.

John Wesley (1703–1791), the joint founder of Methodism, made a practice of recording in his journal accounts of unusual dreams; as we shall see in the next chapter, he had only one significant (in paranormal terms) dream himself, and even that one wasn't spectacular (see page 317). However, his journal contains a number of interesting references, which mustn't be taken too seriously. One must remember that, while Wesley was recording the dreams in good faith, he was only too willing to accept that paranormal events did indeed take place, and had no notion of the fact that it might be worth his while to check up on a few points before accepting what he was told as being the complete truth.

Here's an account from 31st November, 1772:

> A young man of good sense, and an unblameable character, gave me a strange account of what (he said) had happened to himself and three other persons in the same house. As I knew they all feared God, I thought the matter deserved a further examination. So in the afternoon I talked largely with them all. The sum of their account was this:
>
> Near two years ago, Martin S—— and William J—— saw in a dream, two or three times repeated to each of

them, a person who told them there was a large treasure hid in such a spot, three miles from Norwich, consisting of money and plate, buried in a chest between six and eight feet deep. They did not much regard this, till each of them, when they were broad awake, saw an elderly man and woman standing by their bedside, who told them the same thing, and bade them go and dig it up between eight and twelve at night. Soon after they went; but, being afraid, took a third man with them. They began digging at eight, and, after they had dug six feet, saw the top of a coffer, or chest. But presently it sunk down into the earth, and there appeared over the place a large globe of bright fire, which, after some time, rose higher and higher, till it was quite out of sight. Not long after the man and woman appeared again, and said, 'You spoiled all by bringing that man with you.' From this time both they and Sarah and Mary J———, who live in the same house with them, have heard, several times in a week, delightful music for a quarter of an hour at a time. They often hear it before those persons appear; often when they do not appear.

They asked me whether they were good or bad spirits; but I could not resolve them.

'Treasure-hunting' dreams like this one and John Chapman's are not uncommon features of folklore (we shall encounter one or two later when we look at clairvoyant dreams), and they have an uncanny habit of permitting the treasure-hunters to fail to find the treasure, for one reason or another. I once came across an original manuscript by a dowser who claimed that through a combination of dowsing and dreams he'd been able to unearth a treasure buried by a convent at the time when Henry VIII was despoiling the monasteries. On my quizzing the dowser further, he confessed that he'd novelized the account a little, solely for commercial reasons and without changing the main facts. The truth of the matter was that, despite all efforts, the treasure had stubbornly refused to be unearthed; furthermore, it was unlikely that there had ever stood a convent near the site he'd dreamed about. But the main *facts* hadn't been changed, you understand!

A rather more intriguing dream – one which M. R. James might have been proud to have invented – comes from Wesley's journal for 19th April, 1784:

> I went on to Ambleside, where, as I was sitting down to supper, I was informed notice had been given of my preaching, and that the congregation was waiting. I would not disappoint them, but preached immediately on salvation by faith. Among them were a gentleman and his wife, who gave me a remarkable relation. She said she had often heard her mother relate what an intimate acquaintance had told her, that her husband was concerned in the [Jacobite] Rebellion of 1745. He was tried at Carlisle, and found guilty. The evening before he was to die, sitting and musing in her chair, she fell fast asleep. She dreamed one came to her and said, 'Go to such a part of the wall, and among the loose stones you will find a key, which you must carry to your husband.' She waked; but, thinking it a common dream, paid no attention to it. Presently she fell asleep again, and dreamed the very same dream. She started up, put on her cloak and hat, and went to that part of the wall, and among the loose stones found a key. Having, with some difficulty, procured admission into the jail, she gave this to her husband. It opened the door of his cell, as well as the lock of the prison door. So at midnight he escaped for life.

Since this is a story told at *fourth* hand, and since it is packed with improbabilities (think of the incredible stoicism of a wife who sits comfortably dozing the night before her husband is to hang!), the most charitable thing one can say is 'Hmmmf!' and roughly the same sort of judgement must be accorded to the following, which Wesley reported in November, 1772, as having been told to him by 'a gentlewoman':

> Mrs B———, when about fourteen years of age, being at a boarding-school a mile or two from her father's [house], dreamed she was on top of the church steeple, when a man came up and threw her down to the roof of the church. Yet she seemed not much hurt, till he came to her again and threw her to the bottom. She thought [i.e., dreamed] she looked hard at him, and said, 'Now you have hurt me sadly, but I shall hurt you worse,' and waked. A week after she was to go to her father's. She set out early in the morning. At the entrance of a little wood she stopped, and doubted whether she should not go round instead of through it. But, knowing no reason, she went straight through till she came to the other side. Just as she was going over the stile a man pulled her back by the hair. She immediately knew it was the same man whom she had seen in her dream. She fell on her knees and begged him, 'For God's sake do not hurt me any more.' He put his hands round her neck and squeezed her so that she instantly lost her senses. He then stripped her, carried her a little way, and threw her into a ditch.
>
> Meanwhile her father's servant, coming to the school and hearing she was gone without him, walked back. Coming to the stile, he heard several groans, and, looking about, saw many drops of blood. He traced them to the ditch whence the groans came. He lifted

her up, not knowing her at all, as her face was covered with blood, carried her to a neighbouring house, and, running to the village, quickly brought a surgeon. She was just alive, but her throat was much hurt, so that she could not speak at all.

Just then a young man of the village was missing. Search being made, he was apprehended in an alehouse two miles off. He had all her clothes with him in a bag, which he said he found. It was three months before she was able to go abroad. He was arraigned at the Assizes. She knew him perfectly, and swore to the man. He was condemned, and soon after executed.

One of the most horrifying horror stories I know concerns a young woman who has been raped. She is driving with her husband and a friend when, suddenly, she spots the rapist walking along the pavement. The two men leap out of the car and, under cover of darkness, castrate the rapist: a fitting, if illegal, revenge. Breathless from their exertions, they climb back into the car and drive on. Five minutes later, the woman spots the rapist walking along the pavement . . .

I can't help feeling that the villain in this dream, assuming he ever existed (and, indeed, that the dream did), might just have been one of the 'rapists'.

The Lord himself, sometimes as Christ, not infrequently appears in dreams, His purpose being either to cure people or to convert them to Christianity. Wesley records two such cases, the first being that of a happy atheist:

Mr Holloway, a neighbouring exciseman, invited us to breakfast with him. He once began to run well [i.e., saw God], and now resolved to set out afresh; I trust we were sent to him for good.

His wife bitterly opposed this till, one day, as she

> was sitting in her house, a flash of lightning killed a cat which sat just by her, and struck her to the earth, scorching her flesh in many parts, and yet not at all singeing her clothes.[5] When she came to herself she could not but acknowledge the loud call of God. But her seriousness did not continue long; her acquaintances soon laughed her out of it.
>
> Yet God called her again, in dreams and visions of the night. She thought [i.e., dreamt] she was standing in the open air, when one appeared in the clouds exceeding glorious, above the brightness of the sun. She soon after saw a second, and then a third. One had a kind of spear in his hand; the second a besom [broom], wherewith he was going to sweep the earth; the third, an hourglass, as though time were short. This so deeply affected her that she began from that time to seek God with her whole heart . . .

Shades of Saul of Tarsus. In fact, this dream is a lot more credible than the others which Wesley cites: the woman was obviously deeply troubled by her lack of faith – not surprising, in that age – and finally her unconscious told her so. We'll be looking at mystic and religious dreams shortly, but here's an example of another subtype of them, the type in which Christ appears to effect a cure. Again in Wesley's words:

> Here [Oldham] a young woman, of unblameable character (otherwise I should not have given her any credit), gave me a remarkable account. She said: 'I had totally lost the sight of my right eye, when I dreamed one night that our Saviour appeared to me; that I fell at His feet, and He laid His hand upon my right eye. Immediately I waked, and from that moment have seen as well with that eye as with the other.

One can draw a parallel here between this case and that of St Porphyrius, who died in A.D.420. A wealthy Greek by origin, St Porphyrius was a hermit first in the deserts of Egypt, then later on the banks of the Jordan. He reluctantly accepted the position of Bishop of Gaza, which see he administered with astonishing skill. His biography, one of the most important of 5th-century documents, was written by his disciple, Mark the Deacon.

Porphyrius was extremely ill when he sent Mark to sell all his (Porphyrius') possessions, in order to give the proceeds to the poor. When Mark returned, he was astonished to find that Porphyrius was in the best of health: he naturally asked how come? According to Sabine Baring-Gould, Porphyrius replied:

> Forty days ago, being in extreme pain, I made a shift to reach Mount Calvary, where, fainting away, I fell into a kind of trance, during which, methought I saw our Saviour on the cross, and the good thief hanging beside Him. I said to Christ, *Lord, remember me when Thou comest into Thy kingdom*: whereupon he ordered the thief to come to my assistance, and he, raising me off the ground on which I lay, bade me go to Christ. I ran to Him, and He coming off His cross, said to me, *Take this wood* (meaning the cross) *into thy custody*. In obedience to Him, methought I laid it on my shoulders and carried it some way. I awoke soon after, and have been free from pain ever since, and without the least appearance of my having ever ailed any thing.

Mark was not unnaturally impressed, and set down this piece of dialogue for posterity. One is tempted to produce an ostentatious scenario in which Porphyrius subconsciously realized what was wrong with himself, so that his dream not only performed a diagnosis but also effected a cure. If Porphyrius' disease was psychosomatic, which all the symptoms seem to suggest it was, then this is exactly the kind of thing which one might expect to happen. Assuming, once again, the whole thing isn't just a legend.

One dream which Wesley records probably did occur – or, at least, the person who told him about it was convinced that it did. It turns up in a letter to Wesley from one of his acolytes, a certain Richard Moss, dated 28th June, 1745:

> On May 31 I went to Sykehouse and exhorted the people at all opportunities. On Monday, June 3, about three o'clock in the morning, [William] Holme came to me and said, 'Brother Moss, I have been just awaked by a dream that the constables and churchwardens came to press you for a soldier. I would have you get up and go to Norton.' I did so, and he walked with me about half a mile. At his return the constables and churchwardens were come. They asked him, 'Where is the preacher?' He said, 'I have just carried him away; but have you a warrant to press such men as these?' They answered, 'Yes, we have; and will press him if we see him here again.' He replied, 'You shall see him again in that day when the Lord shall judge the world in righteousness.'

It's hard to tell whether this was a prophetic or a clairvoyant dream. My own sneaking suspicion is that it was neither. My guess is that Holme heard that there was a plot afoot to pressgang the nonconformist troublemaker, and that he passed on his quite natural forebodings to Moss. Somewhere along the line, Moss got the impression that those forebodings were born out of a premonitory dream. But mine is an unromantic interpretation of the events.

Sometimes, as in the case of John Chapman, the Swaffham tinker, our incredulity is aroused because a dream-tale is just too good. For the final dream in our 'pretty blasted dubious' category we'll look at one of these, a very curious example of 'double dreaming' recorded in an 1873 report which came before the London Dialectical Society.

A certain Cromwell Varley and his wife went to stay with his wife's sister, who was extremely ill, in order to help her about the house. The first night that they were there, Varley dreamt that he woke to find himself paralyzed from head to foot. His sister-in-law then came into the bedroom (which was odd, of course, because she was completely bedridden) and told him that he'd die if he didn't move. He tried, but without success. She suggested that if she did something to terrify him he'd be startled out of his paralysis, but this failed, too, until she cried: 'Cromwell! I'm dying!' He was jolted out of both his paralysis and his sleep.

This woke his wife, too, and he told her about the dream. (Proof that it really was a dream included the fact that the bedroom door was bolted on the inside.) They noted the time was a quarter to four, then dozed off.

In the morning, Varley persuaded his wife not to tell the sister-in-law about the dream, on the grounds that it would be interesting to see if she had had a similar or related one. And indeed she had. She told exactly the same story of having startled him out of paralysis by shouting that she was dying, and said that her version of the dream had occurred, she knew, between half past three and four in the morning.

The only trouble is that I don't believe this account: I think it's a fabrication. Why was the Varleys' bedroom door bolted? – to protect them from the maraudings of a bedridden woman? What on earth induced Varley to think that his sister-in-law might have had a complementary dream to his own? Surely that's the last thing he'd have suspected – unless he was a dedicated psychic investigator, which it doesn't appear that he was. The whole story simply doesn't hold water once you begin to think about the circumstantial details . . . and yet it appears in various of the 'wow!' books on paranormal dreamings as if it were all thoroughly verified. This despite the fact that the only corroborative witnesses were the three people involved, one of whom was dying.

## *Curios*

It's all too easy to invoke the paranormal when we have curious dreams. The ethologist Mireille Bertrand has described a pet monkey living in Paris which clearly had dreams of the clairvoyant sort. While asleep, but only while asleep, it would occasionally give vent to cries known as 'leader calls', barking noises made by young males of its species as they leave their family group. In the wild, this occurs when they are aged about six; and sure enough the pet monkey was about six years old at the time that it displayed this behaviour.

The conclusion is inescapable: instinct was causing it to dream of a situation which it could never experience in real life, and so it was reacting according to the 'instinctive code'. But what would the 'obvious explanation' have been had a human being dreamt analogously? Instinct certainly wouldn't have been invoked as an explanation: the case would be in the files as one of clairvoyant dreaming.

All sorts of reasons can make people believe they've had paranormal experiences, even ardent sceptics. Sigmund Freud, for example, refused for most of his life to believe in the very possibility of telepathic or predictive dreams, not because he'd thought about the subject, it seems, but simply because the whole notion was anathema to him and because he never had a remotely plausible paranormal dream himself.

But one of his patients produced a case which intertwined Freudian interpretation and precognition so intimately that Freud was persuaded to modify his views. The patient, a middle-aged man, had dreamt that his wife had just had twins. A little later, in real life, he was contacted by his son-in-law with the news that the dreamer's *daughter* had just given birth, a month prematurely, not to one child, as expected, but to twins. Freud couldn't bear to pass up the apparent example of wife-daughter substitution in a dream!

His conclusions on the subject were:

> It is probable that the study of occult phenomena will result in the admission that some of these phenomena are real . . . [but] my personal attitude towards such material remains one of reluctance and ambivalence.

In earlier ages, of course, people weren't nearly so reluctant and ambivalent about the subject, as we have seen in Wesley's case: not only was the paranormal an accepted fact of life, its influence was commonly felt. Paranormal experiences might not happen to you, but they were happening all the time to the friends of the bloke you'd just met in the alehouse. The modern equivalent of this process is the generation of 'urban legends', tales like the one about the granny who died during the family holiday in Spain and so they tied up the body in a blanket and stuck it in the boot but the next night the car was stolen and . . . Even today, some of these tales make it into the newspapers as 'genuine' reports.[6]

In the past, then, the paranormal – and indeed the occult in general – was far more 'respectable' than it is today. It was not uncommon to find people engaged in scientific research which embraced also beliefs which today we find bizarre. Kepler, for example, not only worked out the motions of the planets, so laying the foundations for much of modern physics, he also practised astrology and gave more than a passing nod to the idea of the music of the spheres. We'll look at a couple of 16th-century scientists who were involved also in the occult, and who were much affected by dreams, Cardano and Dee.

Gerolamo Cardano (1501–1576), one of the most remarkable men of the Renaissance, is almost forgotten today. The list of his achievements in the sciences is astonishing, yet most of his discoveries and inventions were to be left rotting for centuries before being developed by other people. He affected the course of British history quite profoundly, firstly by curing Archbishop Hamilton, in effect the Regent of Scotland for the infant Mary Queen of Scots, from asthma; and secondly by (probably deliberately) casting a false horoscope for the sickly Edward VI of England, predicting for him a long and healthy life, and thereby fatally postponing the attempt of John Dudley, Duke of Northumberland, to put Lady Jane Grey on the English throne. It is a tantalizing exercise in 'what if?' to speculate on the future course of British history had Mary of Guise taken over the regency of Scotland, or if Lady Jane Grey had become and stayed Queen of England.

His life is a worked example of the Wheel of Fortune in action. He was born a bastard to a mother who had attempted to abort her unwanted child. Despite the burden of bastardy, he succeeded by dint of sheer intellect and persistence in becoming one of the most renowned scholars of his day, a rich and famous man. He spent the last few years of his life as a penniless beggar, destroyed in large part by his children. His elder son was a thief and murderer, eventually executed for having poisoned his wife (he had been blackmailed into marrying her because of an earlier murder he'd committed). His daughter was a nymphomaniac of appetites outstanding even in those immediate post-Borgian times: she started her career by incest with her elder brother, had her marriage to a nobleman annulled because of her infertility, insatiability and incurable promiscuity, and died of syphilis. And Cardano's younger son was a violent criminal who, at an early age, became a freelance torturer for the Inquisition; later, largely in order to assist his promotion to the position of professional torturer, he played a large part in betraying his father to that institution.

Life in the Cardano family was, therefore, like something on television. The three offspring, by their actions, shredded their father's reputation and reduced his fortune to nothing. The coup de grace was administered by the mathematician Niccolò Tartaglia (*c.*1500–1577), who claimed that Cardano had stolen from him his method for solving cubic equations (it's conceivable that the claim was justified: the details are time-shrouded). Tartaglia it was who engineered the betrayal of Cardano to the Inquisition.

But Tartaglia did worse: he destroyed Cardano's reputation among scientists for centuries – even today, this description of Cardano, found in one popular work, is not atypical: 'He was a thoroughgoing knave and rascal, a gambler, cheat, given to murderous rage, and insufferably conceited . . .'[7]

That the dead should be vilified is one thing – they are, after all, no longer around to have their feelings hurt, or they can scoff at our insults from Elsewhere – but that their achievements should be rejected wholesale is quite another. Cardano was indeed a gambler: he needed the income derived thereby during his struggling years. In order to be a successful gambler, he made the first attempt to work out the Laws of Probability, publishing the results of his attempt, which was partly successful. He was the first to realize that syphilis is a disease distinct from gonorrhea, rather than simply a more savage form – a discovery that was forgotten for three hundred years – and, moreover, he discovered a cure for it. He accidentally discovered the concept of allergies, in his curing of Hamilton's asthma, although he didn't realize the nature of the beast he had by the tail. He invented the universal joint as well as the device called the Cardan shaft, thanks to which your spine isn't shattered to smithereens every time your car goes over a bump in the road at ninety miles an hour.

But in many ways he was an unsympathetic character, largely as a result of his temper and his hypochondria: he would drive friends away by talking for hours about his own maladies, real or imagined. He believed in premonitions and prophetic dreams: thanks to these, and to the horoscopes he case for himself, disaster and death seemed throughout his life to be just around the corner. Disaster came with sufficient frequency that his premonitions seemed always to have been correct. As for death? Well, every time he unexpectedly failed to die, he just went and cast his horoscope again to determine a new death-date.

In his student days he was a prey to nightmares – most of which seem to have been brought on by readings and rereadings of the *Malleus Maleficarum*, that most evil of books, which describes the tortures used by the followers of the Prince of Peace to extract confessions of witchcraft from the poor witless wretches who fell into their hands. Faceless figures, who seemed to be built out of rings of mail, would promenade in front of him. These would be followed by a red-winged screaming cock whose hellish voice would make terrible threats. The meaning of the threats would dissolve as he awoke. All this was, of course, rather milder stuff than the nightmarish material he had been reading.

A more significant dream happened some years later. The tale, which comes from his autobiography, is such a good one that it has to be suspect – it sounds like the romantic exaggeration of an old man looking down all the long days of his youth.

He was living in Sacco when, one night, a comet appeared overhead: instantly he knew that this was a spectre of great significance to him. Once he had calmed himself, he went to bed and fell asleep. He was in a rare and beautiful garden. Through the door opposite him came a fair woman, whom he embraced. As they kissed they were suddenly in complete darkness, the two of them, and he was so filled with a nameless dread that he awoke in a cold sweat.

Not long afterwards, the air was suddenly rent by shouts and yells. There was a fire – the house of the captain of the garrison, Bandarini, was ablaze, although the captain and his family were fortunately not at home. When they returned, they moved into the house next door to the one in which Cardano lived. A few days later he chanced across one of Bandarini's daughters: it was the girl who had been in his dream. As you might expect, they were soon wed.

The whole tale, as I said, seems all to dovetail in a little too well.

Much later, when he and his wife bore their third child (the second son – the one who was to grow up to be a torturer), Cardano dreamt that a great figure appeared to him and rebuked him, saying that it was about time that his literary output began to match the fertility of his loins. He took this to be a signal that he should start writing an important book – possibly his most important – and so, as soon as he awoke, he sat down to work on his definitive treatise on mathematics. Again, this story seems to lack authenticity. Recounted by him years later, it's almost as if he were saying: 'It was God who told me to write this book, so it *must* be good!'

This mathematical text was not his first book. Some years earlier he had bumped into an old university friend who calmly announced that he'd inherited a printing press. Cardano, like so many would-be authors, lusted after the sight of his work in print. Furthermore, as he explained in his autobiography, it fitted in with a recent allegorical dream he had had of his life.

He was one of a vast crowd running towards a mountain. When he asked someone nearby where they were all rushing to he was told they were rushing towards Death. Alarmed – as who would not have been? – he turned aside and saw a slope covered with bare autumn vines; using these as handholds he was able to climb the steep hillside. There were jagged rocks on all sides, and often he nearly fell into deep crevices, but at last he reached the top, to find a barren plain. Crossing the plain he came to a hut. From the hut came a small but wise boy clad in a grey coat.

It's not hard to see the allegory in all this. Leaving aside the rest, the boy – of course! – represented his new-found printer friend, the one who was to carry his name and fame forward into the future. This is all quite impressive stuff . . . except that in the event his friend proved to be such a bad proofreader that the book in question, while a tremendous popular success, brought poor Cardano more than his fair share of academic ridicule. It was to be a while before he was able to salvage his reputation.

His prophetic dreams were, to say the least, unreliable. As with his other premonitions and his horoscopes, they had a habit of warning him of his imminent death. To take just one example: He dreamt that his dead mother came to him and told him that he would be joining her in the following year. This was particularly convincing to him because his horoscope agreed that he was going to die the following year, 1545. In fact, in 1545 he *did* have a brush with death – narrowly escaping being run over by a wagon – but this is hardly a convincing vindication of the dream. Those were dangerous times he lived in – wars, the Inquisition, plague, indiscriminate murder – and it must have been a rare year in which an individual didn't think, at least once during the twelvemonth, that his or her number was up. But as far as Cardano was concerned, he believed that the prophecy had been fulfilled – well, nearly.

We find the same mixture of the rationalist and the bizarre in John Dee (1527–1608) as we do in Cardano. More has been attributed to Dee than to virtually any other figure except, perhaps, Leonardo: if you believe everything you read, he was an accomplished occultist, a spymaster, an astrologer, a mathematician of note, a scryer (with the help of Edward Kelley), a mystic . . . And, naturally, his dream-world was important to him – although it is difficult to separate fictitious accounts of his dreams from the genuine ones. Here is an account of a dream of his which he reported in his diary for 24th November, 1582:

> Saturday night I dreamed that I was dead, and afterwards my bowels were taken out and I walked and talked with diverse [people], and among others with the Lord [Treasurer] who was com to my house to burn my bokes when I was dead, and thought he loked sourely on me.

Although he is said to have had seemingly prophetic or clairvoyant dreams before – for example, dreaming the location of a lost basketful of clothes – it was after his second marriage, in 1578 to Jane Fromond, that his interest in such dreams really began to develop. In his diaries we find records not only of his own dreams but also of hers.

In the main, however, his dreams throughout his life lacked significance – either on the personal or on the larger scale. In one, which Richard Deacon describes in the standard biography, *John Dee* (1968), Dee dreamt of himself naked with

> my skyn all overwrought with work like some kinde of tuft mockado, with crosses blew and red; and on my left arme, above the arme, in a wreath, this word I red – *sine me nihil potestas facere* ['without me it is impossible to make anything'].

Dee was, from time to time, an important man in English affairs of state – especially because of the favour shown to him by Elizabeth I – but his dream-message overstates matters by really rather a long chalk.

But from 1581 for a year or two his interest in dreams was particularly profound, primarily because he was being pestered by nightmares. Or were they all nightmares? Some sound suspiciously to the modern mind like poltergeists – literally 'rattling ghosts' although, if they exist, almost certainly manifestations of the disturbed human psyche.

> The strange noyse in my chamber of knocking, and the voice ten times repeated somewhat like the scrich of an owle but more longly drawne, and more softly, as it were in my chamber . . .
>
> . . . all the night strange knocking and rapping in my chamber . . .

Other, similar, references litter his diaries.

Skipping shyly away from the controversial subject of poltergeists, we come across a much more reassuring dream which his wife had. She dreamt that a celestial being came to her and told her that she was pregnant, and would bear a child called Zacharias. 'Be of good chere,' the celestial creature added, 'he sal do well as this doth.' Of course, depending on the identity of the celestial being, we might have to put this down as an example of a precognitive dream that failed to come true. More likely, since there are so many parallels with the vision experienced by the Virgin, this dream was merely a natural product of the religion-suffused 16th century.

The true significance of Dee's dreams from this period is that it seems likely that they were the critical factor which impelled him to take up his interest in such matters as clairvoyance and scrying. These two activities were to be an important part – sometimes the most important part – of his life for the rest of his years.[8]

We can see that these two men, Cardano and Dee, had each about the same experience of paranormal dreaming: that is to say, not much. Yet Cardano believed that his dreams were indeed of considerable psychic significance and governed his life, while Dee's life probably really was changed by his dreams. There are plenty of cases of dreams having this effect in our own century, as we shall see in the next few pages; and in this context it's perhaps interesting to note that the dreamers in the audience at the television show I mentioned at the beginning of this chapter were almost unanimous in their belief that certain of their dreams were strikingly paranormal and fundamentally important – hence the persistence of the dreamer whose 'precognitive' dreams were little more than mild coincidences. I think this is all part and parcel of the intensified emotion we experience in dreams. When we awaken after a particularly vivid dream, whose images and emotions are etched into our minds, we *know* that it must *mean something*. For example, in *Over the Long High Wall* (1972), J. B. Priestley claims to have had precognitive dreams and then goes on to describe one which has yet to come true. It's not a very dramatic dream – he saw himself confronted by a stranger – but he's sure that it was genuinely precognitive: the quality of the dream experience was quite different from normal. (In autumn 1983 the dream had still not come to pass.) My own guess – and doubtless Priestley would disagree with me violently – is that he merely had a particularly vivid 'different' dream.

Whatever the case, some apparently paranormal dreams have had the effect of changing history. There is persistent rumour that Hitler experienced paranormal dreams, both prophetic and clairvoyant, and that he made his military decisions at least partly in accord with what he saw in his dreams. While I haven't been able to track these stories down to source, I did find that Hitler was frequently visited by nightmares of extraordinary intensity to which he reacted violently and noisily, but then if you'd been responsible for what Hitler had been responsible for you'd have had the odd nightmare, too. Or, at least, I hope you would have.

But I did track down a paranormal dream by the Nazi General Professor Karl Ernst Haushofer (1869–1946) which had a pretty startling effect.

Various factors inspired Rudolf Hess's crazy flight to Scotland, in 1941, where he strove to talk peace between Germany and Britain with the Duke of Hamilton, whom he had met at the Olympic Games in 1936. On a practical level, as Deputy Leader of the Nazi Party, Hess was being outshone by Germany's wartime leaders: he was losing influence and contemporary fame, and the sole way of restoring these seemed to be the 'scoop' arrangement of a peace. Moreover, he had no especial wish to see Britain destroyed (which he was sure would happen otherwise): his conviction was that Britain and Germany could coexist as powerful sister nations – surely the British would see the commonsense of Nazi policies! That he should have attempted the flight at all is testimony to the curiously loony world-outlook of the Nazi leadership during and particularly towards the end of the war. But this does not answer a fundamental question: why did Hess think he had even the slightest chance of success in his mission?

Ignoring the bizarre meanderings of his own already crazed brain, there were two signs which he took, together, as indications that he was bound to succeed. The first was the advice, given late in 1940, of one of his astrologers – possibly Ernst Schulte-Strathaus – that peace would be brought about, and that it would be brought about by him, Rudolf Hess. The second was a curious allegorical dream dreamt by Haushofer, the geopolitician whose notion of *Lebensraum* played a large part in Hitler's thinking and whose son, Albrecht, was a close friend of Hess's. According to Shirer's *The Rise and Fall of the Third Reich* (1959), Haushofer had seen Hess 'in a dream striding through the tapestried halls of English castles, bringing peace between the two great "Nordic" nations'. Hess could not ignore the dream.

Of course, the whole affair was a fiasco. Hess was held as a prisoner-of-war, and later sentenced at Nuremberg to life imprisonment. Albrecht Haushofer was imprisoned under suspicion of complicity in the July (1944) Plot against Hitler's life, and, in the final days of the Reich, shot by the SS as one of a batch of prisoners who, it was felt, were easier to cope with dead than alive. The professor, while under investigation as a war criminal, committed suicide.

Haushofer's dream had the potential to bring the war to a close three or four years early, but, at the opposite end of the scale, there are countless examples of paranormal dreams which are of no importance at all, even to the dreamer.

In 1863 the US manufacturer S. R. Wilmot set sail from Liverpool on the *City of Limerick*, heading back across the Atlantic to his family; he shared a cabin with one William Tait. On 13th October, Wilmot dreamt that his wife came to the cabin in her nightie, hesitated when she saw that there was someone else in the room, but nevertheless came to his bedside and kissed him. Not an unnatural dream for a married man on his way home after a long while.

In the morning, though, Wilmot was astonished when Tait accused him of being a rakehell for having allowed an attractive woman to come into his cabin in the middle of the night, scantily clad, and to kiss him. It transpired that Tait, lying wakeful, had witnessed the whole scene of Wilmot's dream.

Just to make matters extra extraordinary, when Wilmot arrived in New York his wife immediately asked him if he had any recollection of her having visited him. She had dreamt, on the night of the 13th, that she had crossed the ocean until she'd found the right ship, and within it her husband's cabin. She'd gone in, hesitated when she saw there was another man in the cabin looking at her, but nevertheless carried on and kissed her husband. On being questioned, she was able to describe the layout of the cabin in some detail.

A double dream, then – or even a triple dream, if you consider it more likely that Tait, too, was dreaming rather than lying awake.

Well, it's a good story. I can't find any first-hand source for it, but then I may have been looking in the wrong places. But the tale seems to have some remarkable similarities to one told by Stuart Holroyd in *The Directory of Possibilities* (ed. Wilson and Grant – see Bibliography for details). In Holroyd's tale a newlywed Englishwoman was travelling with her husband across the Atlantic to their new home in the USA. Back home, in the kitchen, her mother suddenly realized that the daughter was suffering a violent bout of seasickness, and promptly shot out of her body, over the ocean and into her daughter's cabin, where she suggested a wash, a change of clothes and a stroll on deck. (A very sensible, down-to-earth mum.) As you might expect, 'A few days later [the mother] received a letter from her daughter that confirmed every detail of the strange meeting.'

All very well, but Holroyd gives no dates, names or references for his tale. Come to think of it, we don't know much about the Wilmot story, either . . . Both are, however, examples – even if apocryphal ones – of out-of-body experiences (OOBEs), a topic we'll return to later. (See page 253.)

At the same ultra-trivial level the curious experience of a Mrs Jean Fielding, as recorded in *Phantasms of the Living* (1886), is worth noting as an example of a frequent paranormal phenomenon. One night, after her husband had fallen asleep, she found herself thinking about her girlhood home, which she had not seen for two decades or longer, and in particular about one Harvey Brown, a neighbouring squire. She thought no more about this until the morning, when her husband suddenly announced that he had had a 'strange dream about Harvey Brown, and been at the old home, wandering about it'.

Coincidence? If so, it's a reasonably steep one. Fabrication? Possibly, but a trifle unlikely. Telepathy? Very probably – unless, of course, Mrs Fielding was just plain wrong when she said that neither of them had spared a thought for Harvey Brown for years. It's possible that they had both half-registered a mention of his name in the newspaper, or overheard someone speaking a similar name, or something of this sort. Still, I have to confess that I'm straining a little in my attempts to explain this dream in mundane terms, and I have to confess that telepathy seems an attractive option.

The point about apparently paranormal dreams such as these is not whether they are trivial or not: nothing could have been of less importance to Mr Fielding than dreaming about Harvey Brown. It is that, if they show that phenomena such as telepathy really exist, then their importance is perhaps as profound as Newton's enunciation of the Law of Gravity or Einstein's proposal of the Theory of Relativity. We have been used to regarding the paranormal as either nonexistent or, at best, an irrelevance. It hasn't entered our calculations when we have been plotting the future of the human race. The acceptance of the paranormal 'officially' would require a complete revision of humanity's 'world-view', a revolution throughout all the sciences. So these trivial dreams may be very important indeed.

But the classification of a dream as either trivial or significant depends very much on the individual dreamers themselves. I don't mean just the differing emotive effect which different dreams can have: if I have a particularly vivid and affecting nightmare I don't spend days thinking about its deep meaning or assume that it's important just because it scared the pyjama-bottoms off me. However, other people react differently: to some even the most innocuous and minor of dreams is important, either because dreams are *all* paranormal, or for some other reason which particularly motivates the dreamer concerned. It's all a question of how important you think dreams in general are.

C. G. Jung, whose name litters these pages, thought dreams were of paramount importance,[9] and so it's not really surprising to find that he had a number of dreams which he regarded as being paranormal. That he was interested in precognitive dreams goes almost without saying. Most psychologists do not accept his findings and speculations, regarding them in much the same way as they regard his idea of 'synchronicity' – that 'meaningful coincidences' are the result of the workings of some unknown 'acausal principle', that events need not be linked by cause and effect.

In a famous example, Jung noticed one day that his streetcar number was the same as that of his theatre ticket for the evening's performance, and that the same number was mentioned that day during a telephone conversation. This was, of course, a 'meaningful coincidence'. A much less famous example of the same sort of thing is to be found in Alan Vaughan's delightful diary entry for 19th April, 1968:

> Having read an account of Jung's finding a synchronistic relationship between his streetcar number, his theater ticket number, and a phone number, I studied my streetcar ticket number. It was 096960. Then I realized I was looking at it upside down. But it was the same: 096960. The number of the streetcar could also be read upside down. But instead of finding a third number, like Jung, I nearly tripped over an ashcan with the name JUNG written on it.

But back to Jung, and to an apparently clairvoyant dream of his.

He lay awake late thinking about a friend who had been buried the day before. At some point he fell asleep . . . but suddenly he had the feeling that the friend was in the room with him. Sure enough, there he was at the foot of the bed, beckoning for Jung to go with him; after an internal debate (Jung thought the friend's figure was a fantasy, but if he were *not* a fantasy and yet Jung treated him as such, what brutal ill-manners that would be!), Jung obeyed. The friend led him to his (the friend's) library and climbed up onto a stool to gesture at the 'second of five books with red bindings which stood on the second shelf from the top'. Jung couldn't see what the book was. Then he awoke.

But he was interested enough to approach his friend's widow to ask if he could have a look at the deceased's library. There was the stool, and there the five books with red bindings. The second from the left was Zola's *The Legacy of Death*. The contents were irrelevant, but clearly the title was not.

Jung was wise enough not to make too much of this. Although he claimed that he was unfamiliar with his friend's library, it seems probable that he had been there before – the two houses were only a few hundred yards apart – and while Jung says that in real life he certainly couldn't have seen the book's title on the spine from floor-level, one must be sceptical. Any bibliophile, on entering a room shelved with books, notices 'old friends' along the shelves, even without being able to read the lettering on the spines. (It's a little more complicated than this sometimes. One can half-recognize the book, and have the recognition confirmed by the *shape* of the lettering, even if one cannot recognize the letters themselves.) In this light, it is not especially surprising – and certainly no proof of clairvoyance – that Jung should dream that his recently dead friend should show him a book with the word 'death' in the title.

I find Jung's ideas on the paranormal particularly interesting when he links together two of his main preoccupations, UFOs and dreams. Around the beginning of

1959 a certain H. A. F. wrote to him of a dream in which he had seen a flying swan of which he wished to take a photograph. Just then the swan plunged to the ground, trailing smoke like a shot-down aircraft. Then H. A. F. dreamt of seeing the form of an aeroplane half-obscured by fog or smoke; and next he saw a helicopter-like vehicle approaching him. The occupants of the craft he recognized as beings from another world who were in every sense superior to *Homo sapiens*.

Jung points up the similarity between this account and those of UFO 'contactees' (i.e., people who claim to have chatted with UFOnauts or even been taken for rides around the Solar System) – a point whose validity will be realized, and reinforced, when we talk about the dreams of the Sunderland family (see page 260). He then goes on to interpret the dream as a dream (rather than anything else): The bird is a messenger of the gods, signifying that H. A. F. is about to have his consciousness raised to a 'higher level' by the denizens of that 'higher level'. But the bird/angel falls to Earth, with possibly catastrophic results. The consciousness is befogged and disturbed, and this turns to 'panic and collective psychosis, a fall of the angels with apocalyptic consequences'. Jung claimed that this sort of symbolism was becoming common, and indicated the approaching end of the world.

It is hard to assess quite how literal this interpretation of Jung's was – whether he really believed that such dreams were warnings of the end of the world, or whether he was merely saying that H. A. F. was concerned that the end of the world might be nigh. Remember that the dream was dreamt, and Jung was writing, during the major nuclear-arms build-up of the Cold War. Similarly today, now that a further insane build-up is in progress, 'end-times' reports, including many accounts of dreams containing the symbolism of apocalypse, are proliferating almost as swiftly as the nuclear devices which are at their root. Many of us believe that the holocaust is just around the corner, and that there is nothing that we, or even the organized peace movements, can do to prevent it. (Looking at the half-wittedness and frequent senility of the politicians whose trembling fingers are poised over the nuclear button, these pessimists seem to have a reasonable case.) But dreams of approaching horror do not necessarily signify that precognition is at work: what student has not had the spine-chilling dream of sitting in the exam hall, unable to comprehend any of the questions on the paper, only to pass the exam in real life with ease?

Jung had the idea that in dreams 'nowadays animals, dragons and other living creatures are readily replaced in dreams by railways, locomotives, motorcyles, aeroplanes, and suchlike artificial products' – and herein lies a curious parallel with the UFO phenomenon. In the Middle Ages people 'saw' witches riding the night sky on their broomsticks; in the 19th century they saw airships; in the 20th they see spaceships. Jung suggested that what happened was that wild animals no longer automatically terrified mankind, so that mankind had had to invent new objects of terror. A timid suggestion of mine is that there are indeed lights in the sky, which we lay-people, should we see one, cannot explain (they might be the planet Venus, but then again they might not): onto these lights in the sky we graft our preconceptions of what an inexplicable object might be. Once upon a time, it was a witch on a broomstick; nowadays it's a spaceship. I think it's possible that the same sort of thing happens in dreaming: whereas before we thought that our vivid dreams must have been inspired by God or the Devil, now we think of them in terms of the paranormal or communications from aliens.

Well, I don't, but from what I read it seems likely that you do.

We'll come back to Jung again in the next chapter. Let's look now at someone who had no such conviction that dreams were important, an unfortunate woman who features in a bizarre and rather frightening tale given by William Stevens in his *The Mystery of Dreams* (1950). A friend of his – whom he calls 'Mrs Milland' – dreamt repeatedly that she woke to find a strange man in her bedroom. The stranger looked at her, and then slowly advanced towards her, holding something[10] out; she knew that if he succeeded in touching her with the mystery object she would die, so she shouted at him to go away – which he did.

Some months later 'Mrs Milland' was found dead. A little earlier she had had a fatal fall in her bedroom. In the short time between this and her death she had muttered half-incoherently that she had fallen while struggling out of her bed in order to get away from a spectre.

This may very well be a unique example of a dream-figment – a person who doesn't even exist – committing murder. In other words, the figment gained such a hold over 'Mrs Milland's' mind that in due course it killed her, as surely as if it had been a real stranger lurking in her bedroom with murderous intent.

A paranormal dream or not? I prefer not to think too hard about this dream

## *The Mystic Factor*

It's difficult to know whether mystic and revelatory dreams are paranormal or just plain psychopathic in origin. I've never had one, so I tend to think that people who've had a mystic dream are mentally not all that they could be, but if I have one in the future I know I'll immediately realize that the dreams are in reality messages from the deity.

Jung had just such a dream. Towards the end of 1946 he suffered a very severe heart embolism, which confined him to bed for some time. From his bed he wrote to the Dominican Father Victor White, at that time Professor of Dogmatic Theology at Blackfriars, Oxford, about a dream he (Jung) had had the previous night. The dream seems to have originated – or so Jung believed – in alchemical symbolism: a bright diamond 'like a star high in heaven' is reflected in a tranquil pool of water. To Jung this referred to the alchemical idea that everything above has its reflection below: the diamond is God and the reflection of God in the water is Jung himself. As a very sick man, he took exaggerated consolation from this reassurance.

In his strange, short, poetic book *For a Message* (1974) the British mystic Dr Arthur Guirdham has much to say on dreams, not all of it 100% comprehensible but all of it beautifully expressed. He gives several examples of dreams,[11] one of which we must consider before we make sense of his 'conclusions'.

He tells us that often he is conscious of the presence of his dead father – indeed, that a casual acquaintance has on occasion seen the father with him. One night, staying at an inn which has happy childhood associations for him (and where, in later life, he inevitably experienced great happiness), he was profoundly aware of his father's presence. However, on going to bed, he did not dream about his father, as expected, but instead about a girl who had stayed with the family 25 years before, and whom he had seen only once since. Guirdham stresses that there had never been the least hint of romance between them; only extremely rarely did any memory of her existence come to his mind.

Instead, he felt that the woman had been sent by his father to reveal a truth to him:

> He awakened the presence of this girl because she was beautiful, and he knew that to me there was no truth without beauty.

He claims that he first felt her invisible presence before falling asleep – indeed, that her presence was so strong that he was surprised he fell asleep at all. In his dream they climbed a mountain together, then soared above the mountaintop holding hands; below, on the summit, he could see a snow-filled crevice with a crocus peeping through the snow. Soon they were so high that he could see all the towns and villages that are or ever had been on Earth.

He turned to the woman with a joy that came from beyond her, 'from beyond the gods'. He sensed that he and she were identical; and then she disappeared from his sight by stages, the last vestige being 'the intimation of a smile' – rather like the Cheshire Cat. He felt tremendously alone, but still they journeyed together, up, up, up, to the region beyond the stars.

In the first zone of stars, forms dissolved to leave only patterns of vibrations. In the second zone of stars, there was music which he recognized from childhood – the music of the circling stars themselves. From this he realized that the music was the pure form of sensation; that all our senses are really only different facets of the same, single unified sensation.

She had left him by the time he entered the next 'world', which was filled with silence as by a pent-up breath; where she had been there was 'the inaudible harmony of vibrations cohering', a scenario which is beyond my humble comprehension. In the 'worlds' beyond this one there was no such thing as the individual psyche; while there was individuality, there was no sense of it.

In a further 'world' he found himself thinking in geometric symbols rather than words or images (I'm tempted to draw an analogy with the experiences of Austin Spare – see page 67 – who claimed to have dreamt about impossible geometries). He was looking into 'the creative void . . . the emptiness which is the source of all reality'. This was the seventh of the 'heavens'.

He awoke with the sight of the woman in his mind's eye.

Guirdham claims that dream-figures like the woman are 'messengers' sent to us to grant us revelations. In his case, he says, they always take the form of women – but this is not to imply that there is anything sexual involved; indeed, he says that the 'messengers' can be recognized because in their presence lust dies. While they take the form of women known to him, this is only a matter of form (as it were). They are women because only *via* the Eternal Woman, who lies beyond the realm of God, can one reach the realm beyond even that of the Eternal Woman, that of the ultimate 'nameless principal', whoever that principal might be. Even should the 'messenger' take the form of a man, there would really be a woman inside that male form.

The dreams – 'visions' – in which the 'messengers' appear come only in maturity. The 'messengers' themselves are always beautiful; they have a great childishness and yet great depths of wisdom – wisdom not learnt but a part of them, born from their memories of other lives. They are the children of the great Earth Mother, and they have come to help us to realize Truth.

I have to admit I don't understand it all.

The *Life* of St Teresa of Avila is packed with accounts of her visions – most of which, to don an atheistic hat, seem to have been hallucinations, although some were probably dreams: it's impossible to tell them apart. My guess is that she subjected herself to such privations that she 'saw' all sorts of strange things. Anyway, a couple of her mystical dreams or hallucinations are worth our brief attention.

In one, an encounter with an angel, it is generally believed that there is considerable sexuality involved – that is to say, that she had an erotic dream in which spirituality and carnality were fused, with the dream employing spiritual desire as a symbol for the carnal version. Certainly her reaction to it sounds orgasmic, but I have my doubt as to whether the modish explanation is correct. Other things in life can produce orgasmic feelings than the act of love itself: the thrill of suddenly solving an important long-standing problem, for example, or finally mailing off the manuscript of a book to one's publisher. But see what you think:

> But it was our Lord's will that I should see this angel in the following way. He was not tall but short, and very beautiful; and his face was so aflame that he appeared to be one of the highest rank of angels, who seem to be all on fire . . . In his hands I saw a great golden spear, and at the iron tip there appeared to be a point of fire. This he plunged into my heart several times so that it penetrated to my entrails. When he pulled it out, I felt that he took them with it, and left me utterly consumed by the great love of God. The pain was so severe that it made me utter several moans. The sweetness caused by this intense pain is so extreme that one cannot possibly wish it to cease, nor is one's soul then content with anything but God.

Equally interesting is her account of a visit to Hell:

> The entrance seemed to me like a very long, narrow passage, or a very low, dark, and constricted furnace.

> The ground appeared to be covered with a filthy wet mud, which smelt abominably and contained many wicked reptiles. At the end was a cavity scooped out of the wall, like a cupboard, and I found myself closely confined in it . . .
>
> I felt a fire inside my soul, the nature of which is beyond my powers of description, and my physical tortures were intolerable . . . But even this was [as] nothing to my agony of soul, an oppression, a suffocation, and an affliction so agonizing, and accompanied by such a hopeless and distressing misery that no words I could find would adequately describe it.

This last sentence provides us with a very accurate description of a really bad nightmare. St Teresa gives us several more sentences in similar vein, before describing in equally graphic terms what it was like being crammed into that cavity in the wall.

> It was not the Lord's will that I should at that time see more of hell itself; since then I have seen another vision of frightful things that are the punishments for certain vices.[12]

The point of the whole venture was, of course, to demonstrate to her quite what it was that she had been delivered from, and how grateful she should be for the deliverance.

## *Telepathic Dreamers?*

During World War II John Barnett was stationed in Nigeria – where, indeed, he was to spend some years after the war. His wife Muriel spent the early part of the war in Britain, and then went out on a convoy to Nigeria to join her husband.

At one stage during the journey there was a U-boat

alert, and all the passengers were brought up on deck. It was night, and destroyers cruised around probing the surface with searchlights. Fortunately it was either a false alarm or the U-boats decided that the opposition was too tough to take on: whichever, in due course the all-clear was signalled. Muriel Barnett has described to me the terror of standing impotently on deck, watching the destroyers at work and waiting for the sudden impact of a torpedo.

On her arrival in Nigeria she was met by her husband. One of his first questions was: 'What the hell happened the other night?' He had been profoundly affected by a dream or waking dream. He had sat up suddenly in bed and seen the room filled with rippling lights, like the reflections of light on water; and he had been filled with fear. In due course, the lights and the fear had waned.

The couple compared notes. As far as they could determine, his dream or waking dream had indeed taken place on the night of the U-boat alert – and, more than that, at exactly the same time as it. It was as if he had witnessed the whole scene through his wife's eyes, and felt her terror. One can only assume that Muriel Barnett's experience so affected her that her distressed mind reached out across the miles to 'contact' her husband's.

Or did it? I am very close to this story, because some years after the incidents described the couple gave birth to a son who would one day write this book. I have no reason whatsoever to doubt the account, but I can't help wondering if, over the years, it's gained a little in the telling. I don't mean at all that it has been deliberately exaggerated in any way; but time and again when we read about paranormal dreaming we find that, quite unconsciously, mild coincidences between dream and reality are converted into exact parallels. This is the process we've mentioned before known as 'reading back'.

The answer would seem to be to take people who think that they frequently have paranormal dreams into the laboratory, so that the dreams can be recorded before the dreamer is told what the 'target' is. This is exactly what a team at Maimonides, under Ullman and Krippner, did during the 1960s and later. The dreamer would be placed in one room, sleeping, and being woken up every time his eye movements indicated that he was having a dream. He'd be asked about the contents of that dream, and then his report would be compared with that of another researcher, who had been in a different room staring at a picture. In the morning the dreamer would be shown a selection of pictures and asked to pick from it the one which accorded most with his dream. As you might suspect from such a statistically hilarious procedure, quite often the subject agreed that the 'target' painting, whether or not he had succeeded in picking it out, had something in common with his dreams.

The Maimonides team were a lot happier with their results than I would have been (see page 193). However, on occasion they did come up with someone who could regularly do better than describe incredibly tenuous connections between his dream and the 'target' picture. One such was a young British medium called Malcolm Bessent, who joined the team in 1969. The reason that his results were so much more exciting than the norm was that, when he was being tested, there was no other researcher staring at a picture in a different room. Sometimes the picture in question wasn't even chosen until the following morning. So the obvious conclusion is that Bessent's 'dream-eye' was able to take him not only into the other room, where the pictures were kept, but also ahead in time. At first glance, it would seem that telepathy – always considered the most respectable of the paranormal faculties – wasn't involved . . . unless, of course, Bessent's mind was capable not only of skipping into the future but also of entering into telepathic communication with someone there, possibly himself.

This may sound far-fetched: why opt for a complicated explanation when 'simple' clairvoyance or precognition would serve just as well? The reason is that Bessent's other results seemed to show that he was a telepath.

The most dramatic series of experiments which he was involved in took place in 1971, and was executed with the assistance of the rock band the Grateful Dead. The band was giving six concerts nearly fifty miles from the laboratory where Bessent was to sleep; each of the concerts had an audience of a couple of thousand. Fourteen slides were selected, two being picked at random for each concert; immediately before the concert someone would toss a coin to determine which of the two would be projected in front of the audience. Bessent's name was given to the members of the audience, who were then told to try to 'send' the picture to him during the quarter of an hour or so during which it was on show.

Bessent's best performance was on the night that a picture called *The Seven Spinal Chakras*,[13] by M. K. Scralian, was the 'target'. This shows a man in the lotus position with seven circular motifs running up vertically from his toes to the top of his head; these motifs are brightly coloured, as is the yellow pattern of concentric circles radiating from the top of the meditator's head.

Bessent reported dreaming of being interested in 'natural energy' and talking to a man who had invented a sort of storage box for solar energy. The man seemed to be suspended in midair. In addition, Bessent was certain that a spinal cord was in some way fundamentally important. Not bad: in the picture the meditator does indeed seem to be floating in midair, and the vertical line of motifs up his spine is dominant.

But there was a control at work during the experiment, unknown to the audience. Felicia Parise, who had shown good results in earlier experiments, had her dreams similarly recorded. Her results the night *The Seven Spinal Chakras* was the 'target' are astonishingly unimpressive, although Ullman's team optimistically awarded her a mark of 28 out of 100 for them. Yet a couple of nights later (but still before the results had been correlated) she gave a dream description of *The Seven Spinal Chakras* that is actually much *better* than Bessent's. The relevant transcript has it that

> It was something bright, like a crystal with many facets of colors . . . There is some sort of light or sun or a bright light. It's maybe a man, short like a Buddha . . . like something Aztec, a Mexican totem pole.[14]

This is really an amazingly accurate description of the picture – certainly clear enough to allow you to be able to select the 'target' from a random collection of thousands of other pictures. If there is no trickery afoot – and obviously there were plenty of opportunities for trickery, if Parise was that way inclined – then we can say quite categorically that dream telepathy is a proven phenomenon: to suggest that the dream could have arisen from coincidence alone would be quite untenable.[15]

As I've noted more than once, though, the laboratory reports of telepathic dreaming are always far hazier than the anecdotal ones. Here are a couple of examples of the latter from *Phantasms of the Living* (1886) by Edmund Gurney, F. W. H. Myers and Frank Podmore.

In 1884 Mary Griffith reported that on the night of 11th March, 1871, she awoke in much alarm, having seen my eldest son, then at St Paul de Loanda on the south-west coast of Africa, looking dreadfully ill and emaciated, and I heard his voice distinctly calling to me . . . every time I closed my eyes the appearance recurred, and his voice sounded distinctly, calling me 'Mamma'. I felt greatly distressed all through the next day, which was Sunday, but I did not mention it to my husband, as he was an invalid, and I feared to disturb him . . . Strange to say, he also suffered from intense low spirits all day, and we were both unable to take dinner, he rising from the table saying, 'I don't care what it costs, I must have the boy back,' . . . I mentioned my dream and the bad night I had had to two or three friends, but begged that they would say nothing of it to Mr Griffith. The next day a letter arrived containing some photos of my son, saying he had had fever, but was better, and hoped immediately to leave for a much more healthy station, and written in good spirits. We heard no more till the 9th of May, when a letter arrived with the news of our son's death from a fresh attack of fever, on the night of the 11th of March, and adding that just before his death he kept calling repeatedly for me. I did not at first connect the date of my son's death with that of my dream until reminded of it by the friends, and also an old servant, to whom I had told it at the time.

Startling stuff: why aren't the laboratory dreams so precise as this?

A curiously nauseating example of apparently telepathic dreaming concerns the Reverend A. B. McDougall, who wrote:

On the night of January 10th, 1882, I was sleeping in . . . the house of a friend, into which house several rats had been driven by the excessive cold. I knew nothing

> about these rats, but during the night I was waked by feeling an unpleasantly cold something slithering down my leg. I immediately struck a light and flung off the bed-clothes, and saw a rat run out of my bed under the fireplace.

However, this revolting experience was not suffered by McDougall alone, for a little while later he learnt that

> On the morning of January 11th, a cousin of mine, who happened to be staying in my own home on the south coast, and to be occupying my room, came down to breakfast, and recounted a marvellous dream, in which a rat appeared to be eating off the extremities of my unfortunate self . . . on the 13th, a letter was received from me giving an account of my unpleasant meeting with the rat and its subsequent capture. Then every one present remembered the dream my cousin had told . . .

But not all of the really eyebrow-raising anecdotes date back to the 19th century. The psychologist Dr Jan Ehrenwald has noted a number of curious instances of apparently telepathic dreams experienced by his patients and involving himself.

One patient was a latent homosexual, but had a girlfriend. Some days before the dream in question he had been with her when she had broken her key while trying to unlock the door of her flat.

In the dream the patient was on a clifftop high above a river; he was holding a yellow-metal key with the number 117 on it. Suddenly he dropped the key, but a bush stopped it falling over the cliff-edge, and to his considerable relief he was able to retrieve it.

Ehrenwald interpreted this dream in predictable fashion. The key is a masculine symbol (it 'penetrates' the female keyhole, you see), and indeed the girlfriend had used the metaphor of the key in the lock during loveplay with the patient some while before. Clearly, then, the dream was taking elements from real life and using them as symbols to express the dreamer's concern about his sexual ambivalence and hence his masculinity and virility.

This left the question of the number 117. While pondering on this, Ehrenwald remembered that a week or so earlier he had broken his own key while opening his office door. He pulled from his pocket a copy of the key which he'd borrowed from his wife: it was indeed of the yellow metal described by the dreamer. But what was really surprising was that it bore the number 1017 – close enough in image to 117. Ehrenwald claims that the patient had never seen this or any other key of his.[16]

Just before we get too excited, we should remember that very many keys are made of yellow metal, and that the *sole* reason for invoking telepathy is the approximate coincidence of the numbers 117 and 1017.

In another case one of Ehrenwald's patients described in very great detail a flat which she had visited in a dream. She described the rooms, the windows, the shape, the decor, the furniture – even the type and disposition of the carpets and rugs. What she did not know was that she was describing in detail the flat Ehrenwald had moved into a few days before and which, on the night of her dream, he had been showing off to some visitors. Ehrenwald believed that his patient had been spurred into dreaming telepathically about such a trivial non-emotionally charged issue because a while earlier she had conceived the notion that he felt she wasn't trying hard enough in her analysis.

Ehrenwald found many other examples of his patients dreaming apparently telpathically about incidents in his private life, and he is not the only psychoanalyst to have recorded this. While some of the examples are fairly impressive – like the one I've just cited – others are a little strained and are probably born from wishful thinking. One has to remember, too, that any psychoanalyst will hear countless dreams from his patients over the years, so that by the law of averages some will come pretty close to personal experiences of the psychoanalyst himself. Still, it's hard to believe that mere coincidence could account for the accuracy of the dream about his flat: he was able to count no fewer than thirteen correspondences between the dream and the reality.

Just before we move on to apparently clairvoyant dreaming, we must briefly mention a very well attested case of dream telepathy concerning the novelist H. Rider Haggard and his dog Bob. One night Haggard made so much noise during a nightmare that he woke his wife, even though she had been sleeping in a different room. She rushed through and roused him; and as he awoke he had a separate 'minidream'. In the nightmare proper he had been struggling desperately for his life, as if drowning. In the subsidiary dream, he was beside his dog, which was lying in an odd, contorted position.

The Haggards didn't think too much about the nightmare until Bob failed to turn up the following day. The novelist went out in search of him, and found his body on the bank of a nearby river, seemingly washed up there. Suspecting foul play, he investigated the incident further, eventually proving to his own satisfaction that the creature had been struck by a train on a railway bridge over the river. Haggard concluded that the dying dog, as it floundered in the water in the agony of its injuries, had somehow communicated telepathically with him.

I'm sure there must be countless other examples of apparent telepathy between pets and their owners, but this is the only one I've come across. What worries me about the subject in general is that animals don't seem to think in the same way as humans, so that any putative telepathic communications should be as incomprehensible as someone addressing you in Sanskrit. But maybe I'm wrong.

## *Clairvoyant Dreaming?*

In our discussion of telepathic dreaming we've really reached the conclusion that the evidence isn't unambiguous enough for us to reach a firm conclusion. You may of course disagree withe me, but I've decisively opted to continue sitting on the fence. The same is true of clairvoyant dreaming: indeed, the dividing line between telepathic and clairvoyant dreaming is so blurred that perhaps it isn't really there at all.

An account dated February 1884 by a Mrs Montgomery exemplifies the problem of telling the two types of dreaming apart.

> Nearly 30 years ago I lost a sister. The place where she died being at some distance, my husband went to the funeral without me. I went to bed early, and had a frightful dream of the funeral ceremony. I saw my brother faint away at the service, and fall into the grave. I awoke with the horror of the dream, just as my husband entered the room on his return from the funeral, which had taken place at least eight hours before. I asked him to tell me if anything unusual had happened, as I had had a terrible dream, and I related it. He said, 'Who in the world told you that? I never intended telling you.'

Clearly this dream could be of either of the two types. In the first place, it could have been a telepathic dream: Mr

Montgomery was concentrating hard on the incident for the simple reason that he'd decided not to tell his wife about it,[17] and she picked up his thoughts. Alternatively, it could have been clairvoyant: although the dream occurred eight hours or so after the event, it is common doctrine in the field of the paranormal that the 'travelling mind' is not as restricted by temporal considerations as our workaday conscious mind. There is, of course, yet a third possibility: the dream could have arisen from a mixture of telepathy and clairvoyance. Possibility number four is that the whole story is a fabrication.

Telepathy is probably the best bet of our paranormal trio, for the reason that Mr and Mrs Montgomery, as man and wife, were presumably pretty close. Certainly it seems that spouses are able to communicate *somehow* through the medium of the dream. One partner's dream can affect the other's conscious thoughts; one partner's conscious thoughts can affect the other's dreams; or both can have virtually identical dreams simultaneously. We've already looked at the dream about Harvey Brown; without dwelling too much longer on the subject, let's just cite one more example – from a Mrs Philip Crellin, and dated 1884:

> . . . three weeks ago, I was unable to sleep during the early hours of the night. I thought, amongst other things, of a rather comic piece of poetry which my husband used to repeat years ago. I stuck at one line and could not recall it. However, I fell asleep, and three or four hours after awoke, to find it was time to rise. My husband, after a good night's rest – undisturbed by poetry or prose – awoke also; he stretched out his hand towards me, and repeated the line I had failed to remember in the night, and which did not occupy my thoughts when I awoke in the morning.

Why should Mr Crellin have suddenly come out with a line from a piece of poetry which, as he confirmed, he hadn't even thought about for some considerable while? A long coincidence? Telepathic dreaming? It's very hard to tell. As I say, this sort of communication between spouses is not at all uncommon. Whether or not it is telepathy, as popularly imagined, is another question altogether: it may well be that our right brains are capable of picking up far subtler messages about the people closest to us than we could consciously ever conceive – the merest hints spoken in body language, or something like that.[18] How body language could convey such a subtle message as 'I wish I could remember the next line of that poem you used to recite' is beyond me! Clearly the boundary between subtle perception and 'telepathy' is a hazy one.

The trouble is that, when they happen to *you*, apparently paranormal dreams are particularly convincing. For example, a few years ago the writer Christopher Priest wrote to me at the publishing company I then worked for to tell me about a dream he'd had. (He's not normally given to talking about his dreams.) In his dream he'd conceived a magnificent project: the production of a book of the paintings of the botanical artist Marianne North, whose pictures are on permanent exhibition at Kew. In his dream he knew (quite correctly) that no such book existed, and when he woke up he thought that this would be an excellent idea to pass on to me. (The company I then worked for specialized in highly illustrated books.) Later on, his copy of *The Bookseller*, the journal of the British book trade, arrived: the first advertisement he saw was one from the company I worked for announcing the forthcoming publication of a collection of the pictures of Marianne North.

North is not the best known of artists, so the coincidence was a very long one indeed. Was it a telepathic or clairvoyant dream? I just don't know, but I doubt it. Even though I was directly involved, I could not for the life of me remember whether or not I'd mentioned the book in conversation with Priest. Again, it's possible that he came across some minor mention of it in the trade press, forgot having done so, and then weeks later had a dream based on what he'd seen. In other words, the generation of the dream could have been completely prosaic, rather than in any way paranormal. But, at the time, it *felt* as if the paranormal were involved.

But that can't explain away the feelings of some people that they've had paranormal dreams: sometimes the dreams themselves convince the dreamer and, in turn, must go a long way towards convincing us. Clairvoyant dreams can be especially persuasive when (a) they are concerned with trivial matters yet (b) the circumstances of them are so bizarre that a commonsense explanation is not easily obtainable. Miss R. H. Busk gives us in *Phantasms of the Living* a prime example of such a dream.

> I dreamt that I was walking in a wood in my father's place in Kent, in a spot well known to me, where there was sand under the firs; I stumbled over some objects, which proved to be the heads, left protruding, of some ducks buried in the sand. The idea impressed me as so comical that I fortunately mentioned it at breakfast next morning . . . Only an hour later it happened that the old bailiff of the place came up for some instructions unexpectedly, and as he was leaving he said he must tell us a strange thing that had happened: there had been a robbery in the farmyard, and some stolen ducks had been found buried in the sand, with their heads protruding, in the very spot where I had seen the same.

This is a very, very curious case. It is of course perfectly possible that Miss Busk was simply lying through her teeth; or, on hearing the bailiff's account of the peculiar events, read them back onto a vaguely similar dream which she'd had the night before. The only corroboratory evidence for the dream comes from Busk's sister, who remembered being told about the dream before the arrival of the bailiff; this could have been a false memory or, to be uncharitable, a case of sister backing sister's claim for 'family' reasons.

However, leaving all such suspicions aside, I find this dream supplies perhaps the most convincing evidence of all from dream-clairvoyance. It's all very well to say, 'I had a strange dream the night my father died' and go on to describe an extraordinary coincidence. After all, fathers do die: they generally signal their intentions some time in advance, and the deaths themselves generally have a strong emotional impact on the children. It is only natural that those children should begin to weave together dream fragments until they quite honestly convince themselves that they have had a premonitory or clairvoyant dream of the whole thing. But this just doesn't work in the case of Busk's interred ducks. When you have a dream as (apparently) absurd as this it's only human nature to talk about it over the breakfast plates, so that everybody can join in the laughter. It's unlikely that you'll have any inkling that the dream might be of something that has actually happened. Moreover, whereas you might talk about dreaming that old so-and-so was ill, you'd quite likely forget all about the dream when old so-and-so lived on hale and hearty for the next twenty years (in other words, you generally remember only the 'precognitive' dreams which come true); if like Busk you had something like the 'duck dream' you'd probably remember it for years – as a curio, if nothing else. Had Busk had lots of dreams as (apparently) surreal as this one, she'd have remembered them all; as it was, she thought this one sufficiently bizarre in comparison with her normal dreams that she chattered about it at breakfast.

This sort of trivia seems to be of importance in 'paranormal' dreaming. The idea that only disasters or profoundly emotional events can be either foretold or seen at a distance in dreams is simply not borne out by the records. Here is an account of a clairvoyant dream from one Agnes Bell, dated 21st July, 1884, and once again reproduced in *Phantasms of the Living*:

> In the autumn of 1875, my father and I left home for Perthshire, giving the use of our Hamilton [Scotland] house to an uncle. On Wednesday night, previous to our return home, I dreamt that my cousin had broken the handle of a vegetable-dish, and [that she] said to her sister, 'Don't tell, for I see the soup-tureen handle has been mended, and I shall mend this too.' I told this dream to my father at breakfast on Thursday morning. He laughed, and begged me not to speak of it to my cousins, lest they should say I had been thinking evil of them. However, when we got home on Friday, just as my friends were leaving, I said in a joke, 'Oh! you didn't tell me you had broken the handle of the vegetable-dish.'
>
> My cousin at once turned to her sister, and said, 'Did you tell?' I was amazed, and said, 'You don't mean to say you broke it.' She said, 'Yes, I did, on Wednesday, and I told my sister to say nothing about it to you, and I would mend it like the soup-tureen.'

Again, this is a totally trivial dream about a totally trivial event. I find it a thousand times more convincing than any number of dreams foretelling the Aberfan disaster or the assassination of John Kennedy. The great classics of paranormal-dream lore leave me cold in comparison. I completely refuse to believe in, for example, the dreams of Pope Innocent III.

'Pope Innocent who?' I hear you cry. Well, if you were really up on the lore of parapsychology you wouldn't have to ask the question. Innocent (*c.*1160–1216; pope from 1198) is said to have had two such similar dreams about saints Francis of Assisi and Dominic – respectively the founders of the Franciscan and Dominican orders – that the inevitable conclusion must be, at least for me, that there has been some multiplication or confabulation of legends somewhere along the line.

In 1210 Francis came to Rome to seek papal approval for the 'rule' he had drawn up governing the behaviour of his disciples (who were few at the time, although in several years the Friars Minor, or Franciscans, would be numbered in their thousands). Innocent, it is said, initially was far from interested in Francis' application – especially since some of his cardinals spoke out forcefully against the creation of yet another order. However, in a dream Innocent saw a palm tree grow up at his feet; in a further dream he saw Francis propping up the Lateran Church, which seemed to be in danger of collapse. The combined effect of these two dreams was sufficient to impel him to meet Francis and give him the requested papal approval – although only verbally and informally.

In 1215 Dominic came to Rome for very similar reasons, and once again Innocent and his cardinals were averse to the idea of creating additional orders. However, according to the tale, Innocent dreamt about the tottering Lateran Church yet again, only this time it was Dominic who was propping it up. As with Francis, Innocent gave Dominic verbal approval for the founding of his order. However, owing to Innocent's death in the summer of

1216, it was his successor, Honorius III (d. 1227), who at the end of that year – 1216 – finally gave the papal bull of confirmation.

The lives of both Dominic and Francis were considerably affected by their dreams and visions, if one believes the legends. In most instances it is difficult to tell whether an experience was a dream or a vision; however, each of them seems to have had at least one singularly important dream.

Francis was born John Bernardone in Assisi, near Perugia, Italy, to a rich merchant family; he was nicknamed 'the Frenchman', *Francesco*, for reasons which are obscure and on occasion libellous towards his mother. He grew up to be a hedonistic youth, though not a cruel or licentious one; he is said never to have refused alms to a beggar.

Those were tempestuous times in Italy. After Francis had spent a year in prison thanks to a dispute between Perugia and Assisi, he decided to join the army of Walter de Brienne, which was at the time at war in southern Italy. He kitted himself out magnificently, but not long afterwards met up with a poor man and, moved by the man's raggedy appearance, swapped outfits with him. When he fell asleep that night he dreamt of being in a splendid palace filled with arms of all kinds made from precious metals and each marked with the sign of the cross. A voice told him that these were to be the arms of himself and his 'soldiers'. He seems initially to have taken this dream to mean merely that God was on his side in the ensuing combat, for he continued his journey towards the front. However, on the way he was taken ill, and as he lay in delirium a voice told him to return home, to 'serve the master rather than the man'. This time Francis got the message, and soon after he began to renounce the hedonism of his earlier life and to help the sick and the poor – despite the often violent objections of his father, who had expected Francis to take up the nice safe occupation of merchant rather than run off and be a saint.

Dominic's dream occurred either in 1216 or 1221; the former date seems more likely.[19] He saw that God was angry with the world, and was preparing to display His fury, but that Mary had interceded on behalf of mankind. Mary pointed to two men in particular; one Dominic recognized as himself, but the other was unknown to him. The next day, however, when Dominic was at prayer, a beggar in tattered clothing entered the church, and this beggar Dominic instantly realized was the other figure of his dream. According to the legend, he embraced the man and said to him: 'You are my companion and we must walk together; if we are together, no earthly power can withstand us.' The beggar was in fact St Francis, and thereafter Dominic and Francis worked together, as indeed did the Dominicans and Franciscans.

Frankly, I don't believe that the dreams of Innocent, Francis and Dominic ever happened; but I accept that my belief is as irrational as the fixed belief that every word of such legends is true. I'm pretty sceptical, too, about the tales concerning the Tyler family, even though they're several centuries closer to our own time.

John Tyler was destined to become one of the less remembered presidents of the United States. He was elected vice-president under Harrison in March 1841 and, when the latter died only a month afterwards, took over as president, the first person to assume the office in this way. Although there was some muttering about this, since the Constitution was at the time vague on the issue, Tyler elected to sit out the remainder of the presidential term. His domestic policy was fairly disastrous, and he quarrelled constantly with own (Whig) party, eventually being threatened with impeachment.

Long after he had retired as president, Tyler was in Richmond, Virginia; the Civil War was on. His family were at home, further down the James River. One night his wife Julia dreamt that she was going by boat up the river; she especially noted that it was not the usual river craft, the *Ariel*, but a stranger. Along the riverbank came the mounted figure of a masked skeleton, which in due course raised its mask momentarily so that she could see the face beneath. It was the face of her husband.

Because paranormal dreams were positively commonplace in the family, Julia Tyler took this one seriously. She set off for Richmond; and found out just before she embarked that the *Ariel* had been pulled out of service for repairs and that a different vessel was temporarily standing in for it: the dream seemed to be coming true. There was no horseman on the riverbank, but when she got to Richmond and rushed to her husband's hotel she found that he had suddenly been taken very ill. Within a little over 24 hours he had died.

A good few years later Julia Tyler had a dream premonition of another death: her own. She dreamt that she was lying in bed when her (in reality long dead) mother came into the room. The mother said sweetly that she expected her daughter soon to be coming with her, and left the room again, beckoning as she went. A week or two later Julia Tyler was dead.

Her daughter seems to have inherited the trait of having paranormal dreams. A number of years before her mother's death, Pearl Tyler three nights running dreamt of being with a handsome man outside a cottage on a hillside. Although she had rejected all proposals from her many admirers in real life, the young woman fell in love with her dream-figment at first sight. Some months later, she spotted the man – whom she had never before met outside her dream – at the state capitol and insisted on being introduced. After a brief courtship the two were married; on their arrival back at his home after the honeymoon, Tyler found that it was indeed the cottage she had seen in her dream.

I'm sorry if I'm being unromantic, but I think that a myth-maker has been at work on the lives of the Tyler family.

## *Visitors and Visiting*

However, the idea of other people – living, as in the case of Pearl Tyler, or dead, as in the case of her mother – entering your dreams is a persistent one. Paranormal researchers call cases where you seem to travel out of your body OOBEs, as we've seen; I'm not sure if there's a trendy acronym for cases when someone else seems to come along and be a part of your dream. The dividing line between dreams which seem to be clairvoyant and those which appear to involve OOBEs is a fine one. For example, an experience shared by Constance Bevan and K. Elliott seems, on the face of it, to involve Bevan in some kind of OOBE – or 'astral projection', if you'd prefer that term.

Here are two reports:

*Bevan*: On June 10th, 1883, I had the following dream. Someone told me that Miss Elliott was dead. I instantly, in my dream, rushed to her room, entered it, went to her bedside and pulled the clothes from off her face. She was quite cold; her eyes were wide open and staring at the ceiling. This so frightened me that I dropped at the foot of her bed, and knew no more until I was half out of bed in my own room and wide awake. The time was 5 o'clock A.M. Before leaving my room I told this dream to my sister, as it had been such an unpleasant one.

*Elliott*: I awoke on the morning of June 10th, and was lying on my back with my eyes fixed on the ceiling, when I heard the door open and felt some one come in and bend over me, but not far enough to come between my eyes and the ceiling; knowing it was only [Constance Bevan], I did not move, but instead of kissing me she suddenly drew back, and going towards the foot of the bed, crouched down there. Thinking this very strange, I closed and opened my eyes several times, to convince myself that I was really awake, and then turned my head to see if she had left the door open, but found it still shut. Upon this a sort of horror came over me and I dared not look towards the figure, which was crouching in the same position, gently moving the bed-clothes from my feet. I tried to call to the occupant of the next room, but my voice failed. At this moment she touched my bare foot, a cold chill ran all over me and I knew nothing more till I found myself out of bed looking for [Bevan], who must, I felt, be still in the room. I never doubted that she had really been there until I saw both doors fastened on the inside. On looking at my watch it was a few minutes past 5.

Did Bevan travel out of her body to visit Elliott? Who can possibly tell? The whole thing happened a century ago.

Less unbelievable are cases when people dream that dead friends or relatives come to visit them. We've already seen how Julia Tyler, for example, was 'visited' by her long dead mother, who warned her of her (Julia's) imminent death. As it happens, I don't believe the tale; but I do believe that these visits by the dead can be profoundly affecting. W. Palmer of Barnstaple wrote to me that

> . . . we have recently moved to a new bungalow and I haven't quite settled yet, so perhaps that is why I have had this dream.
>
> I dreamt my mother came and stood by me during the night. I was asleep but I had a feeling someone was standing beside me and she touched my hand. I awoke, not with a start but just normal waking. I lay still, never moved, and she just turned and glided towards the dressing table and disappeared. She was dressed in black. It gave me a queer sensation; I could not go back to sleep again . . .

Another example of a 'ghost' coming to 'visit' a dreamer was reported in 1883 by N. T. Menneer, who recalled a pair of dreams which his wife had had 'some 26 years' earlier. His wife's brother, a Mr Wellington, was at the time of the dream living with the Raja of Sarawak. Menneer recalled:

> I was awoke one night by my wife, who started from her sleep, terrified by the following dream. She saw her *headless* brother standing at the foot of the bed with his head lying on a coffin by his side. I did my best to console my wife, who continued to be much distressed for some considerable time. At length she fell asleep again, to be awoke by a similar dream. In the morning, and for several days after, she constantly referred to her dream, and anticipated sad news of her brother.

In due course, as you might have anticipated, the 'sad news' arrived. Coincidence might be an obvious explanation for the dream, were it not for the fact that, as Menneer pointed out and as it is recorded in *The Raja of Sarawak* by Gertrude Jacob, 'Mr Wellington was killed in a brave attempt to defend Mrs. Middleton and her children'. In fact, Menneer's wife's brother was apparently mistaken for the Raja's son, and so the rebels chopped his head off.

The prophetess Jeane Dixon, whom we shall consider in greater detail in the next chapter, has recalled a curious dream she had (although she didn't describe it as a dream, as such) when her father was dying. One night she seemed to wake from an 'unusually deep sleep' to find her father by her bedside, rather than (in reality) many miles away. He told her that he'd come to say goodbye, and exhorted her to carry on her work, however onerous that might be. Sure enough, when in real life Dixon 'phoned her sister to ask if indeed her father had finally died, he had. Dixon described this as a genuine spectral visit or OOBE on her father's part; my own feeling is that it may qualify as an example of the telepathic dream at work, the father, as he died, communicating with his daughter across the long miles.

Similar instances of the dying coming to 'visit' dreamers are not too uncommon. Here is an example recalled in 1883 by one Lita Jarratt: while it is tempting to dismiss the whole thing as a childhood fantasy, we should note that independent corroboration of the tale was available.

> When I was a little girl, about 10 years old, an old friend of ours, particularly dear to me, a Danish gentleman [called George Hansen] . . . sought to improve his position by going to the city of Mexico. Some months after he left, I dreamed that I saw him sitting in my father's office, and immediately ran up to him, exclaiming, 'I'm so glad you've come back.' He put his hand up, as if to repulse me gently, and said gravely, 'You must not come near me. I am dying in Mexico of the sore throat, and I have come to tell your father.' I

> drew back, grieved and shocked, and woke. The next day I told everyone of my dream, and was well laughed at; but my father had not heard for some time past of our friend, nor did he till three weeks after [when] I overheard a gentleman say to him, 'Well, doctor, have you heard about your friend [Hansen]?' My father having replied in the negative, the gentleman continued, 'I was told he died at Mexico, three weeks ago, of sore throat.'

On being questioned twenty years after the dream, Jarratt mentioned 'the additional detail that even in her dream "sore throat" struck her as an odd thing to die of', reported Edmund Gurney in *Phantasms of the Living*. It could, however, have been something like cancer of the throat.

There seems to be a minor difference between the dying or dead coming to 'visit' you in your dream and you going to 'visit' them. An example of this latter event involves a person called Sisinius who, according to Hermias Sozomenus (Sozomen), the early-5th-century Greek church historian, had a curious dream after the martrydom of St Eutropius, in A.D.404. St John Chrysostom had been banished from Constantinople, much to the fury of his clergy. On the day of Chrysostom's departure the church caught fire, and arson was suspected. Eutropius was a reader in the church, and was haled up before the authorities and required to name the people responsible for the fire. Despite the usual vicious programme of tortures he held his peace – possibly because the suspicion of arson was false. Not long afterwards he died from his tortures.

But, so Sozomen tells us, he was to receive an unusual comfort before his death. Sisinius was Bishop of the Novations. One night he dreamt that he saw a tall handsome man standing near the altar in the Church of St Stephen. This man told him that he had searched all over the city for a man who was truly good and had found only one, a man called Eutropius. In the morning, Sisinius told one of his priests about the dream, and commanded him to track down this Eutropius. The priest immediately guessed that the man in question was the one who had been tortured so viciously, and eventually found the dungeon where he had been incarcerated. The priest told Eutropius of Sisinius' dream, and asked to be blessed by him.

Who was the man in the dream? Was it Eutropius himself? Or was it Christ? Or is this not an instance of the dreamer journeying outside his body to meet up with the similarly journeying spirit of the dying man? Since the whole thing happened over 1500 years ago we shall never know – assuming, that is, that it really happened at all.

People have also, of course, recorded cases of 'visits' not just in dreams but also during their waking hours. Such experiences are beyond the scope of this book; but an interesting subclass of such experiences concerns those events in which the sleeper has the experience immediately on waking – often drowsily accepting the most ridiculous happenings as perfectly normal. The happenings, of course, need not be in the least absurd, as exemplified by the sad experience of M. A. Brooke:

> . . . towards dawn on the morning of August 3rd, 1867, I was roused from sleep to find my brother, an officer in the 16th Lancers, then quartered in Madras, standing by the bed. My impression is that he bent over me, kissed me, and passed quietly from the room, making signs to me not to speak, and that I was full of joy, thinking he had returned home unexpectedly, and lay

awake till the maid called me, when my first words to her were that my brother had come home and I had seen him. I remember my bitter disappointment when at last made to believe that this was not so, and that it was quite impossible I could have seen him . . .

I cannot remember how much time elapsed before the news came by telegram that my brother died suddenly of jungle fever on August 2nd; full particulars did not reach us for weeks later . . .

A couple of points are worth noting. In earlier dreams where I've said that the individual *dreamt* having woken up this is exactly what I think happened; but in Brooke's case I'm not so sure: she says that she 'lay awake till the maid called me'. Of course, it's quite possible that she *dreamt* she lay awake, and then eventually awoke when the maid called her, but I prefer to think that she was indeed awake, and that her dream was hypnopompic.[20]

Brooke concludes that 'I then and now firmly believe my favourite brother came to me at the hour of his death'. In fact, as Gurney points out in *Phantasms of the Living*, detective work shows that the brother 'visited' her nine or ten hours after dying.

A dream – or hypnopompic dream – like this is hard to explain, assuming that everything happened the way Brooke claimed it did. However, we should note that her account is dated fifteen years after the events which it describes, and so one cannot put too much reliance on it.

But the big question is: Was Brooke awake or asleep when she 'saw' her brother?

## *Dreams From Outer Space*

I suppose it's fairly prosaic if the dead come to visit you, but what if the people in your dreams are coming to say 'hello' from the more distant reaches of the Galaxy? All right, so that's a facetious question. But it's certainly true that there's a strong link between 'UFO experiences' and dreaming.

While the more 'down-market' of the UFOlogists carry on trying to persuade us that flying saucers are spaceships and that their occupants are either intergalactic tourists or evil beings from inside the Earth (which is hollow, you see[21]), the more serious investigators seem almost unanimous in their suggestion that the whole phenomenon is at root a psychological or parapsychological one.

There may be something to be said for the proposition. Many accounts of 'close encounters' have a sort of dream-like quality; and in detailed case studies of multiple-encounter contactees it is usually found that some of the encounters occurred during sleep.

One of the most interesting of such studies was carried out a few years back by Jenny Randles and Paul Whetnall, who published their results in *Alien Contact* (1981). It concerns the Sunderland family: Frederick and Marion, and their children Karl, Gaynor, Darren, Nerys and Barry. (In fact, Frederick and Karl had no strange experiences to report: they're included in the list only for the sake of completeness.) To go into the details of all the family's encounters would be impossible: suffice it to say that, while each individual experience can be explained using mundane logic, if on occasion tortuously, the whole complex of them cannot. One is left with only two possible conclusions: that the phenomena actually occurred (even if only in the mind's eye) or that the family is lying through its collective teeth. Randles and Whetnall say that this latter is unlikely, if not impossible: the construction of such an elaborate edifice of lies would be beyond the powers of the members of the family.

But four of the children – Gaynor, Darren, Barry,

Nerys – had vivid dreams allied with their waking experiences. Often it was difficult to disentangle the dream-experiences from the others – which is one of the reasons why some UFOlogists suggest that UFO encounters and dreams can both be traced back to the same psychological phenomenon. There is much attraction in the argument.

One interesting pair of dreams from the Sunderland children will serve as example. In late November 1979 Darren was sleeping deeply when he awoke – or, at least, thought he awoke. The boy is presumably a lucid dreamer, because on this occasion he squeezed his eyes tight shut to see whether or not he was asleep . . . and the next moment he was on a battlefield.

But what a battlefield! Even Ronald Reagan in his wilder moments couldn't have imagined a high-tech battlefield like this. Darren found himself standing by a group of aliens; he had met their type before, while 'awake', so he wasn't frightened. One of them gave him a small replica of the craft they'd used on the earlier occasion and told him that somehow he'd got to carry it across the battlefield and give it to the enemy, for reasons unstated.

The plucky lad dove into no-man's-land, clutching the thing. Soon he was approaching the enemy, who made no hostile move towards him but began shrieking: 'Take it away!' With suicidal bravery Darren went back to 'his' aliens, and they gave him a replacement one, rather like the first. Off went Darren again, but the enemy aliens – humanoids, except with just one eye, and not much more than a metre tall – were every bit as unwilling to accept the new model. Darren looked up at the sky – no doubt in exasperation at his Sisyphus-like chore – and it went blood-red.

And then he was back in bed again. He fell asleep.

Now this dream wouldn't be of much interest on its

own: any kid can watch too much *Star Wars* and dream accordingly. What makes it interesting is the parallel dream which his elder sister Gaynor had that night. She had seen a picture of Darren, head and shoulders, with her own face in the rearground.

> Above their heads were two intersecting triangles creating a six-sided figure. On the left-hand margin of the figure lay a row of vertically spaced signs. From the top downwards these were: four symbols . . . similar to those Darren had seen on the side of his UFO [and like those Gaynor had herself seen on the clothing of other aliens] – a tiny bird – an infinity symbol – a boy – a girl (both in stick symbols) – a small planet (with continents and seas) – a larger similar planet – Darren's entities' hand reaching out to touch Gaynor's entities' hand – the hands joined with the boy and girl sitting together on them – one of the planets cracked in two down the middle – two spheres joined together.

Now, it's not hard to explain this, in some ways. Gaynor had been the family's ace contactee until, as it were, 'her powers began to wane'. As they waned, along came young Darren, keen to be just as interesting as his big sister Gaynor had been. Gaynor is both jealous and generous about this, and her mind is packed with UFO-lore. The UFO-lore not only gives us the appearance in the dream of alien symbols but also all the stuff about aliens' hands and the boy and girl sitting in them. The split planet and the united planets give us the not altogether atypical UFO notion that the Earth will have a great cataclysm but that after that the aliens will become our brothers.

To delve into this last point for a moment: A definitive socio-psychological fact about one wing of the UFO movement is that the aliens are going to save us from ourselves. The extension of the UFO movement, characterized by Erich von Däniken and a good number of other writers who are even worse, that says that aliens swooped godlike around our planet in ancient times, stresses this even more. *The aliens are gods: they're the only ones who can save us*. But before science and technology blasted their way into our everyday lives, *God* was the only one who could save us. Science says – or appears to say – that there's no God, which means that all of us souls who are entangled in the web of human misery have to find some other *deus ex machina*. The aliens! – an especially good choice, since the very science which seems to say that God is *passé* agrees (for the most part) that there are alien civilizations out there in the Universe.

Now add in the factoid that some people instinctively and fundamentally *want* there to be a nuclear catastrophe. I don't mean the politicians; I mean those people, of whom I've met several, who fancy themselves so much in the role of gallant survivor that secretly – perhaps so secretly that they themselves aren't aware of it – they'd be quite happy if the holocaust happened and they were boldly roughing it as one of the few survivors.[22]

Obviously it's impossible for me to say whether or not Gaynor is one of those people: I don't know her. But it seems to me there isn't much difference between (a) 'the aliens are going to save us from the holocaust' and (b) 'the holocaust is going to happen but I'm going to be one of the lucky survivors and *then* the aliens are going to save us'.

All this is reasonably glib. However, there is a worry. Think back to Darren's dream and start putting your powers of amateur dream-interpretation to work on it. There's the *Star Wars* battlefield; the idea of a truce being offered by the wise, good aliens but refused by the humanoids. Hang on a moment: *humanoids*. They're only a little over a metre tall – but then everybody knows that Man is a small-scale event in terms of the Universe as a whole. They've got only the one eye – but this seems reasonable if you think about it at the same time as you think about the modern notion of the divided brain.

Those 'humanoids' are really humans. Humans who have refused – rejected – the aliens. The holocaust goes on. One plucky lad survives it all, trying to act as intermediary: he's the human hero of the piece (and, at a guess, at his age he was a little over a metre tall, too). The aliens are trying to save us but humanity won't let them until it's too late. And then the heroes – the plucky survivors – will welcome the aliens and be embraced by them.

The parallels between the two dreams are obvious – as are the parallels between them and all sorts of mystic, egotistic visionaries of the past. (I don't mean the word 'egotistic' unkindly: egotism, or egocentrism, is part of most people's world-view, and certainly most children's.) But here's the strange thing: the two children dreamt these dreams on the same night. At core, the dreams are identical: that they were dreamt roughly (if not precisely) simultaneously is remarkable.

Not all UFO dreams are so dramatic. Many involve balls of fire – and a selection of Sunderlands had these dreams. In a different book[23] Randles cites the case of one Mike Sacks, who's had a fair number of 'encounters'. She found that when he'd been about 10 or 11 he'd dreamt that

> floating by the bedroom window was a greenish ball, only inches in diameter and seemingly composed of pulsing tiny 'horseshoe' shapes. He remembers communicating with it, as if in a semi-awake state, before

suddenly snapping back to everyday reality. He found himself thinking, 'What am I doing?' and making a lunge for the ball, but it had vanished.

One mustn't put too much weight behind these dreams. That UFO fans should have UFO-type dreams is hardly to be wondered at. The only thing that sticks in the mind is that these glowing balls appear in a good many UFO dreams dreamt by all sorts of different people who come from quite different cultural backgrounds.

## *'Doctor, I've had this dream . . .' 'So have I'*

In 1974 the *Newsweek* journalist Stewart Alsop was dying of leukaemia. Although he held on to his job, he was in and out of hospital, and had been unable to write some of his columns. One night, while he lay in the Solid Tumor Ward of the National Institutes of Health, he dreamt that he woke up in his bed, which was now on board a train. 'We'll be stopping in Baltimore,' he said firmly. He climbed out of bed to look around: fruit, flowers and shoddy furniture. The train was rocking a lot; he had to support himself on the furniture. Then he had to cross a patch of empty floor: a particularly large lurch and he fell over. After a while he got up again, and started opening doors: first a small one, a locker with his clothes in it; next a larger one, a bathroom; finally a much larger one, on the other side of which was what he assumed to be Baltimore station – 'wide platform, dim lights, green tiles'. There was no one to be seen. A whimpering noise in the distance was stilled.

He didn't much like the look of Baltimore, he decided, and so he announced: 'We won't stop here. Start up the train and carry on.' The door closed behind him and he returned to his bed, twice falling over on the way. But he got there in the end, even though getting into the bed was like 'mounting a bucking horse'. He fell asleep again instantly.

When he awoke in the morning he was covered in bruises, but he didn't much care: his X-rays that day showed that the infiltrate which had been spreading across his lungs was now receding. His recovery – although not to complete health – was rapid. He had decided not to stop in Baltimore: he had decided not to die.

It's a pity the story doesn't have a happy ending. His recovery was not permanent, and a couple of years later he went through the big door and down onto the platform of Baltimore station.

Clearly, though, Alsop's dream had effected at least a temporary cure. 'Medical dreaming' is not especially common but, if we believe all that we read, is an accepted fact of paranormal life. The doyen of all diagnostic and curative dreamers was Edgar Cayce, whom we met in Chapter One. Fans of the 'Sleeping Prophet' claim that his subconscious was able to seek out distant individuals – having been given their addresses – diagnose their ailments, and prescribe remedies which always worked. Well, nearly always: 97% of the time.[24]

Cayce worked sometimes in conjunction with more orthodox physicians – or so we are led to believe. In fact, most seem to have been osteopaths, chiropractics or naturopaths of some school; at the time, the whole caboodle seems to have been lumped under the heading of 'homeopathy', which is confusing for a number of reasons. His choice of doctors – or, rather, their choice of him – was inevitable, since the remedies he prescribed fell very much into these disciplines, and included some prescriptions which were homeopathic in the currently accepted meaning of the word.

We have already seen how Cayce went about his

'readings' (see page 26). In a way, he was taught the trick as a boy by a mendicant 'healer' of dubious credentials, one Al Layne. Cayce's very first cure of himself had come about when he had been knocked half-unconscious while playing baseball; he gave instructions for the preparation of a poultice, to be put at the back of his neck, and in the morning he was fine.

But he really learnt the knack one time when he was suffering from loss of voice (the condition affected him on and off through life until he and his wife realized that the bouts coincided with times when he attempted to derive personal profit from his 'gift'). Various techniques, including hypnosis, had been tried; but Layne had the bright idea of using the entranced Cayce's unconscious to do the work. He told it to have a look at Cayce's throat, tell him what was wrong with it, and then to do what had to be done to correct the ailment. This the unconscious happily did, then told Layne to tell the sleeper to wake. Cured!

One of the physicians who worked with Cayce over the years was Wesley Ketchum; he was probably Cayce's most important bulldog in the medical world. Having satisfied himself that Cayce's dream-diagnoses and -prescriptions actually worked, he abandoned any idea of questioning them or criticizing them: he seems to have felt, reasonably enough, that the very fact that they appeared to work was the most important thing.

But sometimes he must have wondered, for some of Cayce's diagnoses reflected bizarre notions from the previous century. And, very often, Ketchum was the muggins who delivered the transcripts of Cayce's 'readings'. In Jess Stearn's biography of Cayce we come across the case of a married woman suffering from some obscure nervous disorder causing paralysis and palsy. Ketchum arrived at her home and read out Cayce's report in front of the woman and her husband. Her problem was that, for some years before her marriage, she had indulged in the 'secret sin' of masturbation. The husband thought all this was a farrago: Stearn seems to think this was because the husband didn't believe that his wife could have done such a thing as masturbate, but it lurks in the back of my mind that possibly the husband's views on medical science had advanced a little from the crank Victorian idea that masturbation among women could cause anything from flat-chestedness and insanity to consumption, death, and even compulsive leg-crossing.

The woman, incidentally, secretly admitted to Ketchum that she had indeed indulged regularly in the 'secret sin' and was thus, extrapolating from modern published statistics, a really shocking pervert – along with some 75% of the rest of the female population.

Conversely, some of Cayce's ideas were ahead of their time. In one case the sleeper advised that a compound fracture of the leg should be treated by simply nailing the bones together. The insertion of screws in such cases is quite familiar to us now, but in those days the idea was pretty startling. And at least one of the remedies he prescribed for cancer seems to have been a hit. He suggested that part of the tumour should be inserted into a rabbit; if the tumour 'took', a preparation should be made from it and injected back into the original patient. In fact, orthodox medical science has since tried this technique; the trick is that the human antibodies reject the injected foreign bodies and then, with luck, go on to treat the original cancer cells in the body as if they were strangers, too.

Cayce seems to be unique among paranormal dreamers. Whether you classify him as a telepath or as a clairvoyant or as something else entirely matters not at all: it is his claimed therapeutic ability which marks him off from all the others. That his remedies were so successful – or, at least, were and are *believed* to have been so successful – has meant that his supporters have swallowed lock, stock and barrel the vast majority of his other pronouncements, some of which, as we have seen and shall see, were very silly indeed.

## *The Curious Case of Ms Grant*

Some paranormal dreamers display such a colossal variety of strange dreams that they are hard to classify. Two such people are the writer Joan Grant, who has published a number of books which are either historical novels or autobiographies of her previous incarnations (take your pick), and Christine Sizemore, whose name is little known but who achieved world renown by being the 'Eve' in the book and film of *The Three Faces of Eve*.

We'll look at Grant's 'reincarnatory' dreams in Chapter Six; here we can meet a diversity of her others.

She claims to have seen ghosts ever since childhood: only in response to a number of promptly delivered thick ears did she stop mentioning them in the company of adults, having before always thought that *everybody* could see ghosts. In particular, as a child during World War I, she frequently encountered in her dreams the ghosts of those hapless young people who had been so recently killed that they had yet to realize that they were actually dead. Her task – her 'war work' – was to tell these fellows there was no need to fear dying: see, they were already dead and they hadn't even noticed.

Some 'cases' were harder. Any man who 'had allowed dogma to infect him with grotesque terrors, or who clung to the agonies which affected his physical body because he thought them the only alternative to oblivion' could be extremely difficult to process, and she would waken with the feeling that she had *been* him, pierced by cruel pain and with the stink of gangrene still in her young nostrils. The worst of it was that, if she tried to explain her nausea to adults, they became worried about the fertile and horrific depths of her imagination. Soon her parents were hiding the newspapers, making a point of never mentioning the war when she was in earshot, and trying 'to convince me that the many friends who had already been killed had all died painlessly with a bullet through the forehead'.

It seems bizarre that seemingly rational adults can glory in the triumphs of war – as in the 1982 Falklands conflict or the 1983 Grenada invasion – and yet be so concerned over a child having nightmares about the reality. There is a very obvious way of getting rid of such nightmares, and it involves no conspiracy of silence.

Her first experience of 'helping people cross over' had happened long before, when she had been a small child accompanying her parents on a trip to New York. Her father, Jack Marshall, had taken her as a treat for a trip on the elevated railway, and to cap the day agreed to her request to be taken for a ride on the subway. However, as they reached the platform, there was a tremendous commotion: a man had fallen or jumped under the train, and all that was left of him now was a ragged, bleeding heap on the platform, beside which, neatly, stood his two boots, the feet still in them.

That night, Joan dreamt that she was back on the platform, but this time alone with the man. She helped him put his feet back on, all the while acting the part of his 18-year-old daughter Agnes, whom he dearly loved. She washed him all over, and youth flowed back into his body. Then she 'took him' to Central Park, where he met his *real* daughter; as they were reunited, the dreaming

Joan lost the form of an 18-year-old woman and became herself, a small child, once more.

In very much later life she was to have a similar dream of having helped someone 'cross over' successfully. A very old gardener whom she knew – 'Old Morgan' – had died peacefully in his bed, having just cheerfully downed a brandy as his farewell to the world. That night she dreamt that she was in a churchyard: Old Morgan was lying happily in a shallow open grave. Since he was there three days before his own funeral, she told him to get up; but this he refused to do, saying that he would stay in his grave until the Last Trump.

It was clearly her duty to help him 'cross over'. The next night she created above his grave a representation of a traditional angel, on the basis that, seeing it, he'd know that he ought to off up out of there and make his way to Heaven. Still he refused to budge.

She then found herself dressed in Edwardian garb, and saying sternly to him that it was ridiculous that he should stay in the grave any longer, since she needed him to help her with her gardens. He climbed out agilely, and in a moment they were both looking over the most magnificent gardens. On seeing these he showed such delight that she knew 'that he had known them when they were planted to translate a dream into reality'; in other words, he was seeing for the first time a garden which he had long ago planted. When he saw that every leaf, every blade, every petal was perfect he said: 'I am in heaven!'

Grant says that, when she questioned Old Morgan's sister about all this, she was told that in his early twenties the man had worked as a junior gardener for a certain duchess; she had remained his ideal of all womanhood for the rest of his life. He had apparently once said that he would refuse even to enter the Gates of Heaven until the duchess told him that he should.

Dreams played a large part in Grant's marital plans, too. She was engaged at a very early age to a nice young man – nice, but too nice to be interesting. She had been driven into the engagement rather against her will, largely thanks to the confident prediction of her mother (who had a name for such predictions: she had foreseen the sinking of the *Titanic*). But Joan was suffering from a severe crisis of conscience: how could she be engaged to one man during her waking hours while at the same time she was spending her dreams in the company of another, one whom she had never met in her waking life but whom she loved profoundly? (See the case of Pearl Tyler, page 252.)

She took an obvious course of action. She broke off her engagement and went on a holiday to Andermatt, Switzerland. She had not long been there when a young man came across her playing on the piano some music which had been taught to her, from beyond the grave, by her grandmother. He burst into the room and said something like 'It's you! I've been dreaming with you for two years! Have you been dreaming with me?' It was of course the man from her dreams.

Naturally enough, they planned to marry immediately: his mother had no objections and her parents put up only token resistance, which evaporated once they had met him. However, for practical reasons, they had to wait – he had to return to the Continent for some months while she remained at her parents' home in England.

On the last night he was to be in England, she was climbing into bed when she heard a voice say: 'You will never see Esmond again.' So she did what most people would have done in the same circumstances: she went and climbed into his bed instead of her own.[25]

She never did see him again. He shot himself dead by accident while cleaning a gun. This she knew thanks to a dream: she saw him looking at the gun in question and being angry with himself for having been such a fool as not to have checked properly that the pistol was empty. The details were confirmed in due course by her friend Leslie.

She continued to dream of Esmond for some while. They were in some enchanted place, of happiness and green fields. In what was to prove the last of her dream-times with him, he explained to her that they were on a different planet – she had noticed that her body seemed lighter, thanks to the lesser gravity – and that, on this planet, one arrived fully grown rather than as a baby. He had decided to stay here rather than have another incarnation on Earth. When she said she would like to join him, leave behind her old body, he replied that her time was not yet.

At length she got over his death and his later disappearance from her dreams. But it was yet another dream which determined her selection of her first husband. She was in a room, looking out of the window, when in came a young woman with two identical small boys. She ushered the twins towards Joan, indicating that she wished her to look after them.

On waking, Joan felt that this was a clear reference to her friend Leslie. His mother had died when he was a child, and he had a twin so like him in appearance that the two could often take each other's places. She went to Leslie and found that indeed his brother Malcolm was ill. She was able to arrange that Malcolm be taken out of the rather seedy nursing home where he had been incarcerated, and that he be allowed to convalesce in a London house which she rented. As a final stage of the cure she and Leslie took him on a Mediterranean holiday – before which she married Leslie in secret. She had thus obeyed the dream by 'looking after' both twins, in their different ways.

The marriage was not, however, to last indefinitely. One of the reasons was, perhaps, that while Leslie recognized her powers, and indeed gave her valuable practical assistance in the writing of *Winged Pharaoh* (see page 383), at the same time his rational mind refused to concede that she was able to psychometrize (tell the history of people involved with an artefact simply by handling it) or relive previous lifetimes. One can understand his dilemma: most readers will face it if they sample any of Grant's autobiographical works. On the one hand, what she has to say is extremely convincing (on the basis that either she's telling the startling truth or she's telling an unbelievably colossal lie); on the other, what she is saying is so mind-boggling that eventually one's intellect begins to protest: 'Oh, come *off* it!'[26]

The Grants were in Iraq, helping on an archaeological dig, when she had an extremely vivid dream about her daughter, who had had to be left behind in England. The child had her arms around Joan's neck and was screaming: 'Don't let them cut my tummy open, Mummy!' At once Joan leapt from the bed, woke Leslie and made for the nearest post office to send a telegram home. The reply they eventually received was reassuring.

Some little while later they had a letter from the child's grandmother (Joan's mother). The little girl had managed to swallow a particularly vicious and large piece of ironwork, but had had the sense to tell her grandmother what she had done. She was fed large quantities of plum cake and was rushed to hospital, where the medical staff said that she would require an operation to remove the offending item. However, before the operation was due, the plum cake did its stuff and all was well.

It's rather hard to know whether this was a clairvoyant

dream, a telepathic dream or – more simply – an astounding coincidence. With a dreamer like Grant, though, there are just too many such dreams for coincidence to be a valid explanation.

## *The Curious Case of Ms Sizemore*

The case of Chris Sizemore became an international *cause célèbre* in 1957 with the publication of *The Three Faces of Eve* by Corbett H. Thigpen and Hervey Cleckley. The famous film, released shortly afterwards, spread her story yet further. In the book and film we learnt of the two personalities, 'Eve Black' and 'Eve White', and their resolution to become a third, dominant and stable, character, Jane.

In fact, this version of Sizemore's story is highly misleading – something which she felt very strongly at the time. Thigpen and Cleckley assumed, for example, that when she spoke of earlier personalities taking her over she was really thinking of different periods when 'Eve Black' and 'Eve White' had been in control. More importantly, and as if to prove the fallacy of this first assumption, Jane was by no means the permanent character they had thought; piece by piece, as other characters came and went in the corridors of Sizemore's brain, Jane was to fade from view until finally, one day, she was gone forever. (It's interesting to note that, while the two psychiatrists thought of Jane as a capable, personable, rational character, Sizemore herself – who 'knew' Jane better than anyone else – thought she was a vindictive scheming bitch.) Add to this that Sizemore's relationships with the members of her family were grossly misrepresented – there was even a suggestion of an incestuous relationship with her father – and it isn't hard to understand why 'Eve' wanted to set the record straight.

For contractual reasons which are – um – obscure, Thigpen and Cleckley exercised considerable control over her efforts to do so. They insisted that she remain anonymous, 'for her own good', when what she really wanted to do was to see her true personal history published without concealments. (One suspects that, in the late '50s, the doctors were actually giving her good counsel in this respect.) And they forced on her other modifications of fact and deliberate omissions. The first result of her efforts, written in conjunction with James W. Poling, was a book called *The Final Face of Eve*, which perpetuated the falsehoods of its forerunner. It was a publishing disaster.[27] To give an idea of the extent to which the two psychiatrists had demanded alterations of straight fact, the book ends with Jane having successfully committed suicide, thereby, of course, killing all the other personalities inhabiting Sizemore's body.[28]

Some very considerable while later, in 1977, Sizemore was able to publish, in conjunction with her cousin and closest friend Elen Sain Pittillo – on whom Jane had modelled herself – what one hopes is the complete, definitive story of this remarkable woman, at the end of which her entire personality is reintegrated to form a competent, capable, whole person. *I'm Eve* (published in the UK as *Eve*) seems sadly to have been less successful than *The Three Faces of Eve*. This may, of course, be a sign of progress: it's possible that the vast bulk of the readers of the earlier book were interested solely in the 'freak show' aspects of the case.

As one might expect, the young Christine Costner (as she then was) had very great difficulty telling the difference between dream and reality. In one case of pique and jealousy, she watched an *alter ego* destroy a special watch of Elen's. When she claimed that the culprit had been the 'other little girl' she was beaten for lying – an occurrence which seems to have been common during her childhood. After all, how could her parents hope to realize that she was already, at that very early age, a victim of the then almost unknown disorder of multiple personality? Even she herself didn't know what was going on: her dream – her nightmare of the wanton destruction – had come true; that was all.

Other dreams – some more conventional, some more bizarre – pock her life history. For a while she went through a sleepwalking phase, during which she dreamt she was flying. Curiously, during her flight she dreamt she was wearing Elen's nightdress; as she and Elen remark in *I'm Eve*, the behaviour and the dream were 'markedly schizoid in character'. She had nightmares about parts of her body turning into snakes; these seem to have had not the usual Freudian origins but to relate to an incident when her uncle, who specialized in 'snakehandling' and snake-killing, got bitten by one of his co-stars. After an aunt had, perhaps foolishly, tried to force her to kiss the dead face of her grandmother as the old woman lay in her coffin, Chris had recurring dreams about this, too – and who can blame her? In much later life, she had a recurring nightmare (or, more correctly, anxiety-dream) about her daughter Taffy. They were in a large room, in the middle of which was a pool of water filled with writhing serpents. Into this pool Taffy fell; the child then began herself to turn into a serpent. Sizemore would jump in to save her, but an aunt would obstruct her, preventing her from climbing out of the pool with the child.

Some of Sizemore's abilities seem to have been alarmingly paranormal – something which has been suggested of other cases of multiple personality, too. Indeed, Colin Wilson has remarked:

It has often been pointed out that the 'controls' of mediums bear the hallmark of secondary personalities – which may seem to suggest that mediumship can be dismissed as a mental illness of the same type as multiple personality. But another striking feature of many cases of multiple personality is that one or other of the personalities often possesses genuine psychic powers.

Leaving aside our natural scepticism, a couple of incidents in Sizemore's life seem difficult to explain in strictly rationalistic terms. In one, as an adult, she was in a fit: deliriously she exclaimed that she was being wounded by a burn on the arm – where, indeed, she had been badly burnt many years before. Relatives applied a cool damp cloth to the by now red and swelling scar of the old burn. When the cloth was removed it was steaming hot. Obviously, this was impossible – but equally obviously it is impossible to doubt the sincerity of those who witnessed the occurrence.

But, more important in our context, she seems to have had a diagnostic dream to rival those of Edgar Cayce. Little Chris Costner had recently lost an aunt and uncle to the scourge of pneumonia, and had been badly struck by it herself. Now her sister lay seriously ill, presumably of the same disease. (Or so the young child thought: in fact, the parents thought it was a bad chest cold exacerbated by a foul dose of croup.) One night Christ dreamt that she met Jesus, and that He told her to tell her mother that Becky, the sister, was suffering from diphtheria, not pneumonia. This the girl did; and thanks to the pressure she put on her parents – despite a certain understandable reluctance of theirs to give their child's dream too much credence – the doctor was called and, his mind directed by the suggestion, diagnosed that Becky was indeed suffering from diphtheria. Had the suggestion not been made, it is likely that the correct diagnosis would not have been forthcoming until far too late to save the girl.

Curiously enough, it was a dream that set the real Chris Sizemore free. For long she had been infatuated by the sad memory of the burial of her infant nephew during her childhood. Towards the time when she and Elen were finishing *I'm Eve*, Chris began to have a recurring nightmare. A child in nappies was picking up a little white coffin – the same coffin her nephew had been buried in, when he was only a few months old. Each time she had the nightmare, Chris would awake, rouse her husband, and say vehemently: 'I didn't kill him! I didn't kill him!'

On being quizzed by Elen, Sizemore admitted that ever since childhood she'd felt that somehow her nephew had died because she had willed him to stop snivelling. If you accept the idea of the paranormal, there is some evidence favouring this explanation: on a different occasion the strong conscious *willing* of Chris that Elen survive a serious illness looks as if it produced a miraculous recovery of the younger woman. If you don't accept the paranormal explanation, then neither event is particularly mysterious. Most of us within near distance of an infant wish it would stop snivelling, so that if the infant should then die the coincidence is not an outrageous one – although young Chris Costner's feeling of guilt over the tragedy is understandable. Similarly Elen may just have spontaneously recovered or, more interestingly, have been inspired by the knowledge that Chris was willing her to live, so that she cured herself.

However, it was the dream, and the discovery of her illogical and long-hidden guilt feelings, which saved Chris Sizemore's life. Of that there can be little doubt.

## *Are We All Psychic?*

Ask anyone and they'll tell you about the curious telepathic, clairvoyant, precognitive or other paranormal dream they once had. A surprising number of people will tell you that they frequently have such dreams. There are only two conclusions to be drawn: either we're all deceiving ourselves or we're all psychics. I find the latter conclusion repugnant for a mixture of logical and illogical reasons.

First, however, we must recognize that we read a lot more mystery into our dreams than is actually there. We've mentioned the phenomenon of 'reading back', in which our unconscious cheats, as it were, by making us imagine false correlations between dreams and subsequent or distant events. We've mentioned coincidence, which certainly accounts for a goodly number of apparently paranormal dreams. Some of the concidences may seem long shots, but you have to remember that most of us do not at gut level really understand the operations of probability. For example, it may seem quite illogical that you need only about 23 people in a gathering for there to be a 50% chance of two of them having the same birthday. Similarly, many of the 'astonishing' coincidences which people describe are really not so astonishing: when analyzed mathematically they prove to be not such long shots after all.

Even if we accept that some coincidences are mighty odd, there is another reason why we must be careful when we talk about the paranormal: the paranormal phenomena have yet to 'prove themselves'. We have as yet no cast-iron laboratory-derived evidence that there is any such thing as the paranormal. It is easy and trendy enough to scoff at scientists for paying little attention to the paranormal on the grounds that it does not 'fit in' with their current world-view; but it is for precisely this reason that scientists would be betraying all logic if they made a practice of invoking the paranormal in order to explain anything which did not immediately yield to analysis.

For example, when I was discussing the Crellins' experience on page 245 I was conscious of the fact that it must seem as if it is much more logical to explain covert communications between spouses in terms of 'simple' telepathy than in the 'complicated' terms of extremely subtle body language. (Please note: I am not saying that my notion about body language *is* an explanation; I'm putting it forward as an example of the kind of mechanism which may be at work.) You may feel that we might just as well call the experience telepathy as fool around with unproven concepts such as body language; but my response is that in that case you might equally say that balls of lightning are 'really' flying saucers. It's all very well to stagger around gawping at the marvels of the Universe, but it's of very little interest if you just take the phenomena at face value: science is concerned with the 'how it works' of things. In short, there is nothing more deadly to all constructive thought in the field of the paranormal than the 'there are more things in Heaven and Earth' mentality.

This may seem as if I'm trying to explain away all apparently paranormal dreams. This is not quite the case. If we can explain away or cast doubts on the vast majority of such dreams, that still means that we are left with the residue of quite inexplicable dreams – and they're the really interesting ones. Perhaps they, too, have rationalist explanations, or perhaps they really are rooted in the paranormal. I don't know, and neither do you.

Certainly, though, so many dreams can be accounted for prosaically that we cannot say that dreams show that we are all psychic. We *may*, of course, all be psychic, but dreams don't prove it. And this is probably a good thing, because psychics – if they exist – can cause harm both to themselves and to others. A while ago a Scandinavian woman sued Uri Geller because she was pregnant. The old, old story? No. It seems that he'd been demonstrating some spoon-bending while she was nearby, and his psychic emanations had accidentally bent her IUD.

# 5

# *Dreams of Times to Come*

Men, my brothers, men the workers, ever reaping something new:
That which they have done but earnest of the things that they shall do:
For I dipt into the future, far as human eye could see,
Saw the Vision of the world, and all the wonder that would be.
Saw the heavens fill with commerce, argosies of magic sails,
Pilots of the purple twilight, dropping down with costly bales:
Heard the heavens fill with shouting, and there rain'd a ghastly dew
From the nations' airy navies grappling in the central blue.
Far along the world-wide whisper of the southwind rushing warm,
With the standards of the peoples plunging through the thunderstorm;
Till the war drum throbbed no longer and the battle flags were furled
In the Parliament of man, the Federation of the world.

– Alfred, Lord Tennyson,
'Locksley Hall'

When [Pilate] was set down on the judgment seat, his wife sent unto him, saying, Have thou nothing to do with that just man: for I have suffered many things this day in a dream because of him.

– *Matthew xxvii* 19

And so bifel that, longe er it were day,
This man mette [dreamt] in his bed, ther as he lay,
How that his felawe gan upon hym calle,

> And seyde, 'Allas! for in an oxes stalle
> This nyght I shal be mordred ther I lye.
> Now help me, deere brother, or I dye.
> In alle haste come to me!' he sayde.
> This man out of his sleep for feere abrayde;
> But whan that he was wakened of his sleep,
> He turned hym, and took of this no keep.
> Hym thoughte his dreem nas but a vanitee.
>
> – Geoffrey Chaucer,
> 'The Nonnes Preestes Tale'

Everyone believes that they've had a paranormal dream or two, and the most popular of all the types of such dreams is the precognitive one, in which the dream-mind ranges into the future picking up images and information about forthcoming disasters, family deaths or winners of the Derby. It has become almost a heresy to suggest the possibility that the case for precognitive dreaming has yet to be proven.

It seems to me that there is a likelihood that the case will never be proven, one way or another, until a radically new line of research into the subject is initiated. Accounts of precognitive dreams are legion, from the Bible to the bulging files of the Society for Psychical Research; but sceptics argue with some justification that many, perhaps most, of such tales are overtly dubious, being of legendary or anecdotal origin, while many other apparently precognitive events can with varying degrees of difficulty be explained in more mundane terms. In other words, it's all very well having masses of evidence in favour of precognition, but not if the evidence is all poor.

What very few people have attempted to research is how precognition *works*. Until a mechanism for it can be devised it is unlikely that any sceptic will give the matter much credence. Towards the end of this chapter I'll make a very tentative attempt to outline a 'model' for precognition which I think might work; this will of course be a purely theoretical excursion because, of course, I have myself yet to be convinced that precognition actually happens. In the meantime, however, we'll look at some of the tales – from the purely anecdotal to the apparently well documented – which, whether they are well known or obscure, have caught my fancy. Please bear in mind that the selection discussed in this chapter is only a tiny droplet from the vast ocean of claimed precognitive dreams. I may well have missed your favourite – almost certainly so if your favourite is one which you've experienced yourself.

First, though, an example which amuses me of a dream which ought to be precognitive but isn't.

In his *The Dragons of Eden* (1977) the US planetary scientist Carl Sagan, known more usually for his television presentations and for his writings on SETI (the *s*earch for *e*xtra*t*errestrial *i*ntelligence), tells us that once he dreamt he was reading a history textbook, but one with a difference. This one didn't stop at the present: the last chapter or two were about the future, as if the book had been written a century hence and somehow 'time-scooped' back into our era.

Naturally enough, it was the information on the future that Sagan wanted most to read, and so he turned eagerly to the page where the present was discussed, planning to read from there to the end of the book. Alas, he discovered that he was unable to read about the future:

> . . . it was impossible. I could make out individual words. I could even discern the serifs on the individual characters. But I could not put the letters together into words or words together into sentences. I was alexic.

Sagan goes on to say that alexic dreams are common for him; and that most people have some impairment of this nature in their dreams. In fact, as far as I can gather, alexia in dreams is pretty unusual: one of the commonest dream experiences is that of falling asleep while reading, dreaming that one's reading on, and then suddenly realizing that the plot's getting a little strange and waking up enough to switch the light off.

Sagan speculates that this lack of reading ability in dreams may indicate that dreams were born of a time when humanity didn't need to recognize symbols – such as words.[1] But since, as I say, the inability to read in dreams seems not especially common, one wonders if he's on somewhat shaky ground here. However, he does seem to be on stronger ground when he says that similar impairments frequently affect other people. In my own case, it's an inability to distinguish who people really *are*: I frequently wake up thinking that I've dreamt about Fred only to realize that the person labelled 'Fred' in my dream was actually Alf – or even Catherine!

## *The Dreams of the Religious*

Religious dreams abound in the Judaeo-Christian tradition as they do in all other religious traditions. We have already come across a number of such visions and revelatory dreams in earlier chapters. Naturally enough, as soon as martyrs have been put to death, all sorts of premonitory and other dreams are ascribed to them, as part of a general pattern of miraculous occurrences suddenly 'remembered' to testify to their saintliness and courage in death. A fairly typical example is that of St Hermes, who was tortured and burnt at the stake in A.D. 304 along with Sts Philip, Severus and Eusebius, under the persecution of Diocletian. Their crime was the refusal to burn the sacred books of the church at Heraclea, near Constantinople.

While the existence of the saints and their martyrdom are matters of history, Hermes' dream is almost certainly apocryphal. However, it has a certain charm. He dreamt that he saw a snow-white dove fly into his room and land on his head, then move down to perch on his chest. It had in its beak some meat, which it fed to him; the meat was delicious.

When he awoke Hermes knew that this dream had been a message from God, telling him that he was to be honoured by becoming a martyr to the Faith. The delicious meat represented, of course, the Eucharist.

Similar tales of precognitive dreams surround the births of some of the holy. For example, there are many legends concerning the Irish St Columba, who founded the monasteries at Derry and Kells before going on to found that on Iona, from which he directed the conversion of the peoples of northern Scotland. Still on display in Donegal is the very stone, or so it's claimed, on which his mother lay while giving birth to him, in about A.D.521.

The legend of his birth tells us that his saintly glory did not go unheralded. While she was pregnant with him his mother dreamt that an angel came to her carrying a veil which was decorated with flowers of every type and beauty. The veil was caught by the wind, and flew away over broad tracts of the land, unfurling as it flew. The angel told her that she was to bear a son who would 'blossom for heaven', to which blissful abode he would lead uncounted souls.

It's hard to believe that this dream wasn't the product of the poetic imagination of some mediaeval chronicler.

Dreams of and about more recent saints tend to be correspondingly more modest in scope. St Louis Bertrán (1526–1581) is probably best remembered for his work in

South America, where he was sent in 1562. He spread the gospel in what are now Panama, Colombia and parts of the West Indies, all the while doing his best to ameliorate the harsh lot of the natives under their 'civilized' conquerors.

Years before, though, Louis is said to have had an interesting precognitive dream. He saw a friend of his, one Father Raphael Castello, submerged in water up to his neck. Naturally enough, the next time he saw Castello he told him about the dream, saying that he thought it was a warning.

Not long afterwards, Castello was travelling by ship from Majorca to Spain when, near Ibiza, a violent storm blew up. A voice bade Castello jump into the lifeboat, which he did, rowing away as fast as his oars would carry him, leaving all the rest of the people on the ship – including the queen-dowager of Spain – to drown. He survived, although he was indeed soaked up to his neck in thc sca.

I'm sure there's a moral lesson in this tale, but I just can't think what it is . . .

Probably the most famous of all the precognitive dreams in the Judaeo-Christian religious tradition is the one dreamt by the Pharaoh and interpreted by Joseph. The dream is recounted in *Genesis xli*:

> 1. And it came to pass at the end of two full years, that Pharaoh dreamed: and, behold, he stood by a river.
> 2. And, behold, there came up out of the river seven well favoured kine [cattle] and fatfleshed; and they fed in a meadow.
> 3. And, behold, seven other kine came up after them out of the river, ill favoured and leanfleshed; and stood by the [other] kine upon the brink of the river.

4. And the ill favoured and leanfleshed kine did eat up the seven well favoured and fat kine. So Pharaoh awoke.
5. And he slept and dreamed the second time: and, behold, seven ears of corn came up upon one stalk, rank and good.
6. And, behold, seven thin ears and blasted with the east wind sprung up after them.
7. And the seven thin ears devoured the seven rank and full ears. And Pharaoh awoke, and, behold, [it was] a dream.

In the morning the pharaoh sent for his dream-interpreters, but none of them could tell him what the dream meant. Finally the butler piped up. He and the chief baker had spent a while locked up at the pharaoh's whim:

11. And we dreamed a dream on one night, I and he; we dreamed each man according to the interpretation of his dream.
12. And [there was] there with us a young man, a Hebrew, servant to the captain of the guard; and we told him, and he interpreted to us our dreams; to each man according to his dream he did interpret.
13. And it came to pass, as he interpreted to us, so it was; me he restored unto my office, and him he hanged.
14. Then Pharaoh sent and called Joseph . . .

The butler's and the baker's dreams, and their interpretations by Joseph, are recounted in *Genesis xl*:

9. . . . In my dream, behold, a vine [was] before me;
10. And in the vine [were] three branches: and it [was] as though it budded, [and] her blossoms shot forth; and the clusters thereof brought forth ripe grapes:
11. And Pharaoh's cup [was] in my hand: and I took

the grapes, and pressed them into Pharaoh's cup, and I gave the cup into Pharaoh's hand.
12. And Joseph said unto him, This [is] the interpretation of it: The three branches [are] three days:
13. Yet within three days shall Pharaoh lift up thine head, and restore thee unto thy place: and thou shalt deliver Pharaoh's cup into his hand, after the former manner when thou wast his butler. . . .
16. When the chief baker saw that the interpretation was good, he said unto Joseph, I also [was] in my dream, and, behold, [I had] three white baskets on my head:
17. And in the uppermost basket [there was] of all manner of bakemeats for Pharaoh; and the birds did eat them out of the basket upon my head.
18. And Joseph answered and said, This [is] the interpretation thereof: The three baskets [are] three days:
18. Yet within three days shall Pharaoh lift up thy head from off thee, and shall hang thee on a tree; and the birds shall eat thy flesh from off thee.

Sure enough, according to the butler, these things had come to pass: he himself had been restored to his position and the baker had been put to death – this was all in the days before the servant problem.

Joseph was brought before the pharaoh and asked for his interpretation of the dream about the thin and fat cattle and the plump and scraggly grain. He pointed out that the two dreams were equivalent – and, in fact, one suspects that the pharaoh originally had only a single dream, two variant versions of which are contained in *Genesis*. The seven fat cattle and plump ears of corn represented a coming seven years of plenty; the seven lean cattle and scraggly ears represented an ensuing seven years of famine. Joseph volunteered to become the supervisor of a programme to store food during the seven years of plenty so that the effects of the seven drought years would be ameliorated. He got the job; 'See,' said the pharaoh, 'I have set thee over all the land of Egypt.'

The evidence in favour of all this having happened is reasonably slender, if we ignore *Genesis*. This is in large part because records from that era of Egyptian history are anyway very poor. There are odd hints elsewhere, however, that a dream-interpreter did indeed rise to a pre-eminent position in Egypt; and there are plenty of records of seven-year famines following seven years of plenty. Moreover, some of the historical details contained in the *Genesis* story of Joseph suggest that it was written by a contemporary or near-contemporary – at least in its original form. The *Genesis* account may be a conflation of several different events, or it may indeed be a true history. Barring some future archaeological breakthrough, we shall probably never know.

## *Tall Tales and Otherwise*

In his *The Bible in Spain* (1843) George Borrow told of a curious incident. He was on ship to Portugal when one of the sailors remarked to his colleagues that he'd just had a strange dream: he'd fallen from the ship's cross-trees into the sea. Naturally enough, he was rather upset about the dream.

Just then, however, the captain ordered the top-sails to be taken in, and the sailor, along with several others, shinned up the mast. A moment later he had fallen from the cross-trees into the sea. Rescue proved impossible, and he drowned.

This little tale sounds very impressive at first, until one recalls that *The Bible in Spain* is hardly a conventional, formal travelogue: in fact, it's hard to tell which of the events Borrow described in it actually took place and which were products of his excellent imagination. It may well be that the story is true: there's simply no way of knowing.

And this is only one of a whole collection of precognitive-dream stories which appear over and over again in the literature but which seem to be, to put the most charitable aspect on it, dubious.

The tale is told that Cicero had precognitive dreams. One night he dreamt he saw a young man being lowered from the skies on a golden chain to stand in the temple door. The following day Cicero went with Julius Caesar to the Capitol, and there saw the boy of his dream: it was Gaius Octavius, Caesar's great-nephew. It comes as no surprise to learn that the young man became Octavian (Gaius Julius Caesar Octavianus) and later, as Augustus, the first Roman emperor.

Is this a valid historical example of a precognitive dream? Almost certainly not. Rulers have always had a habit of rewriting history in order to justify their own positions of power, and a precognitive dream from Cicero would have suited Augustus just fine. The clincher is probably that Cicero himself spoke out strongly against the whole subject of dream-divination, which he regarded as a nonsense. Although it's *possible* that he could have adopted this stance despite having had a highly significant precognitive dream himself, it's perhaps a little unlikely – especially since his sceptical views on the subject were at the time unpopular.

If the rise of a monarch to power generates precognitive-dream tales, then so does the death of a monarch. The death of France's Henry II is renowned throughout the history of prediction, because it is claimed that it was accurately foretold in one of the 'Centuries' of Nostradamus. The stanza in question is

Le lyon jeune le vieux surmontera
En champ bellique par singulier duelle.
Dans cage d'or, les yeux lui crevera:
Deux classes une, puit mourir, mort cruelle.

('The young lion will defeat the old in single combat on the battlefield. He will pierce his eyes in a golden cage: two wounds in one, then he will die, a cruel death.')

In the spring of 1559 the Peace of Cateau-Cambrésis was agreed, and in order to strengthen it Henry betrothed his daughter, the 14-year-old Elizabeth, to Philip II of Spain. Henry called for a period of junketing in June/July of that year; as part of it, he himself would joust against a whole string of adversaries. One of them was Gabriel, Comte de Montgomery, of the Scottish guard; his lance splintered and crashed through the king's golden vizor, wounding him in the eye. Henry later died of blood-poisoning.

Of course, it's rather rash to notch this up as a successful prediction from Nostradamus. While the lion was an occasional symbol used by Henry, it was in no way connected with Montgomery, so why should he be 'the young lion'? Only one eye was pierced, not both. Montgomery was not dramatically younger than Henry. And so on.

But in our terms the really interesting prediction involved was one from the Marshal of France, Blaise de Monluc. According to the tale, the night beforehand he dreamt that he saw the king's face, blood-covered, while in the background he heard voices shouting. Some cried, 'He lives!', others, 'He is dead!' Sure enough, this was exactly the confusion which reigned in reality, since Henry's wound was so ghastly that many onlookers could not believe that he had survived it. (As noted, it in fact killed him within a few days.)

Again the story is probably apocryphal; and I'm reluctant to give it any higher status than of one of the great classics of predictive dreaming, the Tuchkov story.

The wife of Russia's General Tuchkov dreamt three times in the summer of 1812 that she was in a strange hotel room and that her father came in, leading her small son by the hand and saying that the general had been slain at Borodino. She was disturbed enough by this to tell her husband about it; but in the end they dismissed the dream as of no importance, since nowhere on the map could they find any trace of a place called Borodino.

But in a few months later the countess took a room in an inn near to where her husband was helping in the attempt to fight off Napoleon's armies as they advanced on Moscow. And, sure enough, her father came with her son into the room to tell her that her husband had been killed near the little known village of Borodino.

But there seems to be a minor flaw in the tale. Borodino, where Napoleon defeated the Russians under Kutuzov, is neither remote from Moscow nor obscure and tiny. It is about 110km from Moscow, and is large enough to be shown on even a 1:6,000,000 map.[2] It seems unlikely that the Tuchkovs could have made even the most perfunctory of searches and failed to find it.

Similar stories surround other deaths in battle. One of the less uplifting incidents in the American Revolution was the attempt by General Benedict Arnold to betray to the British the key West Point position in 1780. His accomplice, the British Major John André, was captured behind American lines and hanged as a spy. Arnold, the real villain of the piece, served for a short time on the British side before retiring to England in 1781; he died in 1801.

Some while before this – in the early 1770s – we're told that two friends of the dire poetess Anna Seward, Messrs Cunningham and Newton,[3] heard that she was a friend of the budding poet John André, who was visiting Britain. (He'd been brought up largely in Geneva.) Cunningham and Newton were eager to meet the man, and so Seward arranged afternoon tea for them all.

Cunningham and Newton arrived first and, while they waited for André to turn up, the former mentioned idly a pair of linked dreams he'd had the night before. In the first he had seen a young horseman stopped in the forest and taken prisoner by three assailants; and in the second he had seen the horseman hanged in front of a large crowd of spectators.

Shortly afterwards, Seward and André arrived, and Cunningham paled. This young man, whom he had never met before in his waking hours, was the horseman he had seen in his dreams! And, as we've seen, some years later the dreams were to come true.

That, at least, is the tale. Corroboration of it is hard to come by. Seward's diaries and correspondence are lost to us, and Cunningham seems to have died not long after having had the dreams. It seems overwhelmingly likely that the whole story is just a fabrication or, at best, merely a vastly embellished account of a minor coincidence between dream and reality. However, it has become a part of our modern mythology, and no doubt will remain so for the foreseeable future.

## *Individual Anecdotes*

Most of the probably apocryphal tales of precognitive dreaming fall into the 'rattling good yarn' category. Well, you may say, that's fair enough: they wouldn't be remembered and talked about if they *weren't* rattling good yarns.

There's obviously some justification in this argument but it's noticeable that, the better documented a dream-account is, the less of a rattling good yarn the whole series of events makes.

In ideal circumstances, a person who has a precognitive dream writes it down in detail and gives copies to as many people as possible. Should the dream be realized in practice, and should the real-life details correspond in large part to those of the dream, then a good case can be made for precognition. For obvious reasons – how do you know if a dream is precognitive until it comes true? – such ideal circumstances rarely, if ever, come about. The next best thing is where the dreamer at least talks about the dream before the events come about, and we shall be looking later at some instances of this happening.

Before then, though, it's interesting to consider some dreams which, while they lie on the ladder higher than the apocryphal tales, cannot really be considered properly documented. These are what one might call 'personal accounts'. There is no reason to believe that the people involved are either consciously or unconsciously distorting the truth of the events; but at the same time there is no possible way of verifying the tale. Significantly, however, these stories are generally, like the well documented cases, concerned more with trivia than with anything of substance.

For example, Mrs S. Paskell has told me that a few years ago she dreamt that the British politician Lord Home had died. She mentioned her dream in the morning to her husband: her reason for doing so was that she thought it odd that she should dream about someone of whom she rarely thought during her waking hours. That afternoon the radio carried the news that Home's nephew, the playwright William Douglas-Home, had died.

Audrey Atkinson gives a more detailed account of the

only dream of hers which she considers to have been precognitive:

> About six years ago I moved to [a new town] . . . I was in a rather depressed state and tended to 'hibernate', as it was the wintertime. I knew nobody in the road into which I had moved, and, apart from visiting my family . . . , stayed indoors most of the time. One night, I had the most vivid dream, as follows.
>
> I was in my kitchen on a bright sunny morning and I walked into my lounge, which is elevated, overlooking the road. I crossed to the window and looked down. There at the gate was a hearse, with a coffin. On top of the coffin was a circular wreath and another in the form of a cross. In front of the hearse were two men, peering up at me. This so frightened me – I thought they had come for *me* – that it woke me up.
>
> I telephoned my sister and told her I thought I'd had an omen, and that my time was up! I described the dream to her and she said it was most likely my father, who hadn't been well. (He's still OK!) Anyway, I was quite philosophical about my coming demise, and didn't think a lot more about it. Three months later I was in my kitchen on a bright sunny morning, and walked into my lounge, looked out of the window – and my heart nearly stopped beating. There at the gate was the hearse, the coffin with two wreaths, circle and cross, and the two men peering up. But I realized they were looking at the name of my house (which is on the wall beside the window). As I watched they backed up the road [to a house] where evidently an old man had died.
>
> I immediately 'phoned my sister again and told her it wasn't *me* after all. Since I didn't know the man, or even *of* a man, it made me think that somewhere along the line the future has already happened . . .

In both of these cases, of course, other people do seem to have been told about the dreams before the real-life incidents occurred. However, we have to bear in mind that Paskell's dream was at best a near-miss; that there was little by way of detail; and that it's quite possible that her memory is false (unconsciously so, I stress) in telling her that she mentioned the dream to her husband *before* the news of the death came through. Similarly, after this expanse of time, we've no way of knowing how many of the details of her dream Atkinson told her sister; or how many of them Atkinson unconsciously 'read back' into the dream. If I dream of a hearse and then, the next day, see one in our road, I haven't necessarily had a precognitive dream – even less so if three months go by before the dream 'comes true'.

We must bear in mind, having said all that, that there is no way in which we can prove that the dreams were *not* genuinely precognitive. It's simply that we don't know.

The same has to be said about a story told by Lyall Watson in his *The Romeo Error* (1974); he describes the event as an out-of-body experience (OOBE – see page 253), but it seems more like a clairvoyant or precognitive dream. Some years ago he was in Kenya, travelling on safari, when the minibus he was in did a spectacular double-somersault before landing in a precariously poised position: the crash knocked Watson out. While unconscious he dreamt that he was outside the minibus, looking at it as it quivered dangerously. He saw that one of the party, a lad, had had his head and shoulders thrust through the canvas top of the vehicle during the general chaos. If the minibus rolled further, the boy was dead.

Watson says that he then woke, climbed out of the minibus window, and freed the boy just in the nick of time before the vehicle did indeed take that further tumble.

Again, it could well be that Watson underwent a paranormal experience of some kind. However, the moments after waking from unconsciousness are generally pretty confused ones, and it's often hard to remember the details of them afterwards. It's perfectly possible that Watson's unconscious made up the dream when, a while later, he discovered that he'd saved the boy's life but couldn't remember much about it.

In Charles Dickens' diary we find yet another apparently precognitive dream. He tells us that he dreamt he saw a lady in a red shawl whom he did not know; however, she introduced herself as Miss Napier. On waking, he was puzzled, because he didn't know a Miss Napier and certainly didn't know the woman in the shawl by that or any other name. A few days later, however, after one of his public readings, a few fans came backstage to flatter him. Sure enough, one of them was the woman he had seen in his dream, and her name was indeed Miss Napier.

This is very striking; but one has to remember that the record in Dickens' diary is anecdotal in style. Moreover, it was written *after he had met Miss Napier* and not immediately after he had had the dream. Obviously, it would be only after the 'dream came true' that Dickens would realize that it was in any way significant, and so bother recording it; but we have to remember the phenomenon of 'reading back', the unconscious tendency we all have to help our dreams 'come true'. The trivial coincidence of names – and Napier isn't a particularly uncommon name – could easily have convinced Dickens that the real woman looked exactly like the one in the dream.

Still, most of these dreams are trivial, and their very triviality makes one tempted to take them seriously. Were it not for the fact that they are all uncorroborated, or barely so . . .

Few dreams can be more trivial than one had in 1942 by Laura Dale, of the American Society for Psychical Research. In her dream she was vacuum-cleaning in a strange house. Other people were there, as was her dog. Suddenly the vacuum cleaner began to expand and contract like a living thing, and she fled from the house, leaving the others behind. The vacuum cleaner exploded; later she discovered that a man had died attempting to save her dog.

A couple of days later, at the movies, she saw a cartoon called *The Raven* in which a raven and a dog call upon another dog, ostensibly to try to sell it a vacuum cleaner. While the raven demonstrates the machine, the criminal dog slips upstairs to blow the safe. Suddenly the vacuum cleaner comes to life, expanding and contracting like a living thing, and finally explodes, knocking the dog-householder for six. About the same time, the dog-burglar blows up the safe.

The parallels are astonishing, especially since the whole sequence of events is so improbable: have *you* ever dreamt about a vacuum cleaner coming to life and then exploding? And, even if you've had a dream of similar improbability, do you then expect to see it closely re-enacted at the movies?

But why should Dale dream of something so trivial? Ullman *et al.*, who present this tale in their *Dream Telepathy* (1973), suggest that it was because, earlier on the day of her dream, her unconscious had made a fool of itself in an experiment at the ASPR, and that it was now trying to make amends, as it were. But one can't go too overboard about this: once again, there's no reason to believe that Dale was anything other than totally honest, but it's possible she'd seen and forgotten about the cartoon some while before, or had unconsciously heard other people talking about it, or something of that ilk. Moreover (and I may be wrong), the dream doesn't seem to have been 'logged' before the trip to the movies.

Dale seems certainly to have believed the dream to have been genuinely precognitive. G. M. Glaskin, whose 'reincarnationary' dreams we shall consider in the next chapter (see pages 387–97), records in *A Door to Eternity* (1979) a number of dreams which he, too, quite clearly believes to have been truly precognitive – or, at least, to have contained genuinely precognitive elements. I'm less certain, although it's easy to see why he should so believe.

For example, in one he dreamt about various bizarre events at a reception he was attending in honour of Gough Whitlam (erstwhile prime minister of Australia) and his wife Margaret. A few months later he did in fact receive an invitation from the Whitlams' secretary to meet them at an eve-of-poll junket, but he was unable to accept as he was going to be out of the country at the time. The parallels between dream and reality are not marked.

More significantly, in the same dream he saw a dispute, soon happily resolved, between two friends over the value of a necklace. He claims that later he found out that a similar dispute had in fact taken place between them – but he does not tell us the similarities.

Others of his dreams seem to be self-fulfilling. In one he tells of being invited to see a friend who worked in a shop; when he got there she insisted on serving all the customers first, even those who came in after him. He left in a dudgeon. In real life he was a while later asked to keep an appointment with the principal of the college where he was a writer-in-residence. He found that a number of other people were being shown into the principal's office before him, and the fifteen minutes allocated for his own meeting were soon used up. Remembering the dream, he made another appointment rather than follow his natural inclinations and walk out. Here, clearly, the dream had some effect on his future actions. But precognition hardly seems to have been involved: being kept waiting outside the offices of rude self-important people is a common experience for most of us.

Even less plausible as precognitive dreams are the two he records in which he was in a foreign city – probably London or New York, he wasn't sure – for the launch of one of his books. At the time, he had never been present at such a launch (he lives in Australia); but a year after the dream he did indeed come to London for exactly this purpose. What makes it all less exciting is that Glaskin had already published a number of books. Any author is likely, after he has published several books, to be given a launch party by his publisher. Especially if the author is an Australian making a rare visit to the country in which the new book is being published. Even more especially if the author is paying his own expenses for the trip.[4]

In a rather different category fall some of the dreams of Jack Kerouac, which can be interpreted as foretelling impending doom – in fact, it's surprising that they don't seem to have been picked up by any paranormal investigator.

In his *Book of Dreams* (1961) Kerouac records, for example, having dreamt of an aircraft collision over the New York/New Jersey airport; of civil strife, with a large body of PoWs battling their way down the Mississippi; of watching the destruction of New York during the 'end of the world cataclysm'; and of the setting up, in the centre of New York, of a tower on which a nuclear bomb is to be detonated in a month's time so that the city has to be evacuated now.

Clearly these things have 'yet to happen' – with the

possible exception, by the law of averages, of the 'plane crash. There is no sign that Kerouac himself thought that there was any chance of these events coming to pass. Of course, the fact that a dream hasn't yet come true doesn't necessarily mean that it isn't precognitive, and some of Kerouac's sound frighteningly plausible possibilities for the future.

The important point here is that Kerouac's dreams are not logged as precognitive because they have failed to happen. Lots of us have dreams of impending disaster – even on a large scale. We generally forget these dreams although, as with dreams of other types, they may haunt us for a while. Among these countless foreboding dreams, it's not surprising that a few come true – whether they involve catastrophe or trivia. We remember those that come true, obviously. In other words, we have a selective memory which makes us think that a far higher proportion of dreams come true than is actually the case. This is, of course, only one factor clouding our thinking on the subject of precognitive dreaming, as we have noted.

## *Slumbering Tipsters*

In a letter dated 21st September, 1951, C. G. Jung mentioned a certain Mrs X., whose dreams quite reliably predicted the winners of the Derby. Infuriatingly, he gave no further details.

But such dreaming tipsters, while uncommon, are far from unknown. Stan Gooch is a British writer whose works can probably best be described as lying on the more speculative fringes of psychology: his books are sometimes dismissed as nutcult texts, but this is to do them an injustice. They are too interesting, self-consistent and well thought out to be jumbled in with the writings of some of the more overt pseudoscientists. Gooch's ideas may be totally wrong-headed, but one always has the lurking suspicion that perhaps they're not.

In his *The Paranormal* (1978) he discusses at length some of his apparently precognitive dreams, one of which is relevant here. Roughly the same dream occurred twice in the same night: he and some friends went to see a film called 'Showman's Fair' – at least, that's the title that came up on the screen. The next morning he noticed in the newspaper that an elderly horse of which he had never (consciously) heard was running in a race that day: it was, of course, called Showman's Fair. With some trepidation, he put money on the horse – and it won. A couple of weeks later he again put money on it, and again it won.[5]

Gooch cites in *The Paranormal* three other cases of lucky horse-loving dreamers, one of them being John Godley, Lord Kilbracken, who had a distinguished career as a racing journalist thanks to his precognitive dreams.

In 1946, as an Oxford undergraduate, Godley started to be able with apparent consistency to dream the winners of forthcoming races. In his first such dream the winners were Bindle and Juladdin; on discovering in the morning that horses with those names were indeed running that day, he placed money on both – and in due course was rewarded handsomely. Succeeding dreams were not quite so accurate in their predictions, but he generally had little difficulty in identifying the dream-name with that of the real horse in question.

His powers in due course ebbed, although in an isolated case in 1958 he was able to pick the winner of the Grand National.

In 1977 Colin Wilson devoted a programme in his 'Leap in the Dark' television series to the subject. One reviewer of the programme came out with a pertinent question: what is so *important* about being able to predict in your dreams the winners of tomorrow's races? As Wilson facetiously remarked in his *Mysteries* (1978), to a broke undergraduate interested enough in betting to have an account with a bookmaker, the information is deeply interesting – to the point of genuine importance! Gooch, on the other hand, made a rather more forceful point in *The Paranormal*: it doesn't really matter what it is that dreams actually predict, it's whether or not they genuinely *do so* that's important.

Once again, it's the predictions of trivia that seem most credible. Dreams of doom and disaster lead us into murkier territory.

## *Images of Death*

The predictive dream of Francis Humbertson Mackenzie, the last Lord Seaford, is of especial interest in that it played a notable role in the fulfilment of the final prophecy of Kenneth Mackenzie, the famous Brahan Seer (also known as Coinneach Odhar Fiosaiche, the Warlock of the Glen).

The Brahan Seer is a figure shrouded in some mystery, and all details of his life and predictions should be taken with as many pinches of salt as possible. He seems to have been born early in the 17th century on the island of Lewis, in the Outer Hebrides. There are various versions of how he became a prophet. A typical one is that he had engendered the hatred of a farmer's wife for whose husband he was then working. She planned to poison him, but before dinner on the day on which she planned to strike he fell asleep in a field. On awakening he found a stone with a hole through it sitting on his chest. Through the hole he peeped, and the details of her plan were revealed to him. The stone he kept for the rest of his life, using it as a 'focus' for scrying.

In due course, his fame as a scryer increased. While working on the estate of Brahan Castle, in Ross and Cromarty, he became the object of attention of the Mackenzie family (no relation to him) who bore the title Seaforth. He became their sort of family prophet; but it is claimed that he predicted also such much later events as the building of the Caledonian Canal, the advent of the railways, the Battle of Culloden, and the provisions of mains gas and water to Inverness.

His downfall came about when Isabella, Countess of Seaforth, asked for reassurance that her husband Kenneth, the Third Earl of Seaforth, was alive and well: he had been abroad, in Paris, for much longer than expected, and she had heard nothing from him for months. In front of her retainers and family the Brahan Seer tactlessly announced that he could see that her husband was indeed still in Paris, and that at the moment he was in the process of kissing a pretty woman.

Isabella had him tried for trafficking with the Devil, and he was put to death very barbarously indeed.

Before his death, though, he made some specific predictions about the future of the Seaforths. The last of the line would be deaf and dumb, and would be predeceased by all four of his sons. He would know that he was indeed the last because, by way of confirmation, four of the most important local lairds would be, respectively, half-witted, hare-lipped, a stammerer and buck-toothed. His heir would be a white-hooded woman from the East who would kill her sister. This was, according to the legend, rather more significant than the detailed list of the future family fortunes which you or I might give to someone who was in the process of having us put to death.

And now to Francis' dream. He was 12 years old and at boarding school when there was an epidemic of scarlet fever among the boys. One night, when the nurse was out of the dormitory, she heard a great cry. She rushed in to find Francis nearly hysterical because of a nightmare he'd just had. An old woman had come into the dormitory and moved from bed to bed. Into the foreheads of the occupants of some of the beds she had driven little wooden stakes; when she came to Francis she drove the stakes instead into his ears.

According to the story, the boys whose foreheads he had seen pierced in due course all died, and Francis was left completely deaf, remaining so for the rest of his life. And, in his declining years, his speech deteriorated until he finally was dumb. He had four sons, all of whom preceded him to the grave. His daughter and heir, widowed while in the Orient, was still wearing the white dress of mourning then customary when she came to take up her inheritance; her husband's surname had been Hood. And, while she was driving with her younger sister in a carriage one day, the horse bolted and the sister was killed in the ensuing accident.

Almost certainly, most of the Brahan Seer's composite prediction was made up after the event. But Francis' dream was surprisingly well documented *at the time* – rather than later, as is so common with tales of this vintage – and is therefore rather harder to explain away. One possibility could be that the little boy did indeed have such a dream, but that later the details of *which* lads had their foreheads pierced were doctored to accord with the list of boys who actually died. There are plenty of other possibilities. The truth is, of course, lost to us forever.

During the 19th century records improved. In particular, dream-records improved, probably because people were less likely to assume that every interesting dream was magical (and conversely that few things could be magical unless a sufficiency of interesting dreams were invented to go with them). One dream of Mark Twain's (Samuel Clemens') deserves some attention: it is reasonably well documented and, because of Twain's fame, has a certain fame of its own.

Twain frequently recorded or later wrote of his dreams, one in particular of which, as I say, shows signs of prescience – but see below! At the time of the dream he and his brother Henry were working on the Mississippi riverboats. One night in 1858, Twain had a dream of astonishing vividness. He saw his brother's body in the sitting-room, lying in a metal coffin which was supported between two chairs. On the body's breast was a bouquet of white flowers with a single red flower in the middle. The waking Mark told his sister that he believed Henry was indeed dead, so vivid had been the dream.

Some weeks later, the boiler of the boat on which Henry was travelling exploded, killing Henry and many others (it was only by chance that Mark was not among them: he had travelled on a different vessel from his brother). Henry Clemens, alone among all the casualties, was buried in a metal rather than a wooden coffin – the ladies of Memphis had taken pity on his youth and set up a collection. When Mark first saw his brother laid out, the scene was exactly as in the dream – except that it was in the wrong sitting-room and there was no bunch of flowers on the boy's chest. At that moment a woman entered and placed a bunch of flowers there: it was of white flowers, with a red flower at the centre.

This is, of course, a quite stunning precognitive dream . . . except that its source is Twain's own *Autobiography*. This was a project he tackled on and off over the years: it is less a formal book than a selection of essays, some disjointed and some repetitive, written down by himself or dictated to others. One of the friends who took his dictation commented that Twain's recollections were becoming more like rambling fictions than accurate memoirs, and there seems to have been little contemporary disagreement with this view.

As we shall see, dreaming about the assassinations of major political figures is a popular activity. Alan Vaughan has supposed that this is because certain charismatic leaders fit into the 'king must die' mould: someone like John Kennedy is bound to be assassinated because of the overwhelmingly powerful appeal of his charisma, and the unconscious knows this, so it dreams about it. Another possibility is that people often dream about the 'stars' in the news, who sometimes do in real life get assassinated: on any particular night, there are bound to be one or two people who dream about the assassination of a particular public figure.

People who have had such dreams often become celebrities in their own right; we shall look at them later, when we look at the dreamers who have won general renown as a result of their apparent precognitive powers. Here, though, we shall look at John Williams, a banker of Redruth: he is accredited with the best documented precognitive dream concerning the murder of Spencer Perceval, Prime Minister of Britain, on 11th May, 1812. The records date from well after the assassination: Williams' own account of the dream was written in letter form to the Perceval family in December 1832 and reproduced in *Notes and Queries* in February 1891.

He prefaced his account as follows:

> Being desired to write out the particulars of a remarkable dream which I had in the year 1812, before I do so I think it may be proper for me to say that at that time my attention was fully occupied with affairs of my own – the superintendence of some very extensive mines in

> Cornwall being entrusted to me. Thus I had no leisure to pay any attention to political matters, and hardly knew at that time who formed the Administration of the Country. It was, therefore, scarcely possible that my own interest in the subject should have had any share in suggesting the circumstances which presented themselves to my imagination. It was, in truth, a subject which never occurred to my waking thoughts.

Rather like Mrs Paskell (see page 296), who never thought of Alec Douglas-Home. Anyway, Williams claimed that 'about the second or third day of May, 1812' he dreamed that he 'was in the lobby of the House of Commons (a place well known to me)' when

> A small man, dressed in a blue coat and white waistcoat, entered, and immediately I saw a person whom I had observed on my first entrance, dressed in a snuff-coloured coat with metal buttons, take a pistol from under his coat, and present it at the little man above mentioned. The pistol was discharged, and the ball entered under the left breast of the person at whom it was directed. I saw the blood issue from the place where the ball had struck him, his countenance instantly altered, and he fell to the ground. Upon enquiry who the sufferer might be I was informed that he was the Chancellor, I understood him to be Mr Perceval, who was Chancellor of the Exchequer. I further saw the murderer laid hold of by several of the gentlemen in the room. Upon waking, I told the particulars above related to my wife; she treated the matter lightly, and desired me to go to sleep, saying it was only a dream.

According to Williams' account, he went back to sleep and had the dream again. When he woke up, his wife told him to go back to sleep, which he duly did – only to have yet a third 'performance' of the identical dream.

> So much alarmed and impressed was I with the circumstances above related that I felt much doubt whether it was not my duty to take a journey to London, and communicate upon the subject with the party principally concerned. Upon this point I consulted with some friends whom I met on business at the Godolphin mine on the following day. After having stated to them the particulars of the dream itself and what were my own feelings in relation to it, they dissuaded me from my purpose, saying I might expose myself to contempt and vexation, or be taken up as a fanatic. Upon this I said no more, but anxiously watched the newspapers every evening as the post arrived.

In fact, though, the newspapers were not to bring Williams the sorry confirmation of his dream. On the evening of 13th May his son brought him the news: apparently the account had been written after the papers had been printed, and independently sent down from London to Truro. One tends to forget how slow communications could be in those days: Perceval had been killed on the 11th.

Williams might not have thought *too* much about his dream had it not been that

> Some business soon after called me to London, and in one of the print-shops I saw a drawing for sale, representing the place and the circumstances which attended Mr Perceval's death. I purchased it, and upon careful examination, I found it to coincide in all respects with the scene which had passed through my imagination in the dream. The colours of the dresses, the buttons of the assassin's coat, the white waistcoat of Mr Perceval, the spot of blood upon it, the countenance and attitudes of the parties present were exactly what I had dreamed.

The singularity of the case, when mentioned among my friends and acquaintances, naturally made it the subject of conversation in London, and, in consequence, my friend, the late Mr Rennie, was requested by some of the Commissioners of the Navy that they might be permitted to hear the circumstances from myself. Two of them accordingly met me at Mr Rennie's house, and to them I detailed at the time the particulars, then fresh in my memory, which form the subject of the above statement.

I forbear to make any comment on the above narrative, further than to declare solemnly that it is a faithful account of facts as they actually occurred.

What a mind-blastingly good example of the prophetic dream in action . . . if only I could believe it. There do seem to be occasional little inconsistencies which nag away at my mind. For example, Williams 'hardly knew at that time who formed the Administration of the Country', yet he knew that Perceval was Chancellor of the Exchequer. Is it not mildly surprising that he did not know that Perceval was also Prime Minister? Most people know who the prime minister is at any given moment; except around Budget Day, many people would be pushed to name the chancellor of the exchequer. Moreover, if a single individual should hold both offices, how many people would know of him only as the holder of the lesser one?

But there is a more serious criticism than this. Williams said that, when he bought the print in London, it conformed exactly to his dream. This has to be doubted on two counts. Firstly, it is perfectly possible that, quite unconsciously, a print of a scene rather like the one he had dreamt would become in his mind over the succeeding week or two *identical* with his dream. This is the way the human mind seems to work: it's the phenomenon of 'reading back' again. This artificial identity between the two scenes could only have been reinforced in Williams's mind in the twenty years or so between his account and the written version thereof.

Secondly, and more importantly, the print itself would not have been – almost *could* not have been – an accurate representation of Perceval's death. Prints of 'great events' from that period are notoriously more products of the artists' imagination than representations of reality. If one believes Williams – and I find myself increasingly hard pressed to do so – then the best that one can say is that he foresaw looking at the print, rather than watching the assassination itself.

This may be a point in Williams's favour. Soon (see page 356) we'll look at Dunne's experience of the Mont Pelée disaster.

As we saw in Chapter Four, a good number of the paranormal dreams about imminent death concern members of the dreamer's family. I've chosen, for various reasons, to interpret such dreams in terms of telepathy or clairvoyance: most involve little by way of 'time-displacement' and, in many of the cases that do, the displacement is in the opposite direction to precognition: that is, the death happens before the dream, but the dream happens before the dreamer finds out about the death. In various other cases, however, as we shall see in due course, some degree of precognition seems to have been involved (unless, that is, people were lying, etc.).

Two certainly precognitive dreamers – assuming no dishonesty – had recurring precognitive dreams. Neither of these cases makes happy reading.

In his *The Mystery of Dreams* (1950) William Stevens reports on a correspondent whose recurring precognitive dream was that one of her teeth came out. (Teeth dropping out is a familiar nightmare – see page 141). Whenever the dream occurred someone would die. A back tooth indicated an old person, a front tooth a young person.

The same correspondent had a remarkable dream in which she and all her large family set out for a drive in a big car. Every now and then the car would stop, and one member of the family would climb down and walk off sadly into a nearby graveyard. After a moment the car would move on again. According to the anonymous dreamer the years were to show that, in fact, she had been given a preview of the order in which her relatives would die: a cruel preview indeed.

I confess to some scepticism about this dream, because the writer makes no mention of the most fascinating point of all: what happened when she was the last person left in the car?

Another similar death-dream was recorded in *Phantasms of the Living* by Gurney *et al*. A certain Mrs Burton was apparently the sufferer of a recurring precognitive death-dream. The particular dream was of an infant in a bath, and it always came shortly before the death of one of her relatives or a family friend. The death would follow the dream within about twelve hours, in most cases, although in one instance the delay was as long as eleven days.

Should there be someone standing beside the bath, then that gave her a clue as to who it was that was going to die; otherwise she simply had to wait gloomily for the news, wondering who had shuffled off the mortal coil this time. In one instance, she dreamt that she herself was by the bath and dressed in deepest mourning: just over a day later her husband died.

C. G. Jung's apparently precognitive dreams generally concerned the deaths of those close to him. Two of note concerned the death of his mother (in January 1923). In the autumn of 1922 he dreamt that he was visited by his father – who had died long before, in 1896. Jung was delighted to see his refreshed-looking parent (shades of Kerouac – see page 88), and prepared to tell him all about things that had gone on since his death; but his father was concerned only to find out about the latest theories of marital psychology. This was of especial significance, since Jung's parents had not been happily married; but the significance did not occur to Jung until after his mother's death a few months later. Clearly Papa Jung had learnt little about how to have a happy marriage in the afterlife, and as a last desperate measure before his wife's death was consulting his psychologist son to try to find out how to go about things. Sadly Jung awoke just before giving his father the comprehensive gen.

Some while later Jung dreamt that he was in a wild, primaeval place; fear stalked. Suddenly there was a great crashing in the undergrowth, and there broke into view a huge wolfhound. The terrified dreamer knew that this beast had been sent by the Wild Huntsman (whom Jung identified with Wotan) to gather a soul. He awoke in terror – and later that morning was told of the sudden death of his mother. That his dream should incorporate Wotan suggested to him that her soul had gone to an afterlife more comprehensive, more total, than the one implied by the Christian philosophy.

He adds that, as he afterwards plied his miserable way home on the night train, he had constant fitful dreams of joyous music and merry-making; to the mourners a death is a cause for grief, but to the departed soul it is an occasion for festivity and celebration, a joyful marriage with the afterlife.

Not all of the deaths his dreams seemed to forecast were of people especially close to him. In one he saw his wife's bed as 'a deep pit with stone walls' – i.e., a grave. Someone who looked like his wife, wearing a white gown 'into which curious black symbols were woven', floated heavenwards. Jung woke, and was disturbed enough to rouse his wife to ask her the time: 3.00 A.M. In the morning they learnt that one of her cousins had died at that time.

And as a result of one such dream he experienced the true frustration well known to anyone who's dabbled in the field of precognitive dreams: the frustration born from not being *quite* able to remember the most important data. Jung was at a garden party, as were his late sister and a deceased friend – as well as a number of the living. With the sister was another woman whom Jung knew; even in his dream he was certain that this signified that she was soon to die. But when he woke all he could remember about the unfortunate woman was that she lived in Basel . . . but, however hard he thought about friends in Basel, he couldn't guess who she was.

A few weeks later he learnt that one of his patients had died in an accident: curiously, although she had been a patient of his for a long time, and indeed had the status of 'friend', she was the one person from Basel who hadn't come to mind as he attempted to remember the details of his dream. Yet, now that he knew her identity, his memory of the dream was complete.

Jung found it frustrating that only after the event could he remember the face of the woman in his dream; he still felt that the dream itself was genuinely predictive. An alternative explanation is that he 'read back' the identity of the woman into the dream – which was why he had the experience of suddenly 'remembering' it all. Looked at in this light, the prediction becomes less than exciting: all that the dream said was that a woman-friend from Basel would die. Since Jung seems to have known quite a lot of people from Basel, the chances of one of the women dying within the succeeding few weeks were reasonable.

## *Felled by the Grim Reaper*

John Wesley preached at Congleton for the last time on Tuesday, 30th March, 1790, at five o'clock in the morning. Despite the early hour, crowds assembled to hear him speak. During his sermon he related a recent dream of his. He had been walking down a Bristol street when he had seen an acquaintance. However, when the dreaming Wesley had tried to shake the man's hands he'd found that his own were missing.

Wesley took this dream to mean that his work on Earth was nearly at an end and that his 'intercourse with mortals was about to cease'. Indeed, he died on 2nd March, 1791, just eleven months later. However, we should not go overboard about the predictive success of this dream: Wesley was, after all, in his late eighties and very frail at the time.

But if his own powers of prediction were minimal, this did not stop him from avidly noting the predictive dreams of others, especially those that came true. In particular, he noted an example of the same type as his own just-mentioned dream – a dream which foretold the dreamer's own imminent death. On a Sunday in July 1757 he was on the way to a preaching engagement when one of his fellow-travellers told him that

> A woman of Stockwith told her sister who lived with her, 'I do not think to go to market today, for I dreamed that I was drowned in riding across one of the drains on Haxey Car.' But she was soon laughed out of it, and went. She rode over the Car with many other market-folks, and, in crossing one of the drains, where

the water was scarce a yard deep, slipped off her horse. Several looked on, but none once thought of pulling her out till she was past recovery.

This is of course a much more interesting predictive dream than Wesley's own. Wesley's unconscious must certainly have known the end of life was near; but a similar explanation cannot be used in the case of the Stockwith woman's dream. On the other hand, we must remember that the dream was at least second-hand by the time it reached Wesley: it could well have been nothing more than the 18th-century equivalent of an 'urban legend' (see page 211).

Dreams like Wesley's are not uncommon, and are probably best explained in terms of the unconscious (or right brain) dropping hints to the conscious (left brain), *via* the medium of the dream, that time's about up. A typical example of such a dream was that of the US writer and philanthropist Zöe Anderson Norris. It is of particular note because Norris wrote up the dream and published the account in her magazine, *The East Side*, just a few weeks before her death in early 1914.

Norris's dream has many similarities with Julia Tyler's dream which we discussed on page 252. She was lying on her bed looking down a long hall. Tiny at first, but growing rapidly larger as it came closer, was a black spider-like figure which eventually proved to be her long-dead mother. 'Am I to be the next?' asked Norris, thinking of all the other family members who had died.[6] Her mother shushed her, but seemed to agree. Then Norris awoke.

There is a persistent tale that Abraham Lincoln had a premonitory dream just a few days before his assassination. In the middle of April, 1865, among a small company which included his wife, Mary, and Ward Hill

Lamon, the conversation turned to dreams. In his posthumously published *Recollections of Lincoln* (1895) Lamon claims to have recorded Lincoln's own description of the famous dream *verbatim*.

> About ten days ago . . . I could not have been long in bed when I fell into a slumber, for I was weary. I soon began to dream. There seemed to be a dream-like stillness about me. Then I heard subdued sobs, as if a number of people were weeping. I thought I left my bed and wandered downstairs. There the silence was broken by the same pitiful sobbing, but the mourners were invisible. I went from room to room; no living person was in sight, but the same mournful sounds of distress met me as I passed along. It was light in all the rooms; every object was familiar to me; but where were all the people who were grieving as if their hearts would break? . . . Determined to find the cause of a state of things so mysterious and so shocking, I kept on until I arrived at the East Room [of the White House], which I entered. There I met with a sickening surprise. Before me was a catafalque, on which rested a corpse wrapped in funeral vestments. Around it were stationed soldiers who were acting as guards; and there was a throng of people, some gazing mournfully upon the corpse, whose face was covered, others weeping pitifully. 'Who is dead in the White House?' I demanded of one of the soldiers. 'The President,' was his answer; 'he was killed by an assassin!'

On waking, Lincoln opened up his Bible – presumably hoping for some reassurance – only to find that wherever he looked he found descriptions of dreams and visions. In fact, if he'd paused to think about it, he'd have realized that there are so many descriptions of dreams and visions in the Bible that it's quite hard not to trip over them when browsing through the book.

Now, it's rather hard to know how much reliance can be based on Lamon's account. There is, of course, no immediately evident reason why he should wish to lie; but his claim to have remembered word-for-word Lincoln's fairly long description (of which I've given only a part) must be considered dubious, at best. Moreover, it is not on the face of it particularly unlikely that Lincoln should dream of assassination: with the war ending, he was only too well aware that some fanatic might make a last dramatic gesture, and he several times mentioned that his life might be in danger for exactly this reason. And, interestingly enough, his own interpretation of the dream was that it was not himself but someone else who had been the victim of the dream-assassin's bullet. It seems possible that, quite unconsciously – because people remember what they want to remember – Lamon took a fairly simple dream-account and exaggerated it a little; and that Lincoln's dream, in whatever form, was not so much precognitive as simply an expression of his own quite genuine fears.

It is, then, difficult to verify the tale. In the same category fall accounts of a vision which Lincoln is said to have had in 1860, just after his election: looking in the mirror he saw two images of himself, one of them cloudy and insubstantial. The vision, so the tale goes, signified to him that he would have one full term of office, but would not survive the second.

But it is less easy to dismiss his frequently reported recurring dream of being aboard a ghostly ship heading rapidly towards a dim and distant shoreline. Curiously, this dream seemed to Lincoln to come to him always the night before important military developments, especially great victories. Its last visit was on the night of 13th/14th

April, but this night it heralded no good news for him: it was on the evening of the 14th that he was shot down.

Equally popular in dream-lore is the tale of the poet Percy Bysshe Shelley. Towards the end of his life he suffered a prolonged series of nightmares – although he insisted that these were not dreams but waking visions. (Everyone else at the time thought they were nightmares.) Mary Shelley recorded three of these, in one of which he had the terrifying experience of meeting his *Doppelgänger*.

But the two most famous of his nightmares occurred in a single night; their fame rests on widespread reports that the first of the pair was a prophetic dream of his own death. The Shelleys' friends Edward and Jane Williams, he dreamt, came staggering into his bedroom, all covered with blood, and shouting at him: 'Get up, Shelley! The sea is flooding the house and it is all coming down.' He looked out of the window and, sure enough, there was the sea, tumbling in towards the terrace.[7]

Not long after, Shelley sailed with Edward Williams and a cabin boy, Charles Vivian, from Livorno in the *Don Juan*, heading for Lerici. Soon a sudden storm blew up, and local sailors fled for port; one of the captains reported having seen the *Don Juan* struggling in heavy seas. He had come close and offered them the safety of his own craft, but someone (probably Shelley) had refused the offer. One of the sailors had then yelled that they should at least lower their sails; but as one of them – Williams, so the tale goes – moved to do so the other seized him by the arm to stop him.

As is well known, the *Don Juan* never reached Lerici. Some ten days later the three bodies were washed ashore in a disastrous condition – Shelley's body could be identified only by his trousers, his socks and, in a pocket, a friend's copy of a book of poetry by Keats.

So much for the well documented history of the affair; now let's turn to the mythology.

One writer grimly claims that the lacerations of the bodies were just like those sported by Edward and Jane Williams in Shelley's nightmare: how, I wonder, could the writer tell? Was he in some mysterious way transported back in time to view Shelley's dream? Moreover, the dream quite certainly featured Edward and Jane (unless Mary is lying for some incomprehensible reason), not Edward and Shelley himself. In sum, and rather depressingly, this case of 'precognitive' dreaming is – like so many others – not particularly mysterious once you begin to think about it. Shelley had a nightmare about the sea – a nightmare which, as you might expect, involved two good friends who were staying in his house and who were, presumably, much in his thoughts. A while later he drowned, in the company of one of the people most likely to have been travelling with him.

It's possible that his dream was precognitive, but there seems to be absolutely no reason to think so.

## *Doom and Disaster*

Today people seriously involved in the paranormal tend to believe that, in most if not all cases, predictive dreams don't operate as simply as one would like to think. An individual dream may give a hint, a scintilla of information about a coming disaster; only when the reports of enough dreamers have been put together can the whole picture be seen.

On this principle, the British psychiatrist Dr Alice Buck in 1947 set up a series of experiments to study precognitive dreaming. The research unit thus created was soon to turn into the Buck Research Unit in Psychodynamics, which did some of the most significant work in the field of precognitive (and, occasionally, postcognitive) dreaming.

A typical example of the integration of partial predictions concerns the crash of an aircraft into the Shannon at 3.40 A.M. on 4th September, 1954. Many of the passengers were trapped inside the 'plane as it slowly sank; and it was only thanks to one of the crew, who spent two and a half hellish hours swimming and crawling to nearby Shannon Airport to announce the disaster, that there were any survivors at all.

Buck herself dreamt on the nights of 2nd and 3rd September of an aircraft crash; in particular, the time 3.00 A.M. seemed somehow important. Another experimenter dreamt on the night before the crash of a small group of people fighting against adverse weather conditions. They seemed to be going through a ford when they were engulfed by water. Taken together, these dreams do seem to be pointing at the crash.

The group was involved, in 1952, in research into apparently precognitive dreams by some forthcoming large-scale catastrophe; the workers had been inspired by dream-accounts dating from before the Hiroshima massacre and seeming to predict it. In *The Clothes of God* (1956), Buck and F. Claude Palmer describe some of the dreams from 1952 at length.

*2nd/3rd October*: The dreamer was between two people each of whom had a 'big bowl' which they hoped to clash together at some distant place, thereby destroying that place. The dreamer thought the effect would be like firing protons into the atomic nucleus.

*17th/18th October*: The dreamer was with another person in a skyscraper; they could see through a hatch that the building beneath them was on fire. They pulled a handle to operate some mechanism which would insulate the floor beneath them until the fire brigade could come to the rescue. The dreamer realized with horror that the ladders might not be long enough to reach up to the floor they were on. Badly injured people were brought up from the floor beneath, and the dreamer helped care for them. A clergyman arrived, but he didn't seem to realize there was any danger. 'We said to him, "Do you hear the wind?" He stopped for a moment and listened. There was a throaty steady roar, like wind . . . We said, "It is the fire", which of course it was . . .'

*23rd/24th October*: 'I was a watchdog and I knew there was danger about.'

*29th/30th October*: The dreamer was back in the room at the top of the skyscraper. Smoke was coming in, and everybody was acting with greater urgency.

*30th/31st October*: The dreamer was on an exploration vessel in the Arctic. The mission was dangerous, but caution rather than fear was the watchword. Some of the dogs aboard went mad and were put down. Suddenly 'a frightful wind blew . . . for about 30 seconds, and so the windows were shut'. Then the dreamer was on deck, looking out over the water at a 'shadowy ship' called *Death*. (A sea-legend has it that crews see this ship before meeting their doom.) The captain ordered that the ship be rammed: it was like sailing into a thick, dark cloud. The dreamer realized they were in tremendous danger, but that nevertheless the study of the ship *Death* was vital for the furtherance of human knowledge: no one else had been here before and lived.

On 1st November, 1952, the day after the last in this series of dreams, the USA exploded the world's first hydrogen bomb, removing lonely Eniwetok Atoll from the map. It's not hard to interpret the series of dreams leading up to it as precognitive: the fire, the hot wind, the dogs going mad and being put to sleep, the quest for knowledge leading into the cloud of death, and so on.[8]

However, as always we have to be a little careful before leaping to this 'obvious conclusion'. Remember that in 1952 the Cold War was at a pretty virulent stage, and that the memory of Hiroshima and Nagasaki was still recent and clear. The dream-features which paralleled the circumstances of nuclear explosion could have come from newspaper accounts of these blasts. All in all, it would be slightly surprising if there had not been references to nuclear explosion in people's dreams at the time.

A further point in favour of this more mundane explanation is that the dreams continued *after* the Eniwetok blast. Buck and Palmer trace a further series leading up to the first Soviet test, in 1953, another apparently presaging a 1956 Soviet test, and so on. This is all very well, but the 'Occam's Razor' explanation of the whole thing is that people were dreaming nuclear-bomb-oriented dreams, on the one hand, while simultaneously but quite independently the superpowers were carrying on their lunatic policy of nuclear testing, on the other. The same sort of thing is going on today in response to the growing public awareness of the fact that politicians of both East and West are taking us ever closer to the brink of global cataclysm. To regard the whole of Buck's collection of dreams as belonging to distinct series, punctuated by real-life nuclear testing, is therefore probably to impose an artificial structure on two sequences of events whose relationship is a perfectly rationalist one.

The team were on safer ground in 1954 when they studied apparent dream-predictions of the series of disasters involving the Comet aircraft. The Comet crash of 10th January, 1954, was the third involving the aircraft to have happened in twelve months – the other two had been on 3rd March and 2nd May of the previous year. It was obvious to everyone except the authorities (who on

11th January did ground the Comets, but only temporarily) that such disasters were likely to continue: they couldn't have arisen merely by chance. Buck's group therefore determined to correlate dreams which might give warning of further disasters.

The experimenters had become convinced that precognitive dreams were most accurate and prolific if the dreamers were related to or acquainted with people who might in some way be involved in the predicted events. Buck therefore set herself up as a guinea-pig: she determined to travel on a Comet as soon as the aircraft were allowed to fly again.

Within a few weeks she was receiving reports from the other experimenters which suggested that a further Comet crash was on its way; sensibly, she decided not to travel on a Comet after all. Even after the aeroplanes had been returned to service on 19th March the dream-reports continued – and now they were becoming more precise. The experimenters felt justified in sending a warning to the Ministry of Transport and Civil Aviation giving details. The warning was ignored, which was a pity for the 26 who died in the Comet crash of 8th April, 1954.

In *The Clothes of God* Buck and Palmer give a detailed list of these dream-reports; here we must content ourselves with the barest outlines.

The night of 19th March, when the Public Inquiry had decided to let the aircraft fly again, one of the dreamers had an 'extreme nightmare from which I woke screaming'. Even in the dream he was convinced that he was being given foreknowledge of an aircraft disaster, although in the dream the scene was actually aboard a submarine. Suffering from extreme claustrophobia (which he never did in real life), he realized that his sensations must be much like those experienced by pilots who have lost control of their craft. (Whether or not this is the case, this is what he 'realized' in the dream.)[9]

On the night of 3rd/4th April, another researcher had three dreams, all of which seemed relevant. In the first he saw a Comet making a crash-landing at London Airport. The passengers fled from the craft, but someone reassured them and they went back. In the second he was being driven in a van near London Airport (the research unit had determined that the van appeared as a symbol in many pre-disaster dreams, the dream-pun presumably being with 'van' as in 'vanguard'). In the third he had the simple premonition that something probably to do with aircraft would be on the 8 o'clock news – which, of course, a few days later there was.

After the crash on the 8th the Comets were immediately grounded. However, near the end of 1955 the Comet III, in which craft it was thought all the problems had been ironed out, went on a round-the-world trip. Buck and her group produced beforehand a large number of examples of dreams predicting that the craft would suffer damage from fire but that the crew would be safe. Some of this material was published at the time; some of it was not, although documentation exists to show that there was no hurried forging after the event. Which event was the abortion of the last leg of the journey owing to overheating in one of the engines.

This means that the dreams predicting fire-risk were pretty close to the mark. They were thus more impressive as evidence of precognition than most of the earlier Comet ones: almost anyone could have told you that the Comet was a dud aircraft, and it's not surprising that people undertaking research concerning disasters involving the 'planes should dream about them.

More significantly, however, some of the dreams which appeared to foretell the disasters frequently contained images of rotting, fragile metal, house-fabric or other normally solid materials. We now know that the disasters arose as a result of vibration-induced metal fatigue. So, while we must register a 'don't know' in the case of the apparent precognition of the disasters themselves, these rather precise indications of their *cause* are less easily dismissed. To be sure, the unconscious (right brain) is a clever individual, and might have worked the problem out, but this hypothesis isn't terribly convincing. I suppose you could say that fire is a reasonably frequent cause of aircraft disasters, and so it's hardly surprising that it featured in some of the Comet III dreams, but *metal fatigue*?

Perhaps slightly more ambitious than the Buck Research Unit in Psychodynamics was the Premonitions Bureau started in 1966/7 by Dr J. C. Barker and the science journalist Peter Fairley.[10] It was born as a result of Barker's sorrow and horror over the 1966 Aberfan disaster, in which an avalanche of slurry descended upon the Welsh village of Aberfan, killing 144 people, most of whom were children. Barker, who assisted in the rescue operation, contacted Fairley and asked him to invite readers of the London *Evening Standard*, of which Fairley was then Science Editor, to send in reports of any dreams which they had had which seemed to predict the catastrophe.

Of course, this was a very unscientific way of going about things. If you ask *afterwards* if people have predicted a disaster you're bound to get plenty of people who, honest, guv, dreamt about every last detail of it – well, every last detail that's been in the papers, anyway. However, of the 76 reports received, in 22 cases there were supplied also statements from other people who said that the dreamers had told them about the dream before the disaster had happened.

The saddest dream-case of all was probably that of Eryl Mai Jones, aged 10, a pupil at the Pantglas Junior School in Aberfan. A night or two before the disaster she had a dream which, in the morning, she recounted to her mother. She had dreamt that she was going to school, but found there was no school there: 'Something black had come down all over it.' But, she added, she had not been afraid because she was with two of her schoolfriends.

The three children are, today, buried next to each other.

All in all, the setting up of the Premonitions Bureau, if initially only for a trial period of a year, seemed a good idea. At the end of the first year nearly 500 predictions had come in, of which 18 seemed to be genuinely precognitive. In succeeding years the success rate dropped to virtually zero, although the number of reports received more than doubled. It is curious that the work of the bureau seems somehow to have been lost sight of, somewhere along the way. And something of a pity, too: a genuine organization of this kind, properly funded, might make a significant contribution to our knowledge. Conceivably, too, it might provide us with a way of saving vast numbers of lives. It is sad that the only comparable organization I know is a US one whose concern is making predictions of the fluctuating prices of stocks and shares: profits seem to matter more than people.

No single disaster seems to have been predicted more fervently or frequently than the sinking of the *Titanic*. Blanche Marshall, the mother of the prolific dreamer Joan Grant, was one of hundreds who foresaw the event. In fact, one begins to wonder if there was anyone in the UK or US who wasn't pretty certain, as the ship set sail on its maiden voyage, that catastrophe was just around the corner. Many of these precognitive glimpses came in dream form – so many that even a list would fill several pages of this book. However, one must remember that the vast majority of these reports are uncorroborated, and so such a listing exercise would be pretty futile.

The most famous example concerns a London businessman called J. Cannon Middleton. He had actually booked himself a passage on the ship's maiden voyage, but one night he had a dream in which he saw the *Titanic* 'floating on the sea, keel upwards and her passengers and crew swimming around her'. Not unnaturally, he cancelled the trip – especially when he had the dream again the following night. He told members of the family and friends why he had changed his mind *before* the voyage started, so there is no need to doubt the genuineness of his dream.

In his *The Mystery of Dreams* (1950) William Stevens reports Middleton's dream as well as an account from an anonymous US dreamer. She woke up her husband one night to tell him that she had just seen her mother adrift in heavy seas in a crowded lifeboat. The husband was not impressed: he knew that his mother-in-law was safe at home in England. But he knew wrong. As a special surprise, she'd decided to pop across the Atlantic to visit them – as the couple discovered to their horror when the *Titanic*'s passenger list was published in the newspapers the following morning. (What Stevens does not tell us is if the news of the disaster had already been broken by the time the woman had the dream. If it had, the whole story becomes very much less exciting.)

The tale had a happy ending. The mother was rescued. Later she told her daughter that she remembered quite distinctly being in the crowded lifeboat, pitching and tossing on the waves in the darkness, and thinking constantly about the daughter whom, she believed, she'd never see again. But it's not surprising that she was thinking along these lines, of course. If I were in a similar situation, *my* daughter would feature pretty prominently in my thoughts.

In his *A Sort of Life* (1971) Graham Greene mentions having had various apparently precognitive dreams. In one, as a child of 5, he dreamt of a great shipwreck; it was the night before the *Titanic* went down. And years later, in adolescence, when he was under psychoanalysis and keeping a dream-diary, he found that a dream of his about a vessel going down in the Irish Sea was paralleled that very night by the sinking of a ship there. In 1944 he 'dreamed of a V1 missile some weeks before the first attack'.

Before the war, though, he had what is for me by far the most convincing of his seemingly precognitive dreams. Heinemann had already published a few of his novels, and he was thinking about what was to follow. He was encouraged by a dream in which he received an advance copy of a new novel. It was badly bound, printed on rotten paper, and priced at only ninepence; even so, as soon as he opened the book he was impressed by the writing. A book like this, he thought sadly, will be neither reviewed nor bought . . .

Anyone with a wartime or immediately postwar book on their shelves will recognize the type of book he saw in his dream![11]

As we have seen, most disasters have been accompanied by countless reports of apparently precognitive dreams. As we'll see in a moment, in recent decades assassinations have had their share of the predictive attention. But in his *Over the Long High Wall* (1972) J. B. Priestley makes an interesting point. Noting Countess Tuchkov's dream (see page 294), he points out that events like the Battle of Borodino, or even the sinking of the *Titanic*, are small fry indeed when compared with the two world wars. But where are all the precognitive dreams about the wars? Apparently, nowhere to be found. He suggests that this is because mega-disasters are simply too big and too terrible for the dreaming mind to have anything to do with them: it 'so to speak, recoiled from them'.

I find this argument somewhat unconvincing. It's rather like the argument put forward a while back by one of the UFOlogists: the proof that aliens are visiting us is that there is absolutely no evidence that they're doing so; there would be plenty of evidence were it not for the fact that the aliens suppress it all so well; but in order to do the suppressing they have to be here in the first place. QED.

It seems much more likely to me that dream-minds don't experience world wars because, while they can *imagine* personal catastrophes, like being in a shipwreck, they can't imagine international – and hence depersonalized – disasters, such as wars. They can imagine being *in* a war, of course; but then quite a lot of people have such dreams anyway.

An alternative explanation for the lack of dream-reports might be that, in the early stages of a major war, people have more pressing things to think about than seemingly precognitive dreams.

## *The Professionals*

Once Stan Gooch dreamt that he was trying to chat with Isaac Asimov, whom he has in real life never met, at a party – or at what he knew was a party, even though the surroundings were vague. The two writers found that they really had nothing to say to each other. Gooch noted that Asimov was the taller of the two (he does not know if this is true or not). Floating beside them was 'an old-fashioned hot-water radiator, on item to which I have since been unable to attach any significance'.

A few days later, Gooch discovered to his mild surprise that he'd had a letter published in *New Scientist* – and in the adjacent column was a rather longer letter from Isaac Asimov. The two letters were on totally different subjects, just as the two men had, in the dream, found nothing to talk about. The taller dream-Asimov matched the longer letter. They had been at a party, but the surroundings had been vague: could the other party-goers have symbolized the other letter-writers on the page, of whom Gooch's mind knew little or nothing?

The hot-water radiator bothers me, though. Could it be, perhaps, that one of the other *New Scientist* letter-writers read Gooch's letter next to his own and began to get really steamed up . . .

Gooch falls into that loose category of dreamers whom I describe as professionals. In other words, although he's made his name and fortune as a writer and philosopher, his dreams have in a way contributed to his eminence. We've encountered several such people already; it's only to be expected that 'professional dreamers' will have at least a few precognitive dreams up their sleeves.

Several of them have had dreams about the assassination of one or both Kennedy brothers: this seems almost to be the American Express card of 'professional dreamer-land'. Another vital accoutrement seems to be the ability to get dream-predictions really quite spectacularly wrong. The two characteristics are combined in the person of Jeane Dixon.

Jeane Dixon is generally regarded as the USA's leading prophetess – she predicted, we're told, the assassinations of John and Robert Kennedy and Martin Luther King, the 1967 Apollo fire in which three astronauts died, and so on and so on. She uses – or is used by – various techniques in order to read the future: divine revelation; what she calls 'the psychic way', where the word 'way' is presumably used in its meaning of *tao*; prayer/meditation; telepathy, sometimes using a crystal ball as focus (crystal-omancy); and dreams.

The dream-state in which 'God often reveals things' to her is that on the borderline between sleeping and waking. She believes that her premonitions are not so much in the form of the dreams themselves; more that it is in the dream-state that we have direct access to the unconscious. Moreover, our unconscious is governed by the way in which our conscious is working at the time – that is to say, if you think sin during the day then you'll dream sin at night, and *vice versa*. This is a curiously Victorian idea, and in direct contrast to the findings of most other people. Remember St Hilary of Poitiers and St Margaret of Cortona (see page 152): in both cases, it would seem that an excess of daytime virtue was creating 'sinful' dreams.

Some of Dixon's predictive dreams concern national figures, some concern friends. In an example of the latter, a friend asked if her (the friend's) husband, about to undergo major surgery, would live or die. Dixon dreamt that she saw the couple walking along happily, the wife holding a stub of candle. The wife turned smiling towards the husband, and then the candle went out. Dixon told the woman that her husband would survive until the end of her (the friend's) days. What she failed to think about was that the candle was only a stub: the friend's husband recovered, but the friend herself died soon after.

Perhaps her most famous dream concerns the Kennedy family. She saw Jospeh Kennedy (the father) being embraced sympathetically by the biblical patriarch Job – who, if you recall, lost all his sons because the Lord willed it. From that point on, she knew that Joseph Kennedy would suffer the same fate. In fact, he died in 1969; and Edward Kennedy is still going strong in 1984.

The proof of the pudding, when it comes to prophecy, is in the eating of it some while later. I consulted Dixon's *My Life and Prophecies* (1969) to see if there were any prophecies relating to the years 1969–83. Sure enough they were. Both Bishop James Pike (d. 1969) and Lyndon Johnson (d. 1973) were promised long and successful futures – the former, in particular, can barely have survived the book's publication. (In the UK edition a substitute prediction was hastily inserted in the place of this one.) Castro should have been assassinated or at least ousted by now, having served the purposes of his communist (i.e., Soviet) masters and his communist (i.e., Cuban) followers; isn't Fidel a communist? Nixon is a great and good man without a whiff of corruption surrounding him. Most exciting of all, we should by now have made a breakthrough in the field of space propulsion – 'using magnetic and cosmic forces' – allowing us to travel with ease to distant planets.

In an older book on Dixon, Ruth Montgomery's *A Gift of Prophecy* (1965), we find further examples. The Russians should have been the first to land a man on the Moon. Some time around the middle of 1965 the Soviet leader should have become a man whose name began with 'S' (one could say, to be fair, that the Russian Б, transliterated 'B', does look rather like an 'S'). The Berlin Wall should have been demolished in late 1964. By 1978 the two-party system should have disappeared from US politics. By about now the 'principles of Barry Goldwater' should have been 'vindicated' and 'great honors . . . showered upon him'. And finally Sargent Shriver (remember him?) should have done great things for the USA just so long as he took care not to be assassinated.

Not very impressive. It wouldn't be so bad if we could find in the two books some clear-cut examples of prophecies having come true since publication. All that an apologist can do is find the odd one that sort of came out a bit like she said it might – or one which looks as if it might yet come true.

But even here we have to be chary. In early 1976 she said that Prince Charles would marry (he was already 27); his bride would be British (true, but not startling); he would not enjoy kingship although he would in fact be an excellent king; his brother Andrew would fulfil 'the roles assigned to him in government' so well that he would 'win the respect of those who do not favour the monarchy'; Charles might even abdicate in Andrew's favour around 1990. Since Charles has yet to become king (1984), this implies that his reign will not be a long one. Moreover, it seems likely that Andrew will need more than a handful of years to live down, in the popular mind, the details so lovingly presented in the gutter press of his perfectly orthodox sex life. Still, startling events in the next year or two could banish my doubts.

Dixon predicted at the same time that the Shah of Iran would be ousted in 1977, but then most people expected this; anyway, he clung on until 1979. Moreover, the Shah would after a period of seclusion 'stride' back into the limelight of world attention. He's very secluded at the moment; if he does start any striding then, sure as eggs, he really will be the focus of world attention.

Dixon's prediction of John Kennedy's assassination is widely recorded. After all, in a 1956 *Parade* interview she said:

> I remember standing in front of the statue of the Virgin Mary when suddenly the White House appeared before me in dazzling brightness. Coming out of a haze, the

numerals 1-9-6-0 formed above the roof. An ominous black cloud appeared, covering the numbers, and dripped slowly into the White House . . . I looked down and saw a young man, tall and blue-eyed, crowned with a shock of thick brown hair, quietly standing in front of the main door. I was still staring at him when a voice came out of nowhere, telling me softly that this young man, a Democrat, to be elected as President in 1960, would be assassinated while in office.

Alan Vaughan thought it would be fun to track down the relevant issue of *Parade*, and found to his surprise that this wasn't what the article said at all: somewhere along the road, someone had done a little 'improving'. (This must have been embarrassing for Dixon, since it seems unlikely that she was the culprit. She probably couldn't remember what the article said, and accepted quite happily the version of it put in front of her.)

Dixon makes much of the fact that her predictions arise purely because she is in direct contact with God. This may be true; if so, God is a rich, white, middle-class American. In one vision she saw Blacks on the rooftops of governmental buildings, symbolizing, among other things, that Blacks were being put in positions of power 'long before they were ready for them'. Martin Luther King was, of course, a communist tool – one gets the impression that he couldn't really have been a brilliant man because he was Black. In this context, she describes a luxurious lunch atop one of Washington's hotels not long before a planned civil-rights march on the city. Guzzling the grub, one of the people at the table recalled the good old days when he'd been a congressman in the city, adding: '. . . my love for the city and our way of life was so great that I just couldn't agree with the idea of thousands of people using it for another protest march

. . .' And Dixon cites this approvingly, rather than telling us that she threw her steak *au poivre* at him. The marchers believed, perhaps, that there were more important standards of living to preserve than the freedom to dine in expensive restaurants. I'm surprised God didn't mention this to Dixon.

Let's turn to Edgar Cayce, another of America's great dreaming prophets: we're bound to have better luck with predictions there. Of course, one could say that Cayce's diagnoses and prescriptions (see pages 266–9) were in a way precognitive, in that he claimed to describe in some detail how his patients would be cured were his instructions to be carried out. Unfortunately, though, it's rather hard to assess the accuracy of his more general predictions. Not only have his followers tended – quite naturally – to stress predictions that have apparently been fulfilled, but many of his predictions are so vague in terms of timing that they're virtually meaningless.

This is not the case with all of them, if the popular accounts of his life are to be believed. For example, a stockbroker in spring 1929 was having a series of apparently precognitive dreams about a forthcoming market crash. He consulted the sleeping Cayce and was told to get his money out of the stock market, because it was indeed going to crash soon. In October, of course, it did.

How did Cayce arrive at this solution? He had been interpreting the stockbroker's dreams for him. In one, for example, he dreamt that he was selling every last one of his stocks, that his wife was wearing red and that she was being followed by a bull. Clearly this meant that he should sell the stocks; the red dress was a danger signal and the bull was the bull market. This is comparatively forthright imagery in precognitive-dream terms.

But was the paranormal involved? Although he was a young man, he'd already made a fortune on the stock market (thanks to Cayce's advice, some insist). It is perfectly possible that he had an unconscious hunch that a crash was due, and that this hunch was reflected in his dreams. Although we cannot be sure, Occam's Razor must suggest to us that this is what was happening.

On another occasion, in August 1926, Cayce predicted that between 15th and 20th October that year the weather would be exceptionally stormy and that there would be earthquakes in California and Japan. One of the resulting tsunamis would affect southern Japan. In fact, October *was* a very stormy month, and hurricanes affected the Kurile Islands (which stretch in an arc from the Kamchatka Peninsula to Japan's northerly island, Hokkaido) on the 14th and 15th. Moreover, Japan suffered earthquakes on the 19th and 20th, and California was struck by three temblors on the 22nd. On the face of it, this might seem to be very impressive . . . but the prediction isn't really that smack-on. Moreover, Japan and California are two parts of the world which suffer frequent earthquakes – few of them serious, fortunately – and it would be rather surprising if, at any moment, the weather wasn't pretty stormy somewhere in the world. So the best we can give Cayce on this one is a grudging grunt of 'not proven'.

In 1931, when the Depression was at its height, he predicted that the tide would turn in spring 1933. True enough, in March 1933 Roosevelt took office and initiated the New Deal – and the tide *did* turn. But once again the prediction is not quite as startling as it might seem. In 1931 the incumbent president was Hoover – whom I have described elsewhere as 'one of the most inept men ever to have held the office'. It was patently obvious that he was incapable of handling the problems of the Depression, and hence very probable that there would be a change of administration in spring 1933, one of the first tasks of the new administration being to tackle the main problem. Still, to be fair to Cayce, it was not predictable by normal means that the new incumbent would make such a dramatic success, so let's be charitable and award Cayce a hit.

In other cases where he made fairly specific predictions he was not so successful. In 1943 he said that by 1968 China would be a democratic, God-fearing nation, this transition being most rapid towards the end of this period. The only dramatic event in China's history in the years leading up to 1968 seems to have been the Cultural Revolution of 1966, and that hardly seems to fit the bill. Cayce's similar predictions about the Soviet Union have no timescale attached to them.

Again, in 1932 Cayce was asked how the stone blocks of the Great Pyramid had been transported. 'By the use of those forces in nature as make for iron to swim. Stone floats in the air in the same manner. This will be discovered in '58.' In Jess Stearn's *Edgar Cayce: The Sleeping Prophet*[12] (1967) a 'crack geologist' gleefully reports that in 1958 Professor Joseph Weber had recorded work done on the detection and generation of gravitational waves. Antigravity, using which one could slide stone blocks around with ease, must be just around the corner! Unfortunately, gravity just doesn't work that way. Nevertheless, Stearn quotes this – together with work done on the use of magnetic fields as manipulatory tools – as evidence strongly favouring the accuracy of Cayce's prediction.[13]

Cayce was rather more successful about another roughly contemporaneous scientific advance. He predicted that by 1959 would come the invention – or, rather, 'rediscovery' – of the death-ray used by the Atlanteans. I'm quite impressed that the laser was, in fact, invented in 1960; its predecessor, the maser, was invented in 1954. In fact, the calculations which led to the construction of the first laser were done in 1958, and so it would be quite legitimate to say that this was the true year of the invention.

Spot on . . . except that the laser isn't a very useful death-ray. Granted, the US military instantly seized upon the device as such (much more important to have a death-ray than, say, a surgical tool of exceptional usefulness, you see), and granted that today it has certain military applications. The only problem is that, as David Langford has pointed out in *War in 2080* (1979), by the time you'd built a laser powerful enough to be an effective large-scale death-ray, it would be so big that you'd be better off simply dropping it on the enemy.

Cayce predicted that the period between 1958 and 1998 would be fairly eventful – partly as a result of the Earth beginning to 'topple over' as early as 1936, although the effects would not be manifest until the 1958–98 period. 1936 would see, too, the disintegration of many power blocs, or at least the start of it – and this was true enough in the event. (To claim, as Stearn does, that this was a spot-on prediction of the outbreak of World War Two is, I think, stretching things a little.) At the end of the period, in the year 2000, the gradual process would end as the Earth's poles abruptly flipped.[14]

So what are all these exciting events due to happen in 1958–98? Geological and Man-inspired upheavals are going to lead to the destruction of, *inter alia*, New York, Los Angeles and San Francisco. Parts of Japan are going to slide gracelessly into the sea. Areas of Atlantis should have surfaced from the sea in 1968–9 in the Caribbean; Atlantis should have started emerging elsewhere, too, but so gradually that it'll be a while before we notice. And the period will be marked by lots of wars.

Well, there have been lots of wars: let's hope that the predicted destruction of New York doesn't imply that the last big one is on its way. Los Angeles and San Francisco may well be destroyed before the end of the century, thanks to the San Andreas Fault. Japan, like that fault, lies on the 'Ring of Fire', and so it is not unlikely that it will suffer a major earthquake or volcanic disaster.

As for Atlantis rising, there were volcanic eruptions in the Azores in 1957 and 1964 that created temporary volcanic islands, and several more permanent ones have formed off Iceland. Both the Azores and Iceland straddle the Mid-Atlantic Ridge, so such events are not very surprising. More convincingly, in 1960 Agadir, Morocco, was devastated by earthquakes and the succeeding tsunami. Parts of the nearby seafloor were raised by as much as 3000m. There were other, smaller quakes and seafloor-level changes at around the same time in the Mediterranean (which, to be fair, Cayce had predicted – although without a definite date). All of these events took place, of course, a long way from the Caribbean.

As J. H. Brennan has put it, Cayce's

> modern disciples are occasionally almost touching in their anxiety to make subsequent events fit in with his wilder prophecies, but the simple fact of the matter is that Cayce was no better than the average prophet of cataclysm – and the average is pretty poor.

Cayce did predictive 'readings' for himself, of course, but also he had more orthodox precognitive dreams.

In May 1937, for example, he was having difficulty finding $1375 for his next mortgage payment. He dreamt that he was at a concert and, on leaving, that Edward VIII (by now Duke of Windsor) and Mrs Wallace Simpson preceded him. Jesus appeared, and the four of them went to a restaurant. The young couple had disappeared by the time the bill – for $13.75 – appeared. Cayce found to his embarrassment that he had only $0.03 with him; but

Jesus told him not to worry, that he'd have enough money on the day Edward married Mrs Simpson. Sure enough, on 3rd June there was delivered to him a cheque for $1375, sent by a woman whom he had helped in a 'reading'. If all of this happened exactly as reported, then this is quite a startling case of precognition.

Close to the end of his life he dreamt that he had retired and was on a train to Florida, where he was going to live out his retirement. In fact, he retired to a nursing home near Roanoke, in Virginia.

His retirement lasted only a few months. As long before as 1926 he had had a dream predicting his own demise: he was immersed in very hot water and was being scalded to death. He interpreted this to mean that his body would be immersed in water to relieve its pains, and that he would die like this. In fact, he died of a pulmonary oedema; since an oedema is the accumulation of excess watery fluid, one could just about say that the prediction was on the right track.

But the story of Edgar Cayce is not over: he's going to be incarnated again in the 22nd century in Nebraska – and a much changed Nebraska at that, according to his dream: North America west of Nebraska will be submerged beneath the ocean by then. As a boy, he will announce that he is the reincarnation of Edgar Cayce, and he will be taken around the new-look USA in a cigar-shaped aircraft. He will visit the wreckage of New York, where reconstruction will be under way; he will travel over the submerged areas of Alabama. He will see houses made of glass.

It sounds as though the science-fiction writers of the 1930s and '40s were exactly right about the way the future's going to be . . .

You may have detected that our 'professional' oneiromantics have not, so far, produced a very impressive record. Moreover, that there has been a certain amount of 'improving' of predictions so that they fit subsequent events, or fudging of subsequent events so that they more-or-less match the original predictions. It's rather refreshing, then, to turn to a 'professional' who's much happier to admit his failures; in so doing, of course, he makes his successes all the more impressive.

Alan Vaughan is one of the most respected of modern psychics. An American, he has worked in both the USA and the UK. His claimed precognitory glimpses come to him in various ways, of which the most important are probably during meditation and through dreams.

In his entertaining *Patterns of Prophecy* (1973) – entertaining precisely because he is courageous enough to give examples of failures as well as successes – he tells of several dreams he's had. At one point, indeed, he remarks:

> The web of time through which dreams and events seem to be interrelated in underlying patterns makes me suspect that, in some ways, life is a dream. By that I mean that the elements of real-life situations also can be analyzed and broken down into symbols in the same way as dreams and that they can have the same emotional significance (as well as paranormal significance).

Two dreams which he had on the night of 24th/25th May, 1968, seemed to him to predict the assassination of Robert Kennedy. In the first of these he was a Red Indian killing someone by firing a single rifle shot at them through a grating. In the second dream Vaughan *was* Kennedy, walking through a hallway. It was night. From an overhead grating fell dirt.

Vaughan draws parallels between these dreams and the actual assassination of Kennedy on 5th June, 1968. Some of these parallels are a little strained: in his dream the assassin was in hiding, and in fact Sirhan Sirhan did wait in hiding – but you'd hardly expect a would-be assassin to jump up and down waving a revolver in the air beforehand. Similarly, to make much of the fact that in the dream there was dirt falling in the central hall while in reality the 'dirty deed' was perpetrated in a hallway seems to be stretching significances a little. Other parallels are more striking, though: in the dream there was a group of young people in the first room off the hallway, and this was the case in reality; and so forth.

But there is one curious thing. In the dream, the Indian fired only the one shot, but in reality Sirhan Sirhan fired several. This could of course be no more than a minor discrepancy, were it not for one bizarre fact which emerged in the coroner's report. The bullet which actually killed Kennedy seems to have been fired within three inches of the back of his head. As anyone who's seen newsreel film of the incident will testify, Sirhan never got closer than a few feet of Kennedy, and that was *in front of him*. Was it possible, asks Vaughan, that not one but two potential assassins were lying in wait? The other, of course, could indeed have been hiding behind an overhead grating (if there was one there), and taken the opportunity of Sirhan's demonstrative attack to fire one single, but effective, shot. Well, it's fun to speculate.

Not all of his dreams mirror important events. He tells of a 1970 dream of discovering a package which, according to the label, contained the arm of an Egyptian mummy. But there was a little window in the package, and from it emerged a creature with the body of a goose and the head and neck of a serpent – a flying serpent. Could this be the Aztecs' Quetzalcoatl?

A little later, in real life, he was introduced to an anthropologist who was working in South America. On the wall was a wooden ornament shaped like the head and neck of a goose; later that evening, Vaughan sat in a bar next to a girl who was playing with a metre-long snake. Hmmm. But a week or so after that Vaughan met the anthropologist again; this time he was asked to take some mummy wrappings and try to get psychometric readings from them. (Psychometry is the claimed ability to deduce information about the past of inanimate objects.) He felt that the mummy had been near a temple in which there was the statue of a half-beast/half-man figure, 'like the Egyptian Sphinx'. In fact, this proved to be exactly the case.

Now all of this seems fairly trivial. But in the dream we find a curious mixture of symbols of the Egyptian and Aztec civilizations. In 1970, the notion that there might have been some communication between the two continents was not very popular (although it was around this time that Thor Heyerdahl and friends were crossing the Atlantic in *Ra*), but since then it has gained a little more favour – although, to be fair, it's still not very popular. So the important predictive element of the dream might have been Vaughan's involvement with a piece of evidence favouring the cultural-contact hypothesis.

Alternatively, the precognitive aspects may indeed have been trivial. We've noticed already that the most convincing precognitive dreams of 'amateurs' seem to concern trivia rather than Earth-shaking events, and I'm afraid this seems to be the case, too, among the 'professionals'. Russell Targ is actually involved in a company which specializes in making psychic predictions of stock-market fluctuations. In *Mind-Reach* (1977), by himself and Harold Puthoff, he tells us about two of his own precognitive dreams, which took place in rapid succession and which both seem to have come true.

In spring 1975 he and Puthoff went to Tarrytown,

New York State, for a now-celebrated conference whose subject was the activities of metal-benders such as Uri Geller. The night before going to Tarrytown, Targ dreamt that he was at the conference and that the speaker in action was actually *singing* his speech; he was, moreover, wearing a 'tuxedo, ruffled shirt, and a red carnation in his buttonhole'. The next day, at the conference, sure enough there was a man dressed like this, looking a little puzzled. Targ went up to him and asked if he was going to sing that night. The man replied that, yes, he *was* going to sing, but not until later – he was a singer and bandleader, and had accidentally strayed into the wrong conference hall.

And that night Targ dreamt a young female friend of theirs was being given a ring – not a finger-ring but one of the type you get in loose-leaf binders. He and Puthoff concluded that perhaps his dream was being symbolic, that an engagement or similar ring was what was meant. However, when they had a chance to question the woman herself, she informed them that she had indeed been given a large binder-type ring; it had been presented to her, with exaggerated ceremony, by her room-mate, because she was always losing her keys.

Both dreams are oddly convincing; both are concerned with absolute trivia. Two questions arise. If our precognitive glimpses are always only going to be trivial events, then what is the point of precognition at all? Secondly, if precognition exists, then why does it seem that it *can't* be used to foresee important things?

Sometimes the dreams, although they concern trivial matters, are nevertheless slightly staggering in themselves. Joan Grant, whom we've already met at some length in Chapter Four (see pages 269–75), has been familiar with ghosts since a very early age; similarly, her dreams have been important to her since infancy. A combination of these two characteristics came when, as a young woman, she went with her fiancé to stay with some relatives of his in a castle in Durham.

Before they set off she dreamt that not only was the castle haunted, she was going to meet the ghost. Her fiancé told her to keep quiet about the dream.

After they had been there a couple of nights, Grant dreamt that she had spoken with the ghost. It was that of a youngish woman, clad in 18th-century garb. Although the woman had died at the age of 30, she had lived in the house only during her younger years; moreover, she was surprised to find that it was now green rather than grey, that there were gardens, and that there was no longer a spiral stairway from the corner of the gallery – a stairway which in her day had been haunted by a horror.

Joan Grant blew the gaffe, whatever her fiancé might have said: she told his cousin all about the dreams. The cousin, Norah, was not flummoxed. When her grandfather had bought the house, in the middle of the 19th century, it had been grey rather than green, and there had been no gardens. Moreover, the grandfather had had the staircase in question walled up, on the grounds that it was unsafe.

In addition, there was a story to go with the ghost Joan had dream-seen. The daughter of the man who built the house had eloped to Gretna Green, and he had banished her from his presence forever. When her husband died he would not allow her to return; even worse, when she knew that she herself was at death's door he would not forgive her enough to allow her home. Clearly her ghost had returned to the scene where she had spent so many happy youthful years . . . and Joan had done her a great service by making sure that, in future, she would always be welcome there.

The British spiritualist Jane Sherwood tells us, in *The*

*Fourfold Vision* (1965), of a number of her dreams, including two prophetic dreams which concern rather more important events than the ones we have been considering. In the first case the concern was personal, in the second both personal and international. I find the former more convincing than the latter.

She was worried about her income tax: she thought she had been overcharged. She made an appointment to go and argue the matter out. Before the appointment, she dreamt that on arrival at the offices she was met by a friendly woman in an expensive fur. The woman told her to forget about the problem and to accept the fur as a gift. At that moment the (dream) 'phone rang, and Sherwood awoke.

In real life, Sherwood found that she was going to have to break the appointment, and so 'phoned up the relevant officer. To her surprise, she was answered not by a man but by a friendly woman, who told her not to worry, that she had indeed been overcharged, and that a cheque for the difference would be in the post shortly. (I wish this woman could be transferred to my area.) At that moment, the 'phone went in the tax office; the woman apologized for having to go and answer it, and rang off.

As Sherwood points out, the important elements of the dream are identical with those which subsequently took place in real life, with the exception of her being given a real cheque rather than a dream-fur.

Her other dream occurred in early 1914, just before the start of World War One, in which her husband was to die. Unlike many dreams, it imprinted itself indelibly on her mind – it was a 'different' dream. She was attending evensong in a cathedral on a sunny Sunday; all was placid with her except for the consciousness that her husband Andrew was not with her. Outside, people gathered in friendly groups as they are wont to do after a church service, but she stood alone, watching the late-afternoon Sun. The solar disc grew red, and then plummeted towards the horizon; as it reached the horizon there was a devastating explosion of numbing silence (if that seems a contradiction in terms, think about some of your own dreams), followed by darkness. Desperate to find Andrew, she ran in the darkness down 'dusty corridors of time', kicking aside relics of the past.

'"Dusty corridors of time",' she says, 'is not my own phrase: I came back to consciousness with those words ringing in my ears.'

The prophetic meaning of the dream is clear to her. 1914 was to see the unexpected and sudden end of Europe's long 'sunny Sunday afternoon'; the old world was to be a thing of the past, the old ways to be kicked aside; and Andrew was to be lost to her.

I think this is taking things too far. Which of us has not had the anxiety-dream of losing a loved one, be it spouse, child, or whoever? Just because I have once or twice dreamt of climbing off a train only to realize later that I've forgotten to take my sleeping daughter off the train with me (followed by the usual complications) doesn't mean anything more significant than if I'd left a briefcase or a wad of money on the dream-train. Running along in darkness, tripping over debris, is not only a reasonably frequent occurrence in dreams: it happens often enough in real life, too. (It generally happens to me at four in the morning after too long a session in the pub the night before.) The remaining imagery is exceptional only in the light of hindsight: had the dream occurred in 1920 no one, probably including Sherwood, would have thought anything of it.

Of course, you could easily argue that, while the individual components of the dream are not exceptional, their *combination* makes them so; that is, it renders the dream a genuinely prophetic one. This argument can't be proved one way or the other.

Returning to trivia, Sherwood describes a charming and apparently precognitive dream which her six-year-old daughter had. A couple of nights before her birthday the little girl dreamt that she received from her grandmother two lovely birds in a parcel as a birthday present. Sure enough, on the morning of the child's birthday a parcel arrived from Granny; inside was a partridge and a note from the grandmother saying that this was a gift not only from her (she had dressed the bird) but also from the girl's uncle (who had shot it).

Sherwood claims this as an example of the curious way in which prophetic dreams speak to us: the child dreamt of two birds rather than one because the idea of *two gifts in one* was too subtle for her naïve mind to appreciate. Myself, I'd beware of going too far: the fact that the dream seems successfully to have predicted the very unusual present of a bird for a child's birthday would seem to be quite enough, without introducing further subtleties.

However, some apparently precognitive dreams can be very subtle indeed. Jenny Randles is a British UFOlogist; her interests extend to other areas of the paranormal, including precognitive dreams, and she has done some fascinating work on the relationships between dreams and UFO 'contacts', as we have seen (pages 260–5). She has told me of a recent dream which has a quite incredible complexity.

> . . . on Tuesday, January 4 [1983] I did my first ever Radio City show, and was asked to do a series. By chance there was also an article in the *Daily Express* about me that week . . . I did not know when this was due to appear and was only mildly interested . . . The radio series was

different. This was a big breakthrough, which I felt chuffed about, and so was in a state of excitement ( . . . the possibility significant factor).

My dream that night was apparently meaningless. I had been involved in some kind of war and had joined the rebel camp. But I was feeling unsure about this, and sat in the base worrying about my desertion. Mixed up in the imagery was a newspaper cutting which was somehow (although only vaguely) relevant.

For some reason we had to abandon camp, but I would not go without my cutting, which I took. Outside, as the rebels split up, leaving me, one gave me a golden (wedding-type) ring and said, 'I'll give you a ring.' Then I left, although I was . . . impeded in my way . . . by a car that passed me and drove on. I saw its registration plate and the letters MCK . . . P (numbers forgotten). I happen to know a great deal about the car registration system . . . MCK-P is a mark issued in 'P' year by Preston. It is a *real* one (though MCK-N and MCK-R, for instance, were not issued . . .). Instantly, in my dream, I recognized MCK-P as a Preston mark (one of about fifty to sixty issued by Preston during 'P' year), and said to myself in my dream, 'That car is from Preston.'

I awoke. Obviously I was semi-amused and intrigued by how my sleeping mind had fished a seven-year-old car-registration mark out of my head from all the thousands in there. (I know nobody with a mark remotely like it, or even anyone with a Preston-registered car.)

But I had no time to ponder its meaning because the 'phone rang – indeed it probably woke me up. (I had awoken earlier and fallen back to sleep – a situation I find often precipitates this kind of dream.) The 'phone call was from Radio Red Rose, a new station . . .

based in *Preston*. They had read the *Daily Express* piece – which I then did not know had been published – and found the cutting interesting. They wanted to do an interview.

Immediately I thought of my agreement, just reached, with Radio City (whose listening audience overlaps with that of Red Rose in places) and wondered if, by agreeing to do the Red Rose interview, I would be going against my Radio City agreement. So I told Red Rose I would have to check, and would know in an hour or so. 'OK,' the person said. 'I'll give you a ring.'

All the bits of my (telepathic or precognitive?) dream clicked into place. The importance of the newspaper cutting, my fear about desertion to 'the enemy' . . . the giving of a ring – even a location in Preston: all had been identified in my dream and marvellously symbolized so that a typical (nonsensical) dream energed. But a dream packed with *real* information my mind had absolutely no way of knowing as I slept there, alone in the house.

Radio City gave me the OK to do the interview and Red Rose said they would do it over the 'phone at about 1P.M. I wondered about the MCK-P element, thinking a less obscure clue to Preston might have been possible. Did it have any deeper meaning? I found out when Red Rose called me to do the interview and I learnt who the interviewer was. It was a fairly well known sports commentator whom I had not known to be involved with Red Rose. His name is Keith *Macklin* . . . and you see how the MCK is an abbreviation of this. No other Preston mark contains any of the letters in 'Macklin'. MCK is the only one of 161 marks issued by Preston that relates to the name with all three

> letters. It took me minutes to work that out. My dream did it in an instant![15]

There is, of course, a danger in taking highly complicated apparently precognitive dreams like this one too seriously. On the one hand, we can say that such a welter of complicated detail makes the precognitive interpretation the only viable one; but one could object that this might, as it were, be spurious detail. In other words, the real-life circumstances might have caused Randles, initially interested by mild coincidences between dream and reality, to start spotting further, more obscure, coincidences which arose merely by chance, and which could be related to the dream-situation only by intellectual acrobatics of the Heath Robinson style. In such a case, most of the seeming 'coincidences' are in fact imposed by – even created by – the interpreter.

I confess that I simply don't know the answer to this. Part of me agrees with Randles that the dream really was precognitive (and, once again, it concerned trivia), while part of me is unhappy about the whole idea of precognition. And, if precognitive dreams are so obscure in their meanings that only after they've come true can the dreamer realize they were precognitive, what's the point of the faculty of precognition in the first place? All our other, more prosaic, senses are extremely useful to us. If we accept telepathy, precognition, and so on, as additional senses, then we must expect them to have some practical purpose. But, as we have seen both in this chapter and in the preceding one, all the best examples of paranormal dreaming seem to be those concerned with trivia; and many are so symbolic that they can be interpreted only in the aftermath of the real events. Evolution tells us that creatures simply do not have redundant senses.

Unless, of course, precognition and its fellows *were* important at an earlier stage in our evolution and, like the appendix, are in the process of slow disappearance. Perhaps nowadays only a few individuals have this atavistic faculty; and even among them it is but a pale replica of what it used to be like among our forefathers. I'll take this a little further when discussing possible mechanisms for precognition.

## *The Dreaming Dunne*

The British engineer John William Dunne (1875–1949) has probably done more than any other person in this century to imprint on the modern public consciousness the ideas that (a) dreams seem to display elements of precognition, and (b) the study of this phenomenon is a perfectly respectable enterprise. In his *An Experiment With Time* (1927) he presents us with a fair number of his own precognitive and clairvoyant dreams, dreams which suggested to him that our whole concept of the way that time 'works' is fundamentally flawed, and prompted him to generate a new theory of time, serial time. In detail his theory is as close to incomprehensible as makes no difference. In the most approximate terms, Dunne suggested that there was a Time 2, against which we measure the flow of Time 1, Time 1 being the dimensions which we're normally referring to when we use the word 'time'.

Just in case you're thinking that Dunne was making things obscure which are perfectly plain, bear in mind that we have nothing with which to measure the rate of flow of time. 'A clock!' you cry – but a clock doesn't help. In the famous thought-experiments of Special Relativity, the rate of flow of time is certainly different for the person travelling in the fast spaceship from that experienced by the rest of us here at home. *But* the person in the spaceship will notice the clocks ticking on in the usual way, *and* we at home will see our clocks behaving exactly as usual. A clock will tell us how much local time has passed, but it won't tell us how 'quickly' it has done so.

Let's not get too involved with this. A few of Dunne's dreams are of interest; some less so. We'll look at a couple of the ones which intrigue me, the second of which concerned a fairly major disaster.

The first, however, was concerned with an incident which was 'big news' at the time. Dunne was on the Riviera when he dreamt, one night in 1901, that he was in the Sudan, possibly at Fashoda (scene just a few years earlier, in 1898, of a confrontation between Britain and France which came within a whisker of a major war – all over an oasis which neither of them actually wanted). In his dream, Dunne saw three men approaching from the south; they were dressed like the soldiers with whom he had recently himself been trekking in South Africa during his service in the Boer War. He asked them what they were doing so far north; and they replied that they'd come all the way from the Cape. One added that he'd almost died of yellow fever.

The following morning, Dunne read for the first time of the Cape-to-Cairo expedition, which he had had no idea was in progress (although he'd heard, years before, rumours that someone was trying to mount an expedition of this type). According to the newspaper report, which was out of date by the time Dunne read it, the expedition had reached Khartoum, not far from Fashoda. Later he found a report that three of the whites in the party had died during the journey – but from enteric fever, not yellow fever.

There are many similarities between this experience and his most famous dream, which involved the Mont

Pelée disaster. In spring 1902 he was in South Africa. One night he dreamt that he was on a volcanic island, which was just about to erupt. Krakatoa firmly in his mind, he began to make efforts to have the 4000 unsuspecting inhabitants of the island shipped off it in time. He then found himself in an anxiety-dream, in which he was trying to get French official after French official on a neighbouring island to send ships to evacuate the island. He awoke while clinging to the horses of the carriage of an official who was pointing out that it was dinnertime, and could Dunne call back the next morning. Dunne was shouting: 'Listen! Four thousand people will be killed unless . . .'

It was a while before Dunne next saw a newspaper, but when he did the first headline that met his eyes was VOLCANO DISASTER IN MARTINIQUE. A subsidiary headline read: PROBABLE LOSS OF OVER 40,000 LIVES. The report told of the explosion of Mont Pelée in a Krakatoa-like eruption.

In reality, the loss of life was nothing like 40,000, but this was the figure in the report. The curious thing was that Dunne read the figure as 4000, as in his dream, and it was only some 15 years later that he noticed that he'd misread it. This seemed proof to him that, in the case of both dreams, his precognition was of *himself reading the newspaper reports*. In other words, once again the dreams were foreseeing trivial incidents; for, while the occurrences which had given rise to the reports were far from minor, Dunne had foreseen the quite trivial event of himself reading the newspaper. True, both reports had a lasting impact on him, for obvious reasons, and it's often held that it's the really affecting incidents which a dreamer is most likely to foresee; but this doesn't help us much. Presumably the reading of the reports would have had no particular impact on Dunne *had he not had the precognitive dreams!*

There is a vicious circle – a timeloop – at work here. In fact, exactly this sort of paradox is largely responsible for the dismissal by most scientists of the feasibility of there being such a phenomenon as precognition. People who are convinced that precognition exists, on the other hand, point out quite fairly that, if science cannot easily incorporate the passage of information from the future towards the past, then it is science itself which is at fault, not the phenomenon itself. I'm afraid I sympathize with both factions.

## *How Can Precognition Work?*

It's popular at the moment to ascribe precognition – and virtually every other paranormal faculty – to the operations of the right brain. In case you haven't come across the approach, let me just quickly say that the idea is centred on the apparent fact that the two halves of the brain are far from being merely mirror images of each other; and that there appear to be two 'people' living inside each of us, one in the right-hand part of the brain and the other in the left. These two people have different abilities: the 'me' who is typing these words is the left brain me, my conscious ego, if you like. The left brain is good at things like logical thought, writing, algebra, and so on. The right brain is a different beast: it is good at intuitive thought and, if we are to believe the popular theory, paranormal abilities. In approximate terms, the left brain corresponds to the conscious, the right brain to the unconscious.

Of course, to say that there are two of each of us is to oversimplify, to make it sound as if we were all dual personalities. In a way, we are; but clearly there is some interchange of ideas between the two sides of the brain. This is not to say that they operate as equal partners: although in some people the right brain is allowed more of a voice than in others, in virtually everyone the left brain is dominant, generally ignoring the right brain completely – as if unaware of its existence. Only when the right brain becomes particularly emphatic does the left brain pay much attention; should it still fail to do so, the right brain rebels and the individual suffers a mental breakdown of some kind – or, it is believed, begins to creat havoc *via* poltergeist activity or apparent demonic possession. The right brains of most of us do not seem to be the kind of people you like meeting up dark alleys.

In most of us, of course, things never come to this pass: our left brains pay just enough attention to the right for both of them not to become too unhappy. A typical example of a right brain communication is the hunch, when you suddenly have a feeling which is quite unexplained that such-and-such is the right course of action, or is just about to happen, or whatever. The hunch has been described as the everyday paranormal phenomenon, and playing things by hunch can often be startlingly successful. The other way in which our right brains communicate with our left brains ('us') is *via* the medium of the dream.

This is a very useful model of the workings of the brain: it has a lot going for it, and may actually be a pretty faithful representation of what is really going on. However, simply to lump all the paranormal faculties together and say cheerfully that they're the product of the right brain – which is the general approach of many writers in the field – is not terribly helpful. Before split-brain ideas came along, there would have been howls of indignation had anyone proposed that the paranormal was born from the unconscious, and left it at that. What must really interest us is trying to get closer to some idea of how the right brain does its paranormal stuff – if indeed it does so.

Dreams allow us one avenue of research: they allow us to watch the naked right brain. (In lucid dreaming, both left and right brains play their part.) As we have seen, there seems to be a consistent pattern in paranormal dreaming that the most reliable reports are concerned with trivia: don't worry if you dream about a nuclear holocaust, but do worry if you dream about slipping on a banana-skin. One can dismiss this 'trivia factor' as merely a curio – a frustrating curio, perhaps – or one can use it as a clue to help understand how such things as precognition are 'done'.

We have other clues. Firstly, in approaching the paranormal we should take account of 'Grant's Improbability Law'. This has it that, the more a paranormal event breaches the bounds of common sense and logic, the more likely it is that the paranormal event has actually occurred. For example, the evidence in favour of telepathy is not nearly as good as the evidence in favour of poltergeists; yet telepathy seems virtually commonsensical in comparison with the idea that our right brains can throw heavy furniture around, start fires at a distance, dial telephones at random, and all the other things which poltergeists are reputed to do. Yet poltergeist activity has been photographed; and, at the time of writing, there seems a good chance that a woman in Italy will successfully plead, in her defence against an arson and vandalism charge, that she is a centre of poltergeist activity.[16]

Since it is the 'active' paranormal which most offends common sense (as opposed to 'passive' paranormal faculties such as telepathy), we can say as a general rule that the evidence favours the right brain doing its stuff in an active fashion. It does not, as it were, merely sit around watching what's going on, or receiving telepathic signals from the aether, or whatever; it's out there physically changing its environment.

Yes, but *how* does it do this?

This ought to be the cue for me to plunge into some obscure and implausible theorizing; if I were like virtually every other writer on the subject, I would here give a definitive explanation of the way in which the right brain manipulates its environment, and then sit back waiting for the telegram from the Nobel Committee. Like all the other unorthodox theorists, I'd find it a long wait.[17] I'm afraid, therefore, I'm going to have to disappoint you by simply saying that I don't know.

But I think our clues can help us get some fumbling feeling of how it might happen. Remember the 'trivia factor', and remember the way in which Dunne foresaw *reading the accounts of* the major events, not the events themselves. He was by no means the first or last to have an apparently precognitive dream of this type. A large number of the seemingly telepathic or clairvoyant dreams which we reviewed in Chapter Four can be explained instead in terms of the dreamer foreseeing being told about, or dreaming about, the events concerned. Did Miss Busk (see page 246) have an OOBE in which she stumbled over the interred ducks, or was her unconscious telling her that she was going to hear the story about them?

A couple of more direct examples:

On the night of 27th June, 1928, one Dudley Walker dreamt about a train crash in which, near a station, a little train collided with an express. Most of the bodies thrown out of the express onto the trackside were of women and girls; but a man's mutilated body had somehow landed on top of one of the overturned coaches. Walker told people of his dream and made a brief note of it in his office diary the following day. That evening the newspaper told him that just such a crash had occurred near a station some distance away: seven women and girls had died, and the one dead man's body had been thrown on top of one of the coaches.

As with Dunne, there is a timeloop effect at work here. Walker was much affected by reading about the accident, but only because of the dream he'd already had: without the dream, the reading would have had no more effect on him emotionally than would news of any other train crash.

A similar example occurred to Laura Dale of the American Society for Psychical Research in 1954. She dreamt that she was in labour, but that it was not certain she was actually pregnant: she was told that it could be a false pregnancy but that, if it were a real one, the baby must be extremely small. The following morning she bought a newspaper and noticed at once a bizarre story about a woman who, while out in the car with her family, suddenly went into labour – even though she had had no idea she was pregnant. What makes me use the word 'bizarre' is that the baby proved, on delivery shortly afterwards, to weigh just under 11½ pounds! No doubt it was this factor which made Mrs Dale's reading of the report so significant to her that she 'remembered it in advance', as it were. Conversely, the timeloop was at work again.

How does all this tie in with the idea of an 'actively paranormal' right brain? Well, remember the nursery rhyme

> For want of a nail, the shoe was lost;
> For want of a shoe, the horse was lost;
> For want of a horse, the man was lost;

And so on, right up to the loss of the kindgom, 'And for all the want of a horse-shoe nail'. This indicates that very small actions taken or not taken in the present can have much larger-scale effects in the future. In a Ray Bradbury story a group of people travel back to the time of the dinosaurs; one of the time-travellers steps on a butterfly, but thinks nothing of it. However, on return to their own time, the travellers find that the whole of civilization has taken a completely different track from the one which it had in their own 'time-line'.

I think it possible that the right brain is capable of making tiny alterations to the present such that the future is 'changed' beyond measure. This is not an inherently silly idea – or, at least, I don't think it is. Quantum theory tells us that the observer inevitably induces some change of state in the observed, and that even a change on the most minute level can have the effect of changing the Universe – or, more correctly, of bringing into existence ('reifying') a different alternate Universe from the one which would otherwise have been reified. The right brain could tweak the current circumstances on a scale so small that standing on a butterfly would be an act of violence like a supernova in relation to a sneeze. But that tiny twitch of present reality could have far-flung consequences.

Am I then saying that Dunne's subconscious caused the Mont Pelée disaster? No. What I'm saying is that it made sure that he read the newspaper account. Still, the report wouldn't have been there had the disaster not happened. True, but (a) had the report not been there Dunne would have in due course forgotten about his dream, and (b) the report was false in an important detail, and anyway Dunne misread that detail. So all that Dunne's right brain really ensured was that Dunne read a *particular* report – and badly at that. It is not impossible that his right brain tweaked circumstances minutely such that in due course the incorrect estimate appeared.

This is a view of 'precognition' diametrically opposed to the customary ones, and initially, because of this, one's tempted to dismiss it immediately. I would love to be able to do so – but I can't. All the evidence seems to indicate that our right brains firstly conceive a future situation and then manipulate the present in such a way that that future situation comes about. Of course, we then have an inkling – perhaps through our dreams – of what the future will hold; but exactly the same is true if we pour boiling water onto a tea-bag, or throw a stone at a window. There is nothing paranormal in having foreknowledge that the result will be a cup of tea or a shower of glass; and in the same way there may be nothing paranormal in our other, right brain, glimpses of the future. The only paranormal element involved is the ability of our right brains to manipulate the present in a way, and with a subtlety, which our left brains simply do not understand.

All of this must be considered in the context of the question as to whether or not the paranormal actually exists. For myself, I find that I cannot give either a 'yes' or a 'no' in answer to this question. What I have attempted to do is briefly to give the barest outline of a possible framework within which the paranormal – especially precognition – *could* work. I have produced a possible model for the workings of a possible phenomenon, nothing more. One can, of course, develop the model far further than I propose to do here: this is a book on dreamers, not on the paranormal. My model may turn out to be the most complete nonsense, assuming we ever prove the existence of the paranormal and then discover the mechanism whereby it does its stuff. The sole point of devising such models (and, in its more developed form, this one fares quite creditably) is to show that the paranormal may not be the crazily irrational, inexplicable business that we normally think it is.

There is one further question which cries out for an answer: *why* should Dunne's right brain want to present him with an inaccurate report of a catastrophe which occurred on the other side of the world?

Ah, there you've stumped me.

# 6
## *Dreams of Times Long Gone*

> Real are the dreams of Gods, and smoothly pass
> Their pleasures in a long immortal dream.
>
> – John Keats, 'Lamia'

In Chapters Four and Five I explained at some length my rationalist antipathy – illogical though it probably is – for the paranormal. I also expounded 'Grant's Improbability Law': in the field of the paranormal, the more unlikely something is, the better is the evidence for it. However, when it comes to the idea of reincarnation, I refuse to believe in my own law. Reincarnation is silly, a nonsense, a load of hoo-hah. It just doesn't happen. To say that it does involves believing in souls, survival after death, and an astonishing mechanism whereby the free-floating soul can be deftly popped into a convenient embryo. Moreover, *why* should souls be recycled in this way? If I can't remember what I did wrong in my last life in order to deserve this one, then what's the point of it all? Education works only if you can remember yesterday's lesson.

I once read a science-fiction story in which the scenario was that the age of dying was observed to be dropping dramatically. The rate of the drop correlated with the rate of increase in world population. Our hero suddenly discovers the answer: there are only so many souls to go round. Perhaps that's it. Nature, so profligate in all other respects, economizes on souls by using them again and again. I'm not sure I believe this.

Unfortunately, however much I kick and scream about

it, 'Grant's Improbability Law' appears to hold for reincarnation – if we are to believe our dreamers. Throughout this chapter I will rudely interrupt the discussion with my suggestions as to why 'reincarnatory' dreams *really* happen. Most of my hypothetical explanations partially convince me, even where they wildly conflict with each other, but I'm constantly conscious that there's a little voice at the back of my mind saying: 'Of course, it might just be that souls really are reincarnated.' What the little voice doesn't tell me is *how* the process of reincarnation works, or *why* it should happen in the first place. And the rather louder voice at the front of my mind tells me that the whole thing is nonsense anyway.

In *The Romeo Error*, Lyall Watson comes out with the suggestion – and, to be fair to him, I should stress that it's only a suggestion – that dreams themselves point to the reality of the soul's survival after death:

> . . . in the dream stream of consciousness, we have everything necessary to allow a personality to continue to enjoy internally coherent experiences without the need for additional external stimulation taking place simultaneously. This mechanism would in itself be sufficient to explain complete survival of the intact human personality following clinical death, if it could be shown to be independent of body physiology.

Yes, yes, we can all see that here we have a mechanism for survival, and hence possibly for reincarnation. The only problem is that phrase, 'if it could be shown to be independent of body physiology'. Dreams seem certainly to be born in the brain, and experience has shown that brains have this nasty habit of not working any longer if their owners happen to be dead – indeed, a standard test of clinical death is to see if someone's brain has stopped working. It looks as if 'body physiology' puts paid to Watson's suggestion.

If, then, there's no really satisfactory explanation for the *how* and *why* of reincarnation – and I fail to see any way in which the split-brain ideas we've discussed can help us out in this instance – we're left with a rather nasty conundrum. On the other hand, perhaps we're taking things too much at face value. Perhaps what is going on is only something that *looks like* reincarnation. This seems to me to be a strong possibility; if so, then there's a good chance that our split-brain model can come to our assistance after all.

The answer, of course, lies in dreams: they are our access ports to the working of the right brain. I plan, therefore, to survey a few of the 'reincarnatory' dreamers to see if their experiences can throw some light on the discussion. In particular, I shall look at the extraordinary results of the 'Christos Experiment' conducted by the Australian novelist Gavin Glaskin, and at some of the experiences of the most outstanding 'reincarnation' of them all, Joan Grant.

## *Dream-Memories of Atlantis?*

First, however, I'd like to look at the case of Audrey Atkinson, whom we've already met in the context of precognitive dreaming. She is of especial interest in that she has never made the least effort to have her dreams published – to get into the reincarnation business, as it were. This means that her dream-accounts are 'raw'; they haven't been honed and refined for popular consumption.[1] Let us look at two of them, the first of which requires some advance explanation.

> For about twenty years now, I've always felt a special sort of affinity for my favourite, Ruritanian, folksinger

– and I assumed it was because we both shared the same birth-sign!

In 1975 I went to Ruritania for a month on holiday. I had painted a 'double' portrait of him, showing the man and the minstrel. (I'm an amateur artist.) I took this with me, intending to take it to his manager's office. Three weeks went past and I still hadn't plucked up the courage to take it. But then suddenly, one afternoon around 3.30, I felt I ought to take it straight away. My aunt warned me to wait until the next day, as I'd get caught in the rush-hour traffic downtown. But I *had* to go right then!

I got on and off street cars, and finally found [the manager's] office. Feeling an absolute fool (and old enough to know better!) I went inside. There were two typists in the outer office, and I asked if I could see the manager. They said he was on the 'phone, and would I sit for a moment? I had just seated myself when the outer door opened and in walked the folksinger. (Gulp.) He had just popped in to pick up the time of an appointment he had the following day. As he turned to go again, he smiled at me and said hello. I took a deep breath and asked him if he would accept the painting. He thanked me very much and sat down and chatted for about twenty minutes. He was a lovely chap.

Now, if I hadn't gone exactly when I did, and if the manager had not been on the 'phone, I'd have missed him. It seemed quite incredible to me that I had travelled [several] thousand miles, waited three weeks, and caught him by a couple of minutes (which is all the time he would have spent in the office).

'Kismet!' I cried to myself. Unfortunately, me being a few years older than him and not the stuff that folksingers dream about, he didn't see it that way.

Anyway, a few years after that, and just after my divorce, I met his 'double' . . . although [they had] different coloured hair and eyes, the features, the age, the sense of humour, were almost identical. I also felt an immediate rapport with him. However, this man was to cause me a great deal of pain, one way or another. After it was all over, I went to bed one night wondering why, after the trauma of the divorce, I should have to go through all this.

Now at last we can come to the dream!

It was different [from most dreams] in that *I*, myself, was a spectator to the dream, although I played a part in it, in what seemed a previous lifetime. The dream:

I was in a thick-walled house with brilliant sunshine pouring through the open doorway. I was dressed in Grecian fashion (although *I* felt it to be Atlantean), in a one-shoulder-bare robe. My hair was drawn up into circles of plaits on the back of my head, with one long ringlet hanging down my back. My hair was dark (*I* am fair). I was waiting for my husband to come home and was very happy. He appeared in the doorway and I ran to him and we embraced very lovingly. (*I*, watching, could see he was the 'double'.) He was very excited, as his brother was coming home from his many years of travel, and he couldn't wait to introduce him to me. He wore a short tunic with a leather belt, sandals with thongs tied up around the calf, and a short cape. He removed the cape.

We heard the sound of horses' hooves and he rushed outside. I could see him clasping his brother and they seemed to be very fond of each other. When they came in, arms around each other (*I*, watching, could see he was the folksinger), my husband introduced him to me. There was an immediate rapport between us.

Unfortunately, that rapport soon turned into love.

But, since we both loved my husband, we were very upset by this, and he [the brother] decided he would have to go away again. So that my husband would not suspect anything, he said he would go immediately and I would have to tell him [that] he was called away. As we were embracing, rather passionately, to say good-bye, my husband walked in.

The terrible shock and hurt on his face struck us dumb with horror and, before we could explain, he had reeled out of the door. He leapt on his brother's horse and galloped off. The brother spent days looking for him, while I was distraught with grief.

(Now, *I*, the watcher, could see what they couldn't.)

My husband had rushed off to a brothel, and, in his agony of betrayal by the two he loved best, spent days in drunken debauchery trying to ease the pain. Finally, he deliberately picked a fight with a huge guard, who cracked his head against [a] marble pillar, and killed him.

I woke up sobbing and realized that we indeed 'reap as we sow', however many lifetimes it might take. And . . . the dream seemed to have answered my question!

Now the strange thing is [that] the 'double' in this lifetime is a womaniser, almost as if he is *afraid* to love . . . Also, none of us appears to have had a very happy life this time around. Our karma, perhaps?

As I said, it was a *different* dream, in that I watched it as if it was a film, and it jumped from sequence to advance some time ahead.[2]

Now, whether this was just some sort of wish-fulfilment, or whether it actually was a re-run of a previous life – who knows? *I*, that is, the spectator, felt strongly that it was [set in] Atlantis, but it could have been any Mediterranean land, I guess.

I have quoted this dream at very considerable length because it seems fascinating for various reasons. In the first place, Atkinson is quite right when she says that 'it was a *different* dream', although not just for the reasons she thinks – its vividness and emotional impact. It was 'different' too because it made coherent sense, never violating the rules of waking logic.[3] The second point is that, of course, in many ways this was a problem-solving dream: the waking Atkinson wondered what the hell she'd done to deserve the 'double', and the dream told her that perhaps she ought to stop casting out motes from other people's eyes and start doing something about the beam in her own.

In the third place, though, we have the most interesting point: she felt pretty convinced that this previous life (although she herself is unhappy about the idea of previous lives) had taken place in Atlantis. This is something which she shares with most other 'reincarnations' – to the extent that you're actually quite special if you weren't an Atlantean at one time or another. Of course, Atkinson could have been 'recalling' her life among the Minoans: it is now generally but not universally accepted that the legends of the fall of Atlantis are based on the Krakatoa-like eruption of the Thēra (Santorini) and the consequent destruction of the Minoan (Cretan) civilization.

But I think it's far more likely that Atlantis came to her dreaming mind because it was some vague 'place' in history: the garments were reasonable for classical Greece, but the dream-mind knew that the details were probably wrong. The answer? Just think that things were happening in Atlantis: no one can catch you out on the details of Atlantean garb. In other words, I think it likely that what Atkinson experienced was not a 'reincarnatory' but a problem-solving dream – a fiction which helped her come to terms with her situation.

As we shall see, this sort of glib explanation is seriously challenged by other 'reincarnatory' dream-experiences.

But to continue with the Atlantean issue for a moment. As I've noted, the continent must have been packed with people who were going to remember, in subsequent lives, having been there. This would be all very well, if Atlantis indeed were the fount from which sprang all mankind, but the fossil evidence seems strongly to suggest that Man's cradleland was in Africa, and I've yet to come across anyone dreaming of a past life in Olduvai Gorge. I suppose the reason must be that Atlantis has more sex-appeal, as it were.

One 'Atlantean' worth glancing at here is the popular US novelist (Janet) Taylor Caldwell, who is quite convinced that she has visited the Earth in many previous incarnations. Her novel *The Romance of Atlantis* (1975; revised by Jess Stearn) was written when she was only twelve years old and, according to Stearn's preface, was sent by Caldwell's approving father to her grandfather, a books editor, who,

> promptly horrified, suggested the manuscript be destroyed immediately. He did not feel that any child could have produced so unusually mature a work, intellectually and philosophically. The only alternative that suggested itself was that she had borrowed freely elsewhere. In a way, he was right. She had borrowed from the past, not knowing herself how she was dredging up that past.

I have read *The Romance of Atlantis*, and feel that there may have been another and far less arcane reason for Grandpa's suggestion.[4]

In her postscript to the finally published version of the novel, Caldwell tells us how, after all these years, she began to dream again of Atlantis and her life there as the

Empress Salustra.[5] She expresses surprise that this should be so since, she tells us, she had more or less forgotten that Stearn was preparing the manuscript of her childhood novel for publication. The dreams were of new scenes – i.e., scenes other than those in the novel.

In the first dream she was walking to the grounds of her Atlantean palace, absentmindedly noting the various captive animals, including 'the pit in which squirmed captured reptiles of a breed unknown to this present world, and animals also unknown to us moderns'. There seems to be a mild problem here. If Caldwell was 'incarnated' in Atlantis as many as 20,000 years ago, this is still but a clock-tick in terms of evolutionary time: even if those animal species became extinct, their fossils should be abundant and hence the species far from 'unknown to us moderns'. (Moreover, their descendants would still be around, little different from the Atlantean versions.)

Ah, but perhaps the species were confined to Atlantis? Yet the whole *point* of most Atlantology is that the continent was either close to or actually contiguous with Africa on the east and the Americas on the west, so wildlife would certainly have spread onto those adjacent landmasses. Moreover, Caldwell implies that quite a few species 'unknown to us moderns' were represented in the palace zoo: we might have lost track of the odd one, but *lots*? To me, though, the real crunch comes with the question: 'How did Caldwell *know* that the strange species were "unknown to us moderns"?' There are plenty of animal species that you or I wouldn't recognize: is Caldwell a zoology buff?

But enough of such scepticism: let's get back to the dreams.

'Empress Salustra' walks the gardens, filled with a great grief. She loves the Emperor Signar of Althrustri, the country to the north, but he is not only bent on conquering her own nation but also betrothed to her younger sister. Should she have him killed or should she kill herself? Well, the death of the one she loves would make her life a misery, so she has resolved to kill herself – then at least she won't be around to see what happens to her beloved Atlantis.

Caldwell says that she was so affected by this dream that she wept on waking, and took some ten minutes to reorient herself to present-day reality. She remarks that the younger sister of the dream was in fact a current friend of hers (a jolly odd coincidence, that: it's almost as if she'd grafted the friend into her dream), and that she knows the identity of 'Signar' in this life, but is keeping quiet about it. For some while his 'presence' was so strong that she was unable to work.

A week later she dreamt again. Salustra is throwing a feast for Signar and her sister on a raft in one of the harbours of Atlantis. Above the capital city a volcano is smouldering. Signar is caressing the sister freely, which engenders a fair amount of jealousy and grief in Salustra's throbbing heart, and then he mocks her cruelly. 'Again, my anguish almost overwhelmed me, and I awoke gasping with it, and again I was haunted by it for several days.'

Her third dream was set in a time after the demise of Atlantis – something of which she was conscious during the dream. She is with a smallish band of plucky survivors from the continent's devastation; among the band is Signar, who has come to love her truly (the sister, presumably, being now at the bottom of the Atlantic). All of them, ex-empress and ex-emperor included, do their fair share of hewing and gathering, and Salustra is happy in the knowledge that she and Signar are no longer rulers but people united in simple, carefree love. (It's almost like the ending of a popular romance, isn't it?)

Happy as a skylark, Caldwell woke. She remarks that 'the dreams were more vivid than my present reality, more poignant, more agonizing and more joyful. They haunt me, colouring my whole existence, and I feel deprived and filled with an ancient longing.' (This intensification of emotions is, as we've often noted, quite common in dreams.) To do her justice, she sees the whole sequence as not necessarily a *proof* of reincarnation – and comments that the same is true of her childhood 'knowledge' of Atlantis. But then she comes out with the hackneyed 'more things in Heaven and Earth' bit: oh dear.

Edgar Cayce, the 'Sleeping Prophet', could recall not only his own lifetimes in Atlantis and Lemuria (Atlantis' equivalent in the Pacific) but also those of other people. Moreover, he confidently predicted the imminent reemergence of the lost continents. Cayce fans were delighted by the discovery during International Geophysical Year (which lasted 18 months, 1957–59[6]) of the midocean ridges: these, they believed, were the mountain chains of the submerged continents. Since the advent of plate-tectonic theory, and the general acceptance of the notion that the ridges are fractures in the Earth's crust where molten magma emerges from the mantle, there has been something of a silence from the Cayce camp on this front. As well there might be: the existence of the mid-Atlantic ridge puts paid to the idea of there having been a continent there at any time over the last two or three hundred million years – since long before the emergence of mankind, in fact.

Just before we plunge into Cayce's Atlantean experiences, let's backtrack a little. He was convinced of the reality of reincarnation by an experience he had as a young man. He had dreamt of being one of a band of whites fleeing on a raft down the Ohio River: he and the rest of the party were eventually massacred by Indians, which was probably not altogether a bad thing since they were anyway well on their way to starving to death. Some while later, Cayce was in a barbershop when a small boy climbed onto his knee. The boy's father said words to the effect of 'Don't climb all over strangers, Tommy', to which the boy came out with the startling reply that Cayce was no stranger: 'We were hungry together at the river.'

If true, this is indeed a strange tale – and in fact far more convincing than all the rest of Cayce's reincarnation 'evidence' put together. (It could also, of course, be an example of dream telepathy – only the evidence in favour of that is as poor as that in favour of reincarnation.)

Cayce's sleeping mind, as noted, told of his own and other people's incarnations on the lost continents of Atlantis and Lemuria as well as, rather more respectably, in ancient Egypt and more recent historical periods. It is tempting to dismiss it all as a mere farrago. Hm, very tempting.[7]

Initially the human race was not physical but aethereal. Then humanity began to take on physical form and, some 98,000 years 'before the entry of Ram into India' (an event unfortunately undated), invented sex. I find Cayce's description of all this verging on the incomprehensible: it may be that the spiritual creatures thought that sex would be more fun if they had bodies. Whichever way round the two advances happened, the solidifying thought-forms took on the colour of the stuff of which they were made – the red rocks of Atlantis. That's where Red Indians come from. I think. Since the other colours came along later and are thus obviously more highly developed, all this gives us a good comforting excuse to think of the Red Indians as being somehow inferior to us – shades of Joseph Smith and the *Book of Mormon*.

Cayce's descriptions of Atlantean society are entertaining but irrelevant to our purposes. Atlantis was destroyed, though, in not one but three stages, the last of which occurred in about 10,000 B.C. – this was the one recorded by Plato. Dating the three catastrophes is difficult to achieve with precision. As Cayce's son has pointed out, 'The time of these events is so remote (over 10,000 years ago) that few records remain. Those that do are either undiscovered or unrecognized.' Let's not be too unkind about that remark.[8]

Cayce dream-observed the details of so many other people's previous existences in Atlantis that one wonders why nobody has produced a thesis on the astonishing preponderance of ex-Atlanteans who have been reincarnated into his contemporary America, as opposed to anywhere else.

One's previous life in Atlantis can have a profound effect on one's current existence. Take the case of Robert Dunbar, who had previously lived in Atlantis, Egypt, India and Germany, each time being involved in scientific or engineering work – in India, for example, he learned a way to make explosives that could be used to kill members of other tribes. Dunbar – in his current existence – was a small child when all this stuff came out, and his parents were charged with ensuring that in later life he would put his potentially dangerous abilities to good, constructive use. Indeed, in the course of the years, this is precisely what Dunbar did. After having worked in radar during World War II, he elected to continue his career in electrical engineering outside the aegis of the military, where he could have earned more money.

The catch is that his decision seems to have been coloured by his knowledge of and perusal of the readings Cayce gave him in childhood. In the light of this, it is hardly surprising that Dunbar, who seems a nice, humanitarian sort of chap, opted to use his talents for peace rather than for killing people. It's perhaps rather more surprising that he is, apparently, idyllically happily married, but then by statistical laws every now and then the good guys really do come out on top.

Dunbar's case has been quoted as one of the *strongest* in favour of the truth of Cayce's reincarnation readings!

## *Stranger Lifetimes*

Sometimes people have had previous incarnations in more bizarre and remote locations and eras than prehistoric Atlantis. Here is Audrey Atkinson again:[9]

> I had been reading the Tarot, and I kept getting the Moon, and the book said: 'Your dreams will be significant.' . . . I went to bed that night and said, aloud, 'Well, come on then, let's have a significant dream.'
>
> (I should mention here that thirteen years ago I, along with three others, saw a UFO at fairly close quarters, in that it was very low, although the night was very dark. And I had got the *impression* that the occupants were very tall 'metallic' beings. They had a very kindly disposition. You'll see the point of this [parenthesis] later!)
>
> I started to have this vivid dream and saw three huge tablets of hieroglyphics. They were all sloping backwards and leaning on each other: one at the front, and one on each side. They were also surrounded by glowing light. The stonework was in beautifully delicate shades of pale amber, powder-blue, and soft sage-green. On the left-hand tablet, in the middle of the hieroglyphics, there seemed to be the glyph for Leo, ♌, which stood out from the rest. (I'm a Scorpio.)

I looked at these tablets and said: 'OK, I know I asked for a significant dream, but I don't understand this.' (I *knew* that I was having the dream I'd asked for.)

At this, the tablets of stone disappeared and a huge 'metal' man appeared. I knew, at once, that he was one of the occupants of the UFO [I'd seen]. He was of humanoid form, but much larger, about eight feet tall, and seemed to be covered in soft metal. He emanated wonderful vibrations of love and peace and goodwill. He also had a lovely smile!

He 'shimmered' in and out of focus, as if trying to instil some information into my mind. Then the tablets reappeared for a while, then he came back again. This happened two or three times more, and each time I felt this strange tingling 'force' as he tried to make me understand. But I couldn't!

When I woke up, I felt compelled to write to an author, although I'd never given him a second thought before, and had only read one or two of his books.[10] I thought he might be able to explain, but he couldn't. However, we have corresponded, on and off, since then; and he has very kindly sent me some of his books.[11] He has also helped me enormously to get up out of the awful depressions I used to have. I have also learned a great deal from his work, and it does seem to have pointed me in a new direction in life. I have become far more spiritual and psychic since then, and feel I have evolved quite a bit. Perhaps, when I have gone far enough along the road, I will understand the message!

Another odd thing that came out of all that was that I started to do some automatic writing some time afterwards. It implied that the author and I had been related, he my brother, in a previous lifetime. *But* it was eleven million years ago! On another planet, in another star system, near Sirius!

Whether this was my subconscious playing tricks, I don't know (the handwriting was totally different to mine), but some of what it said about another friend did unfortunately come true a couple of years later, when we least expected it. I suppose, if our subconscious is joined to the 'collective' unconscious, then we surely must know what went on in the past, as well as what will happen in the future . . .

It strikes me that this dream, if thought about as an example demonstrating the reality of reincarnation, probably has a lot going for it. Time and time again we have seen how dreams, like white men, speak with forked tongues. It would be just like the dream-world to give Atkinson the urge to write to an author about an otherwise irrelevant dream, solely in order to put these two once-related reincarnated people back in touch with each other. If, that is to say, there is such a thing as reincarnation: it seems much more likely that the Atkinson right brain recognized a 'kindred spirit' on reading a couple of books by this author, told the Atkinson conscious about it – using the medium of the dream – and the rest took care of itself.

There is, of course, a more fundamental objection to the dream and its repercussions being evidence of reincarnation. It's quite possible that Sirius wasn't there eleven million years ago – or, at least, not there as a nice stable Main Sequence star like our Sun.

Perhaps the Atkinson right brain was merely trying to say 'a long time ago and a long way away'. Certainly this sort of effect seems to happen in a lot of 'reincarnatory' dreams: we'll see an example of it on page 389, dreamt by G. M. Glaskin, when we discuss the 'Christos Experience'. For the moment, we can look at a dream of the

British spiritualist Jane Sherwood, which has the same timeless – or, rather, dateless – quality about it.

In the dream, she is aware that the dream-world she lives in is made up of 'vast and formless expanses of sand and marsh from which a misty ocean of water was receding'. She is an enormous, hideous, but friendly sea-monster stranded on the beach; but then there arrives a group of people (or, more precisely, 'manlike creatures'), and her consciousness travels so that she becomes one of them *as well*. The people are terrified of the monster, and set about destroying it. '. . . I had to experience by turns the anguish of the beast and the fear and anger of the mob' until she awoke, her emotions – understandably – in something of a turmoil.

Just a nightmare, you say, and to be fair she is refreshingly sceptical about the 'reincarnation' aspect of the dream. She allows her 'Communicator'[12] to demolish any suggestion that this, the only dream of hers which might qualify as a 'reincarnatory' dream, is just that. The basis for the demolition is that the ego is unlikely to introduce *actual pictures* from previous lives: it may convey *meanings* from previous lives, but these will be dressed up in visual imagery appropriate to the present life of the dreamer (or to something which he or she has read).

This suggestion of the 'Communicator's' is interesting, especially in that it is a rather neat corollary of the suggestion that I've made (see page 372), that 'reincarnatory' dreams are in fact nothing to do with past lifetimes but are simply problem-solving dreams in which, for one reason or another, the characters appear in historical costume; hence the frequent appearance of vague 'Atlantean' garb. While the two notions seem to be diametrically opposed, in fact there's no reason why they couldn't both be true. Mind you, I can't think of any reason why the

Sherwood right brain should want to imagine being a stranded whale.

## Fictions or Memories?

Someone once cruelly said of Joan Grant[13] that she had been an unsuccessful historical novelist until she announced that her novels were all autobiographies of her previous incarnations, at which point she became a successful historical novelist. This is unfair comment: from the time of the publication of her first 'autobiography of the soul', *Winged Pharaoh* (1937), she has claimed only too vociferously that her works are merely the reporting of what she has seen of her past lives when shifting to a different 'level', whatever that means. In fact, some of her quite bland accounts of what it's *like* to be somebody who can 'remember previous incarnations' are oddly convincing, and give her ideas on the nature of the 'reincarnatory process' added weight.

There are four distinct phases of one's reincarnations, says Grant in *Many Lifetimes* (with Denys Kelsey, 1967), although one may incarnate many times within each phase. In *Stage One* you – or, rather, your 'supra-physical' – have the capacity at the very start to organize no more than a single molecule. However, things improve, so that slowly you work your way up through the mineral kingdom until you enter the plant kingdom (*Stage Two*), go through that to the animal kingdom (*Stage Three*) and finally become (*Stage Four*) a member of *Homo sapiens*. In early human incarnations, the entire personality is involved; but as time goes on the individual becomes so developed that there's no longer 'room' in the single human consciousness for the whole personality – hence the idea of the 'supra-physical', a part of which is manifested through you, yourself, and the rest of which seems to hang around governing your actions to a limited extent. As I understand it, the 'trick' of remembering past lifetimes is to get in touch with your 'supra-physical'.

Every pregnant mother will know that there are times when even your favourite foods make your stomach turn. This is not, as you might expect, a simple matter of your body (including foetus) knowing better than 'you' do what foods it needs: it is your unborn child's 'supra-physical' trying to get the message through to you that it would rather have a lump of coal than a lump of Weetabix for breakfast.

According to Grant, in ancient times everybody knew about reincarnation, and so death lost much of its sting; even if you were dying painfully, you knew that as soon as the pain was over you'd be ready to start a new and, with luck, happier life. In more recent historical eras, however, this knowledge of the many-life cycle has been lost. However, you can still retain vague memories of your previous deaths, in that their viciousness harmed your 'supra-physical'. If you're an alcoholic, for example, there's a good chance that you died from thirst in the desert; or even that you were in agony, waiting for an operation in one of those primitive military scenarios where the only anaesthetic was alcohol: you lay on your bed of pain, watching the cup of rotgut as it went the rounds, and hoping that there'd be plenty left over for you . . . In *this* life, therefore, it's no wonder that your 'supra-physical' ordains that you drain every bottle in sight.

If these pre-birth traumas can be littering your unconscious and causing you hardship, it's no wonder that Grant and Denys Kelsey, a psychiatrist, came to the conclusion that, by helping alcoholics and other mentally ill people to remember details of their past lives, some otherwise impossible psychotherapeutic cures might be achievable. They give some examples of their successes in *Many Lifetimes* (see Bibliography).

Although dreams play comparatively little part in Grant's later work with her 'far memory' of past lifetimes, they seem to have started her off along the road, as it were. In *Time Out of Mind* (1956) she recalls her earliest 'reincarnatory' dreams, which she had when she was only about seven years old. In these she was a French girl, aged usually about ten or eleven, but sometimes in her teens. The girl lived in 'a house with a steep grey roof and faded green shutters in which most of the rooms were shut up', had a huge dog, and had also a carriage drawn by two ponies which were only a little larger than the dog.

The young Joan Grant was at the time a little peeved that her parents had judged her not old enough to go with them on holiday to Paris. Had the French girl of her dreams been there? Indeed she had, as Grant found out one night: At the age of nineteen the girl was taken to Paris and thrown into a twilit dungeon, on her own, where she tamed a rat in a desperate attempt to supply herself with some company. She was never to be in sunlight again, except for the time she was taken for a short ride on a tumbril through the crowded jeering streets of Paris, on the way to Madame Guillotine.

> It might have been a terrifying dream, but oddly enough it was rather comforting; because now I knew that beheading does not hurt at all. There was only a loud thud and a feeling of falling head over heels. The next minute she was jumping over a stream to join two men who were waiting for her on the other side of it . . . two men whom she very much loved.

As I say, in later years Grant relied almost exclusively on what she called 'tuning-in' to recapture the 'memories of her past lives'. However, it's interesting in passing to note that the person whose 'biography' she first dictated in book-length detail, a 'former self' called Sekeeta, who lived in Egypt in the First Dynasty and in due course became a female pharaoh,[14] *herself* had 'true dreams' – that is, not only clairvoyant/precognitive dreams but also dreams of her own previous lifetimes. In *Winged Pharaoh* Sekeeta records many of these dreams, including the information that she dream-travelled to Athlanta (= Atlantis) – i.e., to a period 5000 years before even her own. A dreamer dreaming of being a dreamer!

The novelist Edward Lucas White based many of his stories on his dreams, and in one or two cases it's tempting to think that these might have been 'reincarnatory' dreams. His *Andivius Hedulio*, the tale of a Roman nobleman, contains considerable historical detail which, he found on checking later, is almost completely verifiable. In an afterword to the book he remarked:

> The phrasing of this book is mine; otherwise I am scarcely more responsible for it than would be a secretary who has written it out from dictation. I did not originate the plot; I did not, except in a very few [cases], invent the scenes, incidents, or episodes, or create the characters. I dreamed the entire story . . .

Before we get too excited about this, we have to remember that he was a teacher of Latin and Greek, so that it's perfectly possible – indeed, likely – that his unconscious merely pieced together all that he already knew of Rome to create the background.

A more difficult case is that of F. H. Grisewood, reported in 1947 in the magazine *Country Life*. He dreamt from the age of 12 for a number of years about living on a great estate in the time of Charles I. In particular, he had many adventures with a soldier called Jan, who rode out with him often, pointing out the wildlife and the scenery. The interesting thing here is that Grisewood's dreams weren't just random visits to the estate: each dream took up from where the previous one had left off.

When he was 19 or 20 he went to stay with friends, and during his visit he was taken to the home of friends of theirs. Sure enough, the house they went to was the one in his dreams. Touring the house with the hostess, he was able to describe all sorts of details of the way it had been in 'his time', including – most convincingly – a window which had been bricked up long before and about which his hosts had known nothing until he pointed it out to them.

This series of dreams is explicable only in terms of reincarnation, 'timeslip' or fraud. The third of these possibilities cannot be ruled out since, as far as I'm aware, no corroboration of his story exists. This is a very great pity, since obviously, were it to be proved that everything came about exactly as described, we would have one of the more convincing evidences of the veracity of 'reincarnatory' dreams.

## *Christos: Voyages Through Time?*

By far the most extensive series of 'reincarnatory' dreams has come to us as a result of the so-called Christos Experiment. It is ironic that the Australian novelist G. M. Glaskin is best known for his books on this subject, rather than for his novels. The Christos Experiment (or Experience) involves the conscious induction of 'waking dreams' (or 'astral travel', if you want to be partisan about it), some of which can be interpreted in terms of the dreamer having gone back to occupy the body of a previous incarnation.

The series of experiments began in 1971 when Glaskin

was in the house of a couple of friends, pseudonymously 'Ray' and 'Joy'. He was waiting for them to ready themselves for an excursion when he picked up a cheaply produced magazine called *Open Mind*, whose lead story concerned the techniques of the Christos Experiment. (Some while later he was to discover that the author of the article was a Mrs Jacqueline Parkhurst, who has apparently had some remarkable Christos experiences of her own.)

The technique for 'astral travel to previous lives' involved the dreamer lying down with his/her head on a pillow and his/her shoes off. Then one helper would rub the dreamer's pineal region (centre of the forehead – the fabled 'third-eye region') vigorously with the inside edge of the clenched fist; the other of the two helpers would massage the dreamer's ankles. (Glaskin found that, after a while, he could induce the experience without the aid of the helpers.) After suitable amounts of rubbing, the person in control of the 'run' (*not* the dreamer) would ask the dreamer to visualize himself/herself growing taller, first a couple of inches through his/her feet, then the same length through the head. The lengths would be progressively increased until the dreamer was 'growing' about half a metre in each direction simultaneously. Then the dreamer would be asked to expand like a balloon and to 'go' to his/her front door and describe it in detail. That done, it was up to the top of his/her house to describe the view; and then up into the air a further 500m for yet another description. Then the 'runner' would ask the dreamer to turn the scene from day to night and back again a few times before soaring off in a random direction, finally to land 'in a past life'.[15]

Clearly, unless Glaskin is lying through his teeth (and there's no reason to suppose that he is), the results of following this procedure were startling. The dreamers saw everything in incredible detail and with astonishing intensity – even their own front doors.[16] Glaskin says that it was with a sense of shock that he came across the description in Daphne du Maurier's *The House on the Strand* (1968) of the protagonist's observations on being whisked back in time:

> There was no softness anywhere. The distant hills did not blend into the sky but stood out like rocks, so close that I could almost touch them, their proximity giving me that shock of surprise and wonder which a child feels looking for the first time through a telescope. Nearer to me, too, each object had the same hard quality, the very glass turning to single blades, springing from a younger, harsher soil than the soil I knew.

Throughout, the Christos dreamer is conscious of being in both worlds, can respond to the 'runner's' instructions and questions, and describe what is going on.

Glaskin's first book on the subject – *Windows of the Mind* (1974) – describes 22 'runs' undertaken by, in all, 17 dreamers; he himself, Joy and Ray each had two 'runs', while his assistant Leo van de Pas had three (none of which were very successful). I'll go into some detail about the 'runs', or dreams, so please bear with me.

*Glaskin*: (*1*) A return to what he thought was very ancient Egypt. He was a sort of local guru/chieftain. After tramping around for a while, he went to work on his hieroglyphs, in which he was trying to instil great wisdom for the benefit of posterity. But the hieroglyphs were simply not a flexible enough form of writing for him to be able to do this. He (the guru) fatalistically accepted the situation.

(*2*) He was one of a very primitive, pre-speech race, and was running from his people along a tunnel through a mountain to join the more advanced people at the other end. (The modern Glaskin says that he now thinks that the tunnel was lit by electricity or something better. Several thousand B.C.? 'Again I had a kind of precognition that it was the accomplishment of a prior and much more civilized race that was superior even to twentieth-century man, moon-landings and all notwithstanding.' We seem to have arrived in the happy land of Erich von Däniken.) The prehistoric Glaskin makes it to the other encampment, where he is treated with great friendliness and taught the rudiments of speech.

*Ray*: (*1*) He returned to long pre-Christian times where he was a fisherman in Norway, he thought (in real life, he was of Norwegian stock). It was bitterly cold, there was no one else around, and although he wanted a wife there wasn't a suitable candidate anywhere within reach.

(*2*) Poor Ray! He returned to the same previous life.[17]

*Joy*: (*1*) She returned to the time of the Romans, but instead of occupying a body she occupied the ghost of someone who had just died. The 'someone' was the 25-year-old daughter of some potentate, and was petite and ravishingly beautiful.

(*2*) This time she was a man, living virtuously and chastely, liked by everybody – especially the children. She/he looked after goats or sheep (the transcript of the tape-recording of her report is unclear on this). While she/he is in a nearby village being given a cheese by a well-to-do merchant, Jesus appears, and preaches to the villagers. (Christ is apparently only 23 at the time. As Glaskin – quite fairly – points out, there is no reason to believe that Jesus was not preaching at this age.) Joy, or the eremite whose body she inhabits, realizes that Jesus is likely to change his/her way of life for something completely different; but he/she is happy with his/her eremitic lot, and so dodges away from the public meeting in order to snooze in the sunshine.

*Stephan M*: The first part of his 'run' was a fairly dreary adventure in contemporary Australia, the only thing of note being that he knew, in the dream, that his name was John. In the second part, though, he travelled three years into the future to witness, as Stephan, his own mother's funeral.[18]

*Peter C*: He travelled back into his own childhood, where he ran around at the seaside and discovered why he'd had a lifelong fear of water (aquaphobia). (Perhaps the little boy connected the sight of the water with the uncomfortable feeling that some adult from the future was invading his mind!)

*David K*: This subject flew around for a bit (like a bird or in an aeroplane? – the text isn't clear) before landing in a grove of poplar trees which soon turned into a cathedral. He thought he'd travelled back in time a couple of hundred years.

*David B*: He became a 27-year-old called Peter (he was actually, in real life, 21) who led an eremitic existence in an isolated cottage near a village. He thought that he was in a previous body some 70–80 years ago.

*Leo van de Pas*: (*1*) After many complications, he found himself in what appeared to be the contemporary Netherlands, being driven around on the back of a motorbike by his younger brother or a schoolfriend – he wasn't sure which.

(*2*) A washout.

(*3*) First on a contemporary beach in Australia, then to the contemporary Netherlands.

*Richard B*: A bisexual, Richard B found himself transported back to a Roman baths and 'pleasure palace' where, after dithering over the bodies on display, he opted for being fellated by a beautiful young boy. In this body (the dream-body), Richard B believed his name to be Trimalchio. It is interesting to note that apparently his real-life body failed to display the obvious sign of sexual excitation. Curiously, the *Satyricon* of Petronius, in which homosexuality is a major theme, has a character called Trimalchio – indeed, its most important episode is called '*Cena Trimalchionis*'.

*Ruby B*: This lady found herself flying over empty ocean. In fact, she spent quite a while flying over empty ocean. She decided that in a previous life she had been an albatross.[19] This would explain her real-life phobia about flapping birds, because of course albatrosses don't flap much. Glaskin reports that, since then, her phobia has much ameliorated.

*Colin N*: Three distinct dreams, all in the same 'run'. In the first he was somewhere/somewhen in Australia; in the second he trundled around a lighthouse on an isolated rock; and in the third he was in the middle of a desert. In all three, there was the overpowering feeling of being totally alone.

*Julie W*: She reckoned to have returned about a century, to the USA, where she was a prepubescent tomboy who loved her widowed father and worked with him in the fields, but hated and was hated by the 'housekeeper', who happened also to be her father's mistress. In real life, her father has died and she gets on very well with her stepfather.

*Geoff W*: Julie's husband, an extremely young schoolteacher, had at first a typically jumbled dream-sequence – the sort of thing that we're all used to. Then he became simultaneously a young boy who was in a hole in the ground but planning to climb out of it, and a man who had already climbed out of it.

*Jim McA*: He returned to 13th-century Salzburg, where there had just been an unspecified disaster. He committed suicide by throwing himself over a cliff. Happily, in real life he hasn't done this, and has no intention of doing so.

*John M*: Imagine yourself on a tropical island, all alone except for lots of lovely miniature friendly animals, knowing that you – and most of them – are immortal. That's what John M did. Yes, back on the mainland he'd had a girl, Marie, but that was behind him now. He was living in the future, he felt. Dream-animals, says Glaskin, can represent children; and John M did marry a girl called Marie very soon after his 'run'. This seems to be a straightforward waking dream. Certainly it seems unlikely that it represents a future incarnation: for one thing, how did the elephant, zebra, etc., get to the island?

*David H*: Flying a 'plane, and then the 'plane crashed into the water. David H. failed to survive the crash, yet he saw from outwith his body that a curious stilted stick-man figure emerged. This figure floated off aimlessly, picked up a baby kangaroo, gave it to a remote smallcropper and his moronic son,[19] and then floated on a while longer before the end of the 'run'. David H felt that in some way this was a premonition of his own future.

*Paul L*: Although Glaskin dismisses this dream as being the least important of the whole series, my hunch is that it's the *most* important. Paul L found himself briefly viewing the Panama Canal (I would suggest this was a standard, normal dream) and then trudging among the mountains of . . . Tasmania? New Zealand? Perhaps they were the Alps? He was lost, and so went back to a village he'd just passed through to ask for directions. One of the oldsters agreed to show him the way, but in the end proved to be just as lost as Paul L was. As Glaskin points out, the really curious thing here is that Paul L is 100% pure-blooded Chinese. Yet a short while afterwards, on honeymoon in Norway, he reckoned that he had identified the scene of his dream. Few Chinese people can trace their ancestry to Norway!

Let's look at this last dream in fairly conventional terms. Paul L was a medical scientist whose research had come to a sticking point: he didn't know where to go from here. Should he consult an older worker in the same field? But then the older worker might not know the answer, either. In fact, in real life Paul L *did* consult more experienced workers some while later, and discovered that, like the 'guide' in the dream, they couldn't help him.

In terms of the dream as either wish-fulfilment or means of self-analysis, the Christos Experience is fascinating. Let's skip back through some of those dreams again.

*Glaskin* is a novelist. In his first dream he had the wisdom of ages to communicate, but no way of doing so. I experience this feeling every time I face the typewriter: my ability to manipulate the English language falls far short of whatever facile wisdom I have to communicate at that particular moment. Glaskin's dream seems born from his real-life experiences. In his second dream he was taught language by beings more knowledgeable than himself. The same interpretation applies.[20]

*Ray*, of Norwegian stock, dreamt of being 'back' in Norway – but he was all alone and he didn't like the place much. In real life, he has settled in Australia. Should he go back to the Old Country, where his wife would be unhappy (and hence so would he), or should he . . . ? I leave you to fill in the rest of this amateur dream-analysis yourself.

*Joy* dreamt she was a petite and lovely lady who'd just upped and died. Sounds just like a girlhood fantasy. In her other dream she was a man who rejected Jesus. In real life she has often said she'd like to be a man, and she is at least partly Jewish.

*David K* and *Ruby B* flew. He had great fun buzzing

outcrops and the like; she just wafted about over bleak ocean. A popular interpretation of flying dreams (as enshrined in the title of Erica Jong's unreadable best-seller, *Fear of Flying*) is that they signify sexual frustration, or something . . .

*Leon van de Pas* had little success in the experiment. Glaskin says that this is because de Pas was actually frightened of it. I suspect that it was instead because, in exactly the same way that I would be, he was too intellectually interested in the whole affair. Several times, people – amateurs, to be true – have attempted to hypnotize me, totally without success: while they've been twirling their watches (or whatever) I've been on the edge of my seat wondering *what's it going to be like to be hypnotized*? I think van de Pas had the same problem: he was too interested in the experiment to be able to go into the trance.

*Richard B*: Sex dreams are supposed, according to popular interpretations, to indicate anxiety. He'd been having 'brief encounters' with both men and women, but recognized that these were empty and that it was time for him to settle down, to stablilize his emotional life. Which way should he jump?

*Colin N* felt alone in his dreams and, sadly, felt alone in real life.

*Julie W* saw herself as a tomboy, whereas in real life she is a fastidiously feminine dresser. Conclusion obvious but libellous. Also, she saw a typical dream mirror-image of her family life: mother dead rather than father, and hatred for, rather than liking for, the step-parent.

Her husband, *Geoff W*, saw himself having to make the choice between being a boy and being a man. As a schoolteacher in his early twenties, this is the actual choice that faced him in real life.

*John M* had a wish-fulfilment fantasy, doubtless coloured by his worries about getting 'tied down' to his Marie. If dream-animals indicate children, it's interesting that soon afterwards he opted to become a teacher, having spent some while wondering whether to do this or go into medical technology.

In *A Door to Eternity* Glaskin describes a fair number of his natural, as opposed to Christos, dreams. Two of them he feels may have some element of recollection of a previous existence: in one he was a mediaeval monk who fled when his fellow-monks began to kill each other; in the other he was a seaman arriving on board a very ancient steamship and being given the runaround by an officious junior officer.[21, 22]

Neither of these dreams had anything of the force of the Christos ones; and if one is to take every dream set in historical times as being of 'reincarnatory' origin then much of history would have to be rewritten. Moreover, since it would be unscientific to differentiate between historical and other dreams, then the science-fiction dreams which I have and the nightmares which you may have must all be true, too. I decline to believe that my science-fiction dreams are glimpses of past or future incarnations – especially since there are so many mistakes in the scientific content!

As for the Christos dreams themselves, we can see that in every single case (although, for the sake of space, I haven't included all of them here) the dreamers seem simply to have had dreams which either fulfilled their desires or sorted out a problem for them. One could hazard a guess that this is roughly what the gateway to the right brain – or even the right brain itself – is *for*. In other words, the Christos dreams differ from normal dreams only in that, as Glaskin puts it, the dreamer 'is now consciously receptive to his subconscious without the normal requisite of sleep'; i.e., they are waking dreams.

This means, of course, that if the Christos method actually works it could be used as an immensely powerful psychotherapeutic tool. It is rather surprising that psychiatrists haven't adopted it wholesale. There are two possible explanations for this.

## *Conclusions – Or a Lack of Them*

Now, where does this leave us on the subject of 'reincarnatory' dreams – and on the more general subject of reincarnation itself? Well, 'reincarnatory' dreams seem to fall into two general categories – (a) rattling good historical yarns and (b) problem-solving dreams in which the characters wear historical dress. I don't want to keep harping on about my own science-fiction dreams, but the comparison between them and 'reincarnatory' dreams (of which I've never had any) is, I think, a revealing one.

An important point to remember about the 'reincarnatory' dream is that the dreamer wakes up so powerfully affected by the dream that he or she is *convinced* that the dream is a memory rather than a fantasy. There is no getting away from this. Although obviously there's a chance that some 'reincarnatory' dreamers are just plain frauds, out to make a quick buck or to gain fame for egotistical reasons, all of them are unanimous about the fact that their dreams really are memories; which can be translated to mean that the dreams are very affecting indeed. Not always – the rattling good historical yarns tend to be less affecting than the others – but most of the time.

Unfortunately, the same is true of my science-fiction dreams. On occasion they're just rattling good tales, and I forget them not long after I wake up; but on occasion they colour the whole of my day, and I can remember them quite vividly years later. The affecting dreams are utterly different, qualitatively, from the others. (Over and over again, in personal correspondence with dreamers as well as in their published writings, one comes across a sentence to this effect: 'This was a *different* dream.' A prime example is the dream of Priestley's which I refer to on page 220; it was because the dream was so *different* that he was convinced it was precognitive.) However, as I say, I refuse to believe that those *different* science-fiction dreams of mine are glimpses of my future incarnations, or even of my past incarnations in extraterrestrial (but precisely humanoid) cultures. They mean a great deal to me, personally, and presumably are performing some function or other in keeping me sane; but they are irrelevant to you for the simple reason that you aren't me. To you they are nothing but fantasies; to me they are something more.[23]

Until you understand this qualitative difference between the affecting dreams and the others, there's no way that you can understand the true nature of the 'reincarnatory' dream. But, of course, it's easy enough for you to understand the difference: you're a rare bird if you haven't had similarly powerful dreams yourself, set in past, present or future. Imagine that all your really affecting dreams were set in Atlantis, and that together they seemed to tell a quite coherent story of somebody's life. Wouldn't *you* be convinced that you were really remembering, in your dreams, a prior lifetime? Obviously, the notion would fly in the face of all accepted scientific knowledge – and, indeed, 'common sense' – but it would be difficult for you to refuse to believe the evidence of your dreams.

I think, in our attempts to see if dreams are able to give us memories of previous lifetimes, we can forget the rattling-good-yarn type of dream. But the others are not so easily dismissed. On the one hand, they tend to be problem-solving, so the obvious explanation is that the right brain has decided to tell a fable in order to help the dreamer reconcile him- or herself to something or other. That's all very well, but a different point could be made. The majority of the problems which I solve daily are solved because I've come across something similar before. I know how to put a new lightbulb in, which direction to twist it, becuase I've done the job before; the precise memory of how to do it comes to me when I tackle the task. (Sitting here, not putting lightbulbs in, I can't actually remember whetther the twist should be clockwise or anticlockwise: give me a lightbulb and a socket and I'll be able to put the twist in the right direction without *thinking* about whether it's clockwise or anticlockwise.) Could it not be, therefore, that 'reincarnatory' dreams are examples of people drawing on their 'far memories' (to use Joan Grant's phrase) in order to find out how they solved similar problems in the past? What I'm trying to point out is that, just because 'reincarnatory' dreams tend to solve problems, it doesn't mean that those dreams are necessarily fantasies constructed by the right brain purely in order to solve problems. It could, after all, be the other way round: the dreams are telling the dreamers how to solve problems by recalling how they were solved before.

So where do we find ourselves? Sitting on the fence. There's a possibility that 'reincarnatory' dreams are examples of our remembering previous lifetimes, but it's much easier to believe that they're simply problem-solving dreams dressed up. *I* would like to believe this: it makes more sense in terms of my own world-view. But I get very worried when I come across items like Glaskin's apparent corroboration of his Egyptian dream.[20] There seem to be two possibilities: either Glaskin's right brain knows something which his left brain doesn't, or he really is recalling a prior lifetime . . . and I'm unhappy with both. I think that the right-brain explanation, in this context, has so many holes that it sinks; but I refuse to believe, on the other hand, that reincarnation actually occurs: it just doesn't make sense.

Make up your own mind.

# Epilogue

## *The Role and Function of the Dreamer*

If dreams are made up of symbols, then they can themselves also constitute symbols. In the broadest sense, the course of humanity is made up of dreams and nightmares. Just look around you at the moment. Although their voices are often stilled, the dreamers are there: the people who look to the future, who want to bring peace and happiness to all the world, who want us to walk among the stars.

The idealists. The poor crazy fools. The golden kernel of humanity.

And the purveyors of nightmares are all around us, too: not just the torturers and the dictators and the warmongers, but also the people who portray themselves as the forces of grey practicality and grim reason. These are the 'realists' who stifle the voices of the dreamers more effectively than do even the jackboots.

The dreamers are shackled everywhere. A modern Newton wouldn't see an apple fall: he would be concentrating too hard on his tax return. Our poets aren't published, because poetry isn't 'what the public wants': 'what the public wants, man' is the next cardboard episode of some soft-porn opera or the new mind-rottingly banal quiz game on the television.

Robert Goddard dreamt of flying to the Moon, but the *New York Times* told him not to be stupid: out there in space his rockets wouldn't have anything to push against. And for a long time in the public eye the *New York Times* had won the argument. Its anonymous editorial-writers had faced the facts, bitten the bullet, shown Goddard's dreams as the idle fantasies they were.

The money is taken away from NASA but it's not wasted: it's given to the people who make the weapons that are maybe going to kill my child, rockets that are really 'useful', 'essential'.

Our artists are pilloried in the press when they show distant reaches of the mind which some hack journalist somewhere doesn't believe exist.

A council solves a rates dispute with an artist by seizing *part* of his finest creation.

The misery of poverty for millions, we're told, as the dole queues lengthen, provides a way for us all to find happiness; and some of us *believe* it.

Someone dreams of freedom for their land or their tribe or their race or their sex or their religion, and the 'realists' take the dreams and try to realize them by slaughtering the innocent. And the 'realists' on the opposite side respond by doing exactly the same thing.

In a play a sexual act is simulated on stage to symbolize the rape of a country and the oppression of its people. Strong complaint is made that the play is pornographic, and in all the shouting no one makes a whisper about the plight of the country.

And people whose dream is of peace run the risk of being defended by being shot.

Be average. Silence your dreams. Keep still. Face the facts.

It's a bad time for dreamers, my friends. And in consequence we're a sad and sorry species right now.

But the dreamers won't be silenced. The peace-dreamers are arrested and fined and imprisoned and tortured and killed, all over the world; but still they chant their dreams. The poets write and the artists paint and the musicians sing, and so what if their stomachs are empty when they go to bed each night? The Utopians, defeated yet again, rally themselves for the next time:

they have the courage to believe in the strength of their dreams, that one day the dreams *must* come true. It would be nice to be able to share their confidence.

But can we? The purveyors of the nightmare are dominant – and nightmares have their strengths, too. Look at the ground for too long and you'll convince yourself that there's no such thing as the sky. When someone tells you of a sunrise, you know that they're mad or they're a witch or they're worse: 'Thou shalt not suffer a dreamer to live.' What is *real* is the ground beneath your feet. The sky is a fantasy, a drug-crazed hallucination of someone who 'refuses to face' harsh reality. If Christ returned today we'd crucify him all over again.

We can choose between the dream and the nightmare.

We *must* choose.

Soon.

# Notes

## CHAPTER ONE: INNER SPACEMEN

1 Letter to me dated 21st September, 1983.

2 Letter to me dated 25th August, 1983.

3 From an undated letter sent to me in August, 1983. Stewart reported to me also a rather more detailed variant of this dream (the variant recurred, too): this time the pursuer was a giant crab. 'Giant', but able to change size at will so that, when she locked herself in the bathroom to escape from it, it simply made itself smaller and scuttled under the door, then swelled up to its original size. Once again, when cornered, she'd start being over-courteous to the beast.

4 Letter to me dated 26th August, 1983.

5 Letter to me dated 12th September, 1983.

6 Cayce's interpretation is long and curiously hard to comprehend, so it's possible that I'm misrepresenting him.

7 I've on occasion had dreams which were so plausible that they've been quite confusing – they've become false memories. For example, when I was a small child I dreamt that my mother told me that I could travel upstairs in the bus home from school if I got off at Stop A, which was on the flat, rather than Stop B, which was on a hill but was closer to home. Unfortunately, the dream went straight into my memory-bank: when I awoke, there it was as a memory from the previous evening.

A couple of weeks later – in real life – my mother spotted me travelling upstairs in the bus and gave me hell. She gave me even greater hell when I claimed that she'd told me I could: she thought, quite naturally, that I was lying. When finally we worked out that it was a dream which had confused me, I got into trouble for having clambered off the 'bus at Stop B, rather than Stop A! I was never able to remember *dreaming* the conversation, although at the time I could remember the conversation itself quite clearly.

8 To be fair, the original Malay term means 'man of the

woods'. Also, many local names for various types of 'abominable snowmen' can be translated to mean much the same as 'man of the woods'. Monboddo may have been mixing Bigfoot legends up with real apes.

9 Hah! Tell that to our six-year-old.

10 Yes, this deduction loses me, too.

11 Freud comments that only if the parents made love in this way could the child have seen both sets of genitalia in operation. This displays a touching naïvety on Freud's part. However, the other evidences are consistent with his general picture.
Later Freud realized that basing his whole interpretation on a possibly nonexistent scene was perhaps a little risky, and so he suggested that in fact the boy had seen sheepdogs copulating and transferred this activity onto either a chance sighting of his parents making love in the more conventional, 'missionary', position or, even, of them in a totally sex-free scene. This allowed Freud to back away from the almost incredibly unpalatable notion that civilized couples could have made love with the man behind the woman.

12 The account I've given here follows quite closely Freud's own account of the analysis, as given in 'The Case of the Wolf-Man' (see Bibliography).

## CHAPTER TWO: THE CREATIVE DREAMERS

1 This should not be confused with the unorthodox public school, Dartington Hall, although the two are under the same umbrella.

2 This account is taken from Baring-Gould's *Lives of the Saints* (see Bibliography). I take no responsibility for Sir Ingebrand's rather less than winning way with words.

3 The mare in the picture is, of course, an irrelevance. The 'mare' of nightmare comes to us from the Old French *cauchemar*, meaning 'nightmare'.

4 His notebooks are pretty hard going in their original form. Here and elsewhere I've amended Coleridge's punctuation, etc., to ease comprehensibility.

5 The version I've cited is one of his early drafts of the poem. The revised, published edition is more 'poetic', at the probable expense of honesty.

6 From Coleridge's published introduction to the 'fragment', 1816.

7 I should add that it's particularly presumptuous of me because I don't write very much fiction. Curiously, though, the creative dreams which I find most affective and powerful – and which I can still recall weeks later – are all in the field of science fiction. If I were someone else I'd no doubt conclude that they were in fact precognitive. As it is, I'd much rather agree with my conclusions to this chapter (see pages 130ff).

8 Condensed from the version to be found in Justin Kaplan's excellent *Mr Clemens and Mark Twain* (see Bibliography).

9 Mark Twain, on the other hand, managed to dream a few good jokes. For example, a pun: Queen Victoria was at sea, and annoyed the whole time. That's the origin of the VC. Well, it amused our six-year-old.

10 Compare Lovecraft, page 77.

11 Hypnagogic dreamers are quite rare; although my mother happens to be one. She thought everyone had hypnagogic dreams (although she didn't know the term) until once when, aged about 70, she was helping as a volunteer guinea-pig in a series of experiments being run by the Psychology Department of Edinburgh University. She'd been asked to write things down on the back of a sheet of scrap paper; in an idle moment she turned it over and began to read what was on the other side . . . and discovered, all of a sudden, that she was 'interesting'.

12 All right, so I don't.

13 This sort of a thing has probably happened to most men at parties. It's what comes of being a gentleman when asked to 'comfort' a woman.

14 If you think about it, she might have been kind enough to 'phone up her employer and say she couldn't come to work that day because she had a headache . . .

15 Several times Kerouac mentions that his dreams were assisted/affected by boozing, and that's odd. Alcohol actually inhibits the amount of dreaming we do each night – as well as, for obvious reasons, making it more difficult to remember the dreams in the morning. There seem to be three possibilities: (a) that Kerouac was anyway a much more prolific dreamer (or anyway rememberer of dreams) than most of us; (b) his claims of alcoholic excess were

overstated (Dylan Thomas used to do this); (c) the dreams recounted were experienced after he had fallen *back* to sleep in the early hours of the morning.

The astute reader will have noticed that, despite the parenthesized comment under (b), both Kerouac and Thomas died from drink – Kerouac at the age of 47 from massive abdominal haemorrhaging due to a perhaps deliberate overindulgence of gargantuan proportions during the last years of his life. All one can say is that, had both of them drunk as much as they claimed, they'd both have died even younger.

16 The feat was not a mean one: he was in poor health at the time. Even though *Jekyll and Hyde* isn't a long book, the idea of writing it twice within a single week is pretty daunting.

17 The American novelist William Dean Howells (1837–1920). The book named was published in 1873.

18 In the third of his books on the 'Christos Experience', *A Door to Eternity* (1979), Glaskin tells a curious tale. In 1970, while suffering from an illness that had stopped him from writing, he dreamt that he finished one book and then, as had been his wont, immediately started work on the next. The strange thing was that the beginning of the new book was identical with that of the first, although after this the new book adopted its own character. Once he had finished the second book, he began on a third . . . which again started off in exactly the same way.

At the time he thought this was a subconscious warning to him that his writing was getting too 'samey'. He therefore attempted in succeeding years to diversify, with disastrous results. But his three books on the 'Christos Experience' have all, of necessity, required him to begin with an account of his own first adventure 'back into a previous life' – although all three have been, aside from this, completely different from each other.

In other words, is it possible that his dream was actually a precognitive one? In the words of the great Raymond Drake, 'Who knows?'

19 Especially when I'm the one who's written them.

20 This is not true of what I think to be his best story, 'Moxon's Master', in *Can Such Things Be?* (1883), one of the earliest stories to feature a humanoid robot.

21 In real life, Kepler worked for Brahe from 1597 until Brahe's death in 1601. As we shall see, Kepler then inherited all Brahe's observations, and was thus able to derive his three laws of planetary motion. Building on these, Newton derived his theory of universal gravitation. The Kepler/Brahe liaison could hardly have been more important to the history of human progress.

22 If you're tempted to laugh at Verne, just remember that it has been suggested during *this* century that the other planets of the Solar System are populated because, when Atlantis was blown up, chunks of real estate – with their occupants clinging on for dear life! – were shot across the gulf of interplanetary space.

23 Or so he thought. It sounds as if the young Verne was one of those men who just can't bear the thought of other men enjoying fruits which they themselves can't enjoy.

24 As cited in Jean Jules-Verne's warmly recommended biography, *Jules Verne* (see Bibliography).

25 My wife instructs me to note that wives are reaching their prime when they pass the age of thirty.

26 He almost certainly finished it during a second, but shorter, spell in prison in about 1676–77. It was published in 1678, although the second part was not added until 1684.

27 It begins: 'As I walk'd through the wilderness of this world, I lighted on a certain place, where was a Denn; And I laid me down in that place to sleep: And as I slept I dreamed a Dream. I dreamed, and behold I saw a Man clothed with Raggs . . .' It is generally accepted that the 'Denn' was Bedford Jail.

28 It is perhaps unfair that Kipling is today held in such low esteem (except, of course, by the kids, who always know better than we grown-ups). However, the reasons for his low standing are only too easy to pinpoint. Having spent some years in India, where he first became a professional writer, and having in later years travelled to other parts of the Empire, he developed an ideal of colonialism which, to modern eyes, smacks more than a little of racism. In fact, closer examination of his 'Indian' writings shows few traces of racism, if any: his support for colonialism was based on the idea that the British were helping the Indians in countless practical ways while abjuring the overt political power which they could so easily have seized. While this

paternalism is, in today's terms, rather cloying, it has to be borne in mind that the majority of Kipling's *Indian* contemporaries would probably have agreed with him.
That said, his attitudes towards the black South Africans after he had met Cecil Rhodes leave a sour taste in the mouth, although it is possible to argue that his vehement support of the British during the Boer War of 1899–1902 derived from his conviction that under the British the South African peoples would find justice, India-style, while under the Afrikaaners they would find only repression. He specifically predicted the setting-up of a police state under the Afrikaaners – at a time when many saw them as plucky little groups of settlers fighting for their own well justified freedom.

29 See J. C. Barker's *Scared to Death* (London, Muller, 1968).

30 Readers who wish to follow the story of Frankenstein's monster from its creation to recent movie-making are urged to read John Stoker's light-hearted account in *The Illustrated Frankenstein* (Newton Abbot, Westbridge, 1980).

31 This account is drawn from a letter written to me by Mrs Simpson at the end of August, 1983.

32 It is often said that Niels Bohr devised his model of the atom in a dream: he was standing on a star around which planets, connected with thin threads, orbited. Although my studies of Bohr's writings on the subject are necessarily incomplete, I have consulted a fair number of them, and have found not the remotest hint that the story is true. Similarly, texts on the history of science fail to tell the tale. The only books that do are those in the fields of psychology and parapsychology. It's possible that I've missed something, but it seems likely that we have here an example of modern mythology at work.
That this is the case is made all the more likely by the fact that many scientific texts, while being so strangely silent about Bohr's dream, trumpet gleefully those of Loewi and, especially, Kekulé.

33 The tale is also told that Edison used to take constant catnaps so that he could pinch other people's ideas and inventions *via* the medium of the telepathic dream.

34 My initial reaction, like yours, was that from Loewi's description it sounds as if he had made the discovery not in

a dream but as a 'night thought'. However, elsewhere Loewi is emphatic that it really was a dream.

35 Although, as already noted, many of those everyday consumers would not be around to enjoy Howe's invention were it not for Kekulé's discovery, which has had fundamentally important ramifications in pharmaceutics. Sans modern organic chemistry, your friendly pharmacist would still be offering you a limited range of drugs whose efficacy (or otherwise) had been determined only by the results of trial-and-error experiments. Even worse, you might become one of the errors.

36 As opposed to the less sophisticated and now little used chain-stitch sewing-machine.

37 Do not misunderstand me. I don't mean that he was the greatest *science-fiction writer* of all time.

38 We'll be going into this whole subject in much greater detail in Part Two, when we talk about dreams which seem to involve the paranormal.

39 In the case of both the quantum theory and Relativity the poor old left brain is in a vulnerable position, in that it's a very *logical* sort of a person. Both theories violate that most uncertain of principles, 'common sense', to a very great degree. It's much easier for the right brain to come to terms with them because, of course, it doesn't much believe in silly old 'common sense' anyway.

40 Colin Wilson has produced an excellent Lovecraftish novel which, I think, bears out my point: *The Philosopher's Stone* (1969). The difference between Wilson writing horror and Lovecraft writing horror is that Wilson has packed a lot of provocative and stimulating ideas into his novel, whereas Lovecraft was generally happy to do no more than try to scare the pants off us.

41 In the first, the fundamental horror is that of the dwarf-disguised-as-child. (Why should dwarves be frightening? I don't know. Any more than I know why some people should think them funny.) In the second the two horrors are possession (fair enough) and decapitation after death (but . . . but when you're dead you don't notice if someone cuts your head off – and yet the idea is still a fundamental horror).

## CHAPTER THREE: DREAMING CREATORS

1 A unique literary judgement. Or perhaps Dickens merely means that many of Scott's characters were genuine historical personages.

2 As given in the edition of Latham and Matthews (see Bibliography under Pepys). Extracts from this edition of Pepys' diary are reprinted by permission of A. D. Peters & Co. Ltd., to whom a fee has been paid.

3 This is the only reference that I can find to Pepys having a lucid dream. However, from the context, it could appear that the experience was not an uncommon one for him.

4 In 1665 bubonic plague ravaged London. It is thought that the Great Fire of the following year was largely responsible for finally cleansing the city of the plague. If so, it was a good swap: only eight people are believed to have died in the Fire, whereas the Great Plague, one of the 'parting flourishes' of the Black Death, as Philip Ziegler describes it in *The Black Death* (1969), must have accounted for thousands.

5 The garbling is Pepys', censoring the naughty bits – although one can make a fair guess as to what he's talking about.

6 As in the previous chapter, I have amended punctuation and so on in the extracts from Coleridge's notebooks, since otherwise they're pretty hard going.

7 In the field of books, Colin Wilson has recalled that there was some fuss made when it was found that some of his own books on murder were on the shelves of a particularly nasty Australian killer. Could the books have inspired the crimes? Wilson has pointed out that it was far less publicized that the murderer had as well a whole stack of Agatha Christie's novels. If books can indeed inspire violent crimes, then even the most innocuous of entertainments must be watched carefully.

8 There are many reasons for recommending Martin's *Always Merry and Bright* (see Bibliography). One of them is the astonishing sequence of extracts from Miller's dream-diary to be found on pages 280–284.

9 Although one can't help feeling that the La Touche parents were possibly acting wisely: it would have been no more than realistic to equate the giving of a girl's hand in

marriage to Ruskin with a condemnation of her to a lifetime of sexual and emotional frustration. Matters weren't helped when Mrs La Touche got in touch with Ruskin's ex-wife, Effie, who told her the Awful Truth of it all.

10 The 'heavy shapeless mass' and the beautiful cruel woman lead us straight back to the relationship between nightmares, sexual frustration, and the old concept of incubi and succubi which we discussed on page 160 in connection with one of Coleridge's nightmares.

11 Some spellings and punctuations have been amended.

12 Having come to this conclusion, one is tempted to stretch speculation a little further. If the narrator of *Dream Days* and *The Golden Age* was intended to be the young Kenneth himself – and this seems eminently reasonable in light of the overt similarity in circumstances of the Grahame children and the children of the stories – then it seems likely that Grahame, in later life, was idealizing not only his childhood fantasies but also himself. You see, the anonymous narrator is an *interesting* child, who has all sorts of jolly, adventurous japes. To judge from the reactions of Grahame's own family – his siblings and his other relatives, like the tight-pursed uncle – Grahame was not immensely popular as a boy. Of course, this could have been because he was simply boring, like his dream of the 'room'.

13 There *is* a sort of schizophrenic ethic to the book. Toad is a menace and is roundly condemned by society, and the modern reader might feel that, when this dangerous pest loses Toad Hall, it's a jolly good thing. Yet then we are asked to agree that it is only right and proper that Toad Hall should be returned to its original owner since 'commoner classes', as it were, should not be allowed to appropriate the property of the 'aristocracy', however idiotic – and, indeed, criminal – that 'aristocracy' might be.

14 Compare Mark Twain's similar dream on page 81 of being humiliated at a formal function.

15 For a real-life sick joke which exemplifies our downgrading of the dream, in Martin Luther King's sense of the word, there is a single reason why King's great 'I Have a Dream' speech is not recorded *in extenso* in this book: I could not afford the large copyright fee demanded, and my suggestion that I instead make a donation to the Martin Luther King Foundation was dismissed as absurd.

16 So you don't know these poems either? The poet referred to was Adam Lindsay Gordon (1833–1870), author of the collections *Sea Spray and Smoke Drift* (1867) and *Bush Ballads and Galloping Rhymes* (1870). He died by his own hand.

## CHAPTER FOUR: THE COUNTRY OF THE STRANGE

1 Another nasty mass-murderer, Peter Sutcliffe, who terrorized the north of England for several years before his accidental capture in late 1980.
2 Those were the days when you worried if a letter didn't turn up the morning after posting!
3 *Man With Arrows and Companion* by Bichitir.
4 To be fair, some people trying to pick up the 'voices of the dead' have had results which are rather more difficult to explain; i.e., the recordings are clearer, with little white noise.
5 I'm surprised I've never come across this case in books dealing with spontaneous combustion. The fact that her flesh was burnt but not her clothes would seem to be diagnostic of the phenomenon (if indeed the phenomenon occurs).
6 Two interesting books on the subject are Rodney Dale's *The Tumour in the Whale* (1978) and Jan Harold Brunvand's *The Vanishing Hitchhiker: American Urban Legends and Their Meanings* (1981).
7 From *Asimov's Biographical Encyclopedia of Science and Technology*, Revised Edition, 1972.
8 It's interesting if irrelevant to note that there have been suggestions that Shakespeare, in *The Tempest*, based Prospero on Dee and Miranda on Dee's daughter Katherine.
9 In July 1918 we even find Jung recommending to one Fanny Bowditch Katz that she consult her dreams before deciding whether or not to become pregnant.
10 The nature of the 'something' is unspecified.
11 He distinguishes between 'dreams', which are what we normally have, and 'visions', those profoundly affecting dreams that come along only once in a while. In his own terminology, then, he is talking about his 'visions'.

12 The extracts quoted here from St Teresa's *Life* are from the J. M. Cohen translation (see Bibliography).

13 Chakras are, according to Cavendish's ever-useful *Encyclopedia of the Unexplained* (1974), 'points at which the physical body and the astral or subtle body are connected, and are centres of psychic energy'.

14 As given in *Dream Telepathy* by Ullman *et al.* (See Bibliography.)

15 Parise's description is much more accurate than it might appear here, since I decided against filling a couple of pages with a detailed description of *The Seven Spinal Chakras*. Just to mention one feature, her description 'like . . . a Mexican totem pole'. The chakra-motifs are indeed vertically above each other, just like the faces on a totem pole, in this picture. In others that I've seen on the same theme the symbols are not placed in this way, so that a line through them from head to feet would meander considerably along the way.

16 Although we'd be dishonest if we didn't recognize that Ehrenwald could have left his bunch of keys on the desk some while before, and that the patient might have abstractedly noted the number on one of them, forgetting the whole thing immediately afterwards until his dream-mind brought it back to his attention. This actually makes the dream-interpretation, along Ehrenwald's lines, work much better: the patient, worried about his masculinity, realizes that the psychiatrist he is seeing is the key to his future resolution of the problem. That there is also the key/phallus association would not be surprising: dreams frequently employ this sort of symbolic pun.

17 Possibly a deal harder than if he'd decided he *would* tell her about it. To get an idea of this sort of 'concentration on the negative', try as hard as you can not to think about a gooseberry for the next 30 seconds. You see? Once you try *not* to think of something, it's impossible to banish it from your mind.

18 From personal experience, I'm not wholly convinced that this can be a total explanation – if, indeed, there's any truth at all in it. Excuse me while I blush a little before telling you why. A good number of years ago I had a colleague to whom I was much attracted; unfortunately, the feeling wasn't mutual. One night I dreamt that she and

I were making mad passionate love at the side of a swimming-pool. The next morning in the office, exchanges were naturally somewhat strained between us, since I was so embarrassed. After a while I noticed that she was embarrassed, too; and it finally came out that she had had a similar dream to mine. As you might imagine I found the whole situation of the utmost intellectual fascination, and discussed the beliefs of some primitive societies that dreams should be put into practice in real life. Still no.

19 There are persistent reports that Dominic and Francis were bosom friends. It is of course possible that this friendship was invented by later Church historians, but one is tempted to believe it genuine. If so, the meeting must surely have been before 1221, which was the year of Dominic's death.

20 Hypnopompic dreams are analogous to hypnagogic ones, except that they're experienced on waking rather than on falling to sleep.

21 Some of the flying-saucers-from-inside-the-earth theorists are ingenious. One of them has it that at the end of World War Two lots of high-ranking Nazis fled north and found the entrance-hole at the pole. Nowadays they buzz us in their flying saucers as some obscure kind of revenge for our having won the war.

Another is even more adroit in the art of combining fallacies: the people inside the hollow Earth, who fly the saucers, are the survivors from the destruction of Atlantis. Three myths in one – not bad going. (See my *A Directory of Discarded Ideas* for more of such stuff.)

22 Others want it all to happen even if they don't survive. They have found the human condition so miserable that they want to die, yet recoil from suicide. The easy way out is if *everybody* dies. (I'm grateful to P. J. Poulton for this insight.)

23 *The Pennine UFO Mystery* (1983).

24 It is impossible to establish the validity of this figure. However, it should be noted that it isn't quite as good as it seems. According to a GP whom I consulted on the matter, some 80% of his own cures come about through the use of 'placebo medicine': if the patient believes that sucking his thumb will cure him, then cured he will be. So, if we discount the 80% of cases which Cayce would have cured by the placebo effect, we find his remedies actually *worked*

85% of the time. This is still pretty good – but it should be borne in mind that, statistically, people who consult unorthodox practitioners (e.g., faith healers) are by definition likely to respond more to the placebo effect. Another factor is hypochondria, which many doctors are unsympathetic about (wrongly, in my view); unorthodox practitioners play a valuable role in dealing with hypochondriacs.

25 In *Time out of Mind* she tells us that there was all hell to pay when, after his death, her parents discovered that she was an 'adulteress' – that somehow being a more polite word than 'fornicator'. When she married Leslie Grant, who had known about the whole business, he was rather puzzled to find that she was in fact still a virgin. She confessed that she had been so ignorant about sex that she had assumed that 'sleeping with a man' meant no more and no less than sleeping with him, and that any actual procreation took place while the partners slept.

26 Of course, both could be true, in a way. Christine Sizemore's unconscious 'invented' numerous different characters corresponding to various facets of herself (see pages 275–9). I see no reason why, in a different mind, these characters could not be clad in historical costume. Let me use an analogy. I have many different characteristics, which all jigsaw-fit together to make up the single character who is myself. However, once you've put the jigsaw together and stuck all the pieces fast with superglue, you can take a fretsaw and cut it up into quite different pieces. In other words, while the individual pieces are completely changed, the net result of putting them all back together again would be the same.

Grant's right brain, then, could well be saying: 'If I take a Greek athlete and an Egyptian pharaoh and an Italian strumpet, and so on, and put all these characters together, I will end up with the integrated personality known as "Joan Grant". These are, of course, not the *real* pieces that were fitted together to produce her, but when they're all assembled the effect is the same.' As anyone who has read more than a few pages of this book will realize, the right brain uses symbols in order to express itself in our dreams. There is no reason why it should not, in much the same way, use symbols (e.g., apparently historical personages) in order to express itself through false 'memories' of past incarnations.

This is all speculation, of course, but that something of this kind must have been going on inside Grant seems inescapable. Otherwise one cannot explain her sexual naïvety (mentioned in the previous note): if she were genuinely remembering past lifetimes she'd presumably have known all about lovemaking.

27 The UK edition alone carried the title which Sizemore had wanted: *Strangers in my Body*.

28 In fact, Jane had *attempted* suicide at the time and in the circumstances indicated in the book, but she had been unsuccessful.

## CHAPTER FIVE: DREAMS OF TIMES TO COME

1 To be more precise, his suggestion is that dreams are the product of the right side of the brain, which they very probably are (see pages 132–6). The right brain isn't very good at reading; moreover, it seems in many ways to be an atavism. So Sagan's suggestion is really that dreams are born of that particular type of human intelligence which evolved long before the left brain's intellectualism and subsequent rise to dominance.

2 To be fair, this may be in part because it today lies on the railway between Moscow and Smolensk; but in 1812 it was on the main road between the two cities.

3 I think these two are John Cunningham (1719–1773), a very minor poet who wrote the farce *Love in a Mist* (1747), and John Newton (1725–1807), a clergyman and minor poet, whose partial autobiography of his exciting youth at sea before his conversion had some contemporary popularity. However, I have been unable to track this tale down to a contemporary source, and so my identification of these two is very likely at fault.

4 Glaskin makes an interesting suggestion about the phenomenon of déjà vu. He points out that we forget most of our dreams on waking. Might it not be, when we experience déjà vu, that what's really happening is that we're witnessing the coming to pass of one of our forgotten precognitive dreams.

5 Shelley Rhode, presenter of Granada Television's lunch-time show, 'Exchange Flags', has told me that a while ago, in the half-hour or so leading up to an appearance by Gooch on her show, she decided to call his bluff. She asked him to predict the winner of a 2.00 race (the show starts at 2.00), and he was only too happy to oblige. She was able to tell the viewing audience about the prediction before the results came through; when they did, Gooch was triumphantly vindicated.

Unfortunately for 'sexy' television, she then asked him to try to pick the winner of the 2.15, and when the results came through . . . Still, getting even one of them right was quite impressive.

6 One curious thing which Norris mentioned in her article was that the members of her extended family had died at neat intervals of one every second year. Then there had been a longish gap before one of her sisters died in 1910, and another in 1912. Now that it was 1914, it was Norris' own turn. Probably this was all just a coincidence of dates; but it's interesting to speculate that, musing consciously or unconsciously on the tidy nature of the death-roll, Norris' mind generated the dream as a response to her instinctive feeling that her time was up. Consciously regarding her dream as precognitive, she may then have simply 'given up' and died – a phenomenon which has been widely reported in different contexts (see note 10 below). Thus – if there's anything to my speculations – the dream-prophecy may have been self-fulfilling.

7 The second of the two nightmares found him leaning over Mary's bed strangling her. This dream seems to have made him sleepwalk, for when he came to, awoken by Mary's leaping in alarm from her bed, he found himself in her bedroom.

8 The dream that 'I was a watchdog and I knew there was danger about' seems a little weak: I don't know why Buck and Palmer bothered including it.

9 A doodled sketch of the dream seemed to indicate – but only with the benefit of hindsight – that the disaster would occur somewhere around Italy. In fact, it took place off Naples.

10 Both Barker and Fairley were central to interesting stories concerning precognition.

Barker wrote an interesting book, *Scared to Death* (1966), in which he examined the idea that people could indeed be so convinced that death was imminent that they died; for example, in many primitive tribes a shaman can strike someone dead at a distance by *telling* them that they will die, because the victim believes completely in the shaman's powers. For the sake of a concluding chapter, Barker and a colleague did a survey of various professional predictors, going to see them in the role of average punters and trying to find out how many would tell them how long they would live. Barker was told unanimously that he had a long and happy life ahead of him; the only predictor who refused to make any prediction of this type was the palmist Mir Bashir. Barker in fact died while his book was still at proof stage. (Some years later Bashir told me that, when Barker had arrived for his appointment, he had seen death written all over his face. He also said that he always refused to predict how long people would live. It may of course be that his colleagues/rivals have similar policies, but prefer to work on the basis that, if you can make someone die by telling them they're going to, you can make someone survive in exactly the converse way.)

Fairley, on the other hand, was another of the 'rocking-horse winners'. After recovering from a period during which he had been blind (for psychological reasons), he found that he could pick winners in the races. He made a fair amount of money doing so, and then began to *worry* about the ability. It was at this point that the ability vanished. Colin Wilson has suggested that this was because either the blindness or the trauma which had caused it allowed Fairley 'direct access' to the information from his right brain, but that as soon as Fairley's left brain began to worry about the whole thing – i.e., started to explore it intellectually – the right brain fell back into sulky silence.

11 This dream worries me very considerably, because the night before I wrote these words I had a dream which has certain similarities to Greene's. In my dream, the book you're holding had just been published – to profound critical disgust. If Greene's dream can come true . . . no, I don't want to discuss this any further.

12 It would be sadistic to note every flaw of logic and understanding in this book, cruel to note even a few. Here are a few.

The 'crack geologist' referred to seems to draw most of his frontier information from such hotbeds of scientific debate as *Life* and the *St Louis Globe-Democrat*; and describes 17,000-year-old soils as geologically ancient. In a discussion of the land rising and falling we get the exciting news that after one eruption Etna was 25ft higher than before. Before you start visualizing Etna rising slowly before suddenly blasting off through the stratosphere (a theorist did suggest in the 1850s that comets were nothing more than space-travelling volcanoes), just remember that the increase in Etna's height took place at the *top*: erupting volcanoes often do increase in height because not all of the ejected lava runs down the side of the mountain. Throughout the book, temblors (Earth tremors) are described as 'tremblors' – although this neologism does have a certain charm. As does the idea that the formation of new volcanoes (and hence volcanic islands) along the midocean ridges represents the resurgence from the deep of the lost continents Atlantis and Lemuria.

13 To give an idea of the state of the art of gravity detection, let alone gravity generation:

In 1970, using very sophisticated equipment, Weber detected cosmic gravitational pulses arising from the supernova explosions of stars or the swallowing of stellar masses by super black holes at the centres of galaxies. The scientific community was and still is (1983) concerned that Weber discovered *too many* such pulses for credibility; moreover, others have been unable to duplicate his results (there is not the remotest suggestion that he is being duplicitous; merely that there was a foul-up somewhere in the execution of the experiment or the interpretation of its results). The matter is still unresolved: the required apparatus is expensive, massive and fiddly.

It has been suggested that other cosmic events may produce gravitational pulses – e.g., mass transfer between a supergiant star and an orbiting black hole or neutron star – so allowing Weber's equipment to register far more pulses than expected, but this is speculative.

In summary, in 1983 it is *still* infernally difficult to *detect* gravitational waves. Generation of gravity is something else . . .

And, just in case you're about to say that at least Cayce

predicted the *existence* of gravitational waves, remember that Einstein had already done so, some considerable while before.

14 Discussions of the impracticability of sudden pole-shifts can be found in my *A Directory of Discarded Ideas* and *A Book of Numbers*.

15 This account is taken verbatim from a letter sent to me by Jenny Randles, dated 17th July, 1983.

16 Which she is, unless she's seriously insane – and there's no evidence of that.

17 Come to think of it, even if I didn't come out with some pet crank theory but with something really world-shaking, it'd probably still be a pretty long wait.

## CHAPTER SIX: DREAMS OF TIMES LONG GONE

1 I've quoted extracts from Audrey Atkinson's dream-accounts verbatim from her correspondence with me. I have, however, amended punctuation where necessary and changed the nationality of the folksinger she mentions in order to avoid general embarrassment.

2 In fact, most dreams do exactly this – which is why we can dream a 'story' lasting three hours in only twenty minutes: as in any movie, we skip the unimportant bits. (This is assuming that modern research, which suggests very strongly that dream-time goes by at roughly the same rate as real-time, is correct.)

3 Unless, of course, she had consciously or unconsciously doctored the dream in the light of rationality. But I don't think that this is the case.

4 Another child prodigy, the British writer Jane Gaskell, managed to produce during her teens an Atlantean trilogy (beginning with *The Serpent*, 1963) which bears up well to rereading. So there's no proven reason why children shouldn't be able to produce 'mature' novels set in Atlantis.

5 That's another curious thing about Atlantean incarnations: most of us were royalty.

6 In 1983 the UK had a National Numeracy Week which lasted 8 days.

7 In *Edgar Cayce on Atlantis* (1968) Cayce's son cites, in support of the existence of Atlantis, some astonishing cultural similarities which can be found on both sides of the

Atlantic. One of these is the shared use of a 365-day calendar.

8 Oh, let's. If they're all either undiscovered or unrecognized, how can he claim that *any* remain? And if there are *no* – rather than a 'few' – extant records, then why not say so? Because then it wouldn't sound as if a 'few' records survive in support of Cayce's Atlantean fulminations, that's why.

9 Sounding like a nutcase, which she isn't. She has had a lot of very strange experiences, which she habitually and charmingly mocks. She is quite prepared to believe that they are all merely errors of observation, or something like that . . .

10 Just to avoid any possible confusion, the author in question isn't me – indeed, I don't know who he is. So far as I know, Atkinson hasn't read *any* of my books.

11 Conclusive proof that it's not me!

12 See pages 348ff for a discussion of the way Jane Sherwood does her psychic stuff.

13 No relation!

14 See note 5.

15 This description of the procedure may have lost a little in the condensation. My apologies. Please be assured that I'm not mocking the experiment in any way.

16 I hardly need to repeat that this intensification of sensual experience is typical of the dream-state.

17 Ray estimated that it was 8–10,000 years ago. If it was 10,000 years ago, then it's no surprise that he felt chilly: Scandinavia was then still in the thrall of the last glacial advance of the Pleistocene Ice Age.

18 As Glaskin records, three years after Stephan's 'run' the mother was in fact still in fine fettle.

19 I promise I'm not making this up.

20 In fairness, I have to add that some years later he was to see in the British Museum stēlae strongly reminiscent of the one which featured in the first of his Christos dreams. After some research he was able to pinpoint the setting of his dream as in the Faiyum some 5000 years ago. As he points out, reasonably enough, it seems strange that, never before having had much interest in Egyptology (until visiting the BM he hadn't known what the word 'stēle' meant), he nevertheless managed to have a dream about the period correct in all of the details which he has been able to

check. Later he visited for the first time(?) the site in Egypt which he believed he had seen in the dream, and found other remarkable 'confirmations'.

21 In this same book, Glaskin briefly describes his initial discomfort on performing the experiment with some blind people, one of them congenitally blind. This last person, to Glaskin's horror, proved to be able to dream only in the way that congenitally blind people normally do: his dreams involved only the senses other than sight (see references to Helen Keller, pages 18–21). Could this mean, thought Glaskin, that the Creator was so unspeakably cruel that some souls went through all their long successions of lifetimes incarcerated in sightless bodies? He could not believe that God could be so vicious – and so his whole belief in God crumbled.

Thanks to a chance discussion of cassette recorders, though, he was able to reassure himself. A perfectly recorded tape won't sound up to much if played on dud equipment. Analogously, then, it was the blind man's *present* brain which was failing to reproduce everything as it 'played back' his previous lives. I'm not sure that this analogy holds: there seems to be no reason why the sight-centre of the brain should not function even if there is a fault in the 'input' (eyes and optic nerves) – much as a cassette recorder may no longer be able to record sounds but can still play back with perfect fidelity.

But one takes Glaskin's point.

22 Glaskin discusses, and then rejects, an entertaining idea which seeks to explain why reincarnation should come about in the first place. The Cathars and other sects had the notion that there was indeed a Hell, but that we were actually living in it. In addition, the Catholic Church has the idea of Purgatory, where souls go to be cleansed of their lesser sins. Putting these two theses together, you come up with a much better model, in which it is obvious why reincarnation should come about: we live in Purgatory. Clearly most souls require several lifetimes' worth of human misery before being fitted to go on to better things.

23 I'm a little coy about detailing their contents, not only because I plan one day to turn the more interesting of them into short stories but also because I'm sure that, to any reader versed in psychoanalysis, they will immediately

betray that I'm sexually inadequate, a perverted personality, a necrophile, and so on. I'll keep the full disgusting details of my perversions to myself, if that's all right with you.

# Bibliography

In line with my policy in earlier books, I have indicated by * a book which has a lousy index, and by ** a book without an index at all. Publishers and authors who feel aggrieved about their books being in the * category should try to *use* the indexes concerned. Publishers and authors whose books are in the ** category will no doubt go off into the other room and do the decent thing.


Asimov, Isaac: *Asimov's Biographical Encyclopedia of Science and Technology* (revised edn.), Garden City (NY), Doubleday, 1972

Baring-Gould, Sabine: **The Lives of the Saints*, London, John Hodges, several volumes with varying dates around 1800

Benedictine Monks of St Augustine's Abbey, Ramsgate: ***The Book of Saints*, London, A & C Black, 1966

Birkin, Andrew: *J. M. Barrie and the Lost Boys*, London, Constable, 1979

Boswell, James: *Life of Samuel Johnson,* London, Everyman's Library, 1960

Brennan, J. H.: ***Occult Reich*, London, Futura, 1974

Brod, Max: *Franz Kafka: A Biography* (2nd edn.), New York, Schocken, 1960

Brome, Vincent: *Havelock Ellis: Philosopher of Sex*, London, Routledge and Kegan Paul, 1979

Brook, Stephen (ed.): **The Oxford Book of Dreams*, Oxford, OUP, 1983

Buck, Alice E., and Palmer, F. Claude: **The Clothes of*

*God: A Treatise on Neo-analytic Psychology*, London, Peter Owen, 1956

Buranelli, Vincent: **Edgar Allan Poe* (2nd edn.), Indianapolis, Bobbs-Merrill, 1977

Burd, Van Akin: *The Winnington Letters: John Ruskin's Correspondence With Margaret Alexis Bell and the Children at Winnington Hall*, London, Allen and Unwin, 1969

Buttrick, George Arthur, *et al.* (eds.): ***The Interpreter's Dictionary of the Bible*, Vol. 1, New York and Nashville, Abingdon Press, 1962

Caldwell, Taylor, with Stearn, Jess: ***The Romance of Atlantis*, London, Severn House, 1977

Cayce, Edgar Evans: ***Edgar Cayce on Atlantis*, London, Howard Baker, 1969

Chambers, E. K.: **Samuel Taylor Coleridge: A Biographical Study*, Oxford, Clarendon Press, 1950

Christie, Agatha: *An Autobiography*, London, Collins, 1977

Cloyd, E. L.: **James Burnett, Lord Monboddo*, Oxford, Clarendon Press, 1972

Colloms, Brenda: **Charles Kingsley*, London, Constable, 1975

Cronin, Vincent: *Napoleon*, London, Collins, 1971

Curnock, Nehemiah (ed.): *The Journal of the Rev. John Wesley,* London, Charles H. Kelly, 1909

Dally, Peter: *The Fantasy Factor*, London, Weidenfeld and Nicolson, 1975 (paperback edn. titled *The Fantasy Game*)

Deacon, Richard: **John Dee: Scientist, Geographer, Astrologer and Secret Agent to Elizabeth I*, London, Muller, 1968

de Bono, Edward (ed.): *Eureka! An Illustrated History of Inventions from the Wheel to the Computer*, London, Thames and Husdon, 1974

Dickens, Charles: **The Letters of Charles Dickens* (ed. Madeline House, Graham Storey and Kathleen Tillotson), Oxford, Clarendon Press, 1965–81 (further volumes in preparation)

Dixon, Jeane, with Noorbergen, Rene: **My Life and Prophecies*, London, Muller, 1971

Dunn, Jane: *Moon in Eclipse: A Life of Mary Shelley*, London, Weidenfeld and Nicolson, 1978

Dunne, J. W.: *An Experiment With Time* (5th edn.), London, Faber, 1939

Evans, Christopher, and Evans, Peter: *Landscapes of the Night*, London, Gollancz, 1983

Farber, Eduard: *Great Chemists*, New York, Interscience, 1961

Freud, Sigmund: 'The Case of the Wolf-Man', in Gardiner, *op. cit.*

Freud, Sigmund: *The Interpretation of Dreams* (trans. James Strachey)(revised edn.), Harmondsworth, Penguin, 1976

Fruman, Norman: *Coleridge, the Damaged Archangel*, London, Allen and Unwin, 1972

Gardiner, Muriel (ed.): **The Wolf-Man and Sigmund Freud*, London, Hogarth Press and Institute of Psycho-Analysis, 1972

Gattey, Charles Neilson: **They Saw Tomorrow: Seers and Sorcerers from Delphi Till Today*, London, Harrap, 1977

Gibson, Walter B., and Gibson, Litzka R.: *The Complete Illustrated Book of Divination and Prophecy*, London, Souvenir, 1974 (paperback edn. titled *The Encyclopaedia of Prophecy*)

Gillen, Mollie: **Assassination of the Prime Minister: The Shocking Death of Spencer Perceval*, London, Sidgwick and Jackson, 1972

Glaskin, G. M.: ***A Door to Eternity: Proving the Christos Experience*, London, Wildwood, 1979
Glaskin, G. M.: ***Windows of the Mind: The Christos Experiment*, London, Wildwood, 1974
Glaskin, G. M.: ***Worlds Within*, London, Wildwood, 1976
Gooch, Stan: *The Paranormal*, London, Wildwood, 1978
Grant, Joan: ***Time Out of Mind*, London, Barker, 1956
Grant, Joan: ***Winged Pharaoh*, London, Barker, 1937
Grant, Joan, and Kelsey, Denys: ***Many Lifetimes*, London, Gollancz, 1967
Grant, John: **A Book of Numbers*, Bath, Ashgrove, 1982
Grant, John (ed.): **The Book of Time* (Consultant Editor Colin Wilson), Newton Abbot, Westbridge, 1980
Grant, John: *A Directory of Discarded Ideas*, Sevenoaks, Ashgrove, 1981
Grant, Kenneth: **Images and Oracles of Austin Osman Spare*, London, Muller, 1975
Green, Peter: **Beyond the Wild Wood: The World of Kenneth Grahame*, Exeter, Signatures/Webb and Bower, 1982 (revised edn. of *Kenneth Grahame: A Biography*, 1959)
Greene, Graham: ***A Sort of Life*, London, Bodley Head, 1971
Gribbin, John: **Timewarps*, London, Sphere, 1979
Guirdham, Arthur: ***For a Message*, London, Watkins, 1974
Gurney, Edmund, Myers, Frederick W. H., and Podmore, Frank: *Phantasms of the Living*, London, Society for Psychical Research and Trübner, 1886
Hannah, Barbara: **Jung: His Life and Work – A Biographical Memoir*, London, Michael Joseph, 1977
Hastings, James: ***Dictionary of the Bible* (revised edn.), Edinburgh, T. and T. Clark, 1963

Holmes, Richard: *Shelley: The Pursuit*, London, Weidenfeld and Nicolson, 1974

Jones, Richard M.: **The New Psychology of Dreaming*, Harmondsworth, Penguin, 1978

Jules-Verne, Jean: *Jules Verne* (trans. Roger Greaves), London, Macdonald and Jane's, 1976

Jung, C. G.: *Letters* (ed. Adler, Gerhard and Jaffé, Aniela), London, Routledge and Kegan Paul; *Vol. 1, 1973; Vol. 2, 1976

Jung, C. G.: *Memories, Dreams, Reflections* (ed. Aniela Jaffé), London, Collins/Routledge and Kegan Paul, 1963

Jung, C. G.: ***Modern Man in Search of a Soul* (trans. W. S. Dell and Cary F. Baynes), London, Routledge and Kegan Paul, 1933

Kafka, Franz: *I Am a Memory Come Alive: Autobiographical Writings* (ed. Nahum N. Glatzer), New York, Schocken, 1974

Kaplan, Justin: **Mr Clemens and Mark Twain*, London, Cape, 1967

Keats, John: **Letters of John Keats* (sel. Robert Gittings), London, OUP, 1970

Kerouac, Jack: ***Book of Dreams*, San Francisco, City Lights, 1961

King, Coretta Scott: *My Life with Martin Luther King, Jr.*, London, Hodder and Stoughton, 1970

Kingsley, Frances (ed.): **Charles Kingsley: His Letters and Memories of His Life*, London, Henry S. King, 1977

Koestler, Arthur: **The Act of Creation*, London, Hutchinson, 1964

Koestler, Arthur: **The Roots of Coincidence*, London, Hutchinson, 1972

Langford, David: **War in 2080: The Future of Military Technology*, Newton Abbot, Westbridge, 1979

Lash, Joseph P.: *Helen and Teacher: The Story of Helen Keller and Anne Sullivan Macy*, London, Allen Lane, 1980

Lawton, A. T.: **A Window in the Sky*, Newton Abbot, David and Charles, 1979

Lefebure, Molly: *Samuel Taylor Coleridge: A Bondage of Opium*, London, Gollancz, 1974

Lindsay, Jack: *William Morris: His Life and Work*, London, Constable, 1975

Martin, Jay: *Always Merry and Bright: The Life of Henry Miller*, Santa Barbara, Capra Press, 1978

Mason, Philip: **Kipling: The Glass, the Shadow and the Fire*, London, Cape, 1975

Menzies, Lucy: ***The Saints in Italy*, London, Medici Society, 1924

Montgomery, Ruth: ***A Gift of Prophecy: The Phenomenal Jeane Dixon*, London, Barker, 1966

Napier, John: **Bigfoot: The Yeti and Sasquatch in Myth and Reality*, London, Cape, 1972

Neider, Charles (ed.): *The Autobiography of Mark Twain*, London, Chatto and Windus, 1960

Nicholls, Peter: ***The Encyclopedia of Science Fiction*, St Albans, Granada, 1979

Nicolson, Iain: **Gravity, Black Holes and the Universe*, Newton Abbot, David and Charles, 1981

Oates, Stephen B.: *With Malice Towards None: The Life of Abraham Lincoln*, London, Allen and Unwin, 1978

O'Connor, Richard: **Ambrose Bierce: A Biography*, London, Gollancz, 1968

Pepys, Samuel: *The Diary of Samuel Pepys* (principal eds. Robert Latham and William Matthews), London, Bell, 1970–83

Powell, Nicholas: *Fuseli: The Nightmare*, London, Allen Lane, 1973

Priestley, J. B.: ***Delight*, London, Heinemann, 1973

Priestley, J. B.: *Man and Time*, London, Aldus, 1964

Priestley, J. B.: **Margin Released*, London, Heinemann, 1962

Priestley, J. B.: ***Over the Long High Wall: Some Reflections and Speculations on Life, Death and Time*, London, Heinemann, 1972

Raleigh, Lady (ed.): **The Letters of Sir Walter Raleigh (1879–1922)*, London, Methuen, 1926

Randles, Jenny: *The Pennine UFO Mystery*, London, Granada, 1983

Randles, Jenny, and Whetnall, Paul: *Alien Contact: Window On Another world,* Sudbury, Spearman, 1981

Roazen, Paul: **Brother Animal: The Story of Freud and Tausk*, New York, Knopf, 1969

Rosen, Edward: *Kepler's 'Somnium'* (trans. with extensive commentary), Madison, Milwaukee and London, University of Wisconsin Press, 1967

Rowley, H. H.: ***Dictionary of Bible Themes*, London, Nelson, 1968

Sackville West, Edward: *A Flame in Sunlight: The Life and Work of Thomas De Quincey* (ed. John E. Jordan), London, Bodley Head, 1974

Sagan, Carl: *The Dragons of Eden: Speculations on the Evolution of Human Intelligence*, New York, Random House, 1977

Screiber, Flora Rheta: *Sybil: The True Story of a Woman Possessed by Sixteen Separate Personalities*, London, Allen Lane, 1974

Sherwood, Jane: **The Fourfold Vision: A Study of Consciousness, Sleep and Dreams*, London, 1965

Shirer, William L.: *The Rise and Fall of the Third Reich*, London, Secker and Warburg, 1960

Shulman, Sandra: **Nightmare*, Newton Abbot, David and Charles, 1979

Sizemore, Chris Costner, and Pittillo, Elen Sain: ***Eve*

(published in the US as *I'm Eve*), London, Gollancz, 1978
Smith, Adam: ***Powers of Mind: The Revolution in Human Consciousness*, London, W. H. Allen, 1976
Stearn, Jess: ***Edgar Cayce: The Sleeping Prophet*, Garden City, Doubleday, 1967
Sterling, Richard: ***1,001 Erotic Dreams*, London, Sphere, 1982
Stevens, William Oliver: **The Mystery of Dreams*, London, Allen and Unwin, 1950
Stevenson, Robert Louis: ***Across the Plains, With Other Memories and Essays*, London, Chatto and Windus, 1925
Symons, Julian: *The Tell-Tale Heart: The Life and Works of Edgar Allan Poe*, London, Faber, 1978
Targ, Russell, and Puthoff, Harold: *Mind-Reach*, London, Cape, 1977
Teresa, St: ***The Life of Saint Teresa* (trans. J. M. Cohen), Harmondsworth, Penguin, 1957
Thurston, Herbert J., and Attwater, Donald (eds.): **Butler's Lives of the Saints* (2nd edn.), London, Burns and Oates, 1956
Trevor-Roper, Hugh: *The Last Days of Hitler* (4th edn.), London, Macmillan, 1971
Ullman, Montague, Krippner, Stanley, and Vaughan, Alan: **Dream Telepathy*, London, Turnstone, 1973
Vaughan, Alan: *Patterns of Prophecy*, London, Turnstone, 1974
Walker, Benjamin: 'Dreams', in Cavendish, Richard (ed.): **Encyclopedia of the Unexplained*, London, Routledge and Kegan Paul, 1974
Walker, Benjamin: **Encyclopedia of Metaphysical Medicine*, London, Routledge and Kegan Paul, 1978
Wallace, Irving, Wallace, Amy, Wallechinsky, David and

Wallace, Sylvia: ***The Intimate Sex Lives of Famous People*, London, Hutchinson, 1971

Watson, Lyall: *The Romeo Error: A Matter of Life Death*, London, Hodder, 1974

Webb, James: **The Occult Establishment*, Glasgow, Richard Drew, 1981

Willey, Basil: **Samuel Taylor Coleridge*, London, Chatto and Windus, 1972

Wilson, Colin: *Mysteries*, London, Hodder, 1978

Wilson, Colin: **The Quest for Wilhelm Reich*, St Albans, Granada, 1981

Wilson, Colin, and Grant, John (eds.): *The Directory of Possibilities*, Exeter, Webb and Bower, 1981

Wolf-Man: 'The Memoirs of the Wolf-Man', in Gardiner, *op. cit.*

# Index